The Beginning
Elementary School Teacher

Problems and Issues

Edited by

Walter S. Foster

and

Norman C. Jacobs

Department of Elementary Education
Northern Illinois University
, Illinois

93055

Burgess Publishing Company

426 South Sixth Street • Minneapolis, Minn. 55415

To Gladys and Ruth

Preface

For the beginning elementary school teacher there are many questions that remain unanswered as he prepares to assume professional responsibility. No matter how thorough his training, how broad his preservice experiences, how successful his student teaching, he approaches his first assignment with considerable doubt and concern. This is to be expected, and is justified, for there are numerous situations and problems that have not been encountered, or anticipated, and that only experience can reveal and solve. It is possible, however, to refer to the experiences of others in anticipating what will occur and to develop some guidelines for coping with the many problems that beginners face.

This book has been produced to meet the needs of prospective and beginning teachers. It can be used in education classes to help prepare students for the experiences they will encounter in student teaching and as they begin to do full-time teaching; and it can be used to help new teachers understand and surmount the problems that arise during their first years on the job. An effort has been made to consider those specific problems and aspects of the beginning teacher's responsibility which, of necessity, usually receive insufficient attention during the preservice program.

In planning the organizational structure of the selections, it appeared that to ask significant questions and then place the questions and answers in the logical and psychological order of teacher growth would afford the most useful approach. Accordingly, the following questions served as the main focal points for organization:

1. What are the problems faced as the student teacher finds himself in the final stages of undergraduate preparation and proceeds to look for his first position?
2. What practices, procedures, and problems are of particular significance during the first few weeks and months of beginning teaching?
3. What are the specific teaching skills and out-of-class competencies which characterize the teacher who is in the process of becoming a true professional?

4. What are the attitudes, capacities for positive adaptation, understandings, and skills necessary for productive teaching in a rapidly changing society?

It will be noted that the organizational scheme of the book follows this sequence. Part I is concerned with preparing and beginning to teach, Part II with implementing instruction, Part III with becoming a true professional, and Part IV with teaching in a climate of educational change. For a more detailed insight into the nature of each major division as well as a transition from one division to the next, the reader is referred to the introductory paragraphs for each.

In choosing articles for inclusion in this volume, effort has been made to locate selections that offer the most practical suggestions for actual application of theory. It is not likely that all problems have been foreseen; nor is it expected that solutions to all problems are to be found in the readings. Instead, the beginning teacher will find that others have faced similar problems and have found some practices that have worked for them. From this knowledge should come increased understanding of problem situations and procedures for handling them successfully.

The underlying assumption in selecting the readings is that the practice of elementary school teaching is undergirded by sound theory — theory which has been developed from and is supported by discoveries in the psychology of learning and child growth, and reflections on the nature of democratic society. Thus, methodology and procedure are developed in a sound conceptual basis — in an integrated framework which precludes the mere "bag of tricks" or "secrets of the trade" approach designed as simple response answers to challenging problems and situations. On the other hand, it is believed that the treatment of the problems selected is sufficiently practical to meet the concrete difficulties encountered by most classroom teachers.

We wish to express our appreciation to the contributors who wrote original articles for this book, and to the authors and publishers who granted permission to reprint their copyrighted materials. Specific acknowledgment is made at the beginning of each selection.

W.S.F.
N.C.J.

Table of Contents

Dedication iii

Preface v

PART I
BEGINNING TO TEACH

Introduction 2

Chapter 1. Choosing a Position 3

Self-evaluation Before and During the Interview 4
    Ray H. Simpson

Securing the First Position 11
    T. M. Stinnett

Chapter 2. Preparing for the Opening of School 18

Objectives of Elementary Education 19
    Calhoun C. Collier, W. Robert Houston, Robert R. Schmatz,
    William J. Walsh

A Teaching and Learning Environment 28
    Sara Davis

Preschool Planning 30
    Marie A. Mehl, Hubert H. Mills, Harl R. Douglass,
    Mary-Margaret Scobey

The Lesson Plan 38
    George A. Beauchamp

Chapter 3. Starting the Year 45

Starting the Year Right 46
    M. Genevieve Douglass and John L. Grindle

Teaching Classroom Routines 55
    Robert E. Chasnoff

Discipline and Preventive Techniques 57
    Leslie J. Chamberlin

Contagious Teaching 60
    Elizabeth Teigland

Tort Liability and the Classroom Teacher 63
    Arthur Louis Ferguson

Suggested Additional Readings 65

PART II
IMPLEMENTING INSTRUCTION

Introduction 70

Chapter 4. Utilizing Child Development Research 71

Child Development Research and the Elementary-School Teacher ... 72
Don Dinkmeyer

The Feelings of Learning 78
Walcott H. Beatty

To Keep an Inner Balance 83
Charlotte Haupt

Techniques for Dealing with Children's Behavior 89
Wayne L. Herman, Robert V. Duffey, Elisabeth Schumacher,
David L. Williams, Lillian B. Zachary

Chapter 5. Selecting and Employing Procedures and Approaches 95

Levels of Teaching Performance 96
Norman C. Jacobs

Pupil-Teacher Planning 104
Marie A. Mehl, Hubert H. Mills, Harl R. Douglass,
Mary-Margaret Scobey

Classroom Climate 106
Norma Furst and Marciene S. Mattleman

Teaching and Learning Through Inquiry 110
Byron G. Massialas

Developing Increased Creativity with Children 113
George I. Thomas and Joseph Crescimbeni

The Spark Within 116
Cynthia Jarzen

Chapter 6. Providing for Individual Differences 120

Ability Grouping and the Average Child 121
J. Wayne Wrightstone

Individualizing Instruction 125
Bernice J. Wolfson

Do We Group in an Individualized Program? 128
Dorris M. Lee

The Teacher's Changing Role 132
    Donald Deep

Improving Independent Study 135
    Jeannette Veatch

Guidelines for Developing a Homework Policy 138
    William D. Hedges

Chapter 7. Handling Problem Areas and Trends 145

Early Childhood Education 146
    Mildred McQueen

Sex Education in the Public Schools: Problem or Solution? 153
    Ira L. Reiss

School Grounds Provide Opportunities for Outdoor Teaching 162
    Thomas J. Rillo

The Handicapped in the Regular Classroom 165
    Samuel C. Ashcroft

How to Teach in a Ghetto School 168
    Sidney Trubowitz

Joe Doesn't Pledge Allegiance 173
    Ruth Stephens MacGorman

Christmas in the Classroom 175
    David L. Barr

The Best Start is an Early Start 177
    Annette Grubman

Chapter 8. Evaluating Learning 182

Evaluation Takes Many Forms 182
    Robert S. Fleming

On School Marks 189
    Robert L. Williams

Suggested Additional Readings 194

PART III
BECOMING A TRUE PROFESSIONAL

Introduction 198

Chapter 9. Working with Parents 199

It Still Starts in the Classroom 200
    Ned S. Hubbell

What Do Parents Need to Know? 205
    Maxine Dunfee

Making the Most of a Parent Conference 209
    Harriet B. Cholden

A Beginning Teacher Works with Parents 212
    Susan L. Bromberg

Chapter 10. Working with School Personnel 218

The Teacher and Human Relations 218
    Raymond H. Harrison and Lawrence E. Gowin

Teacher v. Teacher: A Proposal for Improving Relationships 229
    Donald R. Cruickshank

Volunteers in the Classroom 234
    Peter Schrag

Teacher Aides: How They Can Be of Real Help 236
    Wayne L. Herman

Chapter 11. Developing Competency 240

Three Gimmicks That Help Teachers Grow 241

A Classroom Experiment 246
    William L. Camp

How to Use Professional Periodicals 250
    Nancy W. Hanna and John M. Geston

To Be a Very Good Teacher 253
    Elvira T. Garcia

What Teachers Think of Their Teaching 256
    Walter S. Foster

Self-evaluation: Procedures and Tools 259
    Ray H. Simpson

Chapter 12. Improving the Profession 268

Criteria of a Profession 269
    Sidney Dorros

I Speak of a Spark 271
    Frank W. Hubbard

Professional Organizations for Teachers 272
    Walter S. Foster

Educational Power and the Teaching Profession 275
    Arthur F. Corey

Negotiating or Bargaining 282

Chapter 13. Becoming a Citizen of the Community 284

The Teacher in the Community 285
    Robert J. Havighurst and Bernice L. Neugarten

The Teacher and Politics 287
    J. Lorne McGuigan

Teachers in Politics: The Larger Roles 291
    T. M. Stinnett

Suggested Additional Readings 294

PART IV
TEACHING IN A CLIMATE OF EDUCATIONAL CHANGE

Introduction 298

Chapter 14. Deciding What and How to Teach 299

Mandate for Change 300
    Allen Myers

Data for Decisions 303

What Shall We Teach? 308
    Dorris May Lee

Shades of McGuffey 315
    Lou Emma Wright Deen

Parents are Ready 320
    Instructor

The Teacher as a Curriculum Maker 326
    Charles R. May

Chapter 15. Working with Organizational Innovations 329

The Teacher Evaluates Innovations 330
    Gary A. Griffin and Rev. Joseph Devlin, S.J.

The Changing Nature of the Elementary School 333
    George I. Thomas and Joseph Crescimbeni

The Phantom Nongraded School 346
    William P. McLoughlin

Why Teaching Teams Fail 351
    Carl O. Olson, Jr.

Innovations in Education 357
    Raymond B. Fox

Chapter 16. Working with Curricular and Instructional Innovations 366

Let Us Develop Children Who Care About Themselves and Others . . . 367
    Alice Miel

Educational Technology and the Classroom Teacher 372
    Richard I. Miller

Learning Environments for Teaching 376
    Shelt Chastain and Mary Louise Seguel

The Teacher and Computer-assisted Instruction 385
    Patrick Suppes

Chapter 17. Building a Philosophy of Education in Today's World 390

Importance of a Philosophy for Teachers 391
    Fred G. Walcott

Building a Philosophy of Education for the Pace-Setting Seventies . . . 395
    William R. Speer

Suggested Additional Readings 397

Author Index 400

Subject Index 402

Part I

BEGINNING TO TEACH

Introduction

As may be noted from a reading of the preface, the organizational scheme of this book has been determined, first, by asking significant questions about problems generally experienced by beginning teachers, and, second, by placing questions and answers in the logical and psychological order of teacher growth. This first major division, "Beginning to Teach," follows that plan of organization precisely. The fact may be readily observed in the topics selected for the three chapters: looking for and choosing a position; making preparations for the opening of school; and plans and procedures for insuring success in the initial months of teaching.

That the problem of securing a position which fits the beginner's talents and abilities should receive first priority is self-evident. In addition to its coming first in the experience continuum, its importance is reflected in the anxiety and concern generated in the applicant as well as in the thoroughness with which employing school officials proceed with the selection process. Further rationale for inclusion of this topic will be found in the introductory remarks of Chapter 1.

Chapter 2 is concerned with the teacher's preparation for the opening of school. The importance of this matter is underlined by the fact that most school systems have well organized orientation periods for their faculties prior to the opening of each school year, some of which may be several days in length. A further development lending meaning to the topic is the increasing prevalence of a school term lasting eleven months or throughout the year, part of which is to be spent in planning, curriculum improvement, and other preparatory activities. The intent of the chapter is to assist the beginner with the many details to be accomplished during orientation week.

Finally, it would seem logical and desirable to include a consideration of the problems likely to be met during the opening days and weeks of the school year. That this period is crucial in terms of later success is generally recognized. Principals and supervisory personnel may spend the larger part of the first few weeks of the term bending every effort to insure that new faculty members have a successful initial experience. The intent of Chapter 3, therefore, is to present practical helps in the way of procedures and techniques, quite specific yet general enough to be adapted to the various situations encountered.

Thus Part I of this volume lays emphasis on the practical first steps necessary for an orderly transition into the beginning stages of teaching. It covers the necessary groundwork preliminary to the more thorough and detailed theoretical and practical considerations of day-to-day teaching treated in Parts II, III, and IV.

Chapter 1

Choosing a Position

Choosing a position is important both to the beginner and the experienced teacher who is seeking a change. First, the particular position selected may be crucial in terms of personal adjustment and the making of a firm career commitment. Many a young college graduate has shifted from teaching to another field after an unhappy and unsuccessful first year or two in the profession. On the other hand, a successful initial experience tends not only to confirm the wisdom of the choice made during college years, but also opens the door to further useful service and personal fulfillment. For the teacher with a number of years' service, the decision to uproot himself and his family and move to another community and school system also entails far-reaching consequences. Teachers are individuals, each with a unique background and set of abilities, talents, and dispositions. Success in any newly chosen position involves this individual uniqueness in interaction with the school and community environment. It is a complex matter, the end result of which cannot be easily predicted. Hopefully, however, the stage is set for a successful and long-term experience. Thus, whether one is newly graduated from college, or has already built a creditable teaching record and desires to advance, or experiences dissatisfaction in his present situation, the matter of making such a consequential decision— selecting the right position—requires much thought and reflection.

That success in finding a position which fits one's background and capabilities hinges on self-analysis, intelligent inquiry, and vigor of pursuit is clearly stated by Simpson in "Self-evaluation Before and During the Interview." He outlines in considerable detail the kinds of questions that must be asked by the beginner and experienced person as he inquires into a situation and measures his findings against his own outlook and qualifications. Simpson concludes with a pro and con list of questions designed to help in making a decision to accept a particular position.

In "Securing the First Position" Stinnett offers many particular helps in the procedure and technique of finding a position, from the writing of letters of inquiry and application to accepting a position and signing a contract, and, finally, a consideration of the ethical questions involved.

Self-Evaluation Before and During the Interview

Ray H. Simpson

A very important, although too frequently neglected, aspect of seeking a new position is that of preparing credentials carefully and accurately. It is important that the recommendations be requested early of those who are to write them and put on file immediately after a course or other direct contact with the person who is to write the recommendation. Many of those who are writing recommendations deal with hundreds of individuals and after a one- or two-year period it is difficult to recover the impressions that one may have had of a teacher or prospective teacher during contact. Not only should these credentials or recommendations be sought immediately after major contact with an employer or an instructor, but it is very important that credentials be kept up to date even though one is not consciously searching for a new job at a specified time. To keep credentials up to date protects one and gives a type of insurance in that they will be available when needed.

Before going to an interview the following questions may well be used for self-evaluation:

1. Have I learned enough about the school and the community in which I am going to be interviewing, and have I listed questions that I would like to raise with the administrator and/or the teaching committee with whom I am scheduled to talk?

2. Am I prepared to give succinctly my current point of view regarding major educational issues such as discipline, my primary purposes in teaching a particular subject, the roles of the teacher in the classroom, the place of extracurricular activities, the roles of the teacher in working with other teachers, and other similar topics?

3. Have I decided rather specifically what I should say if certain questions are asked such as: Would you accept a contract if I were to offer it to you now? What salary would you expect? Do you believe that teachers should join labor

unions? Do you believe that all teachers should belong to the State Education Association? How do you feel about the NEA?

4. What is my attitude toward administrators as a group? This is a question that has not been carefully thought through by many teachers. Willower[1] found that when teacher trainees were asked whether they generally liked or disliked the school administrator, 32 percent of them volunteered the information that he was sometimes disliked because of his authority, which was resented. When the prospective teachers were asked: "What type of person do you think would like to have a career in school administration?" 67 percent pictured the aspirant for administration as a person ambitious for the prestige of high position who sought leadership responsibility. As one student put it, "The person who would really like to be an administrator is probably someone who likes to be boss and run things; someone who is looking for status and who drives to get ahead." The conscious or unconscious image that the teacher has of administrators is likely to affect not only his initial interview but also the teacher's future professional effectiveness.

Traditionally the administrator has asked all the questions in the interview. Forward-looking administrators as well as teachers are increasingly recognizing that it is important for the teacher to go into a new position with his eyes open to both its challenges and its limitations. Tact in asking questions is, of course, very important. The following questions are illustrative of the types of issues that the teacher may appropriately explore with the administrator in order to make a sensible assessment of working conditions in a prospective position:

1. What arrangements are made for inducting new teachers into the school system? For example, are there workshops prior to the opening of school? If so, who operates these?

2. Is there an active in-service training program during the school year? Is observation of other teachers encouraged? DeVita[2] found that when new teachers observed experienced teachers, when experienced teachers observed experienced teachers, when art teachers observed science teachers, when English teachers observed industrial arts teachers, and when other teachers observed as seemed profitable—all these pairings were found to produce very profitable experiences. The experiences of DeVita as well as other administrators have strongly suggested that observations are profitable not only for the observer but also for the observed in terms of professional development. In the approach described by DeVita, the respect and dignity of each individual teacher were emphasized. The school was not interested in having some teachers sit in

[1] D. J. Willower, "Education Students' Perceptions of School Administrators," *The School Review*, 70 (Autumn 1962), pp. 332-344.

[2] J. DeVita, "A Stimulating Technique—Teachers Observe Other Teachers," *The Clearing House*, 37 (May 1963), pp. 549-550.

judgment on other teachers. Written observation reports concerning the competency of the teacher were not encouraged. No names were used by the observer. No names were to be written on the observation form. The school was not even interested in constructive criticism that might be misconstrued or embarrassing to the teacher. In fact, criticism in any form concerning the work of the teacher was not expected. However, it was found that after five weeks of intervisitation it was almost unanimously declared to be a valuable and worthwhile experience. Such activities may also reflect a very cooperative spirit on the part of various teachers in the system.

3. What is the normal teaching load of beginning instructors? The size of the load, particularly of a beginning teacher, frequently determines his success or failure. Several studies have shown that first-year teachers are generally given heavier loads than more experienced teachers and are sometimes assigned odds and ends, some of which may be subjects outside the teacher's field of preparation.[3] The reason for raising this issue is apparent when it is obvious that an inexperienced teacher is likely to need more time for class preparation, and a reduced or at least not an extra teaching assignment is certainly desirable. However, in many systems across the country the reverse is found where experienced teachers automatically have the first choice of all teaching assignments, and what is left is given to the beginning teachers. It is better to find the answer to the teaching load question before employment rather than after employment.

4. What are nonteaching responsibilities or assignments? In addition to a heavy teaching load, in some school systems the new teacher is given a discouragingly large amount of extra-classroom activity, such as supervision of lunchrooms or halls, bus loading, committee work, school programs, sponsoring of two or more clubs, faculty-meeting preparation. Such activities, while necessary, may so spread the energies of the beginning teacher particularly so that he finds it difficult to accomplish his major classroom duties well.

It is important that the teacher investigate what is expected of him before employment rather than waiting till long after and possibly finding an unfortunate situation. Of course, no teaching situation is ideal. Each position necessarily carries with it some disadvantages. However, both the teacher and the school are likely to profit if the teacher is helped to go into a new position with a fairly adequate appraisal of what he is likely to encounter.

5. Is there a single salary schedule for both elementary and secondary teachers? At what level would I start in the salary scale if I were employed? How much credit is given for outside services in salary adjustments? What are arrangements for absences? What is the sick pay schedule, and is it cumulative?

---

[3] R. H. Nelson and M. L. Thompson, "Why Teachers Quit," *The Clearing House*, 37 (April 1963), pp. 467-472.

Are there insurance or other fringe benefits offered by the system? What deductions are made for all regularly employed teachers? In addition to pensions, what are these for?

6. Are there available written descriptions of school practices, including such things as teacher-transfer privileges, pension arrangements, personnel records, responsibilities of department heads, responsibilities of supervisors, responsibilities of principals, arrangements for workshops, and intervisitation possibilities?

7. What are the opportunities and encouragement for professional development and growth on the job? Is there a professional library available for use by teachers? How is work in extramural classes during the school year regarded? How is work in summer school viewed? Is attendance at various professional meetings encouraged or discouraged? What are expectations relative to membership in professional organizations? Is the school currently participating in the tryout of any of the newer curricular materials such as those of the Biological Sciences Curriculum Study,[4] the Foreign Language Instruction Project,[5] the Chemical Bond Approach Project,[6] or materials developed by any of several mathematics programs.[7]

8. Where do most teachers in the system live? What are representative costs? How much privacy does the teacher have in out-of-school hours? What is the distance to appropriate living quarters? Is there any problem of physical safety in the area?

9. Is there a staff evaluation and development program? For example, Sperber[8] has described a significant evaluation and appraisal program which involves three distinct and important stages. The first of these is the preappraisal stage, which involves the selection and orientation of new employees. This serves to set standards of performance. It also gives new employees opportunities in the previous spring and summer to observe and gather needed materials. In the case of employees joining the school system after the beginning of the academic year, opportunities are afforded for observation prior to taking over a position.

Continuous observation with the minimum of three half-hour observations is recommended. On-the-job performance is considered with regard to such factors

[4] B. Class, "Renascent Biology: A Report on the AIBS Biological Sciences Curriculum Study," *The School Review,* 70 (Spring 1962), pp. 16-43.

[5] M. A. Riestra and C. E. Johnson, "Changes in Attitudes of Elementary-School Pupils Toward Foreign-Speaking Peoples Resulting from the Study of Foreign Language," *Journal of Experimental Education,* 33 (Fall 1964), pp. 65-72.

[6] L. E. Strong, "Chemistry as a Science in the High School," *The School Review,* 70 (Spring 1962), pp. 44-50.

[7] E. Moise, ',The New Mathematics Programs," *The School Review,* 70 (Spring 1962), pp. 82-101.

[8] R. I. Sperber, "A Sound Staff Evaluation Program," *American School Board Journal,* 141 (July 1960), pp. 15-16.

as (1) personal characteristics, (2) planning and preparation, (3) methods of instructions for work, (4) observable results in people, (5) relationships with others, and (6) attitude toward teaching or work. Each observation of on-the-job performance is followed up with a postobservation conference with an appropriate staff member.

Planning for the yearly appraisal stage with a staff member is the core of the preappraisal stage. The appraiser reviews the employee's record folder; considers results of the postobservation conferences; consults with supervisors or department heads; re-examines lesson plans and/or work schedules; reviews appraisee-pupil relationships; reviews appraisee-co-worker relationships; reviews appraisee-parent relationships; and reviews appraisee-community relationships.

The second stage involves the main appraisal or conference session. The following are characteristic aspects of it:

1. It is set up at a mutually convenient time.
2. The appraiser sets an informal friendly climate for the session.
3. The appraiser develops the appraisee's desire to evaluate his own performance.
4. From this self-evaluation, patterns are traced to indicate the appraisee's area of strength, growth, and possible improvement.
5. An attempt is made to arrive at a common agreement as to the steps needed to make improvement providing a free exchange of ideas.
6. All written points in the appraisal session are summarized. A summary of appraisal remarks is sent to the principal's office.

The third and final stage involves a continual follow-up: checks on the effectiveness of appraisal sessions for growth and general cooperative development for improvement.

Another type of rating of teacher performance for self-improvement is described by Cosgrove.[9]   This method presents a procedure for evaluating the relative effectiveness of a teacher's performance in four areas of activities. These areas include:

1. Knowledge and organization of subject matter
2. Adequacy of relations with students in class
3. Adequacy of plans and procedures in class
4. Enthusiasm in working with students

For self-evaluation, phrases descriptive of teacher behavior are grouped, each group representing a phrase from each of the four areas. An advantage of the resulting profile is that the teacher (and his supervisor) can consider his behavior

---

[9] D. J. Cosgrove, "Diagnostic Ratings of Teacher Performance," *Journal of Educational Psychology,* 50 (1959), pp. 200-204.

in terms of each of the four dimensions and the behaviors involved. The profile approach with a grouping of items presents an organized and useful analysis of the rating, giving the teacher a clearer idea of his relatively strong and weak areas of performance. The forced-choice arrangement minimizes bias which is so often evidenced in rating schemes. In completing the form, the students rank the phrases in each set as they apply to the instructor. The end result is a profile showing the relative standing of the instructor on the four areas of teacher activity. This type of evaluation approach can be useful not only to the school system but also to the teacher who wants to know where to begin to work on improving his effectiveness.

Finally, after all information the teacher wishes to get or is able to get has been shaken down into the *pros* versus the *cons* for accepting a particular job, an evaluative decision must be made. Illustrative of that which some beginning and experienced teachers face, as epitomized by Hunter and Amidon,[10] is the case of Andrea Kern, who wished to teach in the town where she and her husband would be living. She had a fine academic and student teaching record, had been a leader in academic and extracurricular activities, "was a fine musician, a creative person, and one who loved people." She had already been offered two jobs elsewhere but the Northpoint School would be the only one with an opening within twenty-five miles of where she would be living.

As Andrea Kern sized up the situation, the *pros* relative to accepting the job looked something like this:

If this job were not accepted, commuting of over twenty-five miles would be necessary.

"We have a school library. . . . The extent to which the teachers use extra library reading is up to them," said the principal.

The salary was adequate, since her husband would also have a salary.

A second car for which the Kerns would not have the money would not be necessary.

The principal said: "You'll get all the help you need from us. . . ."

The *cons* as Andrea Kern perceived them stacked up like this:

An inspection of the physical setup of the school did not impress her. All classrooms were almost identical, with children's seats "in carefully lined rows with the teacher's desk plunk in the middle of the front of the room."

"The children all stood when they 'recited,' and there was a formal and strict air about the school that didn't appeal to Andrea."

The principal said: "We are primarily interested in basic education. . . . We expect our teachers to be firm disciplinarians, and we don't like frills."

10 E. Hunter and E. Amidon, *Student Teaching, Cases and Comments* (Chicago: Holt, Rinehart and Winston, 1964), pp. 147-149.

Only one reading series was used, and "we expect every child to have to read through the two books on his grade level before he can progress to the next grade—with an occasional exception, of course."

". . . In the first three grades, we require the reading groups to meet twice each day; once in the morning and once in the afternoon. We use the view-and-learn phonics system, and this is particularly stressed in the first two grades. And we do insist on three groups in reading. We have found that there is simply not adequate time for more than that if each child is to receive enough drill." (This shook Andrea up a bit, since there had been a great deal of freedom in the two places where she had done student teaching and there had been three or four basal reading series, as well as extensive library reading. Also the groups did not even have to meet once a day, let alone twice, if the teacher considered other activities more important. In the other schools reading was viewed as an integral part of the school day—and as a tool, not an end in itself.)

"Social studies" was divided into two distinct parts—history three times a week and geography twice. A strict time schedule for teaching all units was set up in advance, and Andrea would be expected to follow it closely if she accepted the job. (This depressed Andrea, since "she was used to an emerging curriculum, within broad guidelines, and she was used to having the day flow as seemed appropriate according to the content and the children, not according to some predetermined time schedule.")

The work sounded more clerical than creative.

The principal said: ". . . but you will have to accommodate yourself to us, and not expect our system to fit you."

Should Andrea Kern accept the position?

How does limiting oneself, as Andrea was, affect the teacher? The teaching profession?

How autonomous should the teacher be in making certain kinds of decisions in his classroom?

In what areas is it reasonable to expect the teacher "to accommodate" himself to the school system? In what areas should the system accommodate to the teacher?

Securing the First Position

T. M. Stinnett

Applying for the First Job

There are recognized, legitimate ways of applying for teaching positions. There are also methods that are unprofessional and that bring discredit upon teachers as a group.

For most beginners, the initial contact is through the college placement bureau. Candidates file statements about their backgrounds of preparation and experiences. They furnish the names of references who can speak about their characters, personalities, academic abilities, and experiences with children or in general employment. The college adds statements about proficiencies in student teaching. These papers are bound together into a placement folder, usually prepared before the middle of the senior year.

Employing officials, usually the superintendent for small towns and cities and the personnel director for large communities, write the placement bureau describing their needs and stating the day that they will visit the campus. The placement bureau assembles a number of candidates and arranges an interview schedule. The bureau has the folders of all candidates ready for the employing official when he arrives. They are given to him along with the interview schedule. A small room is set aside for his use. He then interviews the candidates according to the schedule.

During the interview the employing official asks questions about preparation, experience, philosophy, personal life, and almost anything else that occurs to him. It is customary for him to guide the general trend of the conversation. This does not mean that the candidate should not ask questions. On the contrary, a much better impression is made on the employer if intelligent queries are made. A conference or meeting of any kind is a dead affair unless there is a two-way flow of conversation.

The candidate should look upon the interview as an opportunity to evaluate the desirability of becoming a teacher in the community represented by the employing official, as well as a means of careful selection of the right candidates for appropriate jobs. It is a time when one can find out how well the standards proposed in the first part of the chapter are met.

A number of things may result from the interview. The employing official may close it with a vague statement to the effect that he is not yet in a position

Reprinted with permission of The Macmillan Company from *Professional Problems of Teachers*, Third Edition, by T. M. Stinnett, pp. 104-110. Copyright ©by The Macmillan Company, 1968.

to make an offer or that he has a number of other applications to consider. The candidate should recognize that this usually means that a position will not be offered.

If the employer is at least mildly interested and is of a rather cautious type, he will probably ask the prospective teacher to send him a letter of application. If this is done, the candidate may or may not hear further from the employer.

The official may ask the candidate to come to his community to talk things over. In this case there is almost sure to be real interest in the prospective teacher.

There are instances in which employers carry pads of contracts already signed by members of their boards of education. If they want to hire a teacher they simply fill in his name, have him sign, and give him one of the forms.

Accepting a Position

It is wise not to accept a position without some thought and gathering of information. In the previous section, the desirability of finding out everything possible about the community in which one is considering teaching was stressed. It would ordinarily be unwise to accept until one had visited the schools, talked with teachers, and secured every other bit of information that could be gathered. Then the pros and cons should be carefully weighed. One can then decide if a position will probably be satisfactory.

Should the first position that is offered be accepted? It is probably best to have several interviews and several files of information in order to have a basis for comparison. On the other hand, if the position that is tendered seems to be just what one is looking for, there is no point in waiting.

Ethics of Accepting

A teacher should not accept a position without due consideration, but after his word has been given, he should live up to his promise unless a very unusual condition arises. Not to do so brings discredit upon the individual, the institution from which he is graduating, and the teaching profession in general. An old saying is that one's word should be as good as one's bond. Society could hardly function unless most people kept their promises.

Admittedly, a few teachers have been careless about fulfilling their obligations. Some have been known to resign from one position in order to accept another only a few days before school begins. Others have quit at a moment's notice to go to a community nearer home or to one where friends are located. It is hard to justify such actions unless the officials of the district where the teacher has been serving are entirely willing to give releases.

When a beginning teacher, particularly, resigns from a contract signed in good faith, he labels himself as unreliable. He also casts a reflection upon his college, because employing officials may feel that he has not been taught proper ethics. He adds fuel to the charge that teachers are interested only in themselves and not in society.

Personal Interviews

There is much less concern about the dress of candidates for teaching positions than was true a few years ago. It is essential that one be neatly and appropriately dressed and well groomed. Today there is little emphasis upon the kind of dress that a teacher should wear, as long as it is in good taste.

In preparing for an interview, it is well to analyze one's strengths and weaknesses. If the candidate likes children, why not say so? If he feels that he is particularly good at art work, why not bring this out? If he is adept at promoting adequate social adjustments, why not mention it?

There is no need to mention weaknesses, although one should not attempt to conceal them. If he has trouble with classroom management, he should admit it if frankly asked, but it is not necessary to volunteer the information. If he is not good at reports, he should confess this fault when questioned about it. He does not need to bring up this topic himself.

A candidate does not want to sit like a dummy during an interview, but he should be careful not to talk too much. Being a good listener is sometimes difficult but essential. Probably more people have talked themselves out of jobs than lost them by talking too little.

In all that he does say, the teacher should be frank and honest. If he does not know the answer to a question, he should say so. If he has not had the training or experience about which the superintendent may inquire, it is not wise to give the impression that he has. He may, though, give reasons why he thinks that his qualifications more than outweigh any deficiencies that he has.

A Checklist for Securing a Teaching Job. Here is a sequential checklist of things to do to assume employment as a beginning teacher.[1]

1. Register with your college placement bureau well in advance of graduation.
2. Fill out the placement forms, providing references, other required papers, and a photograph.
3. Talk with members of the placement staff about your desires regarding your first position, so that they can be alerted and in a position to suggest your name when an appropriate vacancy occurs.
4. Arrange to attend meetings of seniors, usually held by the placement bureau, to discuss job opportunities, salaries, certification, and interviews.
5. Check the placement bulletin board for schedules of interviews, so that you may arrange a meeting with the school employing officers of your choice.

[1] Adapted from Wilbur A. Yauch, Martin H. Bartels, and Emmet Morris, *The Beginning Teacher.* New York: Holt, Rinehart and Winston, Inc., 1955, pp. 55-61.

6. Study the lists of jobs that have been filed with the placement office.
7. Write letters of inquiry or application, or telephone regarding the jobs in which you may be interested.
8. Respond immediately to notices of vacancies sent to you by the placement office. Do this whether interested or not in the job or jobs listed.
9. Apply for your teacher's certificate. Your placement office or faculty advisor will help you with this.

Letters of Inquiry and Application

Sending out promiscuously a large number of letters of application is probably the least effective way of finding a suitable teaching job. A few letters of inquiry, brief and courteous, addressed to the superintendent of schools or director of personnel of districts in which you feel you would like employment is an acceptable and effective means of determining where vacancies exist. The following is an example of the type:

Dr. Charles E. Heath
Superintendent of Schools
Suburbia, Illinois

Dear Dr. Heath:

This will inquire whether your school system will have a position open for the ensuing school year in the teaching of mathematics.

I shall graduate from Central State College this June, with a Bachelor of Science degree and a major in mathematics. Upon graduation I shall meet all requirements for certification in Illinois in this field. In addition I shall have a minor in physical science.

My credentials are on file in the college placement-bureau office. I shall be pleased to have you request these for examination. Further, I shall be pleased to come for an interview at your request.

Cordially yours,

James Appleton

The formal letter of application may not be necessary. Your placement office may locate suitable vacancies, confer with the employing school officials, and arrange interviews. Also, most school districts now provide their own application forms, and may require only that you execute this form. If a letter of application is judged to be necessary, extreme care should be exercised in form and content. Even if you have to pay to have it done, send the letter in typed form. This is easier to read and makes a better impression upon busy school officials. Write your letter in first-draft form, then polish and repolish, checking words and their spelling until the letter is in correct form and conveys precisely what you want to say. Avoid the lengthy letter and the breezy or smart-alecky type of communication. Make the letter a personal one, addressed to the school official by name and position. Avoid at all costs the "To whom it may concern" salutation. Here is an example of a succinct, yet adequate, letter of application:

Dr. Charles E. Heath
Superintendent of Schools
Suburbia, Illinois

Dear Dr. Heath:

I submit herewith my application for the position of teacher of mathematics in the Suburbia High School. My interest in the position is based upon two considerations: (1) This is the teaching field for which I have prepared and in which I feel that I am competent. (2) I have studied carefully the policies and teaching climate in your school system and am convinced that they are superior.

My credentials are being sent to you, under separate cover, by the Central State College Placement Bureau. Should you desire additional references or other information, I shall be glad to supply them. Too, I shall be pleased to come for an interview if you desire.

Cordially yours,

James Appleton

The Letter May Be Important

The letter is the personal representative of the applicant. A misspelled, poorly written letter is likely to jeopardize chances of employment. No matter how many times it must be rewritten, and regardless of the amount of dictionary work that is involved, it is important that the letter be free of typographical errors, grammatical errors, and misspelled words.

At one time, school employing officials insisted that letters be written in the candidate's own handwriting. Many officials now seem to prefer typewritten letters because of their greater compactness and readability.

The important thing seems to be to present the best effect possible.

Commercial Agencies

Beginning teachers seldom have need to use a commercial teachers' agency. College placement bureaus feel responsible for helping all the current graduates to secure positions. The new crop is, therefore, sometimes pushed at the expense of the old. Experienced teachers sometimes find, although not often, that they get less consideration from their college bureaus than do the beginners. Commercial agencies are, therefore, more for those who have been teaching several years than for the ones seeking their first positions.

Beginners who wish to secure positions in states other than the one in which they received their training often find commercial agencies of value. Some college bureaus do not extend their efforts further than the borders of the state.

The commercial agency is likely to operate on a regional or national, rather than a state, basis.

Cost is the chief disadvantage of the commercial agency. Ordinarily, 5 or 6 percent of the first year's salary is charged.

Other Aids in Finding a Job

For making application to school districts in other states, superintendents' names and addresses can be obtained from the latest edition of *Education Directory*, Part 2, "Public School Systems."[2]

The United States Employment Service provides assistance, without cost, to applicants for teaching jobs. It maintains some 1,800 local and state offices and works closely with college and university placement bureaus and state school systems. Through its clearinghouse arrangement, teachers may be in touch with vacancies wherever they exist in the United States.

A number of state departments of education and state education associations maintain placement or listing services for teachers. Most of these charge placement fees. The following state departments of education maintain teacher-placement services (address is the capital city): Alabama, Alaska, Georgia, Idaho, Louisiana, Maine, Massachusetts, Minnesota, Mississippi, New Hampshire, New Jersey, New Mexico, North Dakota, Oklahoma, Pennsylvania, Utah, Vermont, and Wyoming.

The following state education associations maintain placement or listing services for teachers (address is the capital city, unless otherwise indicated): California (Burlingame; Los Angeles for southern section), Colorado, Illinois, Iowa, Kentucky (Louisville), New Hampshire, North Carolina, Oregon (Portland), South Carolina, Texas, Vermont, Washington (Seattle), and West Virginia.[3] Also, NEA has now established a teacher-position listing service called NEA-Search.

Use of References

It is customary to list a number of references when writing a letter of application and when registering with a college placement bureau or a commercial teachers' agency.

These references should, as far as possible, be persons who have observed the candidate's teaching or have watched him work with children in informal situations such as camp or scout work, recreation activities, or church schools. Next in value are the testimonials of employers or businessmen for whom

---

[2] See *Education Directory*, Part 2, "Public School Systems," published annually by the U.S. Department of Health, Education, and Welfare, Office of Education, and available from the U.S. Government Printing Office.

[3] National Education Association, Research Division, "Obtaining a Teaching Position in the Public Schools," Research Memo 1961-27. Washington, D.C.: The Association, June, 1961, 33 pp.

candidates have worked. The recommendations of college or high school teachers have great weight. Of doubtful influence in employment are landladies, colleagues, and neighbors.

It is only common courtesy to ask permission of a person whose name is to be used as reference. He will feel much more like affirmative statements and will probably give a better recommendation if he has been consulted in advance.

The Contract Form[4]

There can usually be no legal employment without a written contract. While in a few instances oral contracts have been upheld by the courts, oral agreements are difficult to enforce. Teachers should insist upon written contracts and should read them rather carefully before signing.

A contract need not be lengthy or complex. About all that it needs to do is to state the names of the parties, the times of beginning and ending work, the tasks to be performed, and the salary to be paid. To be valid, a contract must be signed by the teacher and by authorized representatives of the board of education.

Contracts that carry a clause permitting cancellation by either party on thirty days' notice are not satisfactory. Many teachers have them, though, and apparently are generally satisfied with such an arrangement.

It is best to watch for clauses such as, "The amount of salary paid may be reduced at any time if the district is short of funds." A statement like this is not good for the teacher, even if the district will probably never use this power.

It is also wise to be sure that no unexpected duties are specified. Teachers sometimes have had to coach senior plays or act as advisers to the school paper because they did not read their contracts. The duties were specified there but were not noted.

---

[4] A contract, as contrasted with a license, is a legal document, binding the school board and the teacher to certain conditions of employment. A contract is for the protection of the teacher and the employing school district against capricious action.

Chapter 2

Preparing for the Opening of School

For the teacher who thinks in terms of the nature of the child and democratic society, the structure of subject matter or discipline he is to teach, and the appropriate methodology, the planning and preparation that take place prior to the opening day of school demand that attention be turned to matters of overall and long-range significance as well as those of immediate and day-to-day import.

In the first selection of this chapter, Collier and his colleagues treat objectives comprehensively by pointing out that teaching is a decision-making process that must be conducted in terms of "an evaluation of the times in which we live." Intelligent decision-making in the setting of a changing society requires that considerable thought be given to the determination of objectives which are specific and operable for child and teacher in the social setting. Citing the well-known work of Bloom, the writers proceed to show how the teacher may intelligently approach the all-important task of setting up objectives in behavioral terms, especially in the cognitive domain.

Davis emphasizes the importance of a dynamic setting for teaching and learning, and how such an environment must be predicated on a sound understanding of child growth and development. She indicates how the relaxed, homelike social atmosphere and the spacing and arrangement of furniture and work centers will create the climate necessary for realization of the behavioral objectives stressed earlier by Collier.

Since the realization of well thought out objectives is, to a high degree, dependent on thorough planning prior to and continuous with the teaching act, the editors have decided to include two authoritative articles on this aspect of teaching, so important to beginners.

Mehl and her associates emphasize the necessity of starting the planning process well prior to the opening of school. Beginning with general orientation meetings, the topic is carried through such steps as consulting instructional guides, becoming familiar with textbooks and teachers' manuals, planning for the year, and constructing the daily schedule.

18

Beauchamp follows with a detailed treatment of the daily lesson plan and the teaching unit. Along with offering workable suggestions, he stresses that all arguments are in favor of planning, whether they come from the experienced teacher or the administrator, and that research shows superior teaching and content achievement to have a strong relationship to the thoroughness with which the task is done.

Objectives of Elementary Education

Calhoun C. Collier
W. Robert Houston
Robert R. Schmatz
William J. Walsh

THE TEACHER AND OBJECTIVES

The diversity of population that constitutes an elementary school, together with an evaluation of the times in which we live, demands that the teacher provide a balanced set of educational experiences. However, in order to build and maintain a balanced curriculum and to have a basis for selecting, organizing, and evaluating learning experiences, the teacher must have a set of carefully developed objectives to serve as guidelines.

Teaching is a decision-making process. A person who occupies a leadership role, and most certainly teaching is a leadership role, cannot avoid the responsibility of making many decisions. These decisions, for the most part, are based on value judgments—values deemed important for today's youngsters and tomorrow's adults.

Objectives direct and refine the teacher's thinking as decisions are made. A teacher utilizes as many resources as possible to guide the formulation of a statement of educational objectives. For instance, it would seem wise to rely on (1) his preparation background for teaching; (2) writings of scholars in such fields as philosophy, psychology, and human growth and development; (3) needs

Reprinted with permission of The Macmillan Company from *Teaching in the Modern Elementary School* by Calhoun C. Collier, W. Robert Houston, Robert R. Schmatz, and William J. Walsh, pp. 25-35. Copyright ©by The Macmillan Company, 1967.

of society; (4) desires of children; (5) professional groups and/or associations; (6) local and state curricular groups; and (7) subject-area specialists.

Although it is important to consider carefully as many factors as possible when formulating a statement of objectives, it is also important that the statement not describe a utopia. The ever-changing needs of contemporary society necessitate continual modification of educational objectives. Schools differ from community to community, and what may be considered a prime objective in one school may not, and perhaps should not, receive a high degree of emphasis in another school. The individual teacher is the keystone to effective definition and modification of objectives, therefore he must continually direct his attention to the determination of significant goals.

EFFICACIOUS OBJECTIVES

What is taught and *how* it is taught ought to stem from answers to the question, "What shall we teach for?" In other words, the direction of the program of curricular experiences needs to be guided by our answers to the questions, "What kinds of persons *are* these elementary school age youngsters?" and "What kinds of persons should they become?"

The following objectives warrant the serious consideration of all teachers. Although they are purposely stated in rather broad terms, it would appear that they are significant for our times and that they can be applied to almost any elementary school or to almost any grade level or subject area in an elementary school.

Intellectual or Mental Development

Elementary schools must concern themselves with the important objective of helping youngsters develop a valid foundation in such fundamental and important areas as science, mathematics, reading, language, fine arts, and social science. For instance, the learner needs to develop a variety of reading skills so he can read and interpret information about many areas. Children also should be helped to develop a love of reading as a source of personal satisfaction and pleasure. Teachers need to be effective in helping *all* pupils develop their full *potential* in areas such as mathematics, science, and social science in order to *make intelligent decisions* in a highly complex society.

Mobility of population increases the need to become competent in the skills of communication—speaking, writing, listening. Understanding man's relationship to man becomes vital. Surely children need to build meaningful broad concepts of history and geography and of how these concepts affect human behavior. The intent in this book is not to develop specific objectives in the many subject areas in an elementary school program, but rather to emphasize the importance of these areas to intellectual development. Each subject area included in today's elementary school has its place, not for its particular intrinsic value but rather for its contribution in terms of knowledges and skills which the individual must utilize to function more effectively. If they are to serve this function, subject areas cannot be viewed as separate entities, but must be perceived in their proper relationship to each other.

Those who teach in the elementary school must be concerned with providing experiences that will equip the child with background, knowledge, information, and methods of securing data as well as with the ability to apply information in making wise judgments in new situations.

Intellectual or mental development is an important objective at the elementary school level; therefore, we need to provide for the development of the fundamental skills in using the tools of learning. Increased knowledge and skills enhance freedom because one has more adequate tools with which to work, more of a selection from which to make wise choices.

Fostering Growth as an Individual

An objective should aid and direct each young person to grow and develop as an independent, adequate individual. Because of individual differences and needs, specific objectives for each child may be unique. This instructional stance was underscored by Wilhelms.

> *Every child is unique, and he has an inalienable right to be himself. The pattern of his life to this day has brought him to us with needs and interests peculiar to himself. He has potentialities that are all his own.*
>
> *If we presume—however subtly or cleverly—to set some pattern before him and say, "This you shall be," we violate him. Furthermore, we risk losing what could have been most distinctive in him, because it was not in our predetermined list. Clearly we must take him as the individual he is and open the way for him to become ever more truly himself.*[1]

A child growing up in a democracy needs to learn how to perform effectively both as an individual and as a member of a group. Efforts within the school are directed toward helping each person develop as an individual, realizing the worthiness of *self* and yet recognizing and respecting the worth and rights of *others*. These ideals are certainly compatible. If a person understands himself and has respect for himself, he is more likely to understand others and to be at peace with them.

In the elementary school emphasis on learning to know one's self—the development of an adequate and realistic self-concept—is important. Each pupil should be assisted in recognizing his strengths and weaknesses and how to use his

---

[1] Fred T. Wilhelms, "Curriculum Sources," *What Are The Sources of the Curriculum? A Symposium* (Washington, D.C.: Association for Supervision and Curriculum Development, 1962), p. 21.

strengths to overcome some of the weaknesses. Human beings strive toward selfhood; therefore, the teacher has a responsibility to help the learner become progressively more adequate in self-direction, self-discipline, and self-evaluation.

In discussing the nature of the learner with reference to the classroom, Macdonald states,

> When the student enters the classroom he brings with him a self, or reflection of his ego processes. . . . If the child's self-perceptions reflect adequate ego strength, he will see himself as adequate to the performance of curricular tasks as well as liking what he sees. He will be open to new experiences, ready to grow, willing to experiment and discover. However, when self-perceptions are negative, they have a debilitating effect. Curricular tasks will be seen as too hard and as imposed unreasonably. [2]

Learning experiences need to be paced so they will be compatible with a pupil's needs if he is to be assisted effectively in developing as an independent, adequate individual whose perceptions are positive toward self, toward learning, and toward society.

Growth of the Individual as a Social Being

This objective involves the development of effective human relationships and sensitivity to civic responsibility. People, whether they are pupils in an elementary school or senior citizens, participate more effectively in our society, both as individuals and as members of a group, when they feel secure and confident.

A child, to grow as a social being, needs to become involved in a variety of experiences—sometimes as a leader, sometimes as a follower, sometimes as a cooperating member of a group. To become an effective social being there needs to be opportunity to develop an awareness of, and respect for, the feelings, opinions, and rights of individuals in the various arenas of life.

A pupil should learn something of the values held by other peoples and societies. He may then test his own values against those of others, and through this process better understand the values of our democratic society.

Most of the children in elementary schools are citizens of the United States by virtue of birth. The schools are not preparing these people to be citizens— they are already citizens! Teachers should view them as citizens and help them better understand the rights and responsibilities that accompany citizenship in a democracy. Education for social responsibility deals with political, economic, and social structures. Yet recent research reveals that very few children below

---

[2] James B. Macdonald, "An Image of Man: The Learner Himself," *Individualizing Instruction* (Washington, D.C.: Association for Supervision and Curriculum Development, 1964), p. 38.

the sixth-grade level are at all familiar with the function of the courts or the structure and processes of government and politics. Education for social responsibility should be directed toward democratic values, such as respect for the worth and dignity of the individual. Social responsibility also involves groups working together for common purposes.

Learning to Live with Change

People must learn how to effectively deal with the drastic changes resulting from the great explosions in knowledge, technology, and population described in Chapter 1. Our highly developed communication media now make it possible for young children to actually witness the inhuman treatment of individuals and minority groups, the horrors of war, the overthrow of a government, the assassination of a president, the launching of an astronaut, the birth of a new nation.

The world in which our children will spend their lives will be radically different from any we have known. Adults do not know what pleasures, challenges, opportunities, and problems today's and tomorrow's youth will face, but there is little doubt that these experiences will be different from ours.

One important objective, then, ought to be that of helping the learner expect, welcome, and learn how to cope with change. He needs to recognize that in reality our problems are the world's problems and the world's problems are our problems. Boys and girls can be helped to understand that there will be many different ways to use what they learn. It is important to provide experience that requires an individual to use his knowledge and abilities in dealing successfully with new problems and new situations. Youngsters need assistance to develop effectiveness in working with others, to deal with change and successive crises. As expressed by Earl Kelley, people need to understand that today is different from yesterday, that tomorrow will be different from today, and to look forward confidently to meeting life on that basis.[3]

Fostering Creativity

Our democratic form of government was conceived from the idea that each individual has a unique personality and a unique contribution to make. This democratic way of life has continued to be nourished and sustained by the diverse and unique contributions of individuals toward a common good. If the elementary school is to meet the needs, interest, and abilities of its pupils, the objective of stimulating, encouraging, and fostering creativity must be given a high priority. Sand and Miller believe,

---

3 Earl C. Kelley, *Education for What is Real* (New York: Harper, 1947).

Creativity has been important in the dynamism and growth of American civilization in the past, and its importance will increase in the future. Creativity will be of growing importance in improving skills, ideas, and products in an expanding market; in the global conflict of democracy and communism; and in providing a personal, therapeutic counterforce to the conformity and cultural homogeneity that are the result of the rapid population growth, the cold war, and a mass society.[4]

It is generally agreed that creativity cannot be taught. However, there is much recent research that clearly indicates that every child comes to school with some creative potential. Creativity is not restricted to a few pupils or to certain aspects of the curriculum. Creativity simply means thinking and doing in ways that are unique or new to the person who is thinking and doing. A climate of freedom that encourages creativity in thought and action may be substituted for stultifying rigidity and conformity. The teacher's job is to encourage and assist the individual to discover and utilize his abilities, together with all resources available to him, in order that he may make his own special contribution for personal satisfaction and for the betterment of others.

MAKING OBJECTIVES OPERATIVE

If objectives are to have any operative significance they must be the guiding forces behind the teacher's thinking and action as he plans, selects, and organizes learning activities into some kind of sequence. To function as effective guides, objectives must be stated in specific and clear terms, terms which describe the behavioral changes we desire the pupil to exhibit. Once the kinds of desirable changes in behavior are clearly understood, action may be taken to translate the set of objectives into a program of experiences that have a good chance of attaining the desired goals or educational outcomes.

Probably the best assurance that objectives will be stated clearly and precisely in behavioral terms is to develop a taxonomy of objectives—a classification of pupil behaviors directly related to the expected outcomes. Teachers will find Bloom's *Taxonomy of Educational Objectives* a helpful guide in planning a set of desired pupil behaviors together with procedures for their evaluation. Bloom defines educational objectives as, "explicit formulations of the ways in which students are expected to be changed by the educative process. That is, the ways in which they will change in their thinking, their feelings, and their actions."[5] A taxonomic classification of objectives can facilitate communication among educators as they plan curricular experiences, instructional

---

[4] Ole Sand and Richard I. Miller, "New Goals in Instruction," *California Teachers Association Journal,* May 1964, p. 27.

[5] Benjamin S. Bloom (ed.), *Taxonomy of Educational Objectives* (New York: McKay, 1956), p. 26.

procedures, and evaluative techniques. Developing a taxonomy of educational objectives

> *requires the selection of an appropriate list of symbols to represent all the major types of educational outcomes. Next, there is the task of defining these symbols with sufficient precision to permit and facilitate communication about these phenomena among teachers, administrators, curriculum workers, testers, educational research workers, and others who are likely to use the taxonomy. Finally, there is the task of trying the classification and securing the consensus of the educational workers who wish to use the taxonomy.*[6]

In developing a taxonomy of educational goals in the cognitive domain (recall or recognition of knowledge and the development of intellectual abilities and skills), intended behaviors of pupils as related to mental acts were classified into six major classes. These were then arranged into a hierarchial order of behaviors from simple to complex. These six cognitive objectives were subsequently divided into subclasses from the simplest behavior to the most complex. The resultant objectives in outline form are:

Knowledge
    Knowledge of Specifics
        Knowledge of Terminology
        Knowledge of Specific Facts
        Knowledge of Ways and Means of Dealing with Specifics
        Knowledge of Conventions
        Knowledge of Trends and Sequences
        Knowledge of Classifications and Categories
        Knowledge of Criteria
        Knowledge of Methodology
        Knowledge of the Universals and Abstractions in a Field
        Knowledge of Principles and Generalizations
        Knowledge of Theories and Structures

    Comprehension
        Translation
        Interpretation
        Extrapolation

    Application

    Analysis
        Analysis of Elements
        Analysis of Relationships
        Analysis of Organizational Principles

[6] Bloom, *op. cit.,* p. 11

Synthesis
> Production of Unique Communication
> Production of a Plan, or Proposed Set of Operations
> Derivation of a Set of Abstract Relations

Evaluation
> Judgments in Terms of Internal Evidence
> Judgments in Terms of External Criteria

Each class and its subclasses were defined in such a way that all who worked with the objectives could communicate with each other.[7]

An efficacious educational objective is applicable, in fact appropriate and desirable, for children who come from a variety of backgrounds. The divergent environments of three elementary school-age youngsters were described in Chapter 1. In spite of the evident individual differences among the three children, it would be extremely difficult to deny the significant relevance of the five broad objectives that have been briefly developed in the past few pages for each of these children. Even though the objectives are applicable we would not expect the three children to progress toward the objective in the same way, at the same rate, or to finally derive equal benefit.

The elementary teacher plans a variety of activities and utilizes diverse procedures to aid each pupil to make as much progress toward the desired objective as his ability and background will permit. However, the purpose of this chapter is not to discuss what learning experiences may be provided but to consider what teachers expect the youngster to be like as a result of some learning experiences—from kindergarten to completion of the elementary school.

As an example, consider the objective *intellectual or mental development.* Once the community and faculty of an elementary school has accepted this as an important objective, each teacher in the school needs to think in terms of both long and short-term outcomes. In terms of this objective, what kinds of reasonable pupil performance should a teacher expect—by the time the child completes the elementary school program; at the end of each year; at the end of a unit; at the end of a month, week, or day?

Before a teacher attempts to answer the preceding questions he should consider carefully the general objective under consideration and decompose it into more specific objectives. Consensus indicates the elementary school provides the child's first formal impetus to a continuing intellectual life. As later learning builds on the work of the elementary school, a teacher is concerned with promoting mental or intellectual growth in many areas. Undoubtedly one of these areas would be mathematics, but the development of intellectual growth in mathematics is still a rather broad objective. Obviously teachers must

---

[7] For a condensed version of the taxonomy see Bloom *op. cit.,* pp. 201-207.

formulate more narrow or specific objectives within the area of mathematics for meaningful translation into action. A more precise objective might well be the development of understandings and the ability to apply these understandings as they relate to the area of measurement.

A list of objectives follows that is stated in terms that describe what the learner will "do" (behavior as performance) as acceptable evidence that he has achieved, or progressed toward the objective at three levels of an elementary education program—lower grades, middle grades, upper grades. The list is offered neither as a complete set of objectives in this area nor as the most important objectives for this learning area, but as an illustration of how objectives can be meaningfully stated in expected behavioral terms.

Table 1
The Concept of Measurement

Lower Grades (K-2)	Middle Grades (3-4)	Upper Grades (5-6)
Can tell time by the hour, half hour, and minute intervals.	Can explain why we need standard units of measure.	Recognizes differences between linear and surface measurement.
Identifies objects grouped by dozen and half dozen.	Tells time to the second.	Measures and determines perimeters and areas.
Differentiates between units of liquid measure such as a cup, half pint, and pint.	Reads map scales.	Uses protractor to measure angles in degrees.
Reads weather thermometer.	States the relation between various units of linear and liquid measure.	Recognizes that all measurement is approximate.
Determines whether one object is longer or taller than another.		Selects appropriate standard measuring unit in terms of what is to be measured and the precision desired.

SUMMARY

If classroom experiences are to be goal-oriented, the program of learning activities and the teacher's methods must be based on carefully considered objectives. Such objectives are based on both the needs of the individual learner and the needs of the general society. When formulating a set of educational objectives a teacher uses all available sources of information.

Greater effort than in the past needs to be exerted by teachers to formulate objectives in terms that concisely describe the behavior desired in the youngster.

A Teaching and Learning Environment

Sara Davis

The right conditions are important for the proper growth and development of all life. A good gardener gives his attention to many factors: texture and components of the soil; water supply; sunlight; heat; natural and commercial fertilizers to stimulate growth; adequate space; and right times for planting, fertilizing and tilling. But he considers these factors in relation to particular plants in a particular location. Not all good gardeners follow the same patterns, nor do they use exactly the same materials in the same amounts; but every good gardener knows the peculiar characteristics and needs of each plant in his garden. He works with the materials and conditions as he finds them, supplementing and enriching as needed, to promote the best growth of each plant.

So it is with the good teacher as he guides the growth and development of children. He teaches a unique group of children in a unique environment with the resources available to provide maximum growth for the children. The teacher himself is the most important element in that environment.

The Teacher

A dynamic setting for learning requires a teacher who understands and likes children, one whose values and attitudes are reflected in a climate for learning which is accepting and challenging and in which every person is treated with respect, appreciated for what he is, and valued as a member of the group. Thus the teacher through his reflected understandings, attitudes, feelings and values creates the classroom atmosphere which the child senses as he enters and lives in that classroom. This may be a feeling of flexibility, warmth and orderliness, or it may be one of coldness and rigidity. The classroom that facilitates learning is arranged to stimulate curiosity and interest in a setting of warmth, friendliness and security. Here too are no patterns to follow, for teachers and children are different and situations vary widely. But the physical arrangement should facilitate the type of learning the teacher wants to accomplish.

A Home at School

The good elementary school classroom is so arranged that children feel at home. Each child feels relaxed, at ease and comfortable. An encouraging and supportive teacher helps create a general atmosphere of mutual cooperativeness,

Reprinted by permission of Sara Davis and the Association for Childhood Education International, 3615 Wisconsin Avenue, N.W., Washington, D.C., from *Childhood Education* 43:271-275, January, 1967. Copyright ©1967 by the Association.

acceptance and friendliness. Elements similar to those in life outside of school are present, a pleasing combination of the familiar to provide security and the unfamiliar to interest and stimulate. Each child feels that school is a challenging place, somewhere between home and a laboratory—a place where learning is a natural by-product because experiences have purpose, the environment is stimulating but not artificial, and the activities are challenging but not overwhelming. Materials and supplies are easily accessible and inviting; furnishings look and feel as though children and their needs were considered when they were purchased. Cozy nooks invite a child to curl up with a book or puzzle, and interesting corners kindle interest and tickle the curiosity. Arrangement and space are open and flexible.

Space and Arrangement

Children need space: space to try out, explore, experiment; space to work in groups, large and small; space to work alone; space to play and create; space to be a functioning group member; space to learn to be one's own best self. New classrooms should be planned with a concern for space for growing. But arrangement can either create space or use it all up. Flexible furniture flexibly arranged can provide space for many types of experiences. Movable table-type desks may be arranged singly or in clusters to serve multiple purposes. Low, adjustable and movable shelves may be used for many purposes: to create interest centers for work and play; to provide a feeling of privacy for individuals and small groups; to control "traffic" in certain areas to provide the quiet and freedom from distracting elements needed for some types of experiences. Bulletin boards, hinged at the bottom and properly fitted with small link chains from wall to top corners, may double as work tables or display centers. Properly protected walls and floors may serve as working spaces for such activities as painting, chart work and map-making. Tool or toy chests and costume trunks may be padded to provide extra seating spaces.

The good teacher uses his imagination to create with what he has the setting which children need for learning.

Interest and Work Centers

Well-planned and stimulating classroom arrangements are important in arousing and sustaining interest in many areas. Provision for exploring, experimenting, creating, constructing, solving problems, and discovering new ways of working are important elements in the good environment for learning. There must be an atmosphere of honest freedom in which children sense willingness and encouragement for them to express themselves. Learning centers can promote the natural drives of children, provide opportunities for children to wonder about and puzzle over things which interest them, and provide situations in which they can search for and discover new relationships.

These learning centers which the teacher arranges must provide a wide range and variety of real experiences in which each child observes and participates in many activities which he can discuss with others. In these centers children need freedom of choice appropriate to maturity levels of their particular group and in keeping with the particular situation. Purposes to be achieved and meanings which may accrue are important considerations.

Such centers include science, literature, art, dramatics, building and constructing, arithmetic, social studies, and play and recreation. Young children need a playhouse corner and a place for building and re-creating their environment with a variety of large and small blocks. Arrangement of furniture can help to create and emphasize these centers. There should be abundant materials and equipment for all children. Important considerations in setting up such centers are balance, selectivity, and pleasing, artistic arrangement.

In summary, the classroom environment should be flexible to provide activities that meet a wide range of interests and maturity levels. It should allow freedom to explore, create, construct and solve problems without jeopardizing the rights of others to the same freedom. It should provide opportunities for self-actualization as well as for participation in group activities. The classroom should have characteristics of both home and laboratory. The teacher arranges this physical and social environment to motivate learning toward achievement of objectives, allowing children to live fully and richly during their years in school.

Preschool Planning

Marie A. Mehl
Hubert H. Mills
Harl R. Douglass
Mary-Margaret Scobey

School administrators, valuing preschool planning, usually require teachers to return to school several days before the children. The days before school opens are bustling with activity. Custodians are putting the final touches on their

Reprinted by permission of The Ronald Press Company from *Teaching in Elementary School,* Third Edition, by Marie A. Mehl, Hubert H. Mills, Harl R. Douglass, and Mary-Margaret Scobey, pp. 128-135. Copyright © 1965 by The Ronald Press Company, New York.

summer housecleaning. Supplies are being organized and distributed. Teachers, busy in special meetings or in their classrooms, are familiarizing themselves with instructional materials, preparing the classroom environment, and making plans for the year. Preschool planning has many facets.

Preschool Orientation

A part of preschool planning is preschool orientation of the teachers new to the school district. Meetings are held a day or two before the arrival of the continuing teachers. For this orientation, administrators plan activities such as these:

1. Greetings and remarks by the superintendent
2. Introduction of administrators
3. Description of central staff services and available materials
4. Tours of the administrative facilities, and sometimes of the school district and community
5. Distribution of general instructional guides and special bulletins
6. A reception, a semisocial affair, at which new teachers may meet each other and become acquainted with district personnel

After meeting with administrators, new teachers go to their assigned school for orientation by their principal. The principal's plans for orientation activities may include:

1. Discussion of the principal's philosophy and management of the school
2. Overview of the school and the community it serves
3. Tour of the school and information about special facilities and resources
4. Presentation of school procedures for requesting materials, bank day, fire drill, playground rules, minimum day, etc.
5. Outline of school schedules such as bus arrivals and departures, recess, physical education, library, P.T.A., and faculty meetings
6. Brief explanation of the course of study, curriculum, and instructional guides
7. Review of bulletins issued by the school and the district

A day or two later, teachers who taught in the school the previous year arrive. The principal extends his orientation to cover the usual procedures for opening school. These may include:

1. Introduction of the total staff including special teachers, custodians, cafeteria workers, librarian, nurse, etc.
2. Calendar for the school year
3. Assignment of class lists
4. Discussion of current changes in the school schedule
5. Allocation of special responsibilities as yard duty and club sponsors
6. Distribution of books, manuals, pupil records, supplies, etc.

A few systems have now departed radically from traditional orientation patterns. In each instance, the change has resulted from a desire to get away from superficiality. At Shaker Heights, Ohio, where a new orientation program started this year covers an eight-weeks period, the switch resulted from reactions given by new teachers a year ago. They voiced the need for a program which would give them a greater appreciation of the continuity of curriculum at various levels.

In addition to the preschool meeting at buildings for new staff members, the Shaker Heights program now includes four late afternoon and evening sessions (with PTA served dinner) held every other week after the fall semester gets under way. The afternoon portion is devoted to curriculum study, while school policies receive attention at the evening session. Superintendent Donald Emery is convinced that the new orientation pattern offers many advantages. "The readiness of a teacher to benefit from an orientation program is significantly greater after the school year starts than before, in terms of curriculum and instruction," he said.[1]

Understanding Instructional Guides

As a basis for intelligent preliminary planning, the teacher gathers as much information as possible. He needs to know what he is expected to teach, and several publications are available to help. His preschool planning includes familiarity with them.

The federal government makes no recommendations regarding curriculum, but almost every state lists content legally designated to be taught in the elementary school. A course of study, published by state, county, or local authorities, outlines this content. In addition to a statement of general philosophy, it specifies the knowledge and skills children should acquire at different grade levels. Total weekly time devoted to each subject may be designated. (See tables on next page.)

Usually, the course of study is a general guideline. It allows for flexibility in planning and creativity by the individual teacher. A teacher is expected to utilize his own experience and training within the broad limits of the course of study.

Special instructional guides for individual subject areas give definite suggestions for content and method. If a district places special emphasis on one of the new math procedures, aids for the teacher are provided. Other guides take the form of teaching or resource units. They include suggested procedures and sources of additional information. Such guides are very helpful in making preliminary plans as well as in continuous planning throughout the year.

[1] National Public Relations Association, "Orientation in Depth," *Public Relations Gold Mine* (Washington, D.C.: National Education Association of the United States, 1963) Vol. V.

Suggested Time Allotments for Elementary School Curriculum*
(in minutes per week)

	Grade Level					
	1	2	3	4	5	6
Reading	325	325	300	300	300	300
English	225	150	150	140	150	150
Spelling	–	75	75	60	70	70
Handwriting	75	75	75	50	30	30
Mathematics	100	150	200	240	250	250
Social Studies	75	75	75	250	250	250
Science and Health	75	75	75	200	200	200
Art	100	100	100	100	100	100
Music	100	100	100	100	100	100
Physical Education	100	125	125	125	125	125
Planning Time	125	125	100	50	50	50
Recess Time	75	75	75	125	125	125

* Source: Mercer Island School District, Washington.

Time Allotments

The following time allotment plan is suggested for use in the Winona Public Elementary Schools, Minnesota. Teachers should use this as a guide in preparing their daily programs. (The time indicated is the total number of minutes per week. Provision has been made here for the teaching of a foreign language which has necessitated changes from previous schedules.)

Activities	Grade					
	I	II	III	IV	V	VI
Reading	600	600	450	325	275	250
Social Studies	75	100	150	225	225	225
Language	150	150	175	225	250	250
Spanish	–	–	–	75	75	75
Spelling	–	75	75	75	75	75
Penmanship	50	75	75	50	50	50
Science	60	60	75	100	125	150
Arithmetic	75	100	175	225	225	225
Music	100	100	100	100	100	100
Art	100	100	100	100	100	100
Physical Education and Health	200	200	200	200	200	200
Unassigned	115	115	100	100	100	100
Total	1525	1675	1675	1800	1800	1800

Becoming Familiar with Textbooks and Teachers' Manuals

One of the first things a teacher should do is become familiar with the textbooks and supplementary books to be used. Some states provide every text used in the classroom. Other states provide money with which schools may buy the particular texts they prefer. In very few elementary schools do pupils or their parents buy the books required. By the opening of the school year, the textbooks will be designated and copies will be available for preschool study and work.

Clues to content and method can be gained from texts. Textbooks provide a framework in that they become guides for long-range goals. The texts used should be carefully analyzed. Having more than one text for a subject allows for greater flexibility than having a single text. The contents of a text may encourage a traditional or a modern approach. For example, a chronological approach to the social studies is more traditional than a topical approach. Texts will also vary in reading level, format, illustrations, and developmental sequence of the content. Some texts are much more up to date than others.

Many publishers supplement their texts with other materials. Films, records, tapes, flash-cards, tests, maps, and diagrams can be purchased to reinforce the content of the text. Teachers' guides are available for almost all subjects in the elementary school. Separate teachers' manuals, as such, are less commonly used than they once were. Today, publishers offer a single teachers' edition that combines both guide materials and text. Lessons are outlined, emphases are made, and relationships are presented. Questions appropriate to various sections may be included, related activities suggested, and supplementary sources of information listed.

Manual materials vary in amount and kind. Some books include so many suggestions that teachers are expected to choose or modify according to the needs of the students and the teacher's preferences. Others outline less material that teachers are likely to follow rigidly.

As a teacher becomes familiar with the texts, he plans approaches and emphases to the content. He notes ways of modifying and supplementing the text. He makes an approximation of the time required to cover sections of the content. He decides how to use supplementary texts and library references.

Planning for the School Year

Long-range planning for the school year is another part of the teacher's preschool task. After he has become familiar with instructional guides and textbooks, he can project outlines of work. For each area of the curriculum, the teacher follows a general pattern in long-range planning:

1. Decides on the scope of the study in terms of objectives
2. Organizes the content by tentative selection of major units or significant problems

3. Makes tentative plans for integration or correlation of subjects
4. Approximates the time allotment for each section of study
5. Outlines content guidelines and teaching methods by which the objectives will be attained

The five steps in long-range planning may be simple or complex according to the content under consideration. The school may use a spelling workbook in which the words to be taught are already organized into practical teaching groups. The teacher's plans in this case may involve ways in which supplementary work may be added. They may also include ways in which the listed words may be studied from a different approach, or how adjustments may be made for exceptional children.

Some schools require requisition of audio-visual materials and library books well in advance of use. Projected plans for field trips have to be submitted to the principal. From these reports, an administrator can ascertain that teachers' use of materials and activities is well balanced.

Plans for art, music, and physical education may depend in part upon social studies plans. When these activities are correlated, the teacher plans lessons that are related. He also allows for technical instruction in needed artistic and physical skills that may not be related to a central curriculum unit.

Although decisions about the general scope of the work can be made in advance, detailed planning should be postponed until the teacher becomes well acquainted with the pupils through his day-to-day contacts with them.

Planning the Daily Schedule

The daily schedule is a framework for procedure that allots time to all the curriculum areas and the special activities of the children. Before school starts, the teacher needs to outline a general plan of daily activities. The daily schedule saves time and facilitates action in several ways.

1. It becomes an organizational reference for the teacher and children by establishing relationships among the various aspects of the day's program. It may also be useful to administrators, supervisors, and other employees, such as special teachers, custodians, and nurses, for their work with the children in the group.
2. It helps pupils adjust their work to the school routine. Activities are scheduled around fixed periods such as recess, lunch, physical education, and library hours.
3. It provides for security through routine. Most people, especially children, like routine. They like to be aware of general expectations. Children want to know what comes next. The teacher and children are freed within the order and routine of the schedule. They can start to work with a minimum of wasted time.
4. It provides balance. A rhythm of active and passive experiences, short

periods and long periods, assures variety and appropriate pacing of learning experiences.

5. The daily schedule, whether flexible or rigid, reflects the teacher's philosophy and educational commitments. Traditional, subject-centered instruction fits well within a rigid schedule, because short time allotments are assigned to individual subjects. Modern instruction, less subject centered and more problem centered, requires a flexible schedule.

When a schedule is flexible, a sequence of related experiences within the day is outlined. Flexibility is achieved through longer blocks of time, unbroken and synthesized by pupils' and teacher's planning together the related activities. Learning does not need to be chopped up in short periods. Experiences can be lifelike; group work or independent action may be scheduled; and emergency modifications within a large block of time are easily handled.

Typical classroom schedules of the flexible type follow:

Suggested Daily Schedule for First Grade

8:45-9:10	Children enter room as they arrive; remove wraps. Teacher greets children as they arrive; also checks attendance and notes health conditions of each child during this time.
9:10-10:00	Social studies and science: Group assembles with teacher in charge; plans are made for work time (5 to 10 minutes); children work (30 to 40 minutes). Evaluation takes place as work period progresses. Materials are put away (5 to 10 minutes). Brief evaluation may be held at close, if necessary.
10:00-10:10	Recess.
10:10-10:20	Rest; nutrition.
10:20-11:00	Reading activities.
11:00-11:10	Recess.
11:10-11:40	Language and literature—may include reading, speaking, listening, writing stories, poetry.
11:40-11:55	Singing; rhythmical activities.
11:55-12:00	Prepare for lunch; dismissal.
12:00-1:00	Lunch hour.
1:00-1:30	Arithmetic.
1:30-1:50	Outdoor play: physical education, including informal play with equipment, games of low organization.
1:50-2:00	Gather on playground or in classroom. Discuss briefly today's accomplishments and tomorrow's plans. Dismiss.

Daily Program for Grade Four, Five, or Six

8:50-9:05	Opening exercises and routine matters.
9:05-10:10	Social studies unit activities, including science.
10:10-10:40	Free play and physical education.
10:40-11:30	Arithmetic groups.
11:30-12:00	Music or foreign language.
12:00-1:00	Lunch, rest, and playground activities.
1:00-1:20	Rest, listening to stories, poems.
1:20-2:00	Developmental reading—for information in social studies and science, for pleasure, for library skills.

2:00-2:10	Recess.
2:10-2:50	Language arts: oral and written expression, spelling, handwriting.
2:50-3:30	Art.
3:30	Dismissal.

Planning for the First Day

The first day is a "get-acquainted day." Children are returning from summer vacations in which their interests have been far removed from classroom work. The teacher's knowledge of his students is limited. Some children are new to the group. Some may attempt to "try out" the new teacher. Some may enter the class with unhappy past experiences in school. Being aware of differences in pupil attitudes and experience, the teacher gives considerable thought to planning a first day that will help him know the children. And that first day should help the children know the teacher: his goals, his expectations, and his organizational plans.

Specific plans can be made for seating arrangements, roll call, and distribution of materials. Well-planned routines may then be worked out between teacher and children that first day. Time may be given to discussion and recording of summer experiences and personal interests. Some art and music that is familiar and fun can be planned, as well as stories and poems to be read by the teacher. Preliminary diagnostic activities for the major subjects may be included. Instructional materials are distributed. The teacher's friendly and business-like manner is important to an effective beginning of the school year.

A teacher plans more than he expects to do. He is in a far better position if he has planned too much than if he suddenly realizes that there is nothing more to do.

An important part of planning for the first day is preparing the classroom for work. Supplies and materials are stored in carefully labeled places. The storage spaces are chosen with consideration for traffic lanes in relation to other activities or quiet study areas. For example, paper and other often used supplies are not stored adjacent to the reading circle, but the reading texts should be there.

Efficiently planned, attractive classrooms are arranged in "centers." In one center, or area, there are the library table, books, and other related materials. Easels and other art supplies are in another area. Science exhibits and equipment are placed in still another part of the room. The teacher's instructional plans may suggest these centers.

For the first day, the teacher arranges attractive bulletin boards and art displays. He has a monitor chart ready for assignments, and supplies ready to distribute. His class list is alphabetized. Furthermore, he plans to arrive very early the first morning.

The Lesson Plan

George A. Beauchamp

The lesson plan is a result of the efforts of a teacher in pre-teaching planning. Although some teachers are able to carry their planning in their heads, the majority use a written plan. As in many things, there are different levels of lesson planning. These different levels are characterized mostly by the thoroughness of the plan. It is safe to say that the most thorough job of preparing lesson plans is done at the student-teaching level. Because of their inexperience and because of the supervision of their work, student teachers are forced to be careful and thorough in planning for their teaching. In most cases they never again have to plan so thoroughly. Great variations in planning are practiced by in-service teachers. Generally, too little planning is done because most elementary-school teachers are in charge of children during the school day, and the time element inhibits planning to a certain extent. Entirely too frequently failure to do good planning has been excused by this argument. We need to ask ourselves whether proper planning is worth the effort. Logically one could plead a case for more and better planning. Most experienced teachers and administrators in elementary schools would testify in the same manner. Research efforts like those reported by Flanders indicate that superior teaching and greater content achievement accompany proper planning.[1] The argument seems to be all in favor of planning, and it is beholden of professional persons to find ways and means for doing it. It is possible to identify at least three levels of lesson planning.

A List of Assignments

Next to no plan at all, probably the lowest level of lesson plan is the simple list of assignments. Here the point of departure for planning is nearly always the textbook. The list of assignments will indicate the name of the subject and the pages or exercises that have been assigned, in the order in which they occur in the school day. For example, the first subject of the day may be arithmetic, and the first fifteen examples on page 176 are assigned. The second subject of the day might be language arts and the assignment might be for the children to write a story about how they spent their weekend, and so forth throughout the school

[1] Ned A. Flanders, "Analyzing Teacher Behavior," *Educational Leadership,* 19:173-80, December, 1961.

day. This kind of planning gives the appearance of being very routine and, unless it is supported by some other kind of planning, cannot be considered effective for good learning. Burton criticizes this level of planning as follows:

> *Despite fifty years of attack by competent critics armed with unlimited, valid evidence, there persists the wholly unexplained assignment aimed only at "covering the text." It would be difficult to devise an educational practice so grossly ineffective, so certainly calculated to interfere with learning, as a page assignment to a single text followed by a formal verbal quiz.*[2]

This statement by Burton is especially pertinent to the type of planning that tries only to cover the text. If effective learning is to take place, something other than the lists of assignments must be the guide for teaching.

The General Lesson Plan

The usual mode of recording a plan for teaching has been called the lesson plan. The format of the lesson plan has varied from place to place in the history of teaching. All of them, however, have certain common characteristics. One of these is that a particular area of work is identified. Second, some tentative objectives are indicated. Third, some notations are made of the teacher's ideas for ways and means of getting the children involved in the work to be done. Fourth, a list is made of possible activities for the children to perform. Fifth, a list of materials of instruction is compiled; and sixth, some techniques and procedures for evaluating the area of work are indicated.

Another way for the teacher to think about the plan is to raise a series of questions such as:

What is the area of study? Its sub-areas?

How do I get this area of experience to my pupils?

What are the most likely needed learning materials? Other resources?

What are some of the activities children may perform? Possible organization?

What do I want to happen to the pupils as a result of their learning experiences?

What do I need to plan with the pupils? How?

What things do I need to do?

When a teacher has answered questions like these, he has a plan for teaching.

Of course there are variations within this general framework. Much depends upon the magnitude of the area of work to be undertaken with children. If, for example, a teacher is launching a study of early colonial life, that area of study

---

2 William H. Burton, "Implications for Organization of Instruction and Instructional Adjuncts," *Learning and Instruction,* Forty-ninth Yearbook, Part I, National Society for the Study of Education (Chicago: University of Chicago Press, 1950), p. 227. Reprinted by permission of the National Society for the Study of Education.

could not be accomplished in a single day. Therefore, the over-all plan as indicated in the paragraph above would become an all-inclusive plan. Then the teacher would be placed in the position of needing daily planning in order to insure forward movement and continuity to the total project. In this case a day's work may be devoted only to the establishment of objectives, for example, and perhaps the selection of activities. Another day might be directed toward organizing children into groups to do the work involved. In those cases the daily plan of the teacher would be directed toward those aspects of the total area of work.

It should be cautioned that whenever an over-all plan is made, and then specific plans are made for daily operation, the teacher's responsibility for planning for the daily operations is equally important with the over-all plan, because carelessness at the operational level can defeat the best of over-all plans.

Occasionally, there are short lessons to be taught that are accomplished within a single day. In those cases all of the features are thoroughly planned. Objectives should be stated, activities planned, and evaluation procedures indicated. The total act of planning is not complete unless these considerations are weighed.

A few specific suggestions for the new or beginning teacher about the development of a lesson plan might be helpful. One of the most critical points in teaching is that point at which a teacher attempts to involve the children in the area of work. It may sound superfluous to suggest that a teacher actually write down leading questions or topics to discuss with pupils as a means of involving them in the discussion; but for many teachers this technique has been extremely helpful in their actual work with children. Until one has had a good deal of teaching experience, he may not be sensitive enough to the types of questions to be asked to keep a plan moving along. However, when these things are thought out ahead of time, the teacher has the security of knowing the direction in which he is going. Obviously a danger in this is that the teacher may not be sufficiently flexible to modify his discussion when things do not go as they were originally planned. To be able to change horses in the middle of the stream, so to speak, is a technique that one usually learns through experience. Occasionally it is desirable for a teacher to try to anticipate the reactions of the children to suggestions and questions. In these cases alternatives should be considered so that a teacher can say to himself, "If this does not work then I will do this."

One of the better ways to involve children in a learning activity is through the kinds of materials that are in the classroom. Reference here is to the kinds of suggestions that were made concerning motivational devices, such as a carefully displayed group of books and pictures that can be referred to in the discussion, or that may be expected to stimulate questions and interest on the part of children. The physiology of the environment can be a very important way of getting children involved in learning activities. A third suggestion is to think of many possible activities so that all children can find worthwhile projects or activities. This not only works in the direction of helping the children find activities, but it also works in the reverse direction so that a teacher is not surprised or dismayed at some of the suggestions that children may make for activity. The two important action questions that a teacher should constantly ask himself in planning are: (1) "What am I going to do?" and (2) "What am I going to ask the children to do?"

The Teaching Unit

The most popular form of teaching plan in modern elementary education is the teaching unit. We ordinarily think of the teaching unit as a means of organizing a series of studies or activities around some central theme or problem. In the thinking of the reader there may be some confusion between the teaching unit and what was referred to in Chapter 8 as the resource unit. The similarities between the two types of units are great. In fact the elements are for all practical purposes the same, but the teaching unit is organized for a specific group of persons, with specific objectives to be achieved, and specific activities organized to achieve those objectives. On the other hand, the resource unit contains objectives and activities for groups of children in general.

The outline of the essential elements of a unit as organized by Adams and presented in Chapter 8 is as good as any. However, it will help the reader to understand more clearly interpretations of teaching units if reference is made to suggestions of others for unit organization. For example, Burton indicates the following for developing teaching units:

1. An overview is presented.
2. Teachers' objectives as clearly recognized by the teachers are stated.
3. An approach, introduction, or orientation is developed.
4. The learners' objective appears, is recognized and stated.
5. A planning period is provided.
6. A working period is provided in which learning is carried forward. Replanning enters here from time to time.
7. The learners' objective is achieved together with some or all of the teacher's objectives.[3]

Another group of authors lists the following features for both a resource unit and a teaching unit, and indicate that the teaching unit should contain the same features as a resource unit, except that it is particularly adapted as previously indicated:

1. Title or topic.

[3] William H. Burton, *The Guidance of Learning Activities,* 3rd Ed. (New York: Appleton-Century-Crofts, Educational Division, Meredith Corporation, 1962), pp. 347-48. Reprinted by permission of the publisher.

2. Introductory statement.
3. Objectives.
4. Content guide.
5. Pupil activities required.
6. Materials and resources.
7. Evaluation procedures.[4]

The structure of a unit is indicated by Shuster and Ploghoft under the following headings:

1. Topic or theme.
2. Development of purposes.
3. Overview of topic or theme.
4. Initiatory or approach.
5. Working period.
6. Culminating unit.
7. Evaluation.
8. Instructional materials.[5]

In actual practice the teaching unit has been constructed by using an organized curriculum guide, courses of study, textbooks, and resource materials as points of departure. Because of the use of various departure points in unit construction, the unit idea has been associated with many forms of organization. In this sense the teaching unit is very flexible. The important consideration, and the thing that makes the teaching unit such a desirable method of organization for teaching, is its insistence that objectives be indicated, activities be selected, materials be planned for, and activities be evaluated in terms of the sought objectives. In this sense the teaching unit provides for a complete cycle in teaching activity, and this cycle is psychologically and educationally good.

By comparing the discussion of the lesson plan and the teaching unit, the reader will note few differences. The closure feature of the unit of work is not mandatory for the lesson plan. The lesson plan can be more open-ended. In the final analysis terminology distinctions here are of little significance. The importance is upon the care of planning.

Long- and Short-Range Planning

All teachers must expect to do both long- and short-term planning. There are really two factors that indicate a distinction between long- and short-range planning. One of them is the interval of time to be covered by the area of study,

---

[4] Herbert J. Klausmeier and Katharine Dresden, *Teaching in the Elementary School,* 2nd Ed. (New York: Harper & Row, Publishers, 1962), p. 139. Reprinted by permission of the publishers.

[5] Albert H. Shuster and Milton E. Ploghoft, *The Emerging Elementary Curriculum* (Columbus, Ohio: Charles E. Merrill Books, Inc., 1962), pp. 117-18. Reprinted by permission of the publisher.

and the other is the immediacy of action to be taken subsequent to the planning. With regard to the matter of time intervals, a teacher needs to think of the year as one interval for which planning is made. Another interval is a block of time encompassing days, weeks, or even months, which is dictated by the magnitude of the unit of work to be undertaken. A third interval is the school day, and a fourth possible interval for planning is a period within a school day.

Long-range planning is usually characterized by the over-all plan for adapting the curriculum materials to a specific group of children. For example, Kyte indicates that the first two steps in initial planning by a teacher at the start of either a new school year or a new unit in the classroom, are to consult curriculum materials or courses of study in order to determine what the general range and framework of activities are to be, and secondly, to study all available data regarding the pupils to be taught, so that he has a basis for making judgments about the adaptation of curriculum materials.[6] Kyte then states:

> *The third step in the teacher's initial planning is the development of an instructional program based upon the information obtained from the first two steps. This step is a complex one, taking into account six items: (1) the specific educational needs of the class and individual pupils, (2) the school time available for meeting these needs, (3) the learning activities that will provide the essential experiences, (4) the instructional aids necessary for implementing the program, (5) the preparation of the instructional environment, and (6) the procedure for cooperative planning with pupils. These six points must be considered separately first and then together in order that the tentative plan may take comprehensive form.[7]*

Short-range planning, on the other hand, is characterized more by planning for specific functions within a day or two, or even within a portion of a day. In this case a teacher needs to plan for her own actions, the anticipated actions of children, and the interaction of teacher and children. To illustrate, Wingo and Schorling indicate the following as being important parts of a good teaching plan:

1. Purpose of the work to be undertaken that day. State precisely as possible what your aims are. It is also a good idea to state the aims of the work as the pupils will see them.
2. Specific activities to be carried on.
3. Time budget. State the approximate time you expect to devote to each activity.
4. Materials needed for the work. This includes books, illustrations, other

---

[6] George C. Kyte, *The Elementary School Teacher at Work* (New York: Dryden Press, 1957), pp. 410-12.
[7] *Ibid.*, p. 412.

audio-visual materials, art and craft materials, or anything else you plan to use.

5. Plans for discussion with the class. Include a few good questions you may wish to use to get the discussion under way and keep it going.
6. Directions for work. Make them clear and specific.
7. Plans for evaluation and discussion of future activities which, of course, will involve the members of the class.[8]

Thus it can be noted that a great deal of common thinking goes into both long-range and short-range planning. The principal difference seems to lie in the specificity of the plan for immediate and impending action. There is one thing that has not as yet been mentioned that a teacher should expect. This is that short-range plans have a tendency to disrupt or to modify long-range plans. Because of this somewhat disruptive tendency of short-range planning, it becomes important for a teacher constantly to keep the long-range plan in mind as the school year unfolds. Wingo and Schorling use an interesting phrase, "strategy and tactics," to describe the relationship between long-range and short-range planning.[9] The strategy refers to the long-range outlook and the tactics are the more immediate plans. Tactics constantly have to be modified by a sort of feedback and correction activity for the over-all strategy to be successful.

[8] G. Max Wingo and Raleigh Schorling, *Elementary School Student Teaching*, 3rd Ed. (McGraw-Hill, Inc., 1960), p. 133. Reprinted by permission of the publisher.
[9] *Ibid.*, pp. 123-24.

Chapter 3

Starting the Year

The old adage that nothing succeeds like success is nowhere more applicable than in the case of the beginning teacher as he starts the task of relating to and working with the children in his first class. Assuming that careful long-range and immediate planning have been accomplished prior to the opening of school, there comes now that crucial period which will have a direct bearing on ultimate success in the profession. The following selections offer many specific and general suggestions which will help both the novice and the experienced teacher work more effectively.

Douglass and Grindle concentrate on the first few days and weeks of activity and conclude with a check-list in the area of human relations. Chasnoff is concerned with the importance of routines in the classroom and shows how the teaching day may be organized into a series of specific and well-delineated episodes. Each such division of the day's activity is to be carefully designed, planned, and directed in a manner similar to that used by the choreographer of the dance. The continuing problem of disciplinary control for the beginner, particularly in the sense of employing preventive techniques, is discussed by Chamberlin.

The chapter is continued on a somewhat different plane with an inspirational and creative letter by Teigland to a teacher who is at the halfway mark in her first year and who is in need of a new look at attitudes and anxieties, the necessity of working with pupils of all kinds, and her stance toward personal and intellectual pursuits.

It is highly important that the teacher be aware of his responsibility for the protection of the children he teaches. Ferguson, in the concluding article, recognizes this concern, discusses the nature of negligence, and recommends provisions for avoiding actions that could result in liability suits.

Starting the Year Right

M. Genevieve Douglass and John L. Grindle

Happy New School Year! Whether you are a beginning teacher with butterflies to quell; an experienced teacher in a new system; or even one about to enter her same room for the fifth or seventeenth year—it *is* the beginning of a new year with new faces and new adventures awaiting you. Are you ready for them? In this booklet are some ideas and suggestions to help you through those very important first days and weeks, to lift you over the rough spots, to remind you of what to expect. Read carefully, check the points you want to remember especially, gather some enthusiasm for a good work-filled year, and settle back to greet this year's set of shining faces.

A GOOD BEGINNING

Some general rules

Be firm but fair from the beginning—Control must be gained at the start if an uphill struggle is to be avoided. It is easier to relax control than it is to impose it after it has been lost.

Know your pupils—Regardless of your school's grouping practices, you will encounter individual differences. Knowledge of the child is the first key. Study all the records. Most important, however, is your own observation.

Plan your work carefully—There is no substitute for good planning.

Observe other teachers—You can learn much from your fellow teachers. They are happy to share their experiences. But be yourself; do not copy.

Do not hesitate to ask questions—A question can often prevent disaster.

Start slowly—A good steady well organized pace is far better than a big explosion that fizzles out. Remember also there are reasons why things are done in a certain way. Study these reasons before making big changes.

Establish routines—Whether it is a form for written work or a procedure for sharpening pencils, children need a way of doing things.

Set standards—Partial learnings, careless work, sloppy behavior, and poor citizenship result from a teaching situation without standards.

This material is adapted from an orientation program prepared for the Woodward Parkway Elementary School, Farmingdale, New York. It was written by John L. Grindle, Assistant Principal, in collaboration with M. Genevieve Douglass, Principal.
Reprinted by permission of The Instructor Publications, Inc., Dansville, N.Y., and M. Genevieve Douglass and John L. Grindle เน ภ *The Instructor* 71:71-85, September, 1961.

Be patient—All children will not grasp your words of wisdom the first time. However, there are few who cannot be reached by patience and understanding.

Be calm—Fear, excitement, anger, and frustration are contagious. A calm teacher is the key to a calm room.

Be prompt with clerical work—You expect pupils to meet their assignments; be careful about meeting your own.

Do not do clerical work in class—The class period belongs to the children; they are your first responsibility.

Keep that sense of humor—It will save many a situation.

Accept and apply suggestions—Observations and suggestions are made to help, never to hinder.

Read professionally—Only a growing teacher can have a growing classroom.

Before opening day

Check your administrative manual—Be acquainted with such procedures as the opening and closing hours, attendance procedures, fire-drill regulations, nurse services, cafeteria regulations.

Acquaint yourself with the building—Locate the exits, principal's office, secretarial office, health office, cafeteria, supply room, auditorium, gym, library, and so on.

Get to know your supervisors—These people have the answers to your many questions and the desire to be of service. Do not be afraid to ask for help.

Make your room attractive—One of the ways to get the year off to a good start is to have a room that is friendly and livable on Opening Day. Put up a few pictures, design an attractive and colorful bulletin board, have some books out, and maybe put a plant or two around.

Have materials for the first day—Make it a real day of school. A good start yields big dividends in control, pupil and teacher security, happiness, and absence of frustration. Have on hand paper, pencils, and other materials you may want to use for getting school under way. Secure the books you need. Proper materials coupled with good planning will get you off to a flying start.

Make a temporary seating plan—You will want to change this many times during the year. However, it will put you in command of the situation on Opening Day and will aid you in quickly learning the names of your pupils.

Make a program for the first day—Teachers in self-contained classrooms need daily programs. Have an order of business for the first few days. You may not even get through it, but have a plan. It is as necessary to your command of the classroom as a road map in a strange territory. Knowing where you are going is nine-tenths of the trip.

Make some definite lesson plans for the first two or three days—There is little justification for the opening (or closing) day to be a holiday. You will find the school year short enough. The wise teacher will eliminate the breeding ground of many control problems by a businesslike first day. Good teachers never teach cold. Planning of some sort is always necessary. Those first plans should be written out in some detail. They will provide you with the feeling of security you need when facing the class for the first time.

Arrange the furniture for the first day—If your room has movable furniture, you will be moving it often. But start with a fairly traditional arrangement until you know your children by name and have established control.

That first morning

Arrive early—Have time to greet your neighbor and get any last-minute questions answered; to go over final plans and preparation; to get needed materials; to relax, unpack the smile, gather up your courage, and make ready to meet your class.

Think over the threefold task you have in the first few days—to establish room control; to establish good work habits; to teach working in groups.

Be in your room when the pupils arrive—This is a necessity in establishing good discipline and effective room standards.

Greet children with a smile—Make no comment other than a pleasant "Good morning," if you like. Encourage children to be seated and remain so.

Have your name on the chalkboard—Children should learn to pronounce and spell it at once.

Insist on children's being seated—Pencils can be sharpened later, stories told, and questions answered. The main things at this point are to establish your control and to avoid confusion.

Make opening exercises brief—Your main goal for this morning is to get down to the business at hand.

Check attendance—Check the attendance according to your class list. Have each child raise his hand as you call the name. This will help you associate names and faces.

Develop room standards—For a safe, sane, and profitable year there must be rules and regulations. There must be a way of getting books and materials, a time and procedure for sharpening pencils, an organized way of entering and leaving the room, ways of working and playing, as well as policies of respecting others' rights. You will want to plan and discuss with the children such points as leaving the room; laughing with people, not at them; voice control (talking softly or not at all). There are others you will want to consider. If you are a wise beginning teacher, you will have only one child out of his seat at a time, except in an organized activity. We cannot emphasize this too strongly: get control of your room first; then relax as children can accept responsibility.

Carry out lessons previously planned—Make the first day of school a meaningful one, with real work, and your children will go home happy.

First few weeks

The first pitch is important in any ball game. That first strike has a great psychological effect. But the outcome of the game depends upon what follows. It is necessary to keep pitching a steady game. A successful first day must be followed by a lot of hard work. Much will depend upon what follows in the first few weeks.

Keep your control—This cannot be overemphasized. No matter how great your store of knowledge and how long your preparation, if you do not have the attention of the class, no learning will take place. Relax any control only when children are ready to assume added responsibility. Have something on the board for children to do when they arrive. You will be pleased how well this atmosphere will carry through the day.

Study the cumulative folders of your pupils—Get to know your boys and girls from personal observation. This is vital. However, you need to know the characteristics, achievements, capabilities, problems, and other data concerning your pupils. Every school has records to help you. Make yourself acquainted with this information. The stronger your background knowledge, the greater your chance of success. Just a word of caution: These records are not meant to be instruments of prejudice. Use the information objectively.

Take advantage of every opportunity to meet parents—Parents can be a very big help. They have a great deal of information concerning the child that is very helpful to the teacher. Don't wait for trouble to arise. Get to know these folks before any problems come up. When you see a problem germinating, bring the parents in for mutual action and understanding. If a parent asks questions, give full, honest answers.

Get some interesting worthwhile activity under way—Children like to be doing things. Purposeful activity will do much to motivate enthusiasm as well as build good working relationships.

Record plenty of observations and grades—One of the hardest tasks is grading your pupils. This you will want to do fairly and professionally. Keep plenty of information in case you must justify your marks. Save a good sampling of papers for conferences.

Spend much time in preparation of daily lessons—There is no substitute for this on the road to success. Many persons fail because of poor preparation. Even the experienced must prepare.

Take full advantage of available help—Your principal, specialists in reading, speech, and other curriculum areas, guidance personnel, the psychologist, the nurse, and others stand ready to share their knowledge.

Take advantage of professional meetings—There will be many in-service curriculum sessions, grade-level meetings, and other professional activities. Be prompt. Give as well as receive.

GOOD ROOM CONTROL

A sense of orderliness—A disorderly and disarranged room has a tendency to make children disorderly also. Arrange furniture to give maximum use of space, at the same time providing for free movement of children. Make sure the pupils can move into reading, science, and other activities without climbing over each other and without upsetting teaching materials. Have a definite place for each piece of material. Provide organization for proper care and maintenance of all materials and books. Make sure all materials are removed when they cease to be functional.

Group consciousness—Every child must become aware that he is a member of a group and that as such he has a responsibility toward that group. If he is to participate in its privileges, he must accept its duties and obligations. As a pupil grows, he learns to associate his actions with their effect upon other pupils in his room and in his school. His group control grows gradually into self-control. The teacher is a pattern of courtesy in dealing with the children and should insist that children be courteous to each other, to guests, and to herself at all times. Have regular times for evaluation of their citizenship.

Security—When children and teacher both have a feeling of security, it is easier to approach harmonious and pleasant working relationships. Create an atmosphere of acceptance. Give praise where praise is due. Complimenting children on their work gives the feeling of achievement which is so necessary for security. Adapt assigned work to the abilities of the children, and make certain they understand what they are supposed to do. Make each individual child feel important to the group. Always be consistent in your treatment of children and their behavior. Carefully avoid sarcasm.

Sincerity—Nothing will disrupt a room so quickly and easily as insincerity on the part of the teacher. Children have a keen sense of fairness and often become aware of attempts to camouflage or to deceive before the teacher even gets started. The teacher in turn needs to develop sincerity on the part of the children. When children subscribe to a rule and are continuously allowed to break it, they are learning insincerity. Sincerity can be developed by following through continuously on every rule or standard which is set up.

Group standards—If the class is allowed to participate in the building of group standards, they are apt to make them more workable than if the teacher arbitrarily lays down a set of rules. It is important that rules be made a few at a time and only when needed to establish procedures and rapport within a classroom.

Helpful techniques

1. Share with the children the idea that everybody makes mistakes, but smart persons do not repeat them.
2. Comment on those who do right.
3. Do not bring your personal problems into the classroom.
4. Help the class to distinguish between legitimate and illegitimate noises in the classroom.
5. Have your materials ready. Groups waiting for materials can be starting points for discipline problems.
6. Treat each child as if he were the mayor's child.
7. Keep a good supplementary library in your room.
8. When possible have forum-plan seating arrangements so that the children do not look at backs of heads all day.
9. Take the clinical point of view on your discipline problems. Your doctor treats your throat but he doesn't take it home with him.
10. Call on all pupils in a discussion. Don't let the extroverts dominate.
11. Have confidence in the child's desire to do the right thing.
12. Help the child to belong to his group. Do not set him apart by such labels as **slow, lazy, and silly.**
13. Seek the child's friendship and give him yours in return.
14. See to it that there is effective teacher planning. Keep children so wholesomely busy that no unwholesome activities can creep in.
15. Be sure children participate in the planning, understand what they are going to do, why, and how to go about it.
16. Make directions clear and complete.
17. Keep your poise and dignity.
18. Watch attention spans; know when to change activities, when to speed up or slow down.
19. Have frequent evaluative sessions.
20. Be businesslike.
21. Avoid all suggestions of criticism, anger, frustration. Make personal corrections in private conferences.
22. Radiate happiness and joy in your work. They are contagious.
23. Be just and fair.
24. Be consistent.
25. Be sensitive to children's feelings.
26. Give children responsibilities which are challenging and interesting.
27. Be aware of everything going on in the room.

28. When children do poorly, be encouraging. Help them understand how the job can be done better.
29. Use common sense at all times.
30. Remember that some problems can be handled by banter or humor. Ignore trivial things entirely.

Remedial treatment

Punishment must never be looked upon as an end in itself. It is merely a means of restoring the individual to normality in the group. The measures should be those most appropriate for the pupil's offense and personality.

1. Isolate the offender between the time of the offense and the settlement, but not in the cloakroom or outside the room.
2. Let a little time elapse between the time of the offense and when you talk to him.
3. Be perfectly frank.
4. If property has been willfully damaged, it should be restored, repaired, or paid for.
5. Never force apologies. Accept those freely given, but impress upon the child that future actions will speak louder than words.
6. Try to let the child decide his own punishment.
7. Do not make threats; but if you do, make sure that in some way the threat is carried out.
8. When a case is settled, drop it.
9. General behavior can come up for group discussion. Individual offenders are not for class discussion.
10. Before making an issue of misbehavior be sure it is worth the effort.

KEYS TO SUCCESS

Know Your Pupils—This means more than names. Get as much background as possible before you meet them. Develop a working knowledge of their needs, interests, and experiences and fit your plans to this knowledge.

Know Your Field—Children will have confidence in you only as you demonstrate your ability. Keep abreast of the latest techniques and knowledge.

Be Prepared—Have a clear, specific purpose for each lesson. Introduce each with a preview. Present your points one at a time and in logical order. Keep related ideas together. Keep language simple and avoid involved sentences. When technical terms are necessary, introduce them gradually and explain each meaningfully. Summarize from time to time. Relate material to everyday experiences. Make plans for drill opportunities. Provide for review.

Control Your Presentation—Set your pace to match the difficulty of the material. Do not be afraid to repeat for emphasis. Use humorous stories or comments to add interest.

Make Your Presentation Effective—When demonstrating, first show whole operation briefly, then show it one step at a time, always explaining as you go along. Emphasize key points. Make full use of instructional aids—models, charts, films, slides, and so on. Make your own if commercial ones are not available. But use aids to improve teaching, not as a substitute for it. Use questions to guide your own teaching and to check pupil progress. Ask questions first and then indicate the person to answer. Make sure of retention. Stay with a correction long enough to be sure it has taken hold. Have a child explain each step as he practices.

Motivate and Maintain Interest—Show enthusiasm. Use variety in your presentation. Make your teaching personal. Help children to see the future uses of what they learn.

Use Your Voice Wisely—Speak clearly and loud enough so all may hear. Speak slowly enough for meanings to be grasped. It is better to cover less and cover it well. A little variation in your voice will avoid monotony. Talk to the class, not to the window or the chalkboard.

Make Sure of Progress—Establish concrete goals, making sure they are something to work for. Know what you can expect from your pupils and hold them to it. Show genuine interest in class and individual progress and keep the group informed of its progress. Use praise frequently.

A WORD ABOUT LAW

Consult your school authorities whenever you are in doubt about legal responsibilities. Laws vary widely but in general you should know these for your state and system:

1. The ages when children *must* attend school. When they *may* attend.
2. The minimum number of days in a school year (including conferences).
3. Whether a child may legally be absent for religious instructions and observances.
4. If a teacher may keep a child after school; administer corporal punishment; suspend him.
5. The rights of probationary teachers and length of the probationary period.
6. The legal privileges and responsibilities of tenure.
7. When a teacher may be liable; what would be considered negligence.

CHECKLIST ON HUMAN RELATIONS

In the Classroom

— Do I accept each child—the poor as well as the rich, the dirty as well as the clean?
— Do I help all children feel they belong?
— Do I show confidence in my pupils?
— Do I let my pupils know I like them?

— Do I make each child feel he has something to contribute?

— Do my pupils bring their problems to me?

— Am I available when they want to see me?

— Do I help my pupils accept one another?

— Do I let everyone express his feelings?

— Do I live up to agreements with pupils?

— Do I succeed in getting all pupils to assume some responsibility?

— Do I help the group form a behavior code?

— Do I work for democratic values?

Outside of Class

— Do I try to develop faculty cooperation?

— Do I avoid petty conversation about my associates?

— Do I do my share in determining and carrying out the system's educational policies?

— Do I aid associates with constructive ideas?

— Do I refrain from interfering with the classroom affairs of an associate?

— Do I refrain from shifting my responsibility to another teacher?

— Do I hold inviolate confidential information about my associates?

— Do I transact all school business through the proper channels?

With Parents and Community

— Do I maintain friendly, cooperative relationships with parents?

— Do I hold all information confidential?

— Do parents feel sure that I deal justly and impartially with every child?

— Do I give all parents their fair share of time, regardless of community standing?

— Do I present a complete, fair, and meaningful evaluation to parents?

— Do I listen to and give fair thought to parents' opinions?

— Do I take an active part in community life?

Maturity

— Do I seek to develop sufficient social skills?

— Am I increasingly willing to accept myself as having worth?

— Do I seek to become more self-directing?

— Do I continually seek to improve my problem-solving technique?

— Do I attempt to face my frustrations?

— Do I recognize my own needs? shortcomings?

— Do I volunteer my special skills?

— Do I try to take disappointments without becoming discouraged?

— Do I seek to control myself and adjust my behavior to the situation?

Ethical Standards

— Do I treat each child without prejudice or partiality?

— Do I respect the confidence of a pupil?

— Do I refuse to use my position to promote partisan policies and sectarian views?

— Do I listen to and weigh parents' viewpoints carefully?

— Do I avoid making remarks that might discredit parents?

— Do I evaluate the attitudes and activities of the community with an open mind?

— Do I take part in community life?

— Do I do my share in keeping the public informed concerning school achievements?

— Do I exercise my right to participate in the processes which determine school policy?

— Do I support school policy to the fullest, once it has been determined?

— Do I keep a legal contract unless canceled by mutual consent?

— Am I kind, tolerant, and loyal in all my dealings with professional associates?

— Do I take pride in the achievements of my associates?

— Do I avoid pettiness, jealousy, rancor?

— Do I criticize with discretion?

— Am I proud of my profession?

Teaching Classroom Routines

Robert E. Chasnoff

This brief essay proposes that classroom routines must be taught as carefully and as deliberately as anything else a teacher would teach his pupils. I believe that at the beginning of the school year a teacher must break down a school day into specific episodes and plan the routines as carefully as a choreographer would plan a dance.

This article presents a positive approach to teaching routines in elementary-school classrooms. Basic to this approach is the premise that a teacher should make plans, in advance, deliberately to teach disciplined ways of working in the classroom.

How does a teacher make such plans so that pupils work and learn in an atmosphere of decorum? Four important steps are suggested for teachers to follow at the beginning of the school year. These steps, I believe, lead to a more productive classroom setting and eventually to greater freedom.

1. The teacher first analyzes the school day into a number of specific episodes. One example of a specific episode is "opening exercises." Another episode is the first formal lesson of the day. Still another episode is one in which the class leaves the room and goes down four flights of stairs to the school auditorium.

2. The teacher determines the kind of experiences he hopes his pupils will have during each of these episodes. Although teachers of varying persuasions differ with regard to the degree of freedom and the opportunities for self-expression that pupils should have, teachers do agree that pupils should experience a feeling of order.

3. The teacher plans the "choreography" of each episode. Choreography is used here in the way that the term is used in the dance. That is, the teacher plans in detail the design of the episode. For each episode the teacher decides the sequence of the instructions he will give. He decides the kinds of behavior which would be appropriate for the pupils. He decides where he, himself, will stand or walk. He anticipates the difficult areas which may need particular attention. In short, he creates a plan for the episode in as much detail as a choreographer would for a scene in dance.

Reprinted by permission of Pitman Publishing Corporation, New York, from *Elementary Curriculum: A Book of Readings*, edited by Robert E. Chasnoff, pp. 87-89. Copyright ©by Pitman Publishing Corporation, 1964.

4. The teacher plans the transitions between episodes. These transitions, themselves, are considered as specific episodes. They, too, are planned in the ways noted above.

Having (1) analyzed the episodes, (2) determined the appropriate experiences, (3) constructed the choreography, and (4) planned transitions, the teacher may begin each episode of a school day with a clear idea of how that episode may look. The teacher is able to teach directly and clearly. If, for example, a teacher is planning to lead his class down several flights of steps, he walks the route *in advance.* He carefully plans numerous places where he will stop . . . turn . . . look at and settle his group . . . before moving to the next stopping place. In this way he is able to plan to communicate kinesthetically, as well as vocally and visually, his ideas of how he would like his group to move. He plans places to stop to say something to the group if saying something is necessary. He certainly plans such stopping places to be those where he can see all his pupils, and his pupils can see him.

And when a teacher plans to hand out books for the first time, he plans in advance where the books will be at the beginning of the episode. He plans who will hand out the books. He plans what each recipient of his book will do. While some teachers might plan merely to instruct pupils what to do with the books, other teachers might plan to conduct a discussion to determine what pupils should do with the books when the books are received. Whether a teacher chooses one of these methods or another, the teacher does plan what the choreography will be.

In conclusion, this article has been delimited to deal with the need to plan in advance for carrying out the so-called routines of classroom living. Other equally important aspects of good discipline have not been discussed. Such considerations include the following: the need for an interesting academic program that makes sense to the teacher and to the pupils; the significance of the teacher's feelings about himself and about his pupils; the fact that not all classes can be handled in the same way; the better methods of teaching toward self-direction and self-discipline; and the ways in which preplanning actually helps the teacher to cope with the many unexpected events which cannot be anticipated in any classroom. All these considerations contribute to a teacher's effective leadership. However, it has been stressed here that the first step to a positive approach to classroom routines is to plan the choreography of the specific episodes within the school day. Finally, I suggest that by planning a possible choreography a teacher will find he need not be as rigid as he might be in a planless situation.

Discipline and Preventive Techniques

Leslie J. Chamberlin

The teacher who learns to avoid, prevent or control classroom situations which lead to disorder, discourtesy or inactivity not only improves his effectiveness as a teacher but also his job security and chances for future progress.

Good teachers realize that modern discipline, which emphasizes self-control and self-direction, is one of the most difficult things a child must master in our rapidly changing, complex social framework. These teachers realize that any contribution they may make towards students' development of character, good citizenship and self-control depends largely on their skill in managing pupils in a manner which conforms to a psychology of self-direction.

Adequate classroom control involves:

(1) providing a learning situation that is free from serious distractions;

(2) establishing and maintaining respect for authority in the classroom and the school;

(3) attempting to develop student ideals, interests and skills which contribute to self-control and good citizenship;

(4) presenting a dynamic, but not dominating, sympathetic and pleasing teacher personality to the pupils.

What can the teacher do to provide a learning situation free from serious distractions which maintains respect for authority and contributes to self-control and good citizenship?

The teacher must realize that problems will not occur if they are not allowed to develop. Establishing mutually meaningful standards is the foundation of good discipline.

Therefore, early in the school term the teacher and the students should discuss the standards which the group will accept. This prevents many problems resulting from ignorance of what is acceptable, from carelessness or from just seeing how far a student can go.

An effective teacher must:

(1) be free from any driving need to be liked by all of the students;

(2) accept the role of the parent figure;

(3) realize that boys and girls do not want to be given absolute freedom to do whatever they please;

(4) be consistent in upholding the adopted standards.

Reprinted by permission of *School and Community,* Missouri State Teachers Association, Columbia, Missouri, from *School and Community* 48:24, 38, October, 1961.

Specific routines will help students take care of many recurring classroom situations. The teacher must accept and perform his part in these routines.

For example, it is a good idea for the teacher to meet his classes at the door of the room every day and each new class period. This permits him to supervise his corridor and to greet his pupils as they come into the room. To be effective, however, the teacher must be at his post regularly.

Routines dealing with book and paper distribution, making assignments or giving directions, student seating and forgotten articles must be worked out. In fact, all small details must receive careful consideration.

Often teachers use student monitors in connection with these various routines. This practice is educationally sound, but a teacher should exercise care since the efficiency of the monitor program depends on the selection of reliable children.

The monitor's function should be carefully defined as assisting the teacher and nothing more. Until controls are established, it is well for the teacher to limit the number of simultaneous classroom activities and to handle most of the details himself.

An inexperienced teacher may want to avoid certain teaching procedures, such as group work and other activities which require a good deal of self-control on the part of students until he becomes more skillful in maintaining good control.

Keeping a class constructively busy has much to recommend it as a policy of maintaining satisfactory classroom discipline. A five or 10-minute assignment written on the board each morning encourages classes to enter the room promptly and to get to work quickly. Such morning work also enables the teacher to attend to the latecomers individually, to make last plans for the day and to complete many other daily duties.

This policy of keeping students busy with interesting, well-planned assignments applies to the last few minutes of the school day, also.

Often teachers talk too loudly, on too high a pitch or simply too much. Good teachers learn to listen to themselves, stop talking, and then to continue in a more conversational tone that is free from anger, annoyance or anxiety.

Children resent being yelled at or screamed at and often will be hostile as a result. Many successful teachers use signals such as the classroom lights, a small bell, or putting a finger to the mouth to request silently that everyone lower his voice.

Teachers need to remember that children's attention spans are short. Often when children work on an activity too long, restlessness and noise seem to grow spontaneously. This should be considered when planning lessons, but should it happen during a lesson, the far-sighted teacher should start a new activity before the noise gets out of hand.

Since many discipline problems arise when a student or a few students cannot do an assigned task, the teachers should try to individualize instruction whenever possible. It is better for the less capable student to complete a modified version of the general assignment than for him to drift into a disciplinary situation.

In the classroom, easily recognizable rewards should follow approved behavior without delay. The wise teacher gives recognition to his students whenever possible for their superior work or behavior.

A child who is hungry or tired is apt to become a discipline problem. The teacher should analyze his class periodically as to proper rest and diet.

Being aware of certain physical and/or mental defects can help a teacher avoid many difficult classroom situations. The school's cumulative records help a teacher learn about a child's physical and mental status.

All teachers sincerely interested in providing a good teaching-learning situation should welcome constructive supervision.

Supervision encourages the teacher to try for better classroom control. It sometimes calls attention to previously unnoticed or flippant or sarcastic remarks or unfriendly looks on the part of the teacher.

Supervisors may notice antagonistic or rebellious pupil attitudes as a result of teaching techniques which invite disorder. If this information is presented to the teacher in a professional manner, he then has an opportunity to take corrective action before serious situations develop.

In summary, proper classroom organization improves the teaching-learning situation by saving time and energy, helping preserve order and contributing to character development. Good teachers devise definite modes of seating pupils, recording attendance, directing traffic, distributing and collecting materials, arranging and caring for equipment, regulating light, heat and ventilation and for seeing that desks and floors are kept neat.

Preventive measures help keep problems from occurring, but when serious discipline problems do develop they should be dealt with objectively and firmly without rejecting the misbehaving child as a person.

Contagious Teaching

Elizabeth Teigland

A Letter from Elizabeth Teigland to One of Her Students

Dear Joan:

Here we are at the halfway mark of your first year of teaching! Remember the day you came to my office ready to change your entire career because of the frustrating, negative experiences you were having as a student teacher? We tried to analyze the difficulties you were having, to determine the causes, and we discovered that much of the problem lay within you—in your attitude, your self-concept, your values. Not only was the feedback you were receiving in the classroom a mirror image of yourself, but the feedback indicated that both your strengths and weaknesses were being "caught" by the students. You were experiencing with dismay the contagion of teaching.

For teaching is contagious, and the contagion that interacts in the classroom can be as negative as the measles or as positive as a smile. It flows from student to the teacher and from teacher to the student. It may be on a conscious level like the enthusiasm of a cheer leader, or it may be unconscious like the anxiety preceding merit rating. No one is immune. Therefore, it becomes important for both students and teachers to be aware of the mental and emotional components they contribute to the classroom environment.

As a beginning teacher you undoubtedly have had many moments—perhaps hours—of anxiety as you have felt yourself alone in this "multitangential" task of teaching. No doubt the problems of discipline loomed very foreboding those first days as you faced thirty or more strangers whose behavior was completely unknown to you. You knew those children were trying you out to determine whether you were fair and consistent. They needed to know if the rewards and punishment meted out by their new teacher were commensurate to their deeds. They also needed to know whether the rules decreed today would hold tomorrow. Their anxiety, while possibly unconscious, was fully as great as yours. Your anxiety came partially from a deep but understandable desire to have the children like you. If you were stern and uncompromising, as some advise the beginning teacher to be, would it create resentfulness instead of acceptance? If you were friendly and permissive would your room become chaotic as the children vied for your attention? Your anxiety was deepened by the ever

Reprinted by permission of the *Peabody Journal of Education,* Nashville, Tennessee, and Elizabeth Teigland from *Peabody Journal of Education* 44:272-275, March, 1967.

present, unexpressed threat of experienced colleagues and supervisors whose approval was very important to you.

The success you experience today in maintaining a controlled, but unstrained, relationship with your class is due largely to the pattern established those first days. You recognized that in all human relationships the desire to be accepted is cardinal. It was as important to each child that you like him as a person as it was important for you to be accepted by all those with whom you were working. Your principal and fellow teachers were each as eager to be accepted by you as you were to win their approval. This relationship was contagious and quickly eased anxiety, replacing it with mutual confidence in your ability to be both teacher and friend.

But anxiety over being accepted is not the only contagious force at work in the classroom of the beginning teacher. Do you remember how you felt after your graduation from college, when you held your diploma and teaching certificate in your hand for the first time? As you read the beautifully printed wording, one word probably stood out in your mind—responsibility. You may have thought, "Yes, it is wonderful to be free of the hurdles and obstacles of the academic program and to feel the approval of the faculty. But am I able to accept the responsibilities of freedom?"

This much coveted freedom was an irritant all through your student teaching. Even as you were feeling the agonies of doubt because of the difficulties you were having, you were tempted to place the blame on the situation which did not give you complete freedom to make decisions relative to teaching. You wanted freedom; you wanted to try—alone. Now you were free to try, but you found it was not all joy. For freedom creates anxiety. Not an anxiety over any one weakness, but a total anxiety which permeates every decision you make. "Am I able?" You undoubtedly have asked yourself this question over and over again these months since you began teaching. Many times you may have wanted to put the burden of decision-making on the shoulders of someone whom you considered more able than you.

This anxiety is contagious also. The teacher who doubts her knowledge of facts in areas where facts are pertinent; the teacher who is unable to justify her decisions with sound philosophy; the teacher who must always point to a source of information for security: this teacher cannot instil in her students a confidence in her ability to teach. To know where to find information is important but it is not sufficient, for it will not inspire students to seek, remember, and apply knowledge.

Careful preparation will relieve this anxiety of not being able and will be rewarded with similar diligence on the part of the student. To make decisions, after careful consideration and calm judgment, is a part of responsible use of freedom and is as contagious as the frustration of anxiety. Your confident response to the responsibility of freedom in teaching has been "caught" by your students, and they have become more confident of your ability to teach and of their ability to learn.

Anxiety is only one contagious aspect of teaching. Have you ever tried to convince a class or an individual of the importance of something when really you did not consider it important? An illustration of this is the teacher who tries to instil in her students a love for reading and an interest in a wide variety of books when she, herself, does not like to read. All the eloquence you can command will not convince a class that wide, extensive reading is essential to intellectual success if you, the teacher, do not read.

When parents ask me how they can help their son or daughter become a better reader, I ask them what books they, the parents, are now reading. Too often the answer is, "Well, I really do not have time to read anything but the newspaper." It does not take long for them to see the incongruity between their desire to have their children become readers and the obvious fact that they feel reading is not essential. If the parents are readers, the children will grow up in an environment and atmosphere of books and will sense that their parents place a high value on reading.

Likewise, the teacher who finds pleasure and challenge in reading will have little trouble relaying this attitude to the class. A genuine enthusiasm for intellectual pursuits, whether reading, mathematics, science, or any other study, cannot be hid. Your class will respond to it whether or not you consciously emphasize it. Enthusiasm is contagious when it is real; when it is forced or untrue, it fails. A first grader came home one day and with a perplexed frown said, "Mommy, why does my teacher get so excited because Sally wore her daddy's rubbers? It's all right to read about it, but I can tell lots of things that are more fun." Be enthusiastic—but be honest. Both are contagious.

Perhaps the most contagious of all classroom interactions is the attitude of the teacher toward individual students. How do you, the teacher, look at your class? Do you see it as one group of slow learners one of average, and one of gifted? Then each child will see himself as one of the group into which you have placed him and will respond accordingly. Do you see children as falling into groups such as mentally handicapped, emotionally disturbed, or visually defected? Or do you see them individually in terms of a classification on a scale—two points above normal, five points below normal? Evaluation is contagious. If you are able to accept each child as an individual, differing from every other and varying from day to day, but always worthy of your respect regardless of his physical, social, or intellectual status, then he will be able to accept himself as he is with areas of strength and areas of weakness, but able to deal with either.

What I am saying, Joan, is that no person is so completely negative that he is not deserving the respect of his teacher. You may not accept what he does, but you must accept him if he is going to accept himself. Only in this way can he develop the self-image which is confident, adequate, and free.

This respect for the person is so contagious that it "backfires." As you develop the ability to accept each child in your class as a person worthy of your respect, you will not only help him accept himself but you will also enhance your self-image. You will see yourself as a teacher capable of developing the "I-Thou" relationship so desirable in a teaching-learning interaction. You will be able to join the company of the teacher who once described her experience in these words: "Ours is a companionship on the road to learning, for he teaches me as much as I teach him, and we are both richer for it."

I could go on describing the many ways in which teaching is contagious. Such things as the attractive classroom, the pleasant voice, the undivided attention, and the ready smile may not seem terribly important; but neither did that one case of three-day measles until fifteen children were absent on the day of the program for the P.T.A. Remember?

Watch out! It's contagious!

Tort Liability and the Classroom Teacher

Arthur Louis Ferguson

Today teachers should be more concerned about the question of tort liability than ever before. Like the policeman on the beat whose authority was rarely questioned until the present decade, the teacher is no longer always "right" in the eyes of parents or the courts. We seem to be living in an era of more concern for individual rights and this trend is reflected in an increase in the number of tort law suits against teacher and school board which now reach the courts as compared to the few that reached the courts in bygone days.

This article will address itself to: (1) the nature of tort liability; (2) how negligence is determined; (3) the areas of the school program which give rise to the majority of court cases involving school personnel; (4) possible consequences of a tort suit on the future of a classroom teacher; and (5) what can be done to minimize the possible adverse consequences of being involved in a tort suit.

1. What is tort liability? Tort liability is generally defined as "the state of being bound or obliged in law or justice to do, pay or make good something as a

Written for this volume.

result of a legal wrong committed upon another person or his property." While the law of torts includes a number of criminal acts such as murder, rape, theft, and arson, to give but a few examples, this field of law also includes a number of other acts which cannot be denominated "criminal acts." Of this last class of torts, those which are not criminal in nature, negligence is the most common and the tort which should be of vital concern to the classroom teacher as well as to other school personnel.

2. What is negligence? Negligence is determined by a standard of conduct which is usually defined as "the conduct of a reasonably prudent man under similar or like circumstances." If injury to person or property results from one's conduct which falls below this standard, a law suit may be filed against the party who committed the act. If negligence is proved and the injured party is free of fault, then a judgment in the form of damages may be awarded against the negligent party. Great weight is usually given to the "foreseeability" of danger. If danger is obvious, a reasonable person is expected to take measures to prevent a foreseeable injury. However, for negligence to be proved a legal duty to exercise prudent or reasonable care must exist between the negligent person and the injured party as in the teacher-pupil relationship. Negligence may result from the doing of something that a reasonable man would not do or the omission to do something a reasonable man would do if there is a duty owed to the injured party to exercise reasonable care not to injure him.

3. What areas of the school program give rise to the majority of court suits involving school personnel? In the educational program of the public schools of the United States there are certain curricular areas which give rise to the vast majority of the negligence suits which go to court. These areas include physical education, recreational programs, and free play periods, shop and laboratory activities, and school bus transportation. Commonly cited grounds for suit are failure of the teacher to supervise properly and failure of the teacher to forewarn pupils of inherent danger. Many accidents will happen even though teachers exercise prudent judgment and for these accidents they will not be held liable, but imprudent judgment causes accidents and for these accidents liability may attach.

4. What are the possible consequences of a tort suit on the future of a classroom teacher? The first consequence would seem to be obvious: the financial loss of payment in damages. Of course, the amount of the judgment would determine the degree of hurt to the teacher. A successful negligence suit against a teacher may result in loss of employment. Some state laws include negligence as one of the grounds for dismissal from employment. In view of such dismissal another position may be difficult to obtain.

5. What can be done to minimize the possible adverse consequences of being involved in a tort suit? First of all, teachers can be made aware of the nature, scope, and consequences of imprudent judgment or behavior and certain steps

can be taken to minimize the causes of injury to pupils. Pupils can be supervised properly at all times and warned of inherent dangers in certain activities. Permission slips, signed by parents, should be required before pupils are allowed to engage in some activities such as athletics and field trips. Although permission slips do not relieve the teacher of liability, the parent's consent does discourage legal action. Personal liability insurance policies should be purchased by teachers if coverage is not provided by the school district or through membership in some professional organization such as the National Education Association.

In keeping with the times, more and more state legislatures or state supreme courts are imposing tort liability on school districts for the negligent acts of their employees. This school district liability makes the school district answerable for damages resulting from acts of teachers and other employees, thereby protecting teachers and employees from financial loss for damages. Even in many states which still enjoy traditional tort immunity the legislatures have enacted laws permitting local school districts to purchase liability insurance to protect all school personnel. A few states have enacted "save harmless" laws which require school districts to pay any damages assessed against a teacher employed by that district. The majority of the states are still immune in tort for the negligence of their personnel. This encourages suit against the individual teacher because the injured party has no other recourse. The legislators of these immune states should be encouraged to consider this problem and to enact necessary laws to protect all school employees.

The classroom teacher should make a point of finding out what provisions have been made by his school district to protect him against financial loss. If no provisions have been made at the school district level, personal initiative is required. The local district should be encouraged to make provisions for insurance coverage or insurance should be secured by the individual teacher. It has been said that "accidents always happen to the other guy." This can also be said of tort suits. One successful tort suit against a teacher or anyone else could be one too many.

Suggested Additional Readings

Abraham, Willard. "On Your Way," pp. 9-18 in *A Handbook for the New Teacher*. New York: Rinehart and Co., Inc., 1960.

Adams, Sam, and John L. Garrett. "How Do We Plan for Teaching?" pp. 142-160 in *To Be a Teacher: An Introduction to Education*. Englewood Cliffs: Prentice-Hall, Inc., 1969.

Butler, Alfred L., Jr. "Discipline: How to Get Control on the First Day of School." *Grade Teacher* 86:164-170, September, 1968.

Chasnoff, Robert E. "A Plan for Lesson Plans," pp. 643-648 in *Elementary Curriculum: A Book of Readings.* New York: Pitman Publishing Corp., 1964.

Dawson, Esther. "First Days—for the Beginning Teacher." *The Instructor* 70:24, 76, September, 1960.

Filbin, Robert L., and Stefan Vogel. "The First Day," pp. 46-56 in *So You're Going to Be a Teacher.* Great Neck, New York: Barron's Educational Series, Inc., 1962.

Friedman, Daniel. "How to Find the Job You Want in Education." *The Instructor* 77:77, January, 1968.

Garvey, James F. "The What and Why of Behavioral Objectives." *The Instructor* 77:127, April, 1968.

Gerhard, Muriel. "Behavioral Outcomes: What the Child is Able to Do and Does as a Result of the Teaching-learning Experience." *Grade Teacher* 84:92-95, April, 1967.

Harrison, Raymond H., and Lawrence E. Gowin. "Records and Other Routine Duties," pp. 185-198 in *The Elementary Teacher in Action.* San Francisco: Wadsworth Publishing Co., Inc., 1958.

Haskew, Laurence D., and Jonathon C. McLendon. "The Place to Work," pp. 202-208 in *This is Teaching.* Chicago: Scott-Foresman and Co., 1962.

Howard, Alvin W. "Teacher Liability and the Law." *The Clearing House* 42:411-413, March, 1968.

Hunter, Madeline C. "The Agony and the Ecstasy of Teaching." *NEA Journal* 56:36-38, February, 1967.

Nerbovig, Marcella H., and Herbert J. Klausmeier. "The Challenges of Teaching in the Elementary School," pp. 3-29 in *Teaching in the Elementary School,* Third Edition. New York: Harper and Row, Publishers, 1969.

———. "Curriculum Organization and Planning," pp. 106-147 in *Teaching in the Elementary School,* Third Edition. New York: Harper and Row, Publishers, 1969.

Peters, Herman J., Collins W. Burnett, and Gail F. Farwell. "Careers in Professional Education," pp. 206-236 in *Introduction to Teaching.* New York: The Macmillan Co., 1963.

Richey, Robert W. "Legal Liabilities and Responsibilities of Teachers," pp. 294-321 in *Planning for Teaching: An Introduction to Education,* Fourth Edition. New York: McGraw-Hill Book Co., 1968.

Sylwester, Robert. "Only 179 Days to Go!" *The Instructor* 72:33, 119, September, 1962.

Taba, Hilda. "Translating General Objectives into Specific Ones," pp. 228-230 in *Curriculum Development: Theory and Practice.* New York: Harcourt, Brace and World, Inc., 1962.

Townes, Alta Lu. "Getting Them Started." *NEA Journal* 56:69-70, October, 1967.

Ward, Carolyn Elizabeth. "In Time Smart." *NEA Journal* 57:65-66, March, 1968.

Yauch, Wilbur A., Martin H. Bartels, and Emmet Morris. "Getting Ready to Start the Job," pp. 144-170 in *The Beginning Teacher.* New York: Henry Holt and Co., 1955.

———. "Getting Started on the New Job," pp. 171-195 in *The Beginning Teacher.* New York: Henry Holt and Co., 1955.

Chapter 4

Utilizing Child Development Research

That school practice tends to lag considerably behind research knowledge about children is frankly admitted by Dinkmeyer in the opening article "Child Development Research and the Elementary School Teacher." Proceeding from this point, he presents a succinct summary of the latest and most authentic information from experts in the field. He stresses findings about such meaningful and useful topics as classroom climate in relation to the child's early years, what is known about individual differences and their bearing on grouping practices, and how sex differences affect learning in the classroom. By placing this article at the beginning of the chapter, it is hoped that the importance of basing teaching practices on the foundation of sound scientific research will be brought to both the beginning and experienced teacher.

The chapter then moves into a series of three articles which highlight the importance of every teacher's understanding the child's inner life. That schools in their sometimes exclusive emphasis on intellectual development have been guilty of serious neglect is aptly discussed by Beatty, in "The Feelings of Learning." Citing relevant research about children's emotional life, he points out that a child's success in school is dependent on the teacher's belief in his worth and capability, and that the teacher's every act must be predicated upon this belief. Haupt carries this theme further by showing that the failing child suffers psychological damage and needs success experiences in order to restore his inner balance. Herman and his colleagues, in comparing teaching practices of today with those of forty years ago, conclude that although progress is evident in the way in which teachers apply knowledge of growth and development to the handling of behavior problems in the school, only a beginning has been made.

Child Development Research
and the Elementary-School Teacher

Don Dinkmeyer

Elementary education has been engaged in looking at methods in arithmetic, science, and other curriculum areas and at the improvement of learning. I believe it is vital at this time to concentrate on the child as the significant subject for the elementary-school teacher.

Here I should like to focus on the most important subject in your classroom—the child. Most teachers enter elementary-school teaching because of their love and concern for children. In a short period of time, however, teachers become involved with the curriculum.

American education is increasingly becoming involved in research. How much of this research has filtered down to the classroom and affected the educational process? Members of the American Educational Research Association tend to agree that current school practice is falling considerably behind the research evidence already available about children.

There is a vast spectrum of research. Here I shall be considering the climate of learning, the nature of the child, discouragement, intelligence, motivation for achievement, and their relationship to classroom- and curriculum-planning.

The Climate

First, let us look at the teacher-pupil relationship in any given classroom. Evidence is mounting that a number of children learn primarily because of the relationship they develop with the significant adults in their environment. The teacher becomes the significant adult in the classroom. Research by Lewin, Lippitt, and White indicates that children achieve individual goals as well as group goals more effectively in a democratic climate than in an autocratic or a laissez faire climate (1). Group discussion tends to encourage a democratic climate. There should be regular opportunities in the classroom for the child to express himself, to listen to others, and to take part in pupil-teacher planning and pupil-teacher evaluation. Jennings established experimentally that an improved social climate resulted in higher achievement (2).

If a democratic climate is to have significance for an individual, the individual must perceive the climate as democratic. Some of the research by Thomas and

Reprinted by permission of the University of Chicago Press, publisher, and Don Dinkmeyer from *The Elementary School Journal* 67:310-316, March, 1967. Copyright 1967 by the University of Chicago.

his group indicates that child-training practices appear to produce varied results depending on the nature of the child (3). Thomas' research makes us aware that the child does more than experience sensation. He perceives and conceptualizes. He has within himself the creative capacity to give meaning to his experiences and to interpret. His past experiences and his value system help him evaluate all experiences. As teachers we must recognize that the child may not give the same meaning to an experience that we give to it.

A child's discouragement about his ability to perform adequately in school reduces his productivity. How he sees his capacities and his chance of functioning adequately is more important than the reality of the situation. Discouragement usually results in failure to function in the useful tasks of life, and sometimes accompanies misbehavior. Teachers must constantly be aware that their goal is to help shape the child's concept of self as an achiever. Interaction between teacher and pupil set up certain anticipations, and eventually the child operates on these assumptions as if they were fact. Does the school plan success experiences at appropriate levels of academic achievement for each child to help him feel adequate? Early in the school year every teaching staff might well study each child's assets to shift the diagnostic focus from an overconcern about what is wrong with the child. An inventory of assets can obviously become the basis for a good relationship and provide a strong motivational tool.

The child's view

Davidson and Lange found that children's perceptions of their teacher's feelings toward them had a positive, significant relation to their self-perception (4). The child who had the most favorable self-image was usually the child who perceived his teacher's feelings toward him as being favorable. The more positive the child's perceptions of his teacher's feelings, the better the child's academic achievement and the more desirable his classroom behavior as rated by the teacher. This finding gives us insight into the relationship between the teacher's evaluation of the child's work and his behavior.

Inadequate concepts of self with their accompanying lack of confidence and mastery of the environment usually accompany deficiency in the child's school performance.

In a study of fifth- and sixth-grade children Coopersmith found a coefficient of correlation of .36 between a positive self-concept and school achievement (5). The child who has a poor self-concept tends to be more anxious, less adjusted, and less effective in groups than the child who has a more adequate self-concept.

Perceptual theorists such as Combs indicate that a person cannot behave any more intelligently than he believes he can (6). A child who is convinced that he cannot do arithmetic, spelling, or reading may act in accordance with these convictions. Teachers can help him use his capacity only as they change his convictions.

Intelligence

Psychological research is making us aware that children vary considerably in the rate of mental development and in the emotional factors significant in influencing test scores (7).

We must give increasing attention to the evidence that there are kinds of intelligence and that single scores are relatively meaningless in educational planning. Guilford has indicated some of the kinds of intelligence—concrete intelligence, abstract intelligence, and social intelligence, to name a few (8). He has identified as many as fifty specific intellectual factors.

Teachers, in particular, should be cautious about making educational decisions based on the results of intelligence tests given in the primary grades. Intelligence is a developing function, and research shows us that the stability of measured intelligence increases with age (9).

Teachers need to consider a variety of intellectual factors significant for the learning process. Educators must develop and use more sensitive measures of creativity in school. Torrance estimates that if one were to identify gifted children solely on the basis of intelligence tests, about 70 per cent of our most creative children would be eliminated from consideration as gifted (10). The difference between the creative and those who get high scores on intelligence tests is most clearly illuminated in Torrance's findings. In a group study, the highly creative ranked in the upper 20 per cent on creative thinking but not on intelligence, while the highly intelligent ranked in the upper 20 per cent on intelligence but not on creativity. A very small group rated high on both intelligence and creativity.

A sense of accomplishing

Achievement is one of the major purposes of the school. Psychological research has impressed us that it is important to arrange situations that provide success experiences, and to use the past success experiences in motivating the child (11). For some children developing skill, competence, and success are motives in themselves for continuing an activity (12).

The mutual alignment of goals and purposes is basic for effective teacher-pupil relationships. Too frequently the pupil has one objective and the teacher another. If progress is to be made, alignment of goals is necessary.

Teachers must become familiar with methods of encouragement to help the child believe in himself (13). Effort should be recognized. The child's strengths and assets should be used to facilitate instruction. It is important to convey to the child the feeling that he can perform and that it is safe to try.

Page made an interesting study of the effect of teacher's comments on student's performances (14). Although the study was done in secondary school, there are implications for elementary school. Page found that specific encouraging comments had a positive effect on the student's efforts.

The child's self-concept and his level of aspiration were considered in research by Sears (15). His work demonstrated that self-confident, successful children have similar reactions when level of aspiration is evaluated. Unsuccessful children who lack self-confidence may adopt one of a number of behavior techniques in coping with situations. When children achieve near the level they expect of themselves, their future expectations of performance are quite realistic. One task of teacher-pupil planning is to identify tasks near the achievement level the child expects of himself.

Individual differences between boys and girls should be considered. Crandall's research indicates that the motivation for achievement in boys and girls is quite different (16). Girls appear to be more motivated by the approval and the affection of others. Boys are more motivated by internal demands and a need for self-approval.

The Fels Research Institute has carried out an interesting longitudinal study which indicates that by early elementary-school age the achievement behavior of girls as well as boys is predictive of adult behavior (17).

The early years

The results of current longitudinal research reaffirm the importance of the teacher in the primary grades. Bloom (9: 127), in summarizing some of his research, states, "The absolute scale of vocabulary development and the longitudinal studies of educational achievement indicate that approximately 50% of general achievement at grade 12 (age 18) has been reached by the end of grade 3 (age 9)."

This finding points to the great importance of the preschool period and the first few years of school in the development of general achievement and learning patterns. Bloom suggests the need for a highly effective school environment in the primary grades and questions the value of educational remedial measures at a later stage.

These findings certainly urge the wisdom of providing early guidance and counseling experiences for the elementary-school child.

Grouping

Research in child development also poses a caution for school administrators. Considerable attention has been given to homogeneous grouping. The advent of computers and mechanical methods of grouping has caused some of us to put unwarranted faith in grouping children on the basis of test results. Homogeneous grouping has rested on the assumption that traits are closely related within an individual so that, for example, a bright child is equally superior in all his cognitive functions. Research does not support this idea, however. Butt found that the variability in reading and arithmetic in students at a given grade level, sectioned on the basis of general intelligence, was about 80 per cent of the range for all children in that grade (18). In other words, grouping did not solve the problem of variability of traits within the individual. Individual differences are more than intellectual. Children differ in various talents, in physical capabilities, in maturity, and in the capacity to adjust to the tasks of living. Thus, homogeneous grouping may be a serious fallacy in our educational planning, if it leads the teacher to believe that she is dealing with individuals who are quite alike in their approach to learning tasks.

We should certainly raise some serious questions about the use of norms and standards as applied to human beings. B. Hughes found in his research that the norm described only 13 per cent of the group studied (19). In another study of norms and standards, DeLong found several grades in which no children fit the description of the average. Only 25 per cent of other groups were described by the average when the average was interpreted broadly enough to include a range eight times the standard error of measurement (20). This finding has led to the suggestion that each individual's pattern of development—not the average of the group—be considered as a standard for him.

Cook has pointed out that when a random group of six-year-olds enter first grade, 2 per cent will be below the average of four-year-olds in general mental ability, and 2 per cent will be above the average of eight-year-olds (21). If the extremes are disregarded, a four-year range in general intelligence appears in first grade. By the time this group reaches the age of twelve, or sixth grade, the range in general intelligence alone will have increased to almost eight years.

Individual differences

Administrators and teachers often preach the doctrine of individual differences. They are aware of individual rates of learning, yet there are few indications that individualized rates are taken into account when learning experiences are planned. Suppes conducted an extensive, accelerated mathematics program with a group of gifted first-graders (22). He found a tremendous range in rate of learning. At the end of the first four weeks the fastest child covered half again as much material as the slowest. This was in a group that was preselected as gifted. His data indicate that the greatest gains in subject matter learning come primarily through adjusting to individual differences in rate of learning.

Boys, girls, and teachers

The significance of the interaction between the teacher and the pupil cannot be denied. Meyer and Thompson did an interesting study of classroom interaction between boys and girls and the teacher (23). The researchers reported that boys received significantly more blame and disapproval from teachers. These investigators suggest that because of basic biological and social differences, boys are more active and less conforming in the classroom. Teachers who attempt to force boys in their classes to conform to classroom standards by dominating behavior generate more aggression, withdrawal, nervousness, and loss of self-confidence.

An emotionally healthy atmosphere in school encourages achievement. Spaulding collected data about children from fourth grade through sixth grade in ten elementary schools in a California suburb (24). He concluded that there was a significant positive relation between the adequacy of the child's self-concept and the degree to which teachers were calm and accepting, in an atmosphere where there was a socially integrated, learner-centered group. There was a negative relationship between the adequacy of the child's self-concept and the degree to which teachers were domineering and threatening. Achievement gains were positively related to the consistency, the routine, and the orderliness of the classroom teacher's behavior.

Some elementary schools have used the guidance counselor as a consultant on child development. In this role the counselor helps the teacher recognize the significance of child development in understanding an individual child.

Research on child development has considerable import for teachers—their role and their function—in the classroom. Teachers need to be made aware of the significance of this research.

REFERENCES

1. K. Lewin, R. Lippitt, and R. White. "Patterns of Aggressive Behavior in Experimentally Created 'Social Climates'." *Journal of Social Psychology,* 10 (1939), 271-99.
2. H. Jennings. *Sociometry in Group Relations.* Washington, D.C.: American Council on Education, 1951.
3. A. Thomas, H. Birch, S. Chess, M. Hertzig, and S. Korn. *Behavioral Individuality in Early Childhood.* New York: New York University Press, 1963.
4. H. Davidson and G. Lang. "Children's Perceptions of Their Teachers' Feelings toward Them Related to Self-Perception, School Achievement, and Behavior," *Journal of Experimental Education,* 29 (December, 1960), 107-18.
5. S. Coopersmith. "A Method for Determining Types of Self-Esteem," *Journal of Educational Psychology,* 59 (1959), 87-94.
6. A. Combs. "Intelligence from a Perceptual Point of View," *Journal of Abnormal and Social Psychology,* 47 (July, 1952), 662-73.
7. T. W. Richards. "Mental Test Performance as a Reflection of the Child's Current Life Situation: A Methodological Study," *Child Development,* 22 (1951), 221-33.
8. J. P. Guilford. "Three Faces of Intellect," *American Psychologist,* 14 (August, 1959).
9. B. Bloom. *Stability and Change in Human Characteristics.* New York: John Wiley and Sons, 1964.
10. E. P. Torrance. *Guiding Creative Talent.* Englewood Cliffs, New Jersey: Prentice-Hall, Inc., 1962.
11. R. White. "Motivation Reconsidered: The Concept of Competence," *Psychological Review,* 66 (1959), 297-333.
12. H. W. Stevenson and L. C. Snyder. "Performance as a Function of the Interaction of Incentive Conditions," *Journal of Personality,* 28 (1960), 1-11.
13. D. Dinkmeyer and R. Dreikurs. *Encouraging Children To Learn: The Encouragement Process.* Englewood Cliffs, New Jersey: Prentice-Hall, Inc., 1963.

14. E. Page. "Teacher Comments and Student Performance: A Seventy-four Classroom Experiment in School Motivation," *Journal of Educational Psychology,* 49 (August, 1958), 173-81.
15. P. Sears. "Levels of Aspiration in Academically Successful and Unsuccessful Children," *Journal of Abnormal and Social Psychology,* 35 (1940), 498-536.
16. V. Crandall and Others. "Motivational and Ability Determinants of Young Children's Intellectual Achievement Behaviors," *Child Development,* 33 (1962), 643-61.
17. H. Moss and J. Kagan. "Stability of Achievement and Recognition Seeking Behaviors from Early Childhood through Adulthood," *Journal of Abnormal and Social Psychology,* 62 (1961), 504-13.
18. Cyril Burt. "The Differentiation of Intellectual Ability," *British Journal of Educational Psychology,* 24 (1954), 76-90.
19. B. Hughes. Address, Child Development Research Seminar, Walden Woods, Michigan, August, 1955.
20. Arthur DeLong. Paper to Michigan Academy of Science, Arts and Letters, February, 1955.
21. W. Cook. "Individual Differences and Curriculum Practice," *Journal of Educational Psychology,* 39 (1948), 141.
22. P. Suppes. "Modern Learning Theory and the Elementary-School Curriculum," *American Educational Research Journal,* 1 (March, 1964), 79-93.
23. W. Meyer and G. Thompson. "Teacher Interactions with Boys as Contrasted with Girls," in *Psychological Studies of Human Development,* p. 510. R. Kuhlen and G. Thompson (editors). New York: Appleton-Century-Crofts, 1963.
24. R. Spaulding. "Achievement, Creativity, and Self-Concept Correlates of Teacher-Pupil Transactions in Elementary Schools," in *Readings in Child Behavior and Development,* p. 313. C. Standler (editor). New York: Harcourt, Brace and World, 1964 (second edition).

The Feelings of Learning

Walcott H. Beatty

Stop says Superego, you know you should
I would says Ego, but id [it] feels so good.*

It is a commonplace statement that the child is born with no knowledge of the world. But, he arrives with a number of characteristics that will play key roles in what knowledge he will get and how he will act upon it. We are all

Reprinted by permission of Walcott H. Beatty and the Association for Childhood Education International, 3615 Wisconsin Avenue, N.W., Washington, D.C., from *Childhood Education* 45:363-366, March, 1969. Copyright ©1969 by the Association.

* I do not know the source of this poem, but I have quoted it because I think it captures the problem that arises when we try to split feeling off from intellect rather than recognizing that they are both essential for healthy human functioning.

familiar, to some degree, with the complex nervous system. It is already well developed at birth. It has begun to feed data from all over the body, generated both internally and externally, into memory banks and directly to the motor controls that shape the observable responses of the child. This system, with its potential for modification and increased complexity, is the basis for what we call *intellect.* There is another characteristic of humanness that is just as basic and equally important with which we are less familiar. Data about the condition of the organism and of the changes in bodily functioning are also fed into the central nervous system. These are changes in internal secretions, the tensing of muscles and the changes in level of metabolism of groups of cells or of whole systems of organs and tissues. These changes are noted in our awareness as feelings or emotions. Almost all of the behavior of the young child, including that which we designate as *intellectual,* has but one purpose—to optimize the level of the feeling data, to achieve the feeling of being satisfied.

The Self-Concept

With the increasing complexity of the nervous system, as more and more data are fed into it and organized in relation to satisfying behavior, it becomes necessary for us to conceptualize the process in some molar form if we are to understand the behavior of a human being. One attempt to do this is through Self-Concept Theory. The fundamental assumption underlying this theory is that experience is organized around a core of self-regarding attitudes or beliefs. An individual comes to see himself in the world in rather specific ways and his behavior will be consistent with the kind of person he sees and feels himself to be.

The picture an individual has of what he is like is called *self-concept.* It is built up slowly over time from experiences the child has with his own body and directly with the environment. To an increasing degree, as he matures, the critical experiences are the reflected appraisals of other human beings who interact with him. In the early stages, behavior is a rather direct response to the feelings that incoming stimuli evoke in the organism. The young child appears to seek pleasure, to avoid pain, and to be impulsive. He is guided directly by his feelings rather than by the sophisticated interpretations of feelings that we as adults use as guides. As the child begins to use language and use symbols to code his experience, he becomes more responsive to ways in which others are reacting to his behavior. He begins to see his feelings and reactions in terms of words that others (mainly his parents) apply to them. This is the beginning of the self-concept.

The feeling component is the underlying substrate of the self-concept upon which all further development is based. As the appraisals and teachings of adults are perceived, they are perceived with affective tone. The development of the concept of being a boy or a girl, of how one eats, of actions that are "good" or "bad," of whether one is loved or not—the conceptions in all these areas are loaded with pleasant or unpleasant feelings. Literally thousands of reactions from the world outside the child are fed in and stored as a part of the ever-changing picture the child is developing of himself. This part of the self-concept, which defines what he is like now, might be called the *perceived self*. Other data coming in tell him how he might be. Appraisals that set a standard for his behavior are statements such as, "Boys don't cry" or "Big boys don't hit girls." Probably even more important is the fact that Mother and Father are used as models for the child for a picture of what he could be like. This becomes the part of the self-concept that can be called the child's *concept of adequacy*. It is a picture for the child, who initially accepts his parents' behavior uncritically, of what one should be like to be successful or to be an adequate person.

It is clear that these two pictures will not be the same. To the child it would really feel good if he could be adequate. In all areas where appraisals of his self evoke negative feelings, he is strongly motivated to change in the direction of his concept of adequacy. All discrepancies between his perceived self and his concept of adequacy, as he becomes aware of them, are unsatisfying and removing these discrepancies will be satisfying.

Feelings and Learning

To be more specific, it appears that experiences of learning about the self can be organized under one of four areas:

- feelings of self-worth
- feeling of being able to cope with the world's demands
- feeling of being able to express one's self effectively
- feeling of being autonomous.

An individual is motivated to seek experiences that enhance the feelings in each of these areas.

A brief further word needs to be said about each of these to clarify their relevance to learning. Feelings of worth develop from the experiences of being loved by others and included in their activities. Feelings of being able to cope arise as a child is successful in learning skills and knowledge that enable him to act effectively in response to the demands of the world. This has become, unfortunately, almost the sole emphasis of most of our teaching in school. Feelings of being able to express one's self develop as a child is able to verbalize and act out the good and bad feelings he experiences with art, music, body movement and his interactions with other people. A particularly important part of this, which our culture and schools make very difficult, is the expression of strong or negative feelings. Feelings of autonomy grow as an individual develops in each of the three areas and finds that his own behavior and decisions enable him to gain satisfactions in the world and, in a sense, to control his own destiny. Development in each of these areas is vital; in fact, one can define a mature person as one who feels worthy without having to defend himself, feels confident that he can cope with most life situations, is able to be open about his thoughts and feelings, and feels that he can make significant choices to further his own development. A child will be motivated toward any learning that contributes to the development of these feelings.

Relevant Recent Research

The brief space allotted to this discussion has necessarily made it more abstract than I should wish it to be, but perhaps reference to some relevant recent research will clarify the ideas further. First, at a general level, there are many studies which show that problem behavior is invariably associated with negative feelings about the self. Rudolf Dreikurs (1957) says that the major factor underlying most misbehavior is discouragement. The child sees himself as unable to meet the expectations of adults at home and in the school.

With regard to the feelings of worth, a number of studies show that when a child is responded to as being liked or being important he learns better. Kuhlen and Collister (1952) found that students rated by their peers as "friendly," "popular with others," and "cheerful and happy" in the sixth grade were more likely to graduate six years later than the students who had not received these ratings. Page (1958) in a study of the effects of written teacher comments of encouragement on test papers found that students who received such comments improved on the next test. Students who did not receive comments showed no improvement on the next test. This was true for both good and poor students. The point that a person who feels worthy performs better hardly needs documentation, but schools do need to develop ways of increasing the feelings of worth for more students.

Perhaps the studies that are most relevant to the feelings with which one can cope effectively are those that have been made of the "level of aspiration." The study by Pauline Sears (1940) has almost become a classic. Her general finding was that children who were successful in school tended to set personal goals that were reasonable and realistic. Children who had poor records were either overcautious and set goals well below their present achievement or were extravagantly optimistic, setting goals well beyond any actual accomplishments. Adults who present expectations that are reasonable and help children to have successes will foster development in accurate perception of one's ability to cope and confidence that one can learn to cope.

The whole field of therapy offers evidence that healthy functioning is directly related to being able to express all thoughts and feelings rather than suppress them. Carl Rogers (1959) not only clarifies the nature of such expression but shows that it has direct application in the educational process and is not the province of therapy alone. When children are able and encouraged to express their feelings, the teacher gets invaluable information about the effectiveness of his teaching and the child develops a feeling that the teacher is really there to be helpful.

All of these areas of the self-concept continue to develop throughout life, but we tend to be less aware of the development of autonomy until the adolescent and adult periods. However, some of the most critical learnings in this area come very early. The research by McClelland (1953) on the achievement motive makes this clear. He found that parental expectations and rewards for early achievement of independent behavior before school age resulted in a high need for achievement in the child. He further found that the more physical the demonstration of affection as a reward for fulfilling parental demands for independence, the stronger was the drive for achievement. This finding about parental expectations and the importance of affection confirms the statement above that the development of autonomy is dependent upon growth in the other three areas, particularly in feelings of worth.

Success in School

The teacher who understands these ideas of development and believes and acts as though every child is worthy and capable of coping and should be allowed and helped to express himself and become autonomous can make it possible for children to learn and become mature. A recent study by Rosenthal and Jacobson (1968) demonstrates this elegantly. In an investigation of what they call the "self-fulfilling prophecy," they gave to each of a number of teachers the names of five pupils in her class who, they said, on the basis of tests, would probably make unusual intellectual gains during the coming year. Actually, the children named had been chosen randomly and there was no reason to believe that they would do better than other children. However, the five named children in each class did make significantly greater intellectual gains than other children in the class. The teacher's belief and resulting behavior provided a climate in which these children could feel and be successful.

Education has tended to neglect the feelings of children and has often actively attempted to suppress emotions. It is now becoming abundantly clear that such an approach cripples learning and stunts the child's growth toward maturity. It is time we turned major attention to an understanding of emotional development and how it can be fostered. Our curricula should contain experiences designed to produce emotional maturity in equal proportion to those designed to produce an effective intellect.

REFERENCES

Dreikurs, R. *Psychology in the Classroom.* New York: Harper, 1957.
Kuhlen, R. G., and Collister, E. C."Sociometric Status of Sixth- and Ninth-graders Who Fail To Finish High School," *Educ. Psychol. Measmt.* (1952), 12:632-37.

McClelland, D. C., and Atkinson, J. W. *The Achievement Motive.* New York: Appleton-Century-Crofts, 1953.

Page, E. B. "Teacher Comments and Student Performance: A Seventy-four Classroom Experiment in School Motivation," *Journal of Educational Psychology* (1958), 49:173-81.

Rogers, C. R. "Significant Learning: In Therapy and in Education," *Educational Leadership* (1959), 16:232-42.

Rosenthal, R., and Jacobson. "Teacher Expectations for the Disadvantaged," *Scientific American,* 218:4:19-23.

Sears, P. S. "Levels of Aspiration in Academically Successful and Unsuccessful Children," *J. Abnorm. Soc. Psychol.* (1940), 35:498-536.

To Keep an Inner Balance

Charlotte Haupt

A failing child is a suffering child. He hates school because it is the seat of his unhappiness.

Fortunately, there are some remedies for a child's academic inefficiencies that lie within the teacher's realm to help and also antidotes for the crippling changes in a child's personality that have resulted from his repeated failures. The understanding teacher can at least offer first aid. Some hope lies in a special kind of relationship between the teacher and the child. This rapport is a complete openness to and acceptance of the damaged child. It relieves tensions and makes growth possible; however, only a deep comprehension of the factors that produced the harmful changes can make total acceptance possible.

Acceptance and Natural Classroom Environment

When we analyze some of the causes for negative qualities in the so-called doomed "dropouts" or "nonlearners," antidotes seem to reveal themselves. The first mistake made is that a child who has difficulty in learning to read is branded a *failure.* Charlemagne couldn't read! Perhaps our semantics are poor; perhaps we mean to say, "He is failing to read." It is like saying, "He's a bad child" instead of, "He is a fine child who is behaving badly." But the damage is done and the child is not allowed to forget it. Under pressure of the "failure" label, he tries harder and the resulting emotional strain then makes it impossible for him to learn at all.

Reprinted by permission of Charlotte Haupt and the Association for Childhood Education International, 3615 Wisconsin Avenue, N.W., Washington, D.C., from *Childhood Education* 45:391-395, March, 1969. Copyright ©1969 by the Association.

Children are like seeds; they are different and varied, but each with innate characteristics (qualities) and a miraculous upward urge toward self-fulfillment. When conditions are favorable they will flourish and bloom. Some children are sturdy field flowers and can withstand rough weather; others are hothouse plants that need gentle handling . . . but all need warm acceptance and love, the rain and sunshine needed for survival. When life has handled them badly, growth is thwarted and they wither.

By the time many children come to us, they have already found the world hostile and frightening; they have encountered disapproval or rejection. They are either bored, fearful, discouraged, disorganized, confused or apathetic.

The frightened, timid child needs a haven to which he can flee from a hostile environment; the rebellious child, who is making a last-ditch stand to salvage his dwindling ego, needs a battleground where he can win his fight.

Can you transform your classroom into a happy home, where each child has the right to move freely according to his interests (not regimented like a prisoner), where each feels himself a member of a family or group who do things together to attain certain goals but also have freedom to make choices and develop different interests? There should be natural objects—nuts, shells, a bird's nest to examine; boxes of pictures to look at (they can be postcards); boxes of scraps to handle, cloth to feel, soft objects to fondle, bits of fur or velvet; lots of newspaper to tear, fold or cut up to make things or even paint on, and seeds growing in paper cups or something alive to watch. When materials and supplies are limited, paper bags for puppets or masks and odds and ends have to be brought in by you and the children.

Abstractions and Symbols Come Later

Learning by doing comes *before* learning from books. Children are not ready to cope with abstractions and symbols (reading and writing) until they have the readiness that comes from multiple experiences and manipulation of many and varied materials.

Putting ideas and things together in an individual manner becomes a creative way of looking at all things. This helps the child to see the possibilities for change inherent in all life and lets him recognize that there is more than one way of approaching and solving a problem. A child needs lots of play. This is not a waste of time but an important way of learning, for it means involvement, experimentation and testing of his relationship with people and things. A room full of bustling activity and happy, cooperative ventures is a joyful place.

How Did He Become Bored and Apathetic?

A child may have become bored and apathetic for many reasons. He may have sat in on too many lessons that were foreign to his experience and beyond the range of his comprehension. Trying to keep up was impossible. Indifference was his protection and solace. When explanations were beyond his intelligence or experience level, then wrong expectancies on the part of the teacher caused frustration and retreat from tensions with which he could not cope.

If the curriculum had been chosen from the child's daily living experiences, this might not have happened.

It will take some doing to involve such a child in a "lesson." It might be wise to go on a search for some tiny things in which he still is interested. It does not have to be school material—any source will do. Perhaps by going out of doors you could find it. The tiniest spark of interest might be fanned into a flame.

A child may have lost his desire to explore because he was punished for tasting, smelling, touching or investigating things about which he was curious. A timid child would rather not know than be scolded or laughed at. He needs encouragement to provoke his sense of inquiry; to be piqued by intriguing little projects and problems that he can solve alone or with your help.

When a child has never received satisfying answers to his questions he may also lose his curiosity. Sometimes he may even have been given untrue answers to satisfy him for the moment; but such replies create problems in the future and do damage.

Asking Questions and Giving Answers

Have the patience to answer a question, not by a shortcut quick answer but by one that will help a child see why your answer is true. Can you help him figure out an answer by asking him questions that lead to discovery? Children need to be stimulated to think clearly. A generative question can help them focus their attention in such a way that it creates an awareness of new aspects of things. If I ask a child to tell me the shape of an apple, he will say that it is round. If, however, I ask him to tell me the difference between the shape of an apple and the shape of an orange he will be pulled up short; the apple no longer seems round and he must figure out why.

I sometimes wonder how many teachers are aware of the tiny contributions a child might make by giving a wrong answer. If, instead of just saying "That is wrong" and giving his own explanations, he had asked him what made him think of his answer, the teacher might have opened up a whole area of new and interesting teaching material. A good answer can often be something one enjoys thinking about, as in this example:

Grosspapa's home was especially beautiful on summer evenings. After Sunday night supper, blankets were spread on the lawn and grownups and small fry stretched out to gaze at the star-strewn sky.

Dick was four and drinking in the loveliness too.

After some time he asked: "Dad, how far is it to a star?"

His father mused a while, then answered, "Do you remember how fast we drove when we went to Chicago last Easter? Well, son, if we left tonight and drove without stopping, we wouldn't reach a star even when you are as old as Grosspapa."

Dick was silent. That was something for his imagination to ride out on.

Several weeks later he was lying on the bed with his mother. He adored having his back rubbed, like a kitten, and she was indulging him. Dick was almost purring with contentment. Then thoughtfully he asked, "Mother, do you remember what Daddy said about the stars, how far away they are?"

"Yes, I believe I do," she replied.

"Well," sighed Dick, "That's how much I love you."

One never knows how a child will translate knowledge he has acquired. His inner life is not always shared, even with those he loves. He stores the answers to his questions as a squirrel stores nuts, for use as the need arises. Every adult reply is therefore of tremendous importance, since it is source material from which the child's outlook, later decisions and biases may be formed.

Success Needed for EVERY Child

Can you accept every child "as is"—not as you would prefer him to be? Have you the ability to look at him creatively—as a potential of something fine that has not been developed or lies buried? To most people a potato is just a potato, but to the creative cook this humble "spud" has qualities that can be transformed into an unlimited number of tempting dishes.

The failing child may have suffered from his own inability to meet expectancies of his parents or teachers; pressures brought frustration and increased his failures. What he had thought of as his tiny successes had gone unnoticed, unrewarded. This increased his hopelessness. He may have been ridiculed or punished for his shortcomings and was no longer willing to take a chance on exposing himself; he would rather not know than to feel threatened. When even the smallest measure of success in any area has eluded him, he feels utterly defeated and finally accepts the verdict that he is stupid. Pulling a child out of such a defeated state requires an immense amount of compassionate understanding and constant reassurance of your belief in him as a good and valuable person. *Every child needs to feel successful at something in order to keep an inner balance.* Someone will have to find something or some area where success is possible, then lure him out of his pitiful isolation, back into the world of childhood.

Are you able to reveal yourself to children as a warm, open person by sharing your little joys, sorrows, jokes, or fears and failures in a way that lets them sense your willingness to accept theirs? A child will not come out of his shell unless he feels very sure that no criticism will be forthcoming.

In a clay experience with seven-year-olds, I told the children they might make whatever they wished. I moved quietly around the room, encouraging only the few who could not decide what they wanted to make and passing up the rest. Finally, one little fellow pulled my sleeve as I passed and said, "Don't you want to know what I'm making?" "Of course I do," I said, as I looked at what I thought might be a heap of hot dogs. "Dog dirt!" he beamed at me. "That's fine," I said, "go right ahead!"

I never tell this story to teachers without seeing frowns of disapproval on their faces. Dog dirt is, however, a part of some people's experience! If that was the child's interest at the moment and he was sharing it with me, I was flattered and delighted. Any disapproval from me would have ended the confidence he had in me. At the end of the clay experience, I said to him, "What does one usually do with dog dirt? Do you save it?" "No," he said, "we wrap it up and throw it away." So I made a cardboard shovel and together we put his work back in the bucket. Fun and trust. I don't remember if we held our noses as we did it.

A trusting relationship with a damaged child is a fragile thing, not easy to establish or to maintain since life has made him unduly suspicious of all relationships. I find that I must repeatedly show him that I fail in one way or another, that I make mistakes or forget.

Once a child is confident that no effort on his part, whether successful or not, will ever result in your rejection of him, he may lose his fears and open up.

Alleviate Anxieties Before Teaching Skills

Often a teacher feels so pressured about getting the required academic work done that he becomes more involved with the skills than with the children. Somehow the book material takes precedence over the individual child. He fails to notice the child's changing moods. Things happen to the child, in and out of school, that lift or depress him. His joys, worries or defeats affect his ability to learn. If a child is loaded with anxieties when he comes to school in the morning and you cannot alleviate them, or at least let him know that you are in tune with him, he will learn nothing all day—no matter how hard you may try to teach. Repetitions, explanations will be of no avail. If he is emotionally upset he hears only the sound of your words but cannot grasp their meaning.

Disadvantaged Children: Defeated and Disorganized

In working with disadvantaged children, I found them regimented and disciplined beyond the point of necessity for safety and comfort; I found them unable to distinguish between the proper time for talking or making noise and the proper time for silence. They were so disciplined that they never opened their mouths. Sometimes they were told to sit quietly for long periods without reason and they simply obeyed. Children should know some of the reasons for asking them to do things. The same is true for their academic work. If a child is read to and enjoys it, then he may also wish to give pleasure to younger children by reading to them. If he sees no practical value for knowing arithmetic, he will not be motivated to apply himself. Take time to *tie each new skill to some practical application* that has meaning for the child.

Often a defeated child wanders aimlessly, cannot stick to anything, never sees anything completed and seems totally disorganized. If you could let him help plan an activity and follow through with him, step by step, he might see how one thing follows or leads to another. He could also learn that there are reasons for doing things in a certain order. It might help him to be more organized if he learned how to classify objects by sorting them (all nails of one kind in a particular box, all screws in another), discovering that each has a special use and that finding what one needs quickly is satisfying.

Sometimes I have found that confusion exists because of unclear concepts. Perhaps teaching proceeded too fast for a child; new concepts may have been presented before older ones were fully understood. When there is some doubt as to whether something is clear, it is helpful to approach it from a different angle—the same thing in a new connection. Also, a good analogy may be worth a thousand words.

When a child is encouraged to use all his five senses for learning about things, he gains firsthand sensory experiences that give him something with which to back up his opinion about things. The failing child may never have been asked his opinion about things and often has docilely accepted whatever he was told. He may not have developed any skill in making decisions. If encouraged to observe carefully and often asked for *his* opinion, he will develop self-reliance which in turn will elevate his self-image.

In working with blind children I have found that because of their limited experience with actual objects (many things are too delicate to handle, like a spider's web, or out of reach, like the sky) they have had to accept inadequate verbal descriptions that only serve to give these confused, distorted concepts. Certainly this makes for insecurity. The blind child does not wish to expose his ignorance and often will hesitate to ask questions. The more he learns through his own sensory pathways, the more self-reliance he develops and this in turn raises his self-image.

If these suggestions look like a "tall order," remember that every step in the right direction moves us closer to our goal. No pleasure is greater than seeing a stifled, intimidated child transformed into a sunny, confident person! It is like watching a Walt Disney time-lapse picture of the slow and marvelous opening of a flower. Witnessing such a miracle brings deep and abiding joy.

Techniques for Dealing With Children's Behavior

Wayne L. Herman
Robert V. Duffey
Elisabeth Schumacher
David L. Williams
Lillian B. Zachary

An elementary-school teacher's job is concerned chiefly with instructional processes, but often children's behavior gets in the way. If the teacher is to be effective, he will have to take action to meet the behavioral differences in children. He will have to help the child who relies on the teacher too much, the child who is easily discouraged, and the child who is disliked by other children.

A study by Wickman published in 1928 revealed that teachers and clinical psychologists differed in their rankings of the importance of certain child behaviors (1). The clinical psychologists rated recessive and withdrawal characteristics such as unhappiness, unsocialness, and resentfulness as evidence of serious problems of adjustment. The teachers listed such behaviors as dishonesty, transgressions against authority, and immorality—for example, heterosexual activity, masturbation, or "toilet talk"—as the gravest child behaviors. Teachers also considered lack of application to school tasks, disorderliness in the classroom, aggression, and extravagance more important than recessive and withdrawal behaviors.

A report on a similar study by Stouffer was published in 1952. He found that teachers had become more aware of the implications of emotional and social maladjustments, but were still inclined to evaluate behavior much the same as their counterparts had in 1928 (2).

Lewis reported a study in which teachers were requested to name the children in their classrooms whom they considered retarded, geniuses, or problems (3). An analysis of the children listed in the problem group showed that they were children who disturbed or upset the management of the classroom and resisted the authority of the teacher. Children who were extremely shy and withdrawn, whom the clinician would rank high on the list of children with problems, were overlooked.

In a study of 157 elementary-school teachers, Stendler used twenty-five free-response statements describing various behavior patterns of elementary-

Reprinted by permission of the University of Chicago Press, publisher, and Wayne L. Herman from *The Elementary School Journal* 69:198-203, January, 1969. Copyright 1969 by the University of Chicago.

school children (4). She asked teachers how they would cope with the behavior described. A large per cent of the teachers said that talking to the child or moralizing and adjusting the classroom work were the best ways of dealing with aberrant behavior. Studying the child to find causes of his behavior was the unanimous choice of mental hygienists who also took the test.

Stendler's statements describing behavior patterns of elementary-school children were used in a study by Porter. He presented the statements to a relatively small sample of high-school seniors, college students, and in-service teachers. The subjects were asked how they would cope with the behaviors. Porter reported that older groups tended to move more toward the mental hygienists' view of seeking the cause of the behavior (5). The responses of the in-service teachers were almost equally divided among the various categories: take punitive measures (17.3 per cent), talk to child (19.9 per cent), adjust the work (23.7 per cent), and study the child (17.9 per cent).

How far has teacher education come in twenty years? Have teachers moved toward constructive ways of dealing with behavior problems? Are teachers more prone or less prone to take punitive measures or to reprove a child? Are teachers inclined to search for the reasons underlying children's problems? The present study was undertaken to find answers to these questions.

Twelve of Stendler's twenty-five items were used in the present study:

1. the child who continually fights with other children
2. the child who bites his fingernails
3. the child who relies on the teacher too much
4. the child who continually shows off in class
5. the child who is easily discouraged
6. the child who never pays attention to the teacher
7. the child who is a bully
8. the child who is always unhappy and moody
9. the child who always talks back to the teacher
10. the child who is disliked by other children
11. the child who is timid and shy
12. the child who continually disobeys the teacher

Four items dealt with problems that affect only or chiefly the child himself—numbers 2, 5, 8, and 11; four items presented problems that affect other pupils—numbers 1, 4, 7, and 10; and four presented problems directly affecting the teacher—numbers 3, 6, 9, and 12.

The respondents were instructed to "write the *one best, specific* way that *you* as a teacher would deal with each problem." All responses were anonymous.

The responses to the twelve items were classified into seven categories:

1. Punish the child—any punitive measure
2. Reprove the child—scold, censure, rebuke

3. Talk to the child—counsel, moralize, confer
4. Adjust the environment and/or praise or encourage the child—changes within the classroom, often including some supportive statement or act by the teacher
5. Seek the cause of the behavior—inquire of the child himself, or his other teachers; peruse school records
6. Refer the child—send child to physician, personnel worker, clinic, principal
7. Miscellaneous

Table 1. Distribution of Teachers' Responses to Twelve Items Describing Children's Behavior in the Stendler Study and in the Current Study

	Per Cent of Responses	
	Stendler Study	Current Study
CATEGORY	(1949)	(1968)
1. Punish the child	13.9	3.9
2. Reprove the child		2.2
3. Talk to the child		
Moralize	33.4	13.2
4. Adjust the environment	22.5	46.3*
5. Praise or encourage the child	9.1	
6. Seek the cause for his behavior	14.6	16.3
7. Refer the child	2.7	1.3
8. Miscellany: ignore the behavior, talk to parents		12.6
9. No answer	3.8	4.2

* In the 1968 study, Category 5, "Praise or encourage the child," was combined with Category 4, "Adjust the environment," because praise and encouragement were commonly used with an adjustment in the environment.

When teachers gave more than one response to an item, as a few did, only the first response was tabulated. Reliability of coding was established by having all the investigators independently code a common set of ten answer sheets. Discrepancies were discussed, and guidelines evolved for uniform classification of responses.

Two hundred and forty-three in-service elementary-school teachers—thirty-four of them men—responded to the items. All the teachers were enrolled in courses offered by the Department of Early Childhood—Elementary Education in the University of Maryland during the 1967-68 academic year. Eighty-five per cent of the teachers had at least a bachelor's degree. Forty per cent taught primary grades; 40 per cent taught intermediate grades. The remaining 20 per cent taught music, reading, or special classes. Seventy per cent of the teachers had been teaching in their present positions from one to four years. Sixty per cent of the teachers were parents.

Table 1 summarizes the results of Stendler's study and the results of the study reported here. One striking difference between the two studies is the reluctance of teachers in the current study to deal with pupils' problems by taking punitive measures. Only 3.9 per cent of the responses suggested some kind of punishment. As Table 2 shows, the child who continually disobeys the teacher was singled out for punishment in 17.2 per cent of all the responses. Teachers may be more knowledgeable about research findings, which generally reveal that punishment has little lasting influence in changing behavior.

In the Stendler study "talking to the child" accounted for a third of the responses. In the current study this was not a popular technique, although it accounted for 30.0 per cent of the responses when a child talked back to a teacher. With this marked decrease in trying to deal with behavior problems by talking to the child has come an appreciable increase in trying to change behavior by adjusting the environment. Nearly half of all the teachers' responses to all test items called for adjusting the environment. Teachers strongly supported this method of responding to the discouraged child (91.5 per cent), the timid or shy child (85.5 per cent), the child who is prone to be dependent

Table 2. Distribution of Responses That 243 Elementary-School Teachers Made to Twelve Items Describing Children's Behavior*

Statements	Per Cent of Responses							
	1.	2.	3.	4.	5.	6.	7.	8.
	Punish the Child	Reprove the Child	Talk to Child	Adjust the Environ- ment	Seek the Cause	Refer the Child	Miscella- neous	No Answer
1. the child who continually fights with other children	10.2	2.4	21.0	27.0	29.6	1.2	7.4	1.2
2. the child who continually shows off in class	2.0	2.0	9.0	54.7	9.0	....	20.5	2.4
3. the child who is a bully	7.5	10.2	20.1	33.3	13.5	....	13.5	1.6
4. the child who is disliked by other children	....		10.2	53.9	25.5	....	6.5	3.7
5. the child who bites his fingernails	....		15.2	34.9	24.2	.8	20.9	3.7
6. the child who is easily discouraged	....		4.8	91.5	2.4	....	1.2	....
7. the child who is always unhappy and moody	....		8.6	37.0	33.3	3.2	12.7	4.9
8. the child who is timid and shy	....		2.4	85.5	4.1	....	4.5	3.2
9. the child who relies on the teacher too much	....		8.1	80.8	2.8	....	8.1	....
10. the child who never pays attention to the teacher	2.8	1.6	5.3	54.3	16.0	2.4	11.1	6.1
11. the child who always talks back to the teacher	4.9	6.1	30.0	10.2	11.1	1.6	23.4	12.3
12. the child who continually disobeys the teacher	17.2	4.1	16.8	14.8	16.0	5.3	15.2	10.2

* Items 1 through 4 describe pupils' behavior that affects other pupils.
Items 5 through 8 describe behavior that affects only the pupil himself.
Items 9 through 12 describe behavior that affects the teacher.

(80.8 per cent), the inattentive child (54.3 per cent), the show-off (54.7 per cent), and the child disliked by other children (53.9 per cent). Among the popular responses were assigning work or offering opportunities for success and self-reliance.

The use of Category 6, seeking the cause of the behavior, was about the same for both studies. In the current study teachers often listed this response as the best way of working with the unhappy and moody child (33.3 per cent), the combative child (29.6 per cent), the unpopular child (25.5 per cent), and the child who bites his fingernails (24.2 per cent).

The categories adjusting the environment, praising or encouraging the child, or seeking the cause of behavior denoted direct attempts by teachers to help the child. In the current study these constructive efforts in Categories 4 and 6 account for 62.6 per cent of the responses. The result represents a 16 per cent gain over the responses of the teachers in the Stendler study.

The per cent of responses for referring the child to a clinician or the principal were comparable in the two studies. Teachers rarely used this category in their responses. When they did, it was usually for the child who continually disobeys the teacher (5.3 per cent). "Ignore the behavior" accounted for most of the miscellaneous responses, which made up 12.6 per cent of all responses. Among the behaviors eliciting this response were always talking back to the teacher (23.4 per cent), biting fingernails (20.9 per cent), and continually showing off in class (20.5 per cent). While there appeared to be marked improvement in the teachers' use of other categories, responses of "ignore" raise serious questions about teachers' judgment. When teachers ignore certain behaviors, they seem to be tacitly supporting the idea that the behavior is relatively unimportant or that it may eventually disappear if it is permitted to pass unnoticed long enough.

Table 3 summarizes the three classifications of statements. Punishment and reproof were used sparingly. No teacher suggested using these methods when a child's problem did not directly affect other pupils or the teacher. There is similarity across the board in treatment of pupils' problems of interaction with other pupils and pupils' problems that involve the teacher. When a child had a problem—such as discouragement, shyness, or unhappiness—that did not affect others directly, teachers were more inclined to adjust the environment (64 per cent) and less likely to sit down with him to discuss the problem. Categories 4 and 5—adjust the environment and seek the cause of his behavior—which represent constructive techniques of treatment, show the heaviest concentration of suggested treatments. The respondents, however, were less willing to be constructive when children's problems affected the teacher.

In all three categories, referring the child was rarely used as a way of dealing with behavior. This finding raises some serious questions:

Do teachers think of referring as jeopardizing their reputation as competent teachers?

Table 3. Distribution of Responses That 243 Elementary-School Teachers Made to Twelve Items Describing Children's Behavior, Classified by Type of Behavior

Type of Behavior	Per Cent of Responses						
	1.	2.	3.	4.	5.	6.	7.
	Punish the Child	Reprove the Child	Talk to Child	Adjust the Environment	Seek the Cause	Refer the Child	Miscellaneous
Behavior Affecting Other Pupils— Items 1-4 in Table 1	5.0	3.4	15.6	43.4	19.9	.4	12.3
Behavior Affecting Only or Chiefly the Pupil Himself —Items 5-8 in Table 1	. . . .	8.0	64.3	16.5	1.1	10.1
Behavior Affecting the Teacher— Items 9-12 in Table 1	6.7	3.2	16.3	43.3	12.4	2.5	15.6

Do teachers know when a child's problem is serious enough to be referred?

Do teachers know appropriate persons and agencies for referring?

Do teachers have confidence in these resources?

Are these resources too limited, remote, or expensive?

This study sought to determine whether teachers in 1968 have more insight in dealing with child behavior than teachers did twenty years ago. The findings revealed some changes of a positive nature. Teachers in the study reported here were less inclined to use punishment and more disposed to do something constructive, usually in adjusting the environment in some way or other, in the treatment of child behavior. They depended less on talking to the child and moralizing. No positive changes were found in teachers' willingness to seek reasons for the child's misbehavior or to refer him for treatment.

REFERENCES

1. E. K. Wickman. *Children's Behavior and Teacher's Attitudes.* New York: Commonwealth Fund, 1928.
2. George W. Stouffer. "Behavior Problems of Children as Viewed by Teachers and Mental Hygienists," *Mental Hygiene,* 36 (April, 1952), 271-85.
3. W. D. Lewis. "Some Characteristics of Children Designated as Mentally Retarded, as Problems and as Geniuses by Teachers," *Journal of Genetic Psychology,* 70 (March, 1947), 29-51.
4. Celia B. Stendler. "How Well Do Elementary-School Teachers Understand Child Behavior?" *Journal of Educational Psychology,* 40 (December, 1949), 489-98.
5. Robert M. Porter. "Student Attitudes toward Child Behavior Problems," *Journal of Educational Research,* 52 (May, 1959), 349-52.

Chapter 5

Selecting and Employing Procedures and Approaches

No other questions are of more importance to the beginning teacher than those concerned with methodology and basic approach to teaching and learning. Although at the outset he may proceed rather conservatively, relying on time-tested procedures and strategies, sooner or later he will want to venture into more creative, innovative, and potentially more fruitful methods, such as some of those discussed in the following six articles.

The first article sets the stage by bringing to the reader an overall view of the levels of teaching performance which are possible. Beginning with a consideration of traditional memory level teaching, the article then treats teaching for understanding and meaning, and, finally, creative teaching and learning. The purpose of the article by Jacobs is not only to clearly delineate levels of performance, but also to show their connection with learning theory and provide a kind of framework in which the teacher may strive for continuous improvement of his competence.

The topic of pupil-teacher planning, as viewed by Mehl and her associates, continues the theme of learner involvement in the educative process. The cooperative activities discussed cover a broad range of practices from the organization of classroom routines to the planning and execution of major learning units. Furst and Mattleman see the importance of good questioning techniques, adept introduction of subject matter, and building on the child's previously accumulated knowledge as making a direct contribution to the establishing of classroom climate for learning.

Inquiry teaching, recognized as perhaps the most potentially fruitful new learning procedure to appear in recent years, is clearly defined by Massialas. Of particular importance and help to the neophyte and experienced teacher is the outlining and explaining of the various roles of the teacher in the inquiry process.

The next topic, creativity, closely related to inquiry teaching in terms of teacher attitude toward children and classroom procedures, hardly needs a rationale. Thomas and Crescimbeni point out the importance of the teacher's doing something about developing increased creativity rather than merely giving lip service to the cliche in a rapidly changing world, and then proceed to outline the basic strategy to be employed in the classroom. The topic and chapter are brought to a close with Jarzen's delightful personal presentation of the creative process arising out of the depth of a teacher's experience.

Levels of Teaching Performance

Norman C. Jacobs

The beginning elementary teacher, approaching his position after an extended period of general and professional education including meaningful laboratory experiences, is seriously concerned about the level of performance he may achieve. Unlike his predecessors of a century and more ago, and even some of his contemporaries, he has high hopes that his classroom behavior will reflect what is known about the learning and teaching processes rather than be limited to unexamined heritage and tradition. The purpose of this article is to clarify the exact nature of three levels or styles of teaching performance on which the beginner might operate, reflect on them in the light of learning theory, and thereby contribute to self-analysis, understanding, and improvement. The three levels of teaching to be considered are: memory level teaching, teaching for understanding, and creative teaching and learning.

Memory Level Teaching

The prevailing style of teaching in elementary schools throughout the nineteenth century was reflected in what is known to educational historians as the memoriter school.R2:176 Teacher behavior followed the time-honored pattern of transmitting to pupils the separate and discrete facts of a particular subject area, the sum total of which constituted a segment of known, highly regarded knowledge. Methodology was limited mainly to lecture or telling and assigned reading of the textbook with the immediate goal of literal comprehension, repetition, commitment to memory, and instantaneous recall. The form and structure of the elements of knowledge outlined in the syllabus or textbook provided the day-to-day framework within which the teacher operated. The

Written for this volume.

restricted and unimaginative concept of child behavior accompanying such practices combined with the teacher's authoritarian stance and repressive discipline tended to produce a pupil who was passive in attitude.

Pure memory-level instruction[B1:316] has always had for its rationale a belief in the importance of knowledge and the psychological processes of cognition, memory, and convergent thinking, but has stemmed from no particular theory of learning or school of psychology in the modern sense. It has received some support from interpretations of stimulus-response (SR) or connectionist psychology which conceived learning as simple responses to specific stimuli. Thus school subjects could be broken up into simple fact or skill elements which depended largely upon the memory function for mastery.

A plane of performance geared to memory is, of course, not undesirable in every respect and may even have its uses. As pointed out by Bigge, it may help to promote intelligent behavior insofar as memorized facts are available when needed for the solution of problems.[B1:317] On the other hand the use of such knowledge accumulated in school isolation rarely has any significant bearing on the future thought and action needs of the individual concerned. There tends to be little or no emphasis on the understanding of major ideas, while the instances of creative thinking by teacher or pupil are few. Although it still constitutes a fundamental posture and approach to teaching among many practitioners today, accumulated knowledge and insight into the teaching process have thoroughly exposed its inadequacy.

Teaching for Understanding and Meaning

A second and more advanced level of teaching performance has been variously characterized as "understanding level teaching,"[B1:318] "teaching for meaningful relations,"[S2:351] and "the climate of thinking."[S1:20] The one outstanding characteristic of this level is stress on the importance of main ideas rather than discrete facts as is the case in memory level teaching. Thus whether the teacher is at the stage of long-range planning or is engaged in the more detailed task of constructing daily operational plans, his basic approach will be to, first, effect an intelligent overview of the whole range of factual material to be taught in order to see its general pattern or structure. Second, he will determine what concepts need to be developed, and, finally, what major generalizations or general principles are to be arrived at if pupil understanding is to result.

Emphasis on Structure—The general procedure of intelligent overview as the initiatory step, valid for both teacher and pupils, is derived from Gestalt psychology which stresses pattern perception, insight attainment, and structuring as the essence of all cognitive learning. This view leads to the premise that the general structure and main elements of content in a subject field or discipline rather than its details should be emphasized. However, structuring of material, important as it is in enhancing understanding, is further justified psychologically in terms of more efficient learning. The fact that the general structure is more easily grasped, can be perceived at the outset, and remains longer in memory than the details, is supported by considerable evidence. Stephens points out that structured material may be learned in one-fourth to one-eighth of the time required to learn material that is unpatterned or meaningless.[S1:353]

In classroom practice this principle suggests procedures such as presenting the general pattern or main outline, and overviewing the whole before going into details. Once the pattern is perceived, additional material should be presented in relation to it, and, finally, meaningful relations within the material should be brought out.[S2:356]

Emphasis on Major Ideas—The last point concerning the pupil's perceiving meaningful relations within the material is integral in cognitive learning. It must be borne in mind, however, that understanding as the seeing of relationships encompasses not only the relationships between facts as such, but how facts are grouped under a "single overarching idea."[B1:319] Such an inclusive category of knowledge may be termed a generalization.

Although a generalization well developed is supported by many particulars, an important intermediate step in the continuum from facts to generalizations is the development of concepts. Concepts are meanings which extend beyond specific facts or objects and take the form of classes or categories. For example, in the realm of the social studies, experience and factual knowledge lead to the formation of simple concepts such as *river, city, weather,* or more advanced concepts such as *transportation, nation, civilization,* and, in the more abstract category, *justice, liberty,* and *democracy.* An inductive procedure leading to conceptual knowledge of various levels of sophistication is of course integral to science and social studies curricula.

But understanding, in the fullest sense of the term, is achieved only when children acquire the ability to generalize from their knowledge and experiences and arrive at more inclusive meanings. Thus a generalization may be said to express relationships among facts and concepts, and emerge as a kind of end product in the form of a conclusion, general rule, principle, or truth. It too is best developed inductively, that is, by proceeding from the particular concepts or facts to the concluding larger idea. For example, after a study of the particulars of different forms of social life children may arrive at the generalization that people's ways of living are conditioned by their natural environment. Or, once having acquired the concept of *transportation,* children, through further study, may finally generalize that a complex and highly developed transportation network is crucial to life in an industrial and technological society.

Emphasis on Goal or Purpose—Perceptive teachers have long been aware that true understanding involves more than the seeing of the relationships of a particular fact to a general principle. If teaching is to be most effective the learner must, in the view of cognitive field psychology, see how his efforts will help him to achieve some personally meaningful purpose or goal. Thus only if the development of larger ideas or generalizations occurs in some such personal frame of reference will the pupil arrive at what Bigge terms full, true, or functional understanding.[B1:322] One need not delve very far into cognitive field psychology, especially as developed by Lewin and as reflected by other psychologists, to appreciate the importance of linking insight with goal or purpose in understanding individual behavior.

Emphasis on Experience—A fundamental factor in cognitive learning is experience. Firsthand experience provides the basic raw material in the formation of concepts and generalizations and should be employed whenever possible. A classic example in the teaching of reading is the practice of having children recall their own personal experiences related to the theme or main idea of a story for the purposes of motivation and further understanding. Care must be taken in the development of concepts which tend to be abstract in nature—what Stephens calls "unanchored abstractions."[S2:369] Experiences and illustrations, especially for children of deprived background, may be supplied by the teacher.

Implementation—If the main thrust of teaching is to be the perception of pattern or structure and the search for the big ideas, the teacher will ask, "What behavioral steps are necessary for effective performance on this level?" A summary answer might be the following. First, conduct an intelligent overview of the material to be taught in order to determine its general outline and develop an organizational pattern for teaching. Second, determine the concepts, both concrete and abstract, which need to be developed. Third, determine the generalizations, principles, or truths which should emerge in the minds of pupils as a result of the study. The beginning teacher's problem in rising to understanding level teaching has been well summarized by Shumsky, who states that in terms of objective the teacher will be primarily concerned with making sure that pupils understand "the distinction between data and structure and move as quickly as possible from the first to the second."[S1:22] Put in other terms by Jerome Bruner, the task is to make sure of in-depth understanding by stressing relatedness and the fundamental principles "ordering" a discipline.[S1:22]

Intelligent ordering of material taught and attention to ideational development may be unfruitful, however, if acclimatizing factors are neglected. In contrast to a climate geared to fact accumulation and teacher imposition, the teacher attitude and stance will be less authoritarian, less demanding in terms of specifics. For if true understanding is the objective there can be no absolute control in the traditional sense. A freer atmosphere will need to prevail in order that pupils may be more involved mentally. The stress will be on a higher level of discussion with encouragement of pupil questioning and contributing. And since larger ideas rather than particulars are of major concern, the goals of teaching will tend to be geared to the long-range rather than the short-term or immediate.

Other practical procedures and techniques which facilitate pupil understanding include: keeping the overall objectives clear; the use of meaningful practice rather than repetitive drill in the teaching of skills; and proper pacing, or the keeping of the number of topics covered during the year within manageable limits.

Teacher Background—The question of the teacher's command of his discipline has assumed increasing importance as knowledge has proliferated. In contrasting the requirements for memory plane teaching and teaching for understanding and meaning, the distinction between the two lies in the Gestaltist's view that the teacher's knowledge should have depth extending beyond the basic facts to an understanding of the structure and major generalizations of the discipline or subject taught. As the problem is viewed by Bruner, he must know his subject matter well enough to teach with an economy of time and material; he must make the most economical representation of facts. To do this well, organization and generic learning rather than atomized fact teaching and the "episodic curriculum" will be stressed.[B2:88]

Creative Teaching and Learning

Both levels of teaching thus far discussed are oriented mainly toward pupil knowledge as the major outcome. The more complex form of knowledge sought in teaching for understanding certainly is a viable educational goal, one which demands the best efforts of all teachers. Nevertheless, an exclusive emphasis on knowledge alone fails to meet the demands on intelligence in a society which is complex and rapidly changing. The dynamic world of the present and the future requires the cultivation of man's creative abilities. The schools must rise to the challenge of helping the young to build upon the heritage from the past—to create anew from the known.

The societal condition cited provides the backdrop for the third and highest level of teaching performance which has been variously conceptualized as "reflection level teaching,"[B1:324] "problem solving," "the climate of creative thinking,"[S1:42] or simply "creative teaching." Bruner's stress on crossing the barrier from learning into thinking and generating new knowledge from what is known sums up this level in a general way.

We shall call this third level "creative teaching and learning." Its main characteristic is teacher and learner involvement, i.e., individual, imaginative, and subjective interaction with subject matter in a way which results in a new product of personal significance. The outcomes will assume various forms— problems solved, new problems posed, new knowledge developed, imaginative and artistic products created.

Creative teaching and learning receives its strongest support from cognitive field psychology, a school of thought which not only lays heavy emphasis on pattern, structure, and insight as mental processes, but includes in addition the elements of purpose, goal, and life space—the total psychological environment of the individual. In this context, learning is an active process in which the pupil acquires knowledge but does so in a less direct and obvious way than when the teacher is aiming for understanding alone. The difference lies in the fact that knowledge and understanding are acquired as the pupil solves problems, tests generalizations and principles, and comes forth with new ideas. Knowledge is thus acquired for purposes beyond mere retention. Through learning of more personal significance to him, the individual's cognitive structure and life-space are changed; he sees himself and his environment differently.

Problem-Solving—To some educators and psychologists creative teaching is essentially the employment of problem solving. Bigge, who views the central element of teaching as the use of reflective thinking, posits the teacher's task as one of confronting the pupil with unclear or puzzling situations in the subjects being studied or in some aspect of his own attitudes, values, beliefs, or knowledge. He sees the ultimate goal to be the development of a learner who can achieve new understandings and insights independently of the guidance of the teacher.[B1:234-250] Rightly handled, problem solving will result not only in analytical thinking but will also challenge the pupil to use his imaginative and creative abilities.

Toward the Unknown—Teaching has traditionally been a highly structured process in which the children are expected to proceed from ignorance to knowledge, or from the unknown to the known. In creative teaching and learning, however, the process is reversed. The direction is from the known to the unknown.

As the learner moves in this continuum he creates a problem for the teacher—that of coping with the resulting phase of disorder:

> The learner starts with the known, such as a problem, a story, or a picture, and then experiences a phase of disorder where he moves in divergent directions. He reacts to the stimulus (the known) in his own individualistic way. Not being clear about the direction, he tries different ideas. He may pass an incubation period. Finally, the learner reaches his own insight and orders a new knowledge.[S1:54]

The teacher may find this period of disorder threatening since uncertainty in direction may result in loss of control. Furthermore, he may have to seriously modify or even discard his preplanned procedures and devise a new learning structure when the favorable moment arrives. Instead of operating on a previously determined, closed, and precise order of classroom activity, he will need to proceed with open-ended plans. He will need to evince patience and tolerance of uncertainty.[S1:56]

The meaning of the above is that the disorder phase of class activity is an element for which most teachers are unprepared either through their own experience in school or their professional training. A totally new orientation is demanded.

Divergent Thinking—The tendency of teachers to emphasize pupil responses which are anticipated, specific, and exact is a frequently observed weakness in otherwise strong understanding level performance. While this orientation to external reality is less apparent than in memory level teaching, the teacher's role in the transmission of the cultural heritage and organized knowledge is a powerful determinant of his behavior in this respect.

In contrast, creativity in action requires that the teacher be more attuned to the inner life of the child. He will need to afford latitude for the individual pupil's subjective and personal responses—responses which may take many and divergent directions.[S1:61]

In practice this calls for less teacher specificity in terms of immediate goals and objectives, and, again, more orientation to the unknown and unexpected. Classroom procedures will be more unstructured. In place of their being subordinated to problems and procedures imposed by the teacher, pupils will have more freedom to identify problems and raise questions as well as react to them in their own original and unique ways. Thus pupil thinking will no longer be channeled into narrow avenues but will be free to take its own divergent and many-faceted forms.

Democratic Elements—Democratic teaching has a relationship to creative teaching in that the teacher respects the individual pupil and gives him scope for self-expression. This is noted in two aspects of teaching: task involvement, and cooperative planning.

The learner is task-involved and intrinsically motivated when his activity and the content of his study are of personal significance and meaning to him. The teacher's task is to facilitate this process of relating learning to the pupil's goals, interests, and experiential background. The pupil in turn, rather than submit to total teacher direction, participates in setting his learning task, including goals, content, procedure, and level of aspiration. Such is not the case in memory and understanding level teaching where classroom activity is more teacher-centered.[S1:75-77]

Cooperative planning as an element of democratic education has had and will continue to have its critics. Often it is rightly associated with what may be called a far-out, child-centered school supported by the Rousseauian doctrine of growth as an unfolding of the child's potentialities. In this connection, Shumsky reminds us that growth is the result of the child's experiences and that the teacher must make a wise selection of experiences for classroom learning. This is a refutation of the criticism that cooperative planning means a hands-off teacher attitude and stance. In summary, he sees the whole process of democratic teaching to be a balance between the child-centered and teacher-centered positions, capitalizing on the strengths of each:

> [The teacher] initiates the activity in an authority-centered way. He develops his own interpretation of the subject matter. He directs and structures. However, as the activity proceeds, he permits children, individually and in groups, to come into the planning and develop the lesson in their own divergent ways. He encourages children to move from the known to the unknown, unknown even to the teacher. . .creates a setup and structure for systematic and serious study, which encourages children to learn by identifying with an adult authority and also by developing their own sense of self-direction.S1:73-74

Strategy for the Beginner

It is assumed that understanding and creative levels of teaching are both necessary and valued. Our society today demands of its citizens depth and breadth of knowledge. But the requirements of mere survival on the one hand and a richer life for all on the other pose the need for creative thinking and action. The teacher's responsibility, therefore, is to foster knowledge and understanding with an element of creativity, while avoiding a lapse into the weakness of teaching for memory.

The situation of the first year teacher is made complex, first, because of the many problems he faces in adjusting to his new position; and, second, because of wide variances in temperament, ability, and professional training of the individual. In addition, the particular class of pupils he faces may present special difficulties.

A suggested strategy and stance must therefore be general and flexible. Some unusually creative and adaptable novice teachers may function on a quite creative level almost from the beginning. Others—perhaps most beginners—may need to stress doing an effective job on the understanding and meaning level during the first few weeks and months of the school year while moving gradually toward more creative practices as the situation permits.

REFERENCES

B1 Bigge, Morris L. *Learning Theories for Teachers.* New York: Harper and Row, Publishers, 1964.
B2 Bruner, Jerome S. "Learning and Thinking" pp. 83-92 in MacGintie, Walter H., and Ball, Samuel, *Readings in Psychological Foundations of Education.* New York: McGraw-Hill Book Company, 1968.
R1 Reisner, Edward H. *The Evolution of the Common School.* New York: The Macmillan Company, 1930.

R2 Rippa, S. Alexander. *Education in a Free Society.* New York: David McKay Company, Inc., 1967.
S1 Shumsky, Abraham. *In Search of Teaching Style.* New York: Appleton-Century-Crofts, 1968.
S2 Stephens, J. M., *Educational Psychology.* New York: Holt, Rinehart and Winston, 1956.

Pupil-Teacher Planning

Marie A. Mehl
Hubert H. Mills
Harl R. Douglass
Mary-Margaret Scobey

Pupil-teacher planning has gained increasing recognition as an important part of the teaching-learning process. Through collaboration, the interests and preferences of the children are included in the plan for learning. Having a part in planning helps pupils learn to think and make decisions, discover their own potentials, and develop self-control and self-direction. Pupils are more likely to be interested when they have had a part in planning than when the teacher decides what should interest them.

Acceptance of the idea that the learner should be included in planning has been difficult for many teachers. The theory that the child is immature and therefore is not capable of making important decisions is a common belief that is not substantiated by evidence. Likewise untenable is the notion that one learns self-discipline by being disciplined by others.

The most convincing evidence of the advisability of pupil participation in planning school activities comes from the school where the practice is tried. Pupils have demonstrated their ability and willingness to assume intelligent responsibility for their own acts. Pupil morale has been enhanced. Problems of pupil control have been greatly decreased, and conditions for satisfactory learning have been established. The teacher who encountered difficulty in leading pupils to accept his purposes as worthy has discovered that shared pupil-teacher purposing is an *open sesame* to success.

Reprinted by permission of The Ronald Press Company from *Teaching in Elementary School,* Third Edition, by Marie A. Mehl, Hubert H. Mills, Harl R. Douglass, and Mary-Margaret Scobey, pp. 136-139. Copyright © 1965 by The Ronald Press Company, New York.

The cooperation of pupils in planning activities may be used in practically every aspect of life in the school. In matters pertaining to school citizenship, the subject areas of the curriculum, social activities, and classroom procedure, the pupil's active participation in planning has been effectively utilized.

The teacher has a responsibility to teach children to help plan. A first step is to identify the times when planning is desirable and appropriate. Helping children identify over-all and specific goals is a more difficult task, for it includes an evaluation of what has been accomplished. After clarifying their goals, gradually children develop a plan necessary to achieve the goals. They consider sources of information, needed supplies and equipment, and problems to be solved. They learn to take advantage of all available talents, and they sense when adjustments to ongoing plans are needed. During the planning process, they develop self-direction.

With young children, much of the planning depends on the teacher's ability to guide their participation. As children become more mature, they should be able to assume more of the responsibility. At any level of the learner's development, the teacher is responsible for helping to evaluate the goals and procedures set up, and for guidance when needed.

Pupil-teacher planning takes many forms in the classroom. Perhaps the most common is the daily planning of the day's activities. Each morning, children and the teacher identify the date and follow other routine procedures, schedule activities such as choir practice or a television program, indicate the sequence by which small groups will work with the teacher, and plan what others will be doing at that time. The plans outline assignments for seat work or other activities for individuals and small groups.

Cooperative development of classroom routines and standards is another type of pupil-teacher planning. The most simple routines to be designated are the responsibilities of the classroom monitors and the periodic assignment of individuals as monitors. Standards for behavior on the playground, rules for giving a report, or procedure for learning supplementary spelling words may also be the result of cooperative planning. The following example shows the type of guidelines that might be developed cooperatively:

To give a good report:
1. Know what you want to say.
2. Outline your main points.
3. Speak slowly and clearly.
4. Look at your audience.
5. Use different kinds of illustrative materials.

Other projects conducive to pupil-teacher planning might be classroom plays, auditorium programs, field trips, or culminations of classroom activities. The complete plans will probably not be developed in one discussion. They may involve series of planning sessions related to a sequence of activities, involvement of outside resources, and assignment of responsibilities.

Small groups, too, plan with the teacher. They may be groups preparing a record of an experiment, researching a specific topic, or planning a mural, a time line, or other means of organizing information. The group may simply be a delegation to the principal to request a special service. Careful and considered plans, arrived at cooperatively, evolve from pooling the ideas of all. Sometimes they are made by the small group alone with the teacher. At other times, the small group may make plans with the total classroom group if it is desirable for all to be involved in the planning process. Such plans become most effective means of organization and of developing effective, smooth procedure.

Perhaps the most important type of pupil-teacher planning is that which is inherent in every lesson. Any lesson begins with a motivation-orientation introduction. Involving the children increases interest and participation. Relating the new topic to past experiences gives meaning to the learning. Children need to understand what each person is to do, where materials can be procured, and what to do when work is completed. Such a beginning to the lesson may be brief or in much detail. If established routine and work habits do not give direction, detailed planning is needed. Opportunity is provided to ask questions, clarify misconceptions, and make procedure clear. Timing is established. Then, after the lesson is completed, some means of tying together the experiences and evaluating progress are needed. Again, cooperative effort is utilized to identify progress. Then, steps are projected and essentials for accomplishing them are listed. In such instances, planning is closely related to, and hardly distinguishable from, evaluation.

Classroom Climate

Norma Furst and Marciene S. Mattleman

Almost everyone has seen it happen. Two teachers in the same school teach the same subject matter to classes that are almost identical insofar as pupils' IQ's and cultural levels are concerned. At the end of the year, though, the achievement of one teacher's class is measurably higher than that of the other. Why?

Reprinted by permission of the National Education Association, Washington, D.C., and Norma Furst and Marciene S. Mattleman from *NEA Journal* 57:22-24, April, 1968.

In studies carried on in various parts of the country, observers have reported in elaborate detail on the classroom behavior of hundreds of teachers. In some cases, the studies have been conducted for the specific purpose of finding why some teachers are more successful than others; on occasion, observing teachers' behavior has been incidental to the study of something else—the value of an enrichment program, for instance.

Time and again the observations bear out what many authorities on learning have long believed—that given comparable classes and teaching conditions, the most successful teachers, those in whose classes student achievement is greatest, are the ones who accept their students as worthwhile individuals and make the students conscious of this acceptance.

In order to discover what successful teachers actually do that is different from what unsuccessful ones do, the authors conducted a carefully controlled research study specifically designed to focus on the effects of teaching behavior on pupil achievement. Fifteen social studies teachers in a large metropolitan area taught the same four chapters of a book. Instructional time, class size, and student ability were controlled, but teachers were allowed to teach the material in any way they wished.

Tests administered before and after the four-day experiment showed that students in three classes had learned more than would be expected of children of their ability, those in eight others had learned just about what would have been expected of them had they been left on their own with the book, and those in the remaining four had learned less than would have been expected of them.

The teachers of the highest-achieving group were positive in their approach to the children. They found time to encourage a student even when his answer wasn't the one the teacher wanted. They let students explore content along many thinking levels. The questions they asked were of the "How might things be different in Bolivia if we didn't import their tin?" variety.

The teachers of the classes in which the children learned just about what would have been expected of them had they been left on their own with the book were the teachers who lectured and who concentrated chiefly on factual information. They tended to have a minimum of personal exchange, either positive or negative, with the students.

The teachers of the lowest-achieving group tended to ask the low-level type of question—"How much tin do we get from Bolivia?" They were negative toward the students. If a child would say, "I think this is wrong," the teacher would come back with something like, "How can you say it's wrong when the book says it's right?"

At Temple University, student teachers are analyzing their own teaching and the teaching of others in the light of what observers have seen successful teachers do. They are also experimenting with the effects of different kinds of classroom behavior and are finding out for themselves what happens when they do the kinds of things successful teachers do.

By means of the same sort of analysis and experimentation, experienced teachers might determine whether or not they need to change their own classroom style in order to deal more effectively with their students. The following discussion of teacher behavior, based on our studies and on others made by educators and psychologists all over the country, may be useful to those who decide that some changes are in order.

Teachers vary in the way they tell a child he is wrong. Suppose the teacher asks, "How much is 2 + 2?" and a child replies, "2 + 2 is 5." Student teachers, and many experienced teachers as well, are inclined to say, "No, that's wrong." If the child is a shy first grader and this is his first attempt at answering aloud, the teacher's negative response may discourage him from trying to answer a question tomorrow.

Successful teachers are more likely to try different approaches, such as asking the child how he got his answer, having him demonstrate, or praising his efforts. In response to such treatment, a pupil might venture another try tomorrow.

The teacher who says "No, you're wrong," has put the child on trial and pronounced him a failure. By following a different course of action, the teacher can show respect for the child's effort. In some cases, giving the child another try at the problem in a tone that encourages him to think it through again might give the child a chance to succeed—to prove himself. And if the child simply doesn't know better, the teacher can tell him he's wrong by telling him the right answer—a much more positive response than merely telling him he's wrong.

Successful teachers use praise more effectively than unsuccessful teachers do. Praise can convey the message, "I think you're worthwhile," if the child realizes that he is being praised and feels that he has earned the praise.

"Praise them? That's easy," new student teachers say. When they try to use praise, though, they find that doing so isn't easy at all because it often requires them to create situations that enable the child to act in a praiseworthy fashion.

A teacher whose questions are limited to textbook facts (When did Columbus discover America? What were the names of his ships?) is likely to develop a sort of verbal tic, such as saying "Good" or "OK" instead of giving some meaningful words of praise for a desired response. By contrast, an open-ended question (How is the history of the world very different from what it would have been if Columbus hadn't gone looking for a route to the Indies?) elicits the sort of answer to which the teacher can respond, "Good thinking. That had never occurred to me," or "You've come up with the same opinion that one of my college professors had." Individualized praise convinces the child that the teacher thinks he is worthwhile.

The kinds of questions a teacher asks affect the classroom climate in other ways beside providing occasions for praising. To answer an open-ended question, for instance, a child is obliged to use facts creatively. He learns them by thinking about them rather than by memorizing them, and if he is like the children in the research study, he will do better on an achievement test than if his teacher had used low-level, factual questions.

There are many ways of introducing subject matter. A customary introduction goes something like this: "We're studying percentage now, because we're supposed to study it in fifth grade. I want you to start by memorizing these facts about it."

One teacher used a sharply contrasting method when he introduced percentage to his inner-city, all-boy class by asking, "What's Willie Mays' batting average?" A long and lively discussion followed—about Willie Mays and about batting averages in general. By the time the teacher used the word *percentage,* it had meaning for the boys because they could relate it to something they already knew and cared about.

Successful teachers in general pay more attention to what students already know and to what they think than less successful teachers do. The research study found that the teachers of the lower-achieving groups tend to limit discussion to what is in the book or in the teachers' lectures.

The more successful teachers let discussions take the direction the students' own thinking suggests. If, for example, a child says he thinks something in the text is wrong, the teachers will ask why he thinks so and will listen to his reasons. Even when a child's reasons aren't very good, these teachers don't resort to a flat "That doesn't make sense," but help the child reach a sounder conclusion by making a comment like: "Think about it some more. Now what if—"

Teachers of the high-achieving group depart from the day's lesson plan to explore a child's ideas. Teachers of the lower-achieving groups hold more rigidly to the schedule and insist upon covering a certain block of material each day.

In general, teachers of the lower-achieving groups talk down to their students. They don't ask, "What do you think about it?" or "Would you prefer a true-and-false test tomorrow or one with essay questions?" Sometimes these teachers act as though there were no such thing as a valid excuse. "If you had really studied the lesson last night, nothing that happened on the way to school could have made you forget it," one of them might say.

One of our studies suggests that teachers of this sort are likely to resent programed instruction and to fear such things as electronic teaching devices. Even if aids of this kind are intended for supplementary instruction, these teachers see them as a threat to their absolute authority.

The more successful teachers do not issue edicts. If they must say, "Do it this way, not that way," they explain why. Students' feelings count with this group of teachers and their students know it. "I'm sure you would have done better if you hadn't seen the accident on the way to school," such a teacher might sympathize, adding, "When I get upset, my mind doesn't work right, either."

Most teachers perform the same functions in the classroom. They present subject matter, question, tell students they are right or wrong, and deal with students' ideas and emotions. Whether a teacher establishes a classroom climate in which learning flourishes or one in which it languishes depends upon the way he goes about doing things.

Teaching and Learning Through Inquiry

Byron G. Massialas

In an increasing number of classrooms, the students, instead of remembering isolated facts, are learning how to learn. Their teachers, instead of acting as dispensers of ready-made conclusions, are teaching them to think for themselves and to use the methods of disciplined inquiry to explore concepts in the various domains of knowledge and to study the world about them.

Teaching through inquiry is the process of formulating and testing ideas and implies an open classroom climate that encourages wide student participation and the expression of divergent points of view. A truly inquiry-centered class is a small society whose members utilize the concepts and skills of the arts and the sciences, draw upon their own personal experiences, and attempt to deal judiciously with important natural and social problems. In such a class both teachers and students perform new roles.

The roles of the teacher who stresses the process of inquiry fall into six major categories. These are actual, not ideal, roles, and all teachers, regardless of their subject matter, can perform them. Briefly, the roles are as follows:

1. The teacher as planner. In this role, the teacher carefully plans learning activities for a period of time, possibly a six-week period or a semester. He collects and prepares materials for classroom use and organizes and times the spacing and sequence of these materials. In the absence of readily available published inquiry programs, the teacher either uses imagination to create new ways of utilizing available data or constructs some of his own materials.

Reprinted by permission of the National Education Association, Washington, D.C., and Byron G. Massialas from *Today's Education* 58:40-42, May, 1969.

2. The teacher as introducer. It is important to introduce a new learning experience with material that will serve as a springboard for inquiry and discussion. Timing is important, too. The teacher needs to be able to seize on the "teachable moment."

The introductory material—whether it is haiku, an anecdote, or a math problem—becomes what we call the *discovery episode*. The discovery episode is designed to create a problematic, provocative situation in which the students are prompted to develop concepts and relationships for themselves. Sometimes the students introduce inquiry springboards from their own repertory of experiences.

3. The teacher as questioner and sustainer of inquiry. The teacher's general attitude is that of a fellow inquirer who has no final and absolute answers to give out. Through his style and manner of presentation, he makes clear from the beginning that all statements or claims to knowledge are to be examined and then accepted or rejected in the open forum of ideas. He further develops and reinforces the notion that neither authors of texts nor students and teachers are immune from questioning and detailed probing. Regardless of the age, sex, personality, and cultural-ethnic background of the participant in classroom inquiry, his statements are to be considered on the basis of the grounds that support them. No knowledge claim is ever better than the data on which it stands.

Through a consistent pattern of questioning, the teacher consistently tries to encourage the exploration of different alternatives regarding a problem. For example, he may question the basis for certain positions on social action or hypothesize about an unexplained event.

As a matter of strategy, the teacher usually redirects questions addressed to him. For instance, in a discovery situation relating to political leaders and their patterns of leadership, the teacher presents several unidentified and unexplained pictures of leaders. The students invariably demand information about the cultural origin, the historical period, or the geographic location of the person in the picture. However tempted the teacher may be to supply the answers, he throws the questions back to the students.

In this context, the teacher plays the role of the devil's advocate, constantly prodding the students and making them prove the defensibility of their positions or points of view. His general posture with regard to knowledge and learning is dialectical rather than didactic. He emphasizes the critical exchange of ideas rather than the imposition of ideas on the basis of authority derived from his position.

4. The teacher as manager. The teacher performs such routine management tasks as recognizing students, making announcements, maintaining reasonable order, and keeping attendance records. More important, however, is the

managerial function he performs by using all available concepts, techniques, and data sources to engage students in planning and executing inquiries of their own.

5. The teacher as rewarder. The teacher rewards students for imaginative and creative work and for participation in the process of inquiry. He suggests, encourages, or praises but never commands, criticizes, or punishes. In contrast to a traditional teacher who frowns upon the unorthodox, the inquiry teacher constantly encourages students to play their hunches and praises them when they do. Rewarding the free exchange and testing of ideas in class leads to higher levels of motivation and more student participation.

6. The teacher as value investigator. When dealing with questions of value, the teacher places emphasis on the process of inquiry and on the idea that value judgments must be publicly defensible. He may eventually take a definite position on a particular issue, but he refrains from doing so in the introductory phases of discussion. The teacher operates on the assumption that values are not taught but are examined in the open market of ideas.

The teacher should not be frustrated when a discussion of social issues does not produce definite conclusions. The worth of exercises dealing with human values is not necessarily the forming of conclusions based on consensus. Rather, it is the process of listening to different views and their implications, forming a clear position, examining supporting evidence, judging its relevance, developing objective criteria for validating a recommendation for social action, and, finally, acting upon the recommendation.

For the students, the most important result of learning through inquiry is a change in attitudes toward knowledge. As they engage in the dialogue of inquiry, they begin to view knowledge as tentative rather than absolute, and they consider all knowledge claims as being subject to continuous revision and confirmation. As they try to provide their own answers to difficult questions about man and his environment, they begin to understand the complexity of verifying knowledge and the processes involved in it.

Methods of inquiry and discovery can be used profitably in classes that include students of different academic abilities. Not only superior students but also those who have lower-than-average IQ scores prove to be capable of performing such intellectual operations as defining a problem, hypothesizing, drawing logical inferences, gathering relevant data, and generalizing. Given the appropriate psychological and cognitive climate, these students can perform on a high level and are as highly motivated as those having so-called superior abilities.

Our studies show that the introduction of an issue, whether of a personal or social nature, elicits a great deal of student discussion and the expression of a variety of viewpoints. As they present their ideas, which are continuously challenged by their peers, students begin to see that value judgments cannot be accepted solely on faith. They realize that judgments about the worthiness of a social action, a group project, or personal conduct stand or fall on the basis of the explicit grounds that support them.

Developing Increased Creativity With Children

George I. Thomas and Joseph Crescimbeni

Adults are living in a world which is changing very rapidly. They find it difficult to realize that yesterday is gone and that patterns of thinking and acting which once sufficed are no longer adequate for those who must cope with tomorrow's problems. Some adults refuse to admit that today's children must acquire a broad background of knowledge and skills quite different from those who helped to meet basic needs in the past.

Modern children must be prepared to live in a world of constant change, which calls for flexibility and an ability to adjust to new ideas and new ways of thinking and acting. The school has to help them acquire qualities of independence and creativity along with basic skills if these boys and girls are going to be prepared for life in today's world or that of tomorrow. In a broad sense, the ability of our teachers to develop leadership, initiative, and a creative spirit in their classroom children may be the basis for our very survival.

It may seem trite to repeat the necessity for teachers to foster greater creativity on the part of talented children. Actually, every classroom teacher must refrain from mouthing educational clichés and must begin to do something positive to discover the creative sparks which often exist beneath the surface but which are never allowed to germinate. Pupils with hidden talents that never show themselves are a loss to society. At times teachers may need to develop creativity where it does not actually exist!

Every pupil must be exposed to a curriculum which is broad enough for him to test himself as he searches for answers to old and new problems. He may need to help in discovering new interests, new skills, and new abilities that can become the basis for better living and for a better attack on immediate and future problems. He has to see the world about him from the eyes of many people such as the scientist, the artist, the politician, the statesman, the social worker, the business man, the laborer, and the parent. With good teaching to

Reprinted by permission from the January, 1967, issue of *Education* 87:274-276. Copyright, 1967, by The Bobbs-Merrill Company, Inc., Indianapolis, Indiana.

prod him on, he has to learn to use *all* of his faculties in getting acquainted with his environment.

There will be times when he will find that education can be interesting, but he will have to exert himself if he is to grow and make something of his talents. Teachers will hold him to standards and will often require increased concentration on the problems before him, but these teachers must be ready to use new approaches, new materials, and new concepts in order to present him with challenges that call for clear, intelligent, and creative thinking.

Greater Demands on the Teacher

The skills and understanding which are learned in the modern classroom will often call for a type of teacher and pupil flexibility which is frequently missing in the traditional, teacher-dominated classroom. Modern teachers will find themselves on the verge of a new educational frontier that requires constant courage to continue, while recalcitrant forces within the school and within the community demand a return to the old-fashioned methods of teaching.

Modern teachers may be criticized for demonstrating their ingenuity or creativity as they work with boys and girls. On the one hand they may be told that teachers have to go all out to develop more creative children, while on the other hand they may hear criticized the very activities that will help boys and girls become sensitive to their environment.

Since mastery of facts and basic skills are often considered a criterion of a teacher's success, it behooves the teacher to know her community. If parents want mastery of the fundamentals, teachers must be able to demonstrate their ability to teach these quickly and easily while working towards the realization of other worthwhile and desirable objectives.

Many educators have had to demonstrate that they could achieve goals with their methods of teaching. In some instances, modern teachers have had to guarantee that their pupils would be able to demonstrate academic proficiency if they could use their own approaches and materials, and, fortunately for them, they have often been able to realize approved goals with a minimum of lost time and without sacrificing their educational principles. The secret lies in freeing the teacher and pupil from needless waste motion by teaching to the students' learning levels. In other words, teachers must be creative, in order to free the children to explore their environment and the part they can play in it.

Pupils Not Standardized

Good teaching must be motivated by teachers who can accept the fact that boys and girls are not standardized products that can be placed on a learning assembly line. In teaching a subject, teachers will have specific objectives, but they will not ignore the significance of individual differences in ability, achievement, talent, interest, strength, and motive. These teachers must be ready to test and probe. They have to explore each group of children in search of clues upon which they can build a better foundation or a better background. At times they may have to adjust teaching methods and materials in order to teach on the students' learning levels.

The teacher must be a creative person who can face new challenges with a feeling of satisfaction as children react to her and her teaching. She has to plan activities in anticipation that problems will be encountered as she works with different groups of students. The unexpected problems that teachers and children encounter as they work together are what makes schooling interesting.

At times, both teacher and learner may appear frustrated with the search for answers to their problems, but many of them would be far less happy with their work if everything they planned came out at the proper time and in the proper form. Creative individuals are generally non-conformists, so they will not find continued satisfaction in turning out standardized products. They want to try *different approaches* and *different materials* in their search for answers to both routine and unusual problems.

Many classroom teachers will find boys and girls in their classrooms who are ready and willing to engage in activities which call for research skill, leadership ability, and higher level achievement. These students have the ability to show their creativity if they are placed in situations where creativity is an essential part of the solution to a problem. They need to be placed in many kinds of learning situations that will force them to extend themselves and that will allow them to explore their environment and their own ability to work in it.

Time a Problem

With mass teaching there is always a problem of time, which becomes a barrier to children who have imagination and who have creative potentialities. In a sense, the clock determines whether the teacher or the children are able to engage in what they consider desirable creative activities.

This time factor is also the barrier which modern educators have to contend with as they strive to increase the creativity of school children. It can be overcome only by teachers who have learned to teach on the basis of readiness and interest in new and higher-level activities. Unit teaching and small-group or individualized teaching are helpful here, because the teacher is able to work with more boys and girls at their learning levels. This can result in a tremendous saving of time and energy which can be diverted to new and more challenging areas of study.

The Spark Within

Cynthia Jarzen

"All my children are gifted." I don't remember where or when I heard this thought expressed by a teacher; I do know that, since I did hear or read it, I've liked to believe it. Scientifically, realistically, perhaps, it is not true. And yet if we think of "gifted" as meaning possessing creative potential, at least in certain areas, then it is true, not only of those children of very high intelligence, but of *all* children.

Studies of creativity made at the Institute of Personality Assessment and Research of the University of California and at the University of Minnesota have revealed definite traits of creative people. Most of these traits, I feel, are shown by almost all children, and the teacher must be able to recognize them and to encourage them.

One trait is that of a preference for disorder on the part of the creative person. This trait goes hand in hand, I think, with another one: The creative child is often energetic, curious, adventuresome—a "handful" to his teacher. I have noticed in my teaching that the children who seem to enjoy art and to produce the most creative work are often the noisy ones, the ones who really cannot sit still for very long, and the ones who are often slower intellectually. The quiet, more orderly, faster learners, in contrast, often freeze up, afraid to place the first mark on a sheet of manila paper, and often produce stilted work. Why are they afraid? Perhaps they have been made to hold in their expressions; perhaps a parent or a teacher has made this child feel that good grades or popularity are more valuable than sincerity and spontaneity.

A boy in my class this past year showed a great deal of artistic ability. His mother, unfortunately, did not seem to recognize this. He complained to me one day that his mother did not like to see him drawing all the time. "Don't you want to be popular?" she asked him. He then told me that, when he grows up, he is going to go to England, where he can just draw and no one will bother him. It is important that we help our children feel that they certainly do not need to "go to England."

Another trait associated with originality of thought is independence of judgment, and it is one that the teacher may sometimes find difficult to encourage. A creative child may "stick to his guns," even when he is put under pressure to conform to the opinion of the group.

Reprinted by permission of Ohio Education Association, Columbus, Ohio, from *Ohio Schools* 43:14-16, December, 1965.

I recall an experience that occurred during my first year of teaching. Our discussion in the fourth grade centered on the wonder of man, his intelligence, his superiority. Robert did not seem at all impressed by this fuss over mankind and maintained that the porpoise was the superior creature. I answered by exemplifying man's intelligence—his ability, for example, to build a skyscraper. His retort was, "But, Mis Jarzen, porpoises don't *need* skyscrapers." Well, they don't, do they? The point is that, no matter how deflating, embarrassing, or aggravating a child's ideas may be, we must not stifle them. We must give credit where it is due and encourage continued good thinking, not mere acceptance of what the teacher says. We should allow the child to question and challenge us, but at the same time we must teach him accepted ways of doing these things.

Imaginative Observers

Creative people, studies have shown, are especially observant; they often see things in a different way. A little girl in my class was one day going about the seemingly routine task of watering the plants in our classroom. She watched carefully as she watered the first one, and just could not hold back as she did so: "Oh! Look at it sipping it!" This kind of thing is so nice to hear; and yet, in too-formal a classroom atmosphere, it may rarely be heard.

Studies have also shown that creative people have a tendency to spend an unusual amount of time in the world of imagination. Can much harm be done if we do not immediately snatch the child from his world of fantasy, but allow him to luxuriate there for a while? On the contrary, I believe more harm may be done if we do *not* let him stay.

Since most children at some time do exhibit one or many of these traits, and if, as psychologists believe, all children share to some degree the gift of creativity, what happens to it later on? It is killed, and, unfortunately, the schools are partly to blame for the murder.

We kill creativity every time we overdirect or overprotect our children, when we stifle their outgoing, optimistic attitudes, causing them to become timid through inexperience and unnecessary warnings. We kill it every time we say things like:

"Oh, no, Terry, the diamonds are to be pasted on lying down, not standing up"; "Oh, you've spoiled yours, Mary Lou! It's all messy, and it doesn't have a handle"; "Here's the right color"; "Boys aren't interested in things like this"; or "Girls don't play with chemistry sets."

We kill it every time we condemn a child for answers that, according to "the book," are wrong. When asking, "Why is it better to make buildings of brick rather than wood?" the child who answers that brick is stronger, longer-lasting, safer, etc., will be counted correct. Dare we say that the child is wrong who answers that "brick *isn't* the better material because brick is cold and ugly while wood is warm and beautiful"?

We kill it each time we say "No" to a child who really wants to help out or to add his opinion. If we could catch ourselves before we say "No" to a child and ask ourselves "Why not?" we would not have a good answer to that question. "No" can get to be a nasty habit.

But let's not talk so much about the *don't's* and get on to the *do's* of developing creative potential. There are deliberate steps that we can take to do this.

The atmosphere of the classroom can be conducive to creativity. The importance of maintaining a stimulating classroom environment has been stated repeatedly. Displays should be evident. A library corner, of course, is essential, as well as a variety of materials, both conventional and unconventional. Conventional materials might be such things as maps, globes, construction paper, travel folders, pamphlets, fact cards, etc. Unconventional materials might include wallpaper books, clay, magazines, buttons, Indian corn, feathers, a typewriter (the list is endless) for imaginative uses.

Accepting Responsibility

There are often times when children might be allowed to carry out planning on their own. We need to take advantage of these opportunities for independent work. The first year that I taught, my children developed their own plan for classroom maintenance, with a minimum amount of guidance from me. Classroom chores were tended to carefully, each child seeming to take great pride in his particular duty. The second year that I taught, thinking that I was being most efficient, I provided my new class with a ready-made job board—last year's plan. It was not received with much enthusiasm. I found that I often had to remind certain workers of their classroom chores. In other words, the plan imposed upon my children was not nearly so effective as the plan they formed themselves.

This leads into another approach that may encourage creativity—the "discovery" approach to teaching that enables the child to learn not only the *what's* but, more importantly, the *why's* of his world. This method is more easily adapted to certain areas of study (such as science) than to others. I recently read one report of a group of fourth, fifth, and sixth graders who actually did cancer research. Fantastic, yes; yet who should be joining in cancer research more than the next generation, and as early as they are ready? The "discovery" or "cause and effect" method can be worked into other areas, too. Teaching American history through the study of documents is a good example of this. We must cut down on "fact-stuffing" and build up more good thinking. If we do not, we will be creating masters of known principles and theories but destroying the pioneers who will devise *new* methods, explore *new* ideas.

Certain phases of the curriculum are naturals for creative expression. Art, of course, lends itself easily to our cause; however, precaution must be taken. Often when we ask children to express themselves, we may evoke only imitations and reproductions. I once presented an art lesson in which I asked the children to listen to Tchaikovsky's "Waltz of the Flowers" and to illustrate whatever they imagined as they listened. Several drawings did not show originality at all, but depicted scenes straight from Walt Disney's "Fantasia."

There are hundreds of little ways in which creativity can be enkindled. One way is to list a group of words on the board and to ask the children to create their own stories using these words as a starter. Along this same line is giving students a key word, such as "oyster," and asking them to create a new compound word that is synonomous with it. Not only will the children learn what compound words are, but their imaginations will be stretched to come up with such words as "pearlchest" and "pillowfish."

Asking questions like the following will also stimulate original thinking:

What would you do if you made an emergency airplane landing in the snow-covered mountains?

What are all the possible uses of a book?

What do you think the inside of the Three Bears' house looks like?

We often hear that Americans are time-conscious. I believe this same fault is a serious detriment to our school program and a hindrance to creative development. We often feel that we must "cover" a particular area in a certain amount of time. What we need to do, I believe, is to get more deeply involved, once in a while, in a particular phase of study. We ought to forget about "finishing this today" or "moving on to the next chapter tomorrow" and realize that, in doing so, we may be leaving the children's interests behind. Let's go off on a tangent now and then!

Furthermore, a premature channeling of a child's interests may block his creativity. If a child shows exceptional ability in mathematics, for example, we may tend to play up this ability to such an extent that he will doubt his abilities in other areas. As a result he may become too shy to write a poem, for instance, or to play a musical instrument.

When a child does show originality in his thinking, teachers must show that they appreciate this originality. Simply listening to a pupil's ideas—looking at him straight in the eyes when he talks—can give a child great confidence and encouragement. But, of course, sincerity is all-important. Insincerity can be sensed quickly by a child, and the insincere teacher will defeat his own purpose.

Since each child has the creative spark within him to begin with, let's do our best to help each child sustain it. Let's fan that spark a little so that it may burst forth in great personal satisfaction for him and in new and more beautiful worlds for us all.

Chapter 6

Providing for Individual Differences

Chapter 6 is composed of a series of articles concerning individual differences among children and how teachers and schools meet the challenge posed. Wrightstone leads off with a discussion of how ability grouping affects the average child, citing research conclusions as to its value, when and how to use it, and what dangers might lie therein. The strong current effort to meet the child's needs through individualized instruction is thoroughly explored by Wolfson. She maintains that the teacher, in employing various organizational and instructional innovations, instead of providing truly individualized instruction may be only creating the environment in which it takes place. She goes on to define the process, explore its underlying assumptions, and finally list appropriate classroom procedures and organizations. In extension of this theme, Lee emphasizes the necessity of self-directed learning for each child, while Deep shows that when the teacher individually prescribes instruction, his role changes. He no longer labors under a burden of clerical details and ineffective across-the-board teaching aimed at a fixed middle range of the group, but is free to concentrate on the tasks he is educated and trained to do—teaching, evaluating, and educational decision-making.

The further practical application of individualization emerging in what is known as independent study is analyzed by Veatch. In consonance with the viewpoint espoused by Lee, Veatch asserts that independent study can never consist of teacher-prescribed exercises but must be truly independent in that the child must recognize a problem of his own and devise a means of attacking it. Moving further, into the area of homework assignments, Hedges shows that although results are inconclusive on this controversial topic, there are types of homework which meet the criteria of good teaching and learning. His article "Guidelines for Developing a Homework Policy" completes the chapter.

Ability Grouping and the Average Child

J. Wayne Wrightstone

Children in the typical school population represent a wide range of aptitudes and have diverse educational needs. Is ability grouping—placing together children who, on the basis of intelligence tests, achievement tests, and teachers' judgments appear to have similar capacities for learning—the best means of meeting these diverse needs? Opinions differ on this matter as, indeed, they have ever since ability grouping made its American debut in Detroit, in 1920.

Proponents of ability grouping say that it is easier to teach a group whose abilities are in the same range, pointing out that materials suitable for one member of the group will tend to be suitable for all and that the same will be true of instruction. They claim that the majority of teachers and many parents prefer ability grouping. As their clincher, they submit that the system protects children with high ability from the risk of being held back by those of lower ability.

Opponents of ability grouping counter by citing teachers who prefer to teach classes composed of children who represent a broad range of ability. They add that in any case children grouped homogeneously on the basis of one factor or school subject will not necessarily be homogeneous in other ways and that ability grouping really causes only a slight reduction in the wide range of pupil achievement. They claim that such grouping is basically undemocratic and encourages snobbish attitudes, and quote parents who feel that for their children to be in classes for children of average or low ability stigmatizes them. These foes of ability grouping warn that low-achieving classes run the danger of becoming dumping grounds for disruptive children.

To date, administrators have based most of their arguments pro and con on doctrine rather than on research. What does research say?

Some studies have shown that while having three ability groups at each level reduced the variability of pupil achievement by about 15 to 17 percent, the teacher is more important in the educative process than the device of organizing classes according to ability.

One investigator claims that ability grouping doesn't work because it is based on two erroneous assumptions: that achievement in most school subjects is almost entirely dependent upon intelligence and that the relationship between intelligence and achievement doesn't change. This investigator cites facts and figures to show that in a given school, boys and girls who score the same in an

Reprinted by permission of the National Education Association, Washington, D.C., and J. Wayne Wrightstone from *NEA Journal* 57:9-11, January, 1968.

intelligence test vary widely in their achievement in reading, math, social studies, and science. The variations occur despite identical IQ's because the relationship between intelligence and achievement, influenced as it is by pupil motivation, attitudes, interests, and teaching practice is not static, but dynamic.

In 1966, the Horace Mann-Lincoln Institute of School Experimentation reported results of a comparative study of broad, medium, and narrow range ability grouping in 86 classes organized at the beginning of the fifth grade and remaining intact to the end of sixth grade. After being divided into five ability levels on the basis of IQ scores, some pupils were assigned to homogeneous classes, others to heterogeneous ones.

The general conclusion from this study is that narrowing the range of ability in a class on the basis of some measure of academic aptitude does not produce greater achievement of pupils at any ability level. Average pupils in classes with narrow ranges of ability learned no more than those in classes with the wide ranges. The effect of both kinds of grouping was similar with regard to aspirations and attitudes toward school.

Studies such as these suggest that no plan of grouping makes teaching and learning a simple matter. Any group of 30 or more average pupils, no matter how alike they seem, shows individual differences sufficient to challenge the ingenuity of the most competent teacher.

Classification of ability cannot remove individual differences or the need for adapting instruction to them. Indeed even if all the physical and intellectual factors were equal, the progress of average children in a homogeneous group would be equal only if each of them received exactly the same motivation under exactly the same circumstances with the same material in equal quantity. Even though children seemed to have the identical achievement at the beginning of the school year—in reading, for example—within a month or two, different rates of progress would have widened the range of achievement.

The research discussed so far bears out the thesis that the simple solution called ability grouping cannot meet the varied abilities and needs of the average child. What ammunition does research offer to the opposite viewpoint?

Standard tests of academic achievement, particularly where adaptations of standards, materials, and methods are made, show that pupils make slightly larger gains under ability grouping. The evidence in support of ability grouping indicates that it yields best results in academic learning for dull children; next best, for average children; and least, for bright children. (This conclusion must be regarded as tentative. Some experts claim that the differences may arise because test scores of higher ability pupils, unless carefully controlled, tend to regress toward lower ability levels, hence, the differences reported may not be as significant as they appear at first glance.)

In one study a reading test given to a sixth grade class revealed a range from below fourth grade to above twelfth grade. An intelligence test was then administered to estimate the degree to which pupils were reading above or below their general ability level.

On the basis of the achievement and intelligence tests, pupils were organized into four groups. The first group read from one to four grades above grade level and possessed above average to superior intelligence. The second group read at grade level and possessed a range of intelligence from slightly below average to superior. The third group read from one to two grades below grade level and ranged from below to slightly above average in intelligence. The fourth group read three or four grades below grade level and ranged in intelligence from below average to average.

These basic groups were organized into other subgroups within the class for such specific reading instruction objectives as word analysis, word meaning, rate of reading, and comprehension of paragraph meaning. Later tests showed that this pattern of refined grouping resulted in accelerated and enriched learning for most of the pupils.

Grouping of average children within a classroom may serve several purposes. One purpose is to provide direct instruction of a specific skill needed in reading, writing, spelling, or math. Another purpose is to build on the children's interests. Such groups may be formed within the class when new projects are undertaken or when new interests arise. This type of temporary grouping is frequently found in social studies, science, home economics, or health education. In these areas, effective learning comes through discussion, group planning, and research assignments undertaken by small groups.[1]

Grouping may be arranged for social purposes, on the basis either of sociometric techniques or of the teacher's observations of "who likes whom or who likes to work with whom." Such groups are formed when problems involving social living exist within the classroom and when assignments are so informal that friendship choices are more important than academic abilities or curriculum interests.

Although research shows that classroom teachers have differences of opinion about ability grouping, several studies reveal that a majority of teachers prefer it.

Data regarding the effects of ability grouping upon the personal characteristics of pupils are so inadequate or subjective that no valid conclusions can be drawn.

Parent reaction to ability grouping is sharply divided: Some parents are all for it, but others apparently abhor it.

---

[1] Since grouping in terms of ability and/or achievement does little to reduce the overall range of pupil variability with which teachers must deal, it is not recommended as general practice. However, selective grouping and regrouping by achievement sometimes is useful, particularly at the secondary level.—Recommendation 24 in *Schools for the Sixties:* A report by the NEA Project on Instruction. McGraw-Hill.

In my opinion, ability grouping for the average child is neither a cure nor a calamity. Its value appears to depend upon the teacher who uses it. When it is used without a clear knowledge of the specific learning needs of each average pupil and without the recognition that it must be articulated with carefully planned adaptations in curriculum, grouping can be ineffective or even harmful. It can be harmful when it lulls teachers and parents into believing that ability grouping is providing differentiated education for average pupils of varying degrees of ability, if such differentiation is nonexistent.

Ability grouping is dangerous when it leads teachers to underestimate the learning capacities of pupils at the average ability levels. It can also be harmful when it does not provide flexible channels for moving children from average to higher groups and back again, either from subject to subject or within any one subject as their performance at various times in their school careers indicates.

On the other hand, ability grouping for average children may be used effectively when it grows out of the needs of the curriculum and when it is varied and flexible. Average pupils can be assembled in subgroups for special work, such as advanced content or remedial instruction in a given subject. Teachers can more easily carry out specific plans appropriate for an achievement level without having to provide for other widely divergent pupils for whom the particular content may be inappropriate.

The average child comprises the middle 50 to 60 percent of the pupil population. This represents a wide range of abilities, achievement, attitudes, and skills. No ability group of average pupils will be homogeneous in growth and development in such characteristics as height, weight, intelligence, or academic achievement. An average child's learning is not even; he may achieve well in one area and poorly in another.

For this observer, the answer that research gives is: The effective teacher with excellent pupil-teacher rapport and effective instructional materials will supersede ability grouping in producing effective learning for the average child.

Individualizing Instruction

Bernice J. Wolfson

Consider these classroom activities:

- The teacher reads a story to the class.
- The children work at their seats on different workbook pages, story writing, or projects.
- Four girls arrange a bulletin-board display.
- Two boys share the same book.
- Five pupils listen to a tape-recorded story.
- Twenty pupils listen to a report about the school store.

Are these manifestations of individualized instruction? Perhaps yes, perhaps no. I observed all these activities in a classroom organized for this kind of instruction, but they could have taken place in a classroom that was not actually responsive to individual needs and interests. Indeed, even a one-to-one relationship does not necessarily meet individual needs, for a teacher can direct an individual conference exactly as she conducts work with the group.

Clearly, individualizing instruction does not mean primarily a tutorial arrangement, though a one-to-one relationship is, of course, included. Nor, I think, does it encompass subgrouping on a permanent or semipermanent basis. Whether at the elementary or secondary level, groups should be formed on the basis of a common interest, learning problem, or special task and be disbanded as soon as their purpose is accomplished. Some things, such as planning for shared activities and offering suggestions for solving a general problem, are more reasonably done in groups (sometimes small, sometimes large) than by individuals.

A crucial concept which separates individualized from group instruction is the rejection of the idea that all learners must move through a predetermined, sequenced curriculum. Merely permitting different rates of speed will not provide for individual differences. Essentially, individualizing instruction requires the teacher to encourage individual interests, allow for individual styles, and respond to individual needs.

Two basic facts support the need to individualize instruction. First, as any classroom teacher knows, students vary tremendously. Not only do they differ in shape, size, energy level, and other physical characteristics but also in rate of development, temperament, motivation, previous experience, and style of

Reprinted by permission of the National Education Association, Washington, D.C., and Bernice J. Wolfson from *NEA Journal* 55:31-33, November, 1966.

learning. Second, the human being is an active, seeking organism that does more than merely react to his environment; he also explores and changes it.

Furthermore, the purposes of education, at least as I see them, support the need to individualize instruction. One of these is the development of individuality. The press for conformity is strong in our culture, and certainly some conformity is essential for living in any society. We are not faced, however, with choosing individuality *or* conformity but rather with the issue of balance and meaning.

Other purposes of the school include promoting an understanding of the world and encouraging each child's self-fulfillment and competency. In order to develop individuality and feelings of competence and to move toward self-actualization, children need to learn how to learn, to think independently, to make choices, to plan, and to evaluate.

The history of education is replete with accounts of efforts by sensitive teachers and administrators to cope with the great range of individual differences. Approaches have included individual projects, tutoring on a one-to-one basis, programed learning, and a variety of organizational plans (for example, cross-grade grouping, continuous progress, nongraded classrooms, and multi-age classes). None of these guarantees individualization of instruction. Organization and materials can only provide the environment and arrangements which free a teacher to meet the educational needs of all the pupils in the class.

What a teacher *is* and *does* remains the crucial variable in the classroom. Inevitably one needs to ask: What is the teacher doing in the classroom? What assumptions does he make about the nature of children and how they learn? What attitudes and expectations does he communicate to the class?

Even those who agree on the need to individualize instruction may have different operational approaches based on conflicting sets of assumptions.

One approach views the teacher as a diagnostician who, with the aid of various tests, subject matter specialists and consultants, determines what each student should learn. He then prescribes and assigns appropriate tasks and materials. In some cases, the teacher may bypass much of this operation and allow programs, textbooks, and curriculum guides to take over. But, essentially, the teacher is still making the decisions and carrying out the program.

Another approach assumes that real individualization of instruction, in ways that are meaningful to the learner, requires a good deal of self-selection and self-direction by the learner. The teacher in this operation is primarily a consultant to the learner and a manager of the classroom environment. His role is to help students learn to plan and evaluate, to provide stimulating experiences, to make students aware of many alternatives when making decisions, to supply a variety of appropriate materials.

He responds both to the requests of individuals and to his own hypotheses as to what variety of materials and opportunities might be helpful.

Reflection on the two approaches described above should make it clear that nongraded schools may represent the first or the second kind of operation. Most nongraded schools, as they exist today, are in fact graded by reading achievement. Children are grouped for "likenesses" and put through essentially the same curriculum. By contrast, a nongraded class which is multi-age and heterogeneous may be viewed as composed of thirty unique individuals who, from time to time, have common interests and needs.

Programed learning, as developed to date, is mostly related to allowing for different *rates* of learning. It is the manner in which programs are used in the classroom that determines whether or not they facilitate individualization. Self-selected, relatively short units of work would support individualization; long units required of all pupils would not.

Many of the current innovations and restorations (such as programed learning, special grouping, nongraded organization, and team teaching) allow for minor adaptations to individual differences but rest on the old assumption that there exists a graded body of skills and content which is most appropriately learned in a preplanned sequence. This assumption definitely impedes efforts to individualize instruction.

Another impediment is the fact that parents, teachers, administrators, and even children are inclined to define success and failure in terms of graded expectations. A child who is learning and increasing his competency is often labeled as failing because he hasn't succeeded in the arbitrary sequence set up for all learners in a particular grade.

The alternative to trying to patch up a system which rests on values and assumptions contradictory to those which are behind individualized approaches is to reconceptualize both the organization and the content of schooling. Let me say, without going into detail, that I believe the following assumptions are important in working toward the long-term educational goals basic to individualized instruction.

1. For real learning to occur, the learner must see a purpose and meaning in the learning experience.

2. No *best* method exists for all teachers to use in teaching anything to all children.

3. The way a teacher interacts with children affects the amount they learn, their feelings about learning, and their feelings about themselves.

4. There is no best structure in the disciplines nor a best sequence in skill development.

Classroom procedures and organizations which I think are appropriate include:

1. Grouping for diversity (multi-age, nongraded) with opportunities for *temporary* subgroups to pursue special interests and competencies

2. Self-selection in reading and in interest groups from many alternatives (This requires a wide range of human, material, and audio-visual resources.)

3. Opportunities for independent work, alone and in small groups

4. Individual and small-group conferences with the teacher for pupil-teacher planning and evaluation and for teacher assistance as needed.

In the final analysis, the classroom teacher (supported by administrators and parents) must translate his own values and goals into action.

As far as traditional school content is concerned, during the primary years I would emphasize exploratory activities in the various content areas as well as the development of skills in communication, learning, and human relations. In the intermediate years (with overlap into both primary and upper levels), I would provide opportunities for selecting more systematic approaches to developed knowledge alternating with exploratory activities and discussions of personal meanings.

Today's problem of meeting individual needs and providing for individual differences in our mass education system is extremely difficult to resolve. Although educators may agree on the need to effect changes in this direction, we sorely need to work out some philosophically consistent practices which will develop and support individuality.

Do We Group in an Individualized Program?

Dorris M. Lee

"Hi, Bill! Did you see the notice on the bulletin board? Jim and Kathy are going to discuss Jean Lee Latham's book, *Carry on, Mr. Bowditch,* [1] this morning about 10:00. You wanted to find out about how sailors use sea charts and maps. Let's join the group."

And at 10:05 five boys and three girls join Jim and Kathy in the story-sharing corner of the room. Jim starts by giving the setting and general

Written with encouragement and suggestions from teachers (grades 1 through 8) Mary Crawford, Beaverton; Florence Edwards, David Douglas School District, Portland; Elizabeth Gill, Vancouver, Washington; Carole Lisignoli, Portland; Joseph Rubin, Portland; Lynn Rystogi, Portland; Donna Sposito, Portland.

Reprinted by permission of Dorris M. Lee and the Association for Childhood Education International, 3615 Wisconsin Avenue, N.W., Washington, D.C., from *Childhood Education* 45:197-199, December, 1968. Copyright ©1968 by the Association.

[1] Jean Lee Latham, *Carry On, Mr. Bowditch* (Boston: Houghton Mifflin, 1955).

focus, with an introduction of the main characters and the part they play in the story. Kathy develops the main theme and gives some personal reactions to the author's style and the feeling of reality she has about the characters. Then Jim explains what he has learned about using charts and maps at sea, which is what Bill has joined the group to hear. He begins asking Jim questions about it. Others join in, some with questions, some with comments, and two of them suggest further sources they have found helpful. Kathy then comments on what she has found about Jean Lee Latham's background on this topic and her other biographies. At this point some of the group begins to drift away and back to activities with which they are now more vitally concerned.

Of course there is grouping in an individualized program! The groups are just formed differently, for different purposes, and continue for different lengths of time. But first we must make clear what we consider individualized instruction to be. *Since* a learning situation, to be effective, must be such that each child can bring personal meaning to it, the child must have at least a part in the planning and decision-making. *Since* each learns in his own way and from the framework of his own present understandings, each must have a part in determining his own procedures for learning. Thus individualized instruction of necessity must involve self-directed learning.

Self-directed learning is a far cry from the justly feared do-whatever-you-want variety. Here the learner identifies his own educational needs, decides what he can do to meet them and how he can most effectively carry out his purposes. The teacher may help as little as by raising a question or as much as by extended conferencing. Planning with children helps them learn how to identify needs and procedures in terms of purposes. Individual conferences, in which the teacher can talk with each child about how he can identify needed learnings and how he decides what procedures would meet his purposes, are most useful in developing self-direction.

What Is a Group?

In this context, what is a group? It is those children who at that time have common specific concerns, needs, interests or plans. It may be initiated by one or more of the children involved or by the teacher or by the interaction of teacher and children. The group stays together as long as the specific reason for its establishment still exists. Some children may leave and others join as their immediate needs are met or developed.

Groups in which children have a part in deciding their participation or which grow out of self-directed activity have values that do not accrue from teacher-established and maintained groups. Almost by definition, there is involvement and purpose not otherwise possible. This eagerness and singlemindedness develop unique learnings. Self-selection of an individual or group learning activity brings commitment attained in no other way. The child then feels a responsibility to himself or the group.

- Mr. Swanson finds that Suzy, Bob, Karen, and Billy have difficulty recognizing base words in derived words. Each one also has become aware that he has not yet learned this, mainly through his or her individual conference with Mr. Swanson. So the group is formed to work together with the teacher in clarifying the problem, each suggesting ways of solving it from his own perceptions and reactions. One child after another gains insight, feels he understands, and leaves the group. With only Bob left, the teacher explores *his* thoughts and perceptions related to base and derived words. He discovers that he has always thought "base" meant "bottom" and never really has been able to bring any meaning to the word in this context. Each time he has thought he understood from the examples, he has become confused by the term. Mr. Swanson clears the meaning and Bob moves another step forward.

Purposes for Grouping

Individuals are unique and, while broadly speaking most have common general needs, immediate and specific needs and concerns differ widely. We believe content is primarily for use in developing concepts and understandings about the world of people and things in which the child lives. Further, we believe that a great variety of content may be used to develop needed concepts and understandings. Since children learn most effectively when dealing with material and ideas to which they can bring personal meaning, they will be using a wide variety of content. The number identifying with certain specific content at any one time may vary from one to possibly eight or ten. If the whole group has had a particularly meaningful experience, they may all want to discuss and think together for a while at least. Groups then provide a vehicle whereby those who can relate well to certain content or ideas may work together in a way most meaningful to them.

- A sixth-grade class has been having a variety of experiences that have oriented them to South America's problems, weaknesses, strengths and concerns; to its climates and general geography; to the languages of its people. Their familiarity with names of countries has alerted the children to comments relevant to South American situations in newspapers and magazines, on TV and radio, and by parents and friends. One morning Sarah comes in with a clipping relating the concern of American meat packers to the importation of Argentine beef. She asked her mother about it and in the store that afternoon they checked the canned meat shelves in their grocery store. Now she wants to know more about it. Her questions and concerns attract several others and a group of six expresses interest in finding out what it means to cattlemen both in the United States and Argentina. Since the teacher believes that a study in depth of one or two countries provides more real understanding, as well as develops skills in tackling a problem to find answers, she encourages the group to go ahead. She also recognizes that such exploration leads into virtually every aspect of a country's life—economic, political, geographical, historical.

Another purpose for grouping may be to attain needed skills not developed in other ways. When children live in a fluid, exciting learning environment where eager, purposeful activity is ever present, most acquire many such skills as natural, untaught learnings. However, some needed skills may be missed. When this is noted, by teacher or children, those who need the skills will join a group for the purpose of acquiring them, so that they may more easily go on with what they feel they need and want to do.

● A fourth grade has been working independently and in small groups to find out the various ways animals are useful to man and how man has affected the animals. They have been doing much reading and discussing and thinking, even copying out of books everything that has any relationship to the study, but some of the children are getting bogged down. Judy and Linda come to Miss Jenkins with the problem. Upon questioning the group, Miss Jenkins learns that ten of them are having trouble with notetaking. Although considerable attention was given to notetaking earlier in the year, this group knows they have not mastered the skill to the point of using it effectively.

Miss Jenkins suggests they and any others who wish meet that afternoon to pinpoint their problems. Twelve come to the meeting; specific problems are shared and ideas exchanged. Miss Jenkins gets them to think about their real purpose in taking notes, what they are going to use them for, how they can decide what to take down. After working for twenty minutes, they agree to try out their new understanding the next day and to meet together again on the following day to share progress, to ask further questions, and to check their skills by reading some of their notes to the group.

Groups form, shift membership and dissolve more or less continuously on the basis of common interest. Sometimes they are instigated by the teacher, but more often in a self-directed classroom they develop spontaneously. Such groups may be for a wide variety of purposes and involve a wide variety of activities. Some of them are:

● to work together in writing a story that may be presented to the class or taped for other groups to listen to and evaluate

● to prepare for the reading of a play of their own or one already written, for presentation to their class or another in the school

● to preview and evaluate a film for use of a larger group or the entire class

● to carry out the various functions necessary to the writing and "publishing" of a class or school newspaper

- to decide on significant and challenging questions to pose to a larger group or class for the purpose of stimulating involved discussion dealing with the understanding of main issues in an area of learning
- to use a listening post with tapes either teacher, child or group made for any of a variety of purposes
- to watch film loops, filmstrips or film and record combinations also for a variety of self-identified purposes
- to solve problems of the moment, as when one or two children say, "We need to discuss this with everybody working on our project" or ". . . with everybody playing baseball at noon" or ". . . with those who want to plan what we need to think about when we write stories for first-graders to read."

The Teacher's Changing Role

Donald Deep

The fall of 1967 saw great unrest among teachers across the United States. The unrest itself was not surprising to many in education; however, the reason for the unrest in many instances was quite revealing.

Conscientious teachers throughout our country cried out for improved teaching conditions and the best possible atmosphere for teaching. Teachers demanded that their role become more professional and modern. The classroom teacher no longer wanted to be a clerk, simply an imparter of knowledge, a Jack-of-all-trades, but a teacher—one who guides pupils to their full attainment.

Teachers realized that their pupils were the chief victims of the conditions under protest and that ways must be found to correct the injustice to the children. Teachers sought conditions that would make it possible for each pupil to profit fully from the education extended him. This is nothing new. Teachers everywhere have been striving toward this goal, but only recently have programs been set up that lead to it.

There are many paths to a new challenging role for teachers. The Univeristy of Pittsburgh and the Baldwin-Whitehall School District have launched a program that fits the changing role. The program, only four years old, has won praise from an important critic—the teacher.

Reprinted by permission of the University of Chicago Press, publisher, and Donald Deep from *The Elementary School Journal* 69:84-88, November, 1968. Copyright 1968 by the University of Chicago.

At Oakleaf Elementary School in Baldwin Township just south of Pittsburgh, a number of subjects are taught in an individually prescribed program. The subjects are mathematics and reading from Kindergarten through Grade 6, science from Kindergarten through Grade 4, and spelling in Grades 3-6. Pupils in heterogeneous classes work on different skills simultaneously. In mathematics, one child may be working on geometry, another on addition, another on fractions. More than likely no two pupils will be working on the same topic at the same time. In this program, the teacher must know the subject matter, for in one day she may have to help one child in geometry, another in multiplication, and then another in measurement. Since the class is individualized, the variability of the pupils has increased. In fourth grade, the range of achievement is approximately four years. Clearly, teachers at Oakleaf must have more than a mastery of skills for their grade level. Teachers must be familiar with the entire curriculum. The individualized program has encouraged the integration of mathematics and reading in the primary and the intermediate grades. Confinement to a one-grade textbook has been eliminated.

Just how does the program work? Again, the mathematics program will serve as an example. The curriculum is divided into nine levels—A through I. Most levels are subdivided into units. There are units on numeration, place value, addition, subtraction, multiplication, division, combination of processes, fractions, money, time, measurement, and other special topics. Each unit is designed to develop specific skills called *behavioral objectives,* which the pupils are expected to master. The entire curriculum has more than four hundred behavioral objectives. Here is an example of a behavioral objective from Level E, Unit on Multiplication, Skill 4: "Uses the associative principle for multiplication to multiply more than two numbers with single digit factors."

Once the curriculum has been defined, the next step is to determine where a pupil at Oakleaf should begin work. A series of placement tests is given to each pupil to learn his starting level and unit. Each child is then given a pre-test on that unit to identify the skills he needs to master. A particular pupil may require lessons and drill in only three of six skills. A score of 85 percent or higher is considered mastery.

The teacher evaluates the pre-test and is responsible for writing an individual "prescription" to develop the skills the pupil needs to master. A prescription assigns the child various learning activities. He may be assigned to a teacher for individual tutoring. Or he may be assigned, with a few other pupils, to a teacher for small-group instruction. Or he may be assigned, with many pupils, to a teacher for large-group instruction. He may be asked to do work pages, to listen to a disc, a tape, or a language master. He may be asked to view a film or a filmstrip. After the pupil completes his prescription for the skills in the unit and the teacher evaluates his lessons, the pupil is given a post-test, an alternate form of the pre-test, to check his mastery of the unit. If he has not mastered the unit, the teacher prescribes supplemental work. If he has mastered the unit, he is given the pre-test for his next unit of work. Because the teacher is continually diagnosing each pupil's weaknesses and strengths, children are not subjected to boring drill in areas where they have demonstrated mastery.

In the subjects covered by the program, each pupil is given responsibility for "filling" his prescription. He obtains his own work pages, materials, aids, discs, as prescribed. Most pupils proceed through the prescribed materials with very little direction and instruction from the teacher. Almost all the work is scored by teacher aides or by the pupil himself. The teacher makes the final evaluation of the work. Teacher aides score all tests of diagnostic skill, but the teacher evaluates the test results. Our hope at Oakleaf is that each child will gain a sense of responsibility for the work he is doing and will take an active interest in his progress. Pupils are encouraged to become more self-reliant and independent while working on the individually prescribed instruction programs.

In this program teachers rarely lecture. They are too busy observing the child's progress, evaluating his diagnostic tests, writing prescriptions, and instructing individuals or small groups of pupils who need help. In this program the teacher's role is what experienced teachers have been seeking for years—that of teaching, evaluating, and making important educational decisions. Each prescription for an individual pupil is reviewed by the teacher each day. Most of the prescriptions do not last more than one class period.

An important aspect of the program is complete assurance that teachers have time for planning. Group planning sessions are held weekly for each subject area. At these sessions, teachers discuss specific problems or changes in the program. During the school day teachers have time not only for group planning, but also for individual planning. Most clerical tasks are handled by teacher aides. The aides, who are paid an hourly wage, are housewives in the area who have a high-school education.

Usually the teacher has all the prescriptions prepared before class. At the beginning of the class, the pupils' folders are handed out. Each child looks at his prescription sheet for his day's lessons. Children who need new materials for their lessons get them at a designated place. The teacher then goes about various tasks. She may help pupils who need assistance. She may evaluate pupils' check tests, pre-tests, and post-tests on certain skills. She may help pupils who have a prescription, "See teacher." She may direct one pupil to teach another, oversee pupils in supplemental activities, or write new prescriptions.

This program does not make the job of the elementary-school teacher any easier, but the rewards are immediate and the role is fast approaching professional standard—exactly what it should have been years ago.

Improving Independent Study

Jeannette Veatch

The crux of improving independent study lies in whether or not it *IS* independent. Workbook pages and teacher-made exercises are very much *DE*pendent as they are issued by the teacher. Usually, in the elementary school we refer to independent work as that taking place during the "seatwork" time; i.e., when reading groups are meeting with the teacher.

"Seatwork" centered around such "exercises" will yield little that really educates. The appalling fact is that most teachers, as well as most people who *train* teachers, believe that such paper work is important and educative, a belief not backed up by research data. We read about "well-planned" workbooks. There are no such workbooks; nor can there be, as no author knows what a child in a given class needs at a given time. No planning is good that ignores the children to be involved, so it is nonsense to speak of "well-planned" workbooks. The only hope is that teachers may have a variety of exercises and drill pages to fit a recognized need of a child. This means a dozen different workbooks and hundreds of teacher-made exercises. Even then there is no guarantee that the best-fitting exercise will teach a child whatever that exercise is supposed to teach. We simply do not know *what* workbooks teach, if they teach anything at all. There is little except the opinion of the author of the material to justify their value, even if developed with a modicum of try-outs (but not standardization) with living, breathing children.

To develop improved independent study we need to avoid teacher-assignments of this type. Workbooks are timekillers and should be viewed as such. When and if they should be proven educative, then perhaps will be the time to use them. In the meantime let us discuss learning which can be carried out independently. Children will study independently more often, with greater concentration, and certainly with greater interest when that which they study is of their own choice. Independent study means just that—*independent.* Recognizing a need, the child develops his own means of attacking a recognized problem, seeking the help he needs when he needs it.

Self-recognition of a need is a first step and certainly one of the major laws of learning. When a child *knows* he confuses "b" and "d," he can work on it. When a child realizes he is not sure of certain consonants in the beginnings of

Reprinted by permission of Jeannette Veatch and the Association for Childhood Education International, 3615 Wisconsin Avenue, N.W., Washington, D.C., from *Childhood Education* 43:284-288, January, 1967. Copyright ©1967 by the Association.

words, he can develop a project of cutting out pictures from magazines of objects that start with the needed letter. There are limitless projects in the minds of children.

One point about independent work is that it need not be hurried. When a pupil develops his own project he has the time to work on it during an independent work period without being hounded to finish. When a child is the only one doing a certain thing there is no need on the part of the teacher to rush him through. The child knows when it is time to go out and play or to go home. He can pace his work to the realistic needs of the length of the school day; if he doesn't finish one day, he can plan to stop at such a point so as to finish another. There is a matter of serenity and concentration that must not be ignored. A child works at his own project, and he works on that project at his own pace. While there is no research in independent activities on this matter, there is plenty on self-selection in reading that supports the philosophy of this type of activity.

One interesting master's project[1] showed children, familiar with self-selection practice in reading instruction, to be markedly more independent and resourceful in planning their independent work than were children under a traditional basal reader, workbook program.

Criteria for Improving Independent Study

Independent study requires that children make the choice as to what to do. Does the teacher make suggestions? Of course! Does the teacher check on these activities? If he wants to. But those criteria helpful in leading to the improvement of independent study are generally in the tenor of the following:

● The activities are child-chosen, self-assigned and largely self-directed, although assistance from the teacher or from friends is possible and helpful.

● The activities will require little formal checking, no red-pencil correction, but much teacher approval and knowledge.

● The activities may be long-term or short-term without regard to the length of the period devoted to their accomplishment.

● The activities must absorb children so that there is little need for the child to interrupt himself or the teacher for any purpose short of emergency.

● The activities should use materials that are easily accessible and commonplace. The creative use of ordinary materials should be a hallmark of these activities.

● The activities should be done for the pupil's personal satisfaction, producing enthusiasm rather than the feeling of doing a chore.

---

[1] Davida Scharf Goldweber, "A Comparison of the Attitudes of Independence and Resourcefulness of Students Under an Individualized Program and a Traditional Program in the Same School." Unpublished Master's Thesis. Jersey City State College. 1966.

These activities, however, do not spring full blown out of the thin air. They require a classroom setting full of possibilities for self-determined endeavor. Most useful references[2] describe, in some form, centers of interest that beckon to children.

Centers of Interest

With some variation, the centers of interest are set up around the following areas:

BOOK CENTER—where all the books are kept: trade, text and reference.

WRITING CENTER—where writing supplies of all kinds are kept, hopefully a typewriter or two, and including space for blackboard writing or writing on brown paper on the wall.

ART CENTER—where wet media such as clay, finger paint, water paint can be used with clean-up facilities handy; where dry media such as crayons, colored chalk, pretty paper, paste and scissors have a place of their own.

SCIENCE CENTER—where all manner of equipment such as magnets, batteries, terraria, aquaria, collections and exhibits find a spot.

DRAMATIZATION CENTER—where the unit in social studies lends itself to dramatization and exploration or where, for younger children, playing "house" is possible.

MATERIALS CENTER—where blocks and other creative toys and playthings are available for construction and similar activity.

FOLLOW-UP MATERIALS CENTER—where the teacher can assign specific exercises and other work and where children might find material to work upon for their own benefit.

With classrooms set up along these lines, independent work comes into its own. Teachers and pupils plan together so that children work through the problems that face them.

Using the Centers

Given these centers, what can a teacher expect of young children? Which activity comes when? Is there an order to activities? Briefly, order and sequence depend upon the needs of the independent work period itself. Consecutive activities are usually of two types: (1) those that occur during the reading period

---

[2] The reader is referred to the following:

Constance Carr (Ed.), *Children Can Work Independently* (Washington, D.C.: ACEI, 1952). Out of print; only in bound copies in some libraries.

H. F. Darrow and R. Van Allen, *Independent Activities for Creative Learning* (New York: Bureau of Publications, Teachers College, Columbia University), No. 21 Series. Practical Suggestions for Teaching, 1961.

Jeannette Veatch, *Reading in the Elementary School* (New York: Ronald Press, 1966). Chap. 5.

and (2) those that occur at some other time of the school day. The differences between these two periods lie in the noise level of the activities. In the first, because the teacher needs to be heard by the individuals and groups, a noisy activity cannot be allowed lest there be interference. But when an independent "free" time is set up when no such instruction is required, then pounding, hammering and all manner of noise can occur without causing problems. Planning for either of these two types of work periods should take place when the day is begun in the morning. Teacher-pupil planning comes into its own when there is leeway for pupil-decision.

Sequence of Activities

As far as sequence of independent activities is concerned, the independent work period during the reading time can and should begin with the silent reading of a self-chosen book. Under a program of individualization, self-selection is the motivating force behind reading. Children choose books usable by teachers to improve reading skills. Subsequent follow-up activities can be based on such book choices. A child may prepare his selection to present to his teacher during an individual conference, or he may plan a project that stems from that selection. Beyond those activities that tie directly to reading, there is really no particular need for a prescribed sequence of events. Let the child absorb himself and so be exposed to the excitement of learning independently. The prime test of such an activity is, of course, "What can the activity by itself teach the child?" Upon the answer to this question hangs learning that develops children to their potentials.

Guidelines for Developing a Homework Policy

William D. Hedges

Assigned home study tasks are one source of the misunderstandings that occasionally arise among parents, teachers, and school administrators. Attesting to this statement is the fact that homework is listed by the Educational Policies Commission as one of ten contemporary issues in elementary education.[1]

In addition, interest in homework policies has been rising if the increased incidence in recent years of articles on homework is a reliable indicator.

---

[1] National Education Association and American Association of School Administrators, Educational Policies Commission. *Contemporary Issues in Elementary Education.* Washington, D.C.: the Commission, 1960.

Reference to the *Readers' Guide* and *The Education Index* for a count of articles published during the past six decades yields the information shown in figure 1.

Tabulation of the 292 articles located revealed that they appeared in 120 journals. More than one-third (41%) were published by only nine journals as follows:

Clearing House	22
NEA Journal	17
The Journal of Education	15
School Review	13
High Points	13
Parents Magazine	12
American School Board Journal	10
Grade Teacher	9
The Elementary School Journal	9
Total	120

These data are not intended to be exhaustive, because articles have been published in some state journals, popular magazines, and other periodicals which are not listed in either of the two indexes consulted. It is assumed, however, that the figures are indicative of a general rise in interest in the subject among school and lay people.

Pressures have been increasing during the past six to eight years for teachers to demand more and more of students in the elementary grades. There is an increased tendency in many schools across the country to load children with several hours of homework each evening. Under the American system of public education, principals are necessarily responsive to these pressures. Because of this trend toward more and more homework, a trend which is highly questionable unless there is sound evidence to support the value of homework to youngsters, it occurred to the writer to investigate the extent to which homework practices are based on well designed and carefully executed research studies.

The following material reports the essence of 40 of the 292 references located. The articles reviewed were selected on the basis of two factors: 1) they appeared on a purely subjective basis to be most scholarly; and 2) about three-fourths of them were written within the past decade.

Inconclusive Evidence

The evidence concerning the effects of homework is inclusive. Most of the articles and other reports are nonexperimental, and limitations in such factors as

Reprinted by permission of Department of Elementary School Principals, National Education Association, Washington, D.C., from *The National Elementary Principal* 44:44-47, November, 1964. Copyright 1964, Department of Elementary School Principals, National Education Association. All rights reserved.

adequacy of design, replicability, and scope prevent any sweeping conclusions. Thus, Ruth Strang in a 1955 NEA publication on homework wrote: "Although many opinions exist on the effect of homework upon scholastic success, there has been little research on the subject. The many intangible factors involved have prevented exact and consistent measurement of changes and relationships."[2]

The vast majority of the articles reviewed consisted of the opinions of teachers, principals, professional educators, and popular writers. Happily enough, however, many of these did treat the argument of homework vs. no homework as the strawman it actually is: i.e., they suggested that the fundamental question is *how much of what kind of homework for what child under what conditions and for what reasons?*

It must be admitted, then, that no *definitive* answers can currently be provided to such questions as the amount of time children of various ability and achievement levels should spend on homework and the nature of appropriate home study tasks. This degree of fuzziness is ironical, if not tragic, in view of the millions upon millions of hours spent by students (and parents) each year in completing home assignments and in view of the long span of years over which homework has been assigned in this country.

Without comprehensive and firm research evidence on the various facets of homework, it is easy to see why schools bend with each wave of feeling that washes over the American people. Recently, the wave has been fear—fear of an enemy. How tragic it is that Johnny must now spend longer hours bending over work that may or may not be helping him just because his parents are afraid, and there are no firm, clear guidelines to enable principals and teachers to combat the effects of this fear.

Major Principles

What, then, can be said? What can be said in addition to the statement that the research evidence is inconclusive and even conflicting and that extensive research projects of a longitudinal and comprehensive nature need to be conducted on the specific effects of specific types of home study on particular kinds of children in particular subjects? Some statements can be made, but they can only be made as a basis for helping the principal and his faculty think through the policy they may wish to establish for their school. In this context, major principles presented in the articles reviewed are summarized below.

Arguments Commonly Given in Support of Homework

1. Homework keeps parents in touch with the school program and their child's progress, thus creating a closer bond between home and school.

[2] Strang, Ruth. *Guided Study and Homework.* What Research Says to the Teacher, No. 8. Prepared by the American Educational Research Association in cooperation with the Department of Classroom Teachers. Washington, D.C.: National Education Association, 1955. p. 19.

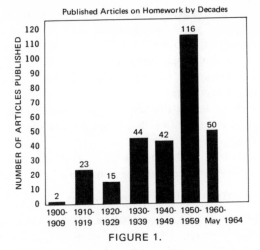

FIGURE 1.

2. It teaches a child to follow directions and helps him learn how to organize his time.

3. It teaches the child to accept responsibility and helps him develop self-reliance in his work—improves study skills and work habits.

4. Struggling with lessons is good discipline and a builder of character.

5. Homework provides constructive use of time which might otherwise be idly squandered; it keeps the child out of mischief after school.

6. It reinforces school learnings and gives needed drill on work taken up in class.

7. The amount of knowledge required by the curriculum simply cannot be imparted during school hours alone.

Arguments Commonly Given Against Homework

1. After a six- or seven-hour school day, a child is tired, and it is too much to expect him to do homework. Not only is there too little time left for play but reading books for seven, eight, or more hours a day may lead to cramped lungs and eyestrain because children may be unable to obtain enough physical exercise.

2. The extra work load may reduce the interest and vigor with which the child faces the next day's work.

3. Homework is often work for the parents instead of the child, and parents frequently do it in a way not approved by the teacher. Thus, the parents just confuse the child.

4. Parents are seldom qualified to supervise home study. It is better for the children to do careful, guided study at school where their needs for special help or further information can be met.

5. Homes do not always provide suitable study conditions or facilities.

6. Other educationally valuable activities such as scout meetings, music lessons, church activities, club meetings, hobbies, recreational reading, educational TV programs, and play may be neglected.

7. Disagreeable tasks are too often assigned for homework instead of creative, interesting assignments.

8. The harmony of family life may be jeopardized, and in cases where the home offers cultural opportunities, its positive influence on the child's development may be reduced.

9. In some schools where homework has been abolished or severely limited, the sum total of achievement does not seem to have been affected.

What Parents Have a Right To Expect from Teachers

1. Parents have a right to expect that teachers will be sure that the child clearly understands the assignment. It should be definite and should always have been explained in class. Preferably, the child *will have started it while in class* and under the guidance of the teacher to make sure he knows what he is to do. Too many assignments are vague.

2. Parents should be able to expect that teachers will *not* give homework for disciplinary reasons.

3. When homework is completed and turned in, parents should know that it will be carefully checked by the teacher or her assistant. Otherwise, it should not be assigned.

4. Parents can properly expect that no homework will be given over weekends or holidays.

5. Parents can expect that assignments will not require the use of books or other materials which are not available in the home.

6. Homework should be assigned only when it clearly serves a purpose. Students often don't know why they are to do this or read that. When assigned reading, for example, they need to be told whether they are to learn specific facts, whether they are to look for the main ideas in the material, whether they are to relate details to the main ideas and identify the author's pattern of thought, whether they are to draw inferences and conclusions, etc. Thus, parents have a right to expect that teachers will not make snap assignments but will plan carefully in terms of the outcomes desired and the time needed to do the work.

7. Parents have a right to expect homework to be within the ability of the child. Otherwise, the child will be forced to "borrow" his classmate's work; prevail on Mom or Dad to do it for him; worry and fret unduly over his being unable to do it; or forget the whole matter with unpleasant results for all.

8. Parents have a right to expect some homework when the pupil has been absent or when he is not working up to expectancy and needs special remedial work.

What Teachers Have a Right to Expect from Parents

1. Teachers have a right to expect that the parents will arrange a quiet, comfortable place, well lighted and with ample work space, for the child to work.

2. If the assignment is reasonable, teachers have a right to expect that the parents will cooperate by encouraging their child to do it. It should be noted that what may seem to be an unreasonable homework load may actually be the converse. A child may have difficulty with homework because he lacks good study habits.

3. Teachers have a right to expect the parents to refuse to carry out the assignment for the child. This does not mean parents shouldn't point out principles involved, help give illustrations, and make some suggestions. Parents should not nag their children and put too much pressure on them. If they take over and force, cajole, bribe, or punish, they may see to it that the studying is done, but hardly in a way that suggests that learning can be an interesting occupation and certainly without helping the child grow in his ability to assume responsibility. It will help a good deal if the parent will take the initiative in finding out what the school actually expects of the student—this is sometimes widely at variance with what a child tells his parents and may honestly believe.

4. Teachers also have a right to expect parents to take a broad view of the values of various types of homework, since the values differ under different circumstances and conditions.

Characteristics of Good Homework Assignments

1. Homework should be carefully planned, with students motivated to complete the assignments—assignments that are definite, interesting, meaningful, and geared to individual abilities.

2. The teacher should take some responsibility for helping the child to form efficient study habits. How to study and learn is, unfortunately, not taught very well—if at all—in most schools. Too many children waste too much of their study time because they have never learned how best to use it.

3. Most homework should be of an informal nature, supplementing formal preparation in the class and following the bent of the child: reading good fiction, poetry, history, popular magazines and newspapers, watching good TV programs, seeing excellent movies, etc.

4. The homework assignments should be made only after children understand the process and have had enough practice in class to do homework on the subject unaided.

5. Most homework assignments should be personalized—geared as far as possible to meet individual needs—and should be within the pupil's range of skill. This means that there should be very little or no regularly assigned drill-type homework for the entire class. Exercises that can be done mechanically

encourage copying, while an assignment that calls for initiative and individual creative effort rules out copying and challenges the student to work effectively.

6. Most homework assignments should be of a type which can be better done away from school. This includes collecting information, sharing ideas with parents, and situations in which children are involved in something like creative writing or preparing reports.

A Suggested Homework Policy and Time Schedule

1. Ideally, a definite, clear-cut policy on homework will have been worked out by parents and teachers (probably through the PTA) with mutually agreed upon statements concerning purposes, amount of homework, policies on weekends, types of home study, etc.

2. A good homework policy means parents should feel free to come to the teacher and discuss with her the child's homework situation without the teacher's feeling defensive—and the converse.

3. A sound homework policy will insure that children are not overburdened with home assignments. It is evident from what has been said that *there is no single time schedule* that will be suitable for all schools or even for the same school over a period of time. Even so, in developing a homework policy, principals and teachers may wish to consider what many authorities believe to be a *maximum* time allotment suitable for the majority of youngsters—assuming the other criteria for sound homework assignments have been met. With these points in mind, the following time schedule for various grade levels may be helpful:

Grade 1—none or at most 10 minutes
Grade 2—up to about 10 minutes
Grade 3—15 minutes
Grade 4—20 minutes
Grade 5—25 minutes
Grade 6—30 minutes

4. The best homework policy will incorporate considerable flexibility depending on varying circumstances and situations, and both school and patrons should be ready to modify it from time to time as deemed advisable.

Conclusion

Because of the limited and inconclusive research on homework in the elementary school and because of the varying needs of children both within and between communities, it is incumbent upon the principal to exert the leadership necessary to develop a policy for his school. It has been the purpose of this article to summarize the thinking of many writers on the topic in the hope that such data may serve as a basis for policy development.

Chapter 7

Handling Problem Areas and Trends

The articles that have been chosen for inclusion in this chapter contain thought-provoking ideas concerning several current problem areas and trends in elementary education. The area of early childhood education is one that is receiving a growing amount of attention. Kindergartens are being introduced into the public school systems of many states; programs such as Headstart, Sure Start, and Operation Follow Through are being developed and expanded; and public school nursery-kindergartens are in operation. Some suggestions as to what and how young children should be taught are to be found in the article by McQueen.

One of the more controversial issues facing teachers today is that of sex education in the public schools. In the second article, sociologist Reiss delineates the task in terms of social, moral, philosophical, and educational perspectives before discussing questions of practical strategy in starting programs, determining qualifications of teachers, and deciding how the subject should be taught.

Although the idea of using the outdoors for educational experiences is not new, for many teachers the practice is innovative. During the past few years, increasing emphasis has been placed on the quantity and quality of outdoor education programs. The article by Rillo is included in this chapter because it suggests to teachers ways they can use the immediate school environment for outdoor experiences.

Increasingly, children with physical impairments are attending school in the regular classroom. Ashcroft's article, "The Handicapped in the Regular Classroom," is designed to help teachers understand the nature and needs of physically handicapped children and to offer suggestions for working with them successfully.

Although considerable thought and attention are being given to the preparation of teachers to teach children who are less advantaged than the majority, many teachers assigned to schools in deprived areas have not been prepared to work with disadvantaged children. "How to Teach in a Ghetto School" will be of special help to them. Trubowitz gives some very specific suggestions for getting to know and understand the children and the community and for using this knowledge and insight in planning and conducting meaningful learning experiences.

In a pluralistic society it is to be expected that there will be many differences in basic beliefs and values among the children. A lack of teacher sensitivity and appreciation of this fact may create problems. At the same time opportunity for enriched classroom experiences exists. The way that one sixth grade teacher used what could have been a difficult situation to help pupils develop greater understanding of individuals and their rights is described in the article "Joe Doesn't Pledge Allegiance." A second concern is that of recognition of religious ideas and religious holidays. The selection by Barr, "Christmas in the Classroom," should help teachers clarify their thinking in this area and cope with problems that arise.

The chapter concludes with an article discussing another question of considerable import: how and when to teach Afro-American history and culture. Grubman's guide to introducing black studies in the primary grades, appropriately titled "The Best Start Is an Early Start," presents activities and materials for teaching about the Afro-American's contribution to our country's history.

Early Childhood Education

Mildred McQueen

Balancing Opposing Theories

Although educators agree on the goals of early childhood education, they do not agree on ways to achieve them. And the arguments about the learning capacities of young children have been going on for centuries. In general, there have been what might be called two extreme schools of thought with entirely different approaches, and over the years the opinions of educators have swung back and forth between them. The advocates of one approach emphasize readiness—the idea that we must not try to teach a child what he is not ready to learn. Advocates of the other approach maintain that the sooner a child is placed in a rigorous learning program the faster he will develop intellectually. Progressive education with its child-centered theories usually gets the credit or blame for the first theory. But actually the root of the idea goes back a couple of

Reprinted by permission of the publisher from *SRA Research Report, Early Childhood Education, Part Two*, 1967, pp. 1-4. ©1967, Science Research Associates, Inc., Chicago.

centuries when people began to rebel against making little children learn as much as could be forced into them under the rigid discipline of a stern headmaster. In the early American colonies, for instance, three- and four-year-olds were often required to learn Latin as well as reading and writing. Then some scholars and philosophers began to say that children were not adults and should not be forced to learn as if they were. From this new belief came the idea, widely accepted for some time now, that children should be taught what they are capable of learning as they become ready for it. In some schools the readiness theory was so rigidly followed that some children were actually held back from learning what they were ready to learn. Development came in fixed stages and that was that. Some teachers, for example, were very much against any attempt to introduce reading to children before they were six years old. Parents took up the idea, too, and even if the child wanted to try to read the words in his picture books, they feared it would impede his later progress in school. Lately some educators have swung to the other extreme. These critics of the readiness approach blame the permissive child development theory for watered-down learning and school failures. They believe the child should be put to work in a rigorous academic program. This theory with its emphasis on an intense academic focus has increased pressure for early reading programs, nursery schools with rigid discipline, and the introduction of science and foreign languages into earlier grades in elementary school. Hartman describes some current studies that proceed on assumptions quite different from those of child development experts as to what makes up an effective preschool program, especially for the disadvantaged. In addition to an intense academic focus, these experimental programs are diagnostically based rather than interest- or experience-oriented. Concern for the child's language difficulties is predominant and it is assumed that if he can handle language and reading effectively after he enters school, many of the psychological and social problems that ordinarily impede his progress will disappear. But many current programs, if one can believe the reports, are giving attention to language difficulties as well as to children's health and emotional problems. And is it logical that psychological and social problems will disappear if no attention is given or no guidance offered? Health problems certainly must be corrected if children's learning is to progress. In addition, those who are against formal learning and highly structured classrooms in the early years say no evidence exists to show that children will benefit in the long run from this heavy load. In fact, there is some evidence to show that trying to force development causes tensions and pressures and may also lead to failure. It also must be kept in mind that children learn in different ways Studies on teaching reading to young children give evidence of these differences. Two longitudinal studies conducted by Durkin during a six-year period with children in California and New York showed that those who learned to read before entering school learned in very different ways. Although all of these preschool readers were read to by parents or brothers and sisters at a very early age, enjoyed the experience, and asked questions, they also carried on self-initiated projects related to reading over extended periods of time. Calendars, food packages, pencil-and-paper projects, and interest in street signs, grocery lists or TV commercials all helped these children learn words. In addition to individual differences there were also masculine and feminine ways of learning to read, at least in vocabulary. Boys and girls were interested in different kinds of words—boys in rocket, jet, and car; girls in words related to playing store or house. Many suggestions for teaching early reading came from the study, and Durkin wishes these could be translated into school practice. But on the basis of kindergarten visits, she was not hopeful. Many kindergartens were copies of those of twenty years ago, with schedules emphasizing play activities and games; others showed changes, but disappointing ones. Workbooks and drill made up their reading programs. Although the readiness theory that children should not learn to read before six is fallacious, Durkin believes the introduction of workbooks and formal teaching into preschool programs is also a mistake. The examples in this reading study clearly illustrate the two extreme schools of thought on teaching young children—the child-centered program in which the child is offered little mental challenge and the formal academic program. An interesting note is that the child development experts are now being called traditional by the advocates of structured academic programs. And the fact that the progressives have become traditional adds a humorous note to the controversy. Perhaps this is what is needed, for humor can often help to destroy extreme ideas and restore balance and common sense. The way out of the controversy, as some educators have wisely concluded, is to pursue a middle course that uses the best of both approaches Young children need and can benefit from a good deal of intellectual stimulation, but they should not be placed in learning stiuations that are too formal. Accordingly, there should be some general principles and techniques to follow that would be helpful in working with all young children. For example, researchers on the culturally disadvantaged have said that techniques effective with them would be useful to other children as well. At the same time, adaptations are necessary for certain groups, such as the culturally disadvantaged, and in the end for each youngster. Good education at any age is simply an adaptive response to the children being educated.

Recommendations

The members of the Educational Policies Commission and other educators have outlined the main goals of early childhood education. These lie in four major areas:

1. **Intellectual Goals.** These include the promotion of curiosity, the growth of language, and preparation for the structured intellectual activities that will

come in later years. They also include the development of the ability to handle concepts. One of the important contributions that early education can make is the extension of the child's span of experience. Under skilled guidance, he can discover new worlds in almost every situation. At first the approach to studying the world will be a simple one. As Fowler points out, the child should progress from the understanding of a single object to seeing the relation between objects and then their relation to a larger structure—the home, store, school, community—as parts of a whole. Law emphasizes that with a wide range of concrete experiences the more abstract concepts of reading, writing, and numbers will begin to make sense. A variety of materials are needed—books, papers, and pencils, of course, and also sand, water, sawdust, dirt, paint, and clay; living things such as worms, plants, insects, and animals; people, such as older children, visitors, and community resource people; and even what Law calls "beautiful junk," which children love, such as dress-up clothes, old clocks, broken radios, scraps of wood, and jewelry. For culturally disadvantaged youngsters, it may be necessary to give more emphasis to language development, cognitive skills, orderly ways of working, visual and auditory perceptual training, and quantitative concepts.

2. **Emotional Goals.** A sense of security, confidence, and self-respect are important to the child's learning and mental health. Extra attention to this area in programs for the disadvantaged is essential. Because most of these children have negative ideas about themselves, they must be helped to develop a more positive self-image; pride in school success must be fostered. To this end, the child must often feel a sense of accomplishment. He must feel that he is respected and his work valued.

3. **Social Goals.** A young child is likely to see himself as the center of the world. If he is to grow into a useful and responsible adult, he must develop a concern for and a responsibility toward others. On the other hand, he must also learn how to speak up for himself so that he does not follow others blindly, he must learn that he, too, can contribute and that he has rights that are to be respected. Early education programs can help youngsters learn how to work with other children and adults, to be more socially acceptable, and, very important, to learn how to share. Culturally disadvantaged children may need to learn how to substitute verbal expression for strong physical aggression in relations with others. Their own rules may allow physical assault when they can get away with it. But these children usually have a fierce loyalty to brothers and sisters and some group cohesiveness that can be used as a basis for learning to work with others.

4. **Health Goals.** Health care should be considered, too. A good deal of attention to the child's physical well-being may be needed in programs for the disadvantaged. Such attention was offered in Head Start programs. About 90 percent of the children got a medical examination. But there has been too little

follow-up on medical problems. When a child's parents cannot do so, the school should provide medical examinations so that health problems can be taken care of. Children should also be helped to develop good health habits.

In addition to recommendations about the goals of early education programs, experts in the field have made some other suggestions for effective programs:

● Continuity with the rest of the school program is vital. No preschool program can produce lasting or effective results all by itself. It must be followed by a good kindergarten and primary curriculum. In February 1967 President Johnson, in a special message to Congress, urged a strengthened Head Start program with special attention to launching a follow-through procedure during the first few school grades. The Educational Policies Commission recommends that the school program for six-year-olds be based on the program for four- and five-year-olds.

● Teachers must be highly skilled in their ability to work with young children. Law suggests a professional with vigor and imagination who can tolerate informality, enjoys children and parents, and has emotional satisfactions independent of them both. Although she may be scholarly, she must be able to use simple techniques with imagination. She must be interested in and curious about the world, and flexible enough to make momentary decisions. There is a critical shortage of qualified preprimary teachers. Although questions about the best preparation for teachers are only partially answered, the Chicago Institute for Early Childhood Education, one of the country's first schools devoted solely to training teachers in preschool education, opened its doors in September 1966 to twenty selected teachers for an intensive one-year course in early childhood development. It is expected to expand after the first year.

● Cooperation with parents is another important part of early education programs. Relations between the home and school are particularly important at the nursery school and kindergarten level. It should be usual practice for parents to share in the program in some way. This parent relationship is essential in working with disadvantaged children, because parents may not understand the program or know how to help their children.

● Early education programs require careful planning, and school systems should not try to set up a program overnight on an inadequate budget. The program should be planned to fit the needs of the community.

Examples of Programs

Most of the programs described currently in educational literature are for disadvantaged groups. But it will be helpful to examine some specific programs to see what approaches are being used:

● The aim of Project Get Set, a giant-size prekindergarten program in Philadelphia, is to give underprivileged children a better chance at a fair start in life. In 91 centers, more than 4000 three- and four-year-olds from disadvantaged homes are participating in the program. At the same time fathers and mothers of the children are gaining experiences that will help them to become better parents. The project employs a staff of 800, including 300 teachers, 300 teacher aides, and 30 home-school coordinators, and conducts its own program of in-service education. The home-school coordinators are trained by professional social workers. Get Set conducts its own programs for medical and dental care and parent education. Although the project receives 90 percent of its funds from the federal government, it operates in an atmosphere of neighborly cooperation; nothing about it suggests big business or big government. The director and her assistants have taught in neighborhoods that now have Get Set centers, so they find it easy to establish rapport with parents. Most of the teacher aides and other nonprofessional employees live in the neighborhoods where they work, and home-school coordinators are usually women who have a record of community work in the neighborhoods they serve. The program emphasizes the personal with both children and parents. Each child is a VIP with his own name marked on the place he keeps his coat. The teacher helps him print his name on his drawings, and it may also be on the wall under the picture of a birthday cake during his birthday month. Classes are small; each class has a teacher, a teacher aide, and a volunteer mother-helper. With three adults to work with each group there is always someone to praise a small child for a special accomplishment. There are fifty male teachers on the staff. And what a treat it is for a little boy from a fatherless home to have a man to whom he can whisper an important secret or to show him how to keep his tower of blocks from falling down! The person-to-person atmosphere of Get Set and the neighborly spirit may be responsible for the wholehearted way parents have accepted the project. They are made to feel they are partners in a plan to help make life better for their children.

• A preschool program for disadvantaged children in New Rochelle, New York, a suburban community near Manhattan, used some approaches that were different. An expanded program grew out of a pilot project for three-and-a-half- to four-year-olds from low-income groups to include five prekindergarten classrooms with an enrollment of 150. An effort was made to reach every child who qualified, but words like *poor, poverty,* and *underprivileged* were never used in press releases, flyers, or speeches. The staff felt that such language might be thought offensive by the very people they wished most to reach. Volunteers were encouraged to see parents as neighbors, not as the unfortunates. Another feature of the program was the use of young people of high school age as teaching aides, and this procedure will probably be expanded. A few people of high school age who volunteered in response to a request for help at a high school summer session have been assigned to paid jobs as teaching assistants. They bring excellent qualities to the classroom: interest, enthusiasm, a sense of responsibility, willingness to learn, warmth and affection for their young charges, sensitivity to the needs of children, and pride in their work. In only one case has a volunteer student had to be relieved of her assignment. New Rochelle personnel emphasize, however, that paid or volunteer assistants will not be effective unless preliminary and inservice training and teacher supervision are provided. In general, the curriculum is planned to be the best kind of program for all children of nursery school age, combined with the basic goals of a compensatory program. Gains were evident after the first month and continued. Vocabulary and intellectual curiosity were increased, creativity was stimulated, social relations developed, and pride in school success was initiated. Trips were planned to encourage curiosity and widen horizons. The major adventure was a bus trip to the Bronx Zoo with parents and aides in attendance. After the visit children told descriptive stories to the teacher and drew pictures of what they had heard and seen. In some cases children drew pictures of animals they had *not* seen, an illustration of fantasy and imagination. One interesting conclusion of the staff is that the zest for learning and class adjustment vary from class to class; they believe this may also be true of different communities. For example, it cannot be assumed that the characteristics of the underprivileged Negro child in New York's Harlem are necessarily those of the underprivileged Italian or Negro child in New Rochelle. The marked verbal reticence reported elsewhere was not found with many children in the New Rochelle project. They did need, however, to expand their vocabulary. The staff feels it would be a mistake to expect characteristics so often described in the literature to be persistent and inevitable and thus found in every prekindergarten project. For this reason staff members suggest that the goal for any prekindergarten program for the culturally disadvantaged should be broadly compensatory rather than specifically remedial, because the instruction must be derived from the working experience and evaluation procedures of each community.

• Many other reports of early education programs have come from communities around the country. Preschool education is a year-round activity in Detroit, where programs focus on language development. Parent involvement, health examinations, and cooperation with social service agencies are part of the program. San Antonio, Texas, modeled its year-round program after the Head Start summer program and serves mainly two ethnic groups: children from Spanish-speaking homes and Negroes. Inservice training for teachers was planned cooperatively with the University of Texas. Lebanon, Oregon, has a program called Sure Start that calls for follow-up of six- and seven-year-olds who continue having difficulty. The Woodward, Iowa, program takes Head Start home to parents. Home Start tries to strengthen the child's educational foundations in the home with parent education and a child development specialist who identifies problems of children that may hinder school progress.

Mount Vernon, New York, gives mothers a vital role and uses Montessori methods and materials in its preschool program for four-year-olds. Instructors were drawn from a pool of forty-five kindergarten teachers who took a thirty-hour Montessori in-service course. Mothers and teaching assistants are trained on the job and after school. The Mount Vernon staff says teachers must be trained in Montessori methods for an effective program and a great deal of preliminary work must be done with mothers. The staff also believes that the early introduction of standard reading readiness materials designed for conventional teaching in the first grade must not be used with four-year-olds. Instead the staff recommends multisensory materials related to verbal symbols in a concentrated approach to language and reading development. A few experimental programs report concentrated academic discipline for young children, with intense drill. On the whole, though, the majority of programs use an approach that combines intellectual stimulation and preparation for more formal learning with guidance and attention to the emotional and physical needs of children.

No matter what decision is reached on universal public education for four-year-olds, there is hope in the ideas being considered about working with young children. Certainly early education programs for disadvantaged youngsters will continue and will be improved by more follow-through. And the movement as a whole will bring renewed efforts to find better ways of helping young children.

Sex Education in the Public Schools: Problem or Solution?

Ira L. Reiss

Within the next decade the majority of our public schools will in all likelihood have some form of sex education program. Whether this change in our public school curriculum will be the solution to existing problems in the area of sex or whether it will create more problems is a vital question that we ought to face up to now. We still have time to assess the way sex education is being

Reprinted by permission of the *Phi Delta Kappan,* Bloomington, Indiana, from *Phi Delta Kappan* 50:52-56, September, 1968. Copyright 1968 by Phi Delta Kappa, Inc.

integrated today and arrive at a judgment on the wisdom of continuing or changing the present trends.

I have had the opportunity to become familiar with much of the material utilized in the public school sex education programs and with the way the courses are taught and integrated into existing school programs. I don't pretend to have taken a representative sample but I have become familiar with a great many sex education programs. The chief impressions that I have been left with are that the key characteristics of the sex education programs that exist in most of our public schools today are: 1) the courses have strong moralistic and propagandistic elements, 2) the courses stress physiological aspects of sexuality, 3) the courses are isolated and sexual materials are not integrated into other relevant courses in the school system, 4) the teachers of these courses are inadequately trained for an inadequately defined task. It should be clear that much of what is said critically about sex education could be said critically about many other aspects of the educational system, but I will leave that broader task to someone else.

The moral aspect of sex education courses is probably their most easily detectable quality. One has only to glance at course descriptions to find frequent references to teaching the students the "value" of chastity, or the "dangers" of going steady, or a list of reasons why one should avoid heavy petting, "excessive" masturbation, or premarital intercourse. On the positive value side one finds the emphasis on married life so strong that the clear implication is that those from broken homes are in a very "bad" situation. The specific values that are stressed vary somewhat, although they are almost invariably the status quo type. What is crucial is not the specific values but the fact that teachers are morally indoctrinating children in the name of education.

This raises the question that many public schools do not seem to have faced. That is the basic philosophy of education under which they operate. As an academician I can answer this question in a broad way quite easily. There is a general philosophy of education that is most accepted in the colleges among those who are in the education departments as well as among most others. The position is that education is aimed at teaching people *how* to think and not *what* to think. Education is not propaganda or indoctrination. If one teaches about politics, one does not teach that the Republican or Democratic party is the best party. Rather, one teaches people how the political processes work so that the students may be able to handle their own life in this area more intelligently. Similarly, if one teaches about American religions one does not teach that Catholicism or Protestantism is the best religion. Rather, one teaches how the religious institution is organized and how it operates in our society so that if the individual has questions regarding religion, this educational background may aid in his handling of them. The same should be true for teaching about sex.

According to this generally accepted philosophy of education, we would not tell the student that abstinence or permissiveness before marriage is the best form of behavior. We would teach how sexual relationships occur and analyze this so as to increase the student's ability to think calmly and rationally in this area and thereby better handle whatever problems may arise.

Of course, no social institution such as the public schools is free of moral judgments. Judgments of value must be made to decide what is an important enough part of our cultural heritage and our current and future life to be included in the school curriculum. It is also a moral judgment that good education is education that is objective and impartial in its treatment of subject. But such judgments do not bias the way a particular topic is treated; they do not allow us to preach in favor of one political party, one religion, or one sexual standard. The moral judgments that schools allow are operational judgments concerning how the school system should function in our society—and that is quite different from moral judgments favoring a particular moral position on the substance covered in a course.

Granted, it is a difficult thing to be impartial and to maintain an interesting presentation and to avoid mere memorization of facts. In the area of sex, when an objective stance is not taken, when we resort to moralizing, the student's typical reaction is to tune out the teacher. Such indoctrination courses often bore the students who have heard the same thing year after year from other adult sources. Students may take such courses because they are easy and because they take little preparation, but they hardly take them for educational reasons. The goal of teaching people how to think without indoctrination is difficult and achieved at best in part only. But if we do not at least try for this goal, the likelihood of failure to be objective and the likelihood of our educational system becoming more propagandistic would increase greatly. The ideal serves to maintain approximation to standards. Such limitation on moralizing would naturally not apply to religious institutions. Sex education within a church would be expected to contain some moral commitment to the church's position.

The question arises here as to precisely how sex should be taught in order to fit into the public schools. At the present time, the heavy emphasis on physiology and the lack of an integrated curriculum regarding sex is in part a result of the fact that the physiology of sex is an area where teachers find it easier to avoid facing their own hang-ups on sex, i.e., their own emotional feelings. But the stress on physiology overlooks the crucial areas of attitudes and social pressures that mean so much in the full explanation of human sexuality. Also, the educational aids, such as the charts showing the fetus during all nine months of pregnancy and the internal and external organs of the male and female, are readily available. Similar educational materials in the psychological, sociological, and anthropological aspects of sex are not so easily available.

However, this is being remedied by publications issued by SIECUS and other groups. In addition, the National Science Foundation has given grants that will soon lead to revisions in our social studies offerings in the public schools. Some of these changes will include more materials on the entire area of family life.

Part of the question of content is the question of the level of sex education and the specific courses utilized. An isolated course on sex education at the seventh-grade level is hardly an effective way to handle the needs for sex education. If we have decided, as most Americans have, according to recent polls, that sex is an important enough aspect of our life that is should be handled in the public schools, then we have to do more than simply insert one course and feel that we have solved the problem. We must realize that the reason there is a felt need for sex education in the public school curriculum is that the curriculum has been denuded of its sexual content over the generations. Almost all disciplines have had the sexual aspects of their fields removed.

This "sex-ectomy" can be corrected. For example, in economics one of the most fascinating areas to study would be the economics of prostitution. To what extent do the classical laws of supply and demand apply here? In history one would gain much by studying the ways in which the sexual codes of society affected the political life of presidents and kings. The question of the illegitimate child of Grover Cleveland, the sexual interests of Catherine the Great, are but two examples of prime relevance. Social problems courses could discuss the relative effectiveness of various birth control methods in controlling population growth in countries like India. English literature is one of the very few areas where sex hasn't been removed as thoroughly as in other fields. This is predominantly so because to remove it would eliminate much if not most of the valuable literature that forms the subject matter of this field. This is one reason why it is in literature courses that some parents find books to which they object. Such parents lack the philosophy of education we have been speaking about and have more of a moral indoctrination philosophy of education.

My point is that the sex-ectomy should be remedied by putting sex back into all fields. In this way it can be viewed in social and cultural context and will not be given undue importance. After all, sex is not an academic discipline; one cannot major in sex. Thus it has no place as a separate course in a public school system unless one wants to take a kind of "driver's education" approach to it. If we want sex education to have the respect of the teachers and the students, then it would seem the best path to follow would be to integrate it into the legitimate existing disciplines. To do otherwise will make it likely to be taught in moralistic fashion. Of course, such total integration into various courses cannot occur without proper teaching materials and properly trained teachers. It is not something that can occur overnight. However, if we lack integration as a goal we may feel that the one seventh-grade course in sex education really is transmitting all the sexual awareness that is needed, and thereby we would fail to achieve an adequate sex education program. In the public schools as well as in other institutions, it is having well-thought-out, long-range goals that leads to progress.

This brings us to the last characteristic of present-day sex education—the poor quality of many of the teachers involved. Partly, this is due to the fact that what is supposed to be done is poorly defined and often is de-defined in ways that are nontraditional in American education. By this I mean that the course is defined as a kind of moral indoctrination which parents hope will cut down on VD, pre-marital pregnancy, and premarital intercourse. Note that such a demand for "practical" consequences would eliminate most of the courses in our current public school system, particularly those in the humanities area.

Why is it that when we add the "new math" to the public school system we use arguments regarding the ease with which the new math can be learned, its better integration with more advanced forms of mathematics, and so forth? We don't find many arguments that ask why bother to get so involved with mathematics, since most of us won't need to do more than count our change at the movie theater. We don't find such arguments because we have accepted the intrinsic value of mathematics as an area of knowledge that is important enough to our civilization for us to preserve a high level of awareness about it. Why don't we use the same reasoning about sex and justify the "new sex" by contending that such knowledge is an important enough aspect of our way of life that we should have a sound understanding of it? Such an approach would lead to better prepared students in our colleges. The answer is, I think, that in sex we allow our emotions to blind us to the educational philosophy that guides us in the case of mathematics. By doing this we take sex out of the usual academic structure; then it becomes a question of who is qualified to teach this unusual type of course. Often the coach or a friendly housewife is given the task. For a moralistic, applied approach to sex such people may well be relevant, but for an educational approach they clearly are not adequate.

From the point of view of educational philosophy, our basic mistake is to think that when we deal with sex in the public schools we must somehow treat it differently than we do all our other subjects. Different subjects may well require somewhat different pedagogical techniques, but the pedagogical requirement of sex is well within the limits of existing methods. Many classes handle emotionally charged subjects (often more emotional to the teacher than the student) when discussing social problems, novels, and cross-cultural differences. Is sex really so different?

The qualifications for teaching sex in the public schools should be the same as the qualifications for teaching in most other fields. A good teacher needs to be able to establish rapport with the class and needs to be sensitive to ways of clearly communicating to that class. A good teacher must know the subject matter thoroughly and must strive to communicate it at a level that can be understood. A good teacher must be able to handle all aspects of the field, and not be emotionally blocked from covering a particular part of it.

Ideally, sex education would be taught in an integrated fashion; materials could be added to the social science units at all levels. I stress all levels, K—12, because it seems best to start before emotional blocks are too strong and to treat sex as a natural part of all instructional levels. It would seem to be psychologically advantageous to discuss common events like menstruation, masturbation, and marriage before they occur. Children of all ages have a sexual quality to their lives and the discussion of sex is something they are "ready for." They are "mature" enough to handle it if it is presented in accord with sound educational principles.

A teacher whose substantive training is in psychology, sociology, and anthropology would be best equipped to see the obvious places that sex could be incorporated into the social science units. A few of the many ways that sex could be brought easily and naturally into the elementary classroom are discussions of the family, in comparisons of courtship in animals and man, in comparisons of different societies, in discussions of different customs regarding marriage, and in discussions of how our self-image affects our sex life. I stress here the social studies units, for the physiological aspects of sex can more easily and clearly be added to the biological science areas without as much difficulty. Home economics and health courses can incorporate the more applied aspects of sex—the problem-centered and direct role preparation aspects. Naturally, the knowledge of sex gained in a variety of other courses has implications for role preparation and should give greatly increased insight to the students, but home economics and health courses can focus more directly on this applied area. Nevertheless, sex education should not be conceived of as predominantly present in these applied fields, but rather as predominantly centered as one integrated part of many fields. This approach puts sex into a broad human context rather than singling it out as an isolated problem area.

The question of practical strategy necessary to get a sex education program adopted makes it likely that a school system may want to start with one course at a certain grade level. However, unless the person running that course plans to get educational materials and to help coordinate the integration of sex throughout the existing curriculum, the course will not really become part of the educational life of the students. One can, of course, have an interdisciplinary applied-type course on sex; but if that is all one gets into the school system, then sex has not been put back into our schools but rather has simply been fused onto the academic educational system. As long as that state of affairs remains, the course will have low prestige. It will thus be poorly staffed and students will take it for "laughs" and easy grades rather than for educational purposes. The faculty in college education departments will also not look favorably upon an applied course and will do little to further the preparation of competent teachers. The same holds true for "family life education" courses; they, too, most often have no disciplinary "home" and are no more readily accepted. Such family life education also needs to be integrated into existing disciplines.

The real danger in America today is that almost all of our schools will add a type of moralistic, unintegrated, and poorly staffed applied course in sex education and then feel that they have taken care of the needs for sex education. This is exactly what I see happening today in our country and unless we take a longer and more careful look at the matter we may have a sex education program on a national scale that really is an anti-sex education program.

Now let us briefly look at some of the key factors which seem to be pressuring sex education toward becoming an educational failure. One very crucial area affecting the popularity and the success of sex education programs today is the attitude of parents toward sex in their own families. An observer from another culture would be immediately struck by the fact that although parents will readily admit the great importance of sex to their youngsters' future lives, they have a noticeable tendency to avoid discussing sex with their children. It would be difficult to find a comparable situation in any other pattern of American socialization. For example, parents who feel that religion is an important part of their child's present and future life do not hesitate to talk about religion. They do not wait to be asked and then just answer a direct question and go no further. The modern parent seems to do just this on sex. He may rationalize this position by statements about the "readiness" of his child. He may feel that he will give the child "ideas" about sex if he raises the topic. The practical consequences of such an approach are to lessen the influence of the parents and increase the influence of one's peers on one's sex life. By minimizing talk about sex, one does not end the sexual interests of one's child. The child still plays the usual sex games of curiosity and exploration with other children. Sexual information, accurate or not, and sexual attitudes of various sorts inevitably filter down from the older boys and girls to the younger boys and girls. There is no way for parents to stop this; there is only the possibility of extending the parental influences by a more concerted effort to deal with the topic of sex even if the child doesn't initiate it.

Obviously, one key reason for the hushed approach to sex is that the parents haven't yet come to terms with their own attitudes. Also, the parent may feel he doesn't have the needed information. He may feel inadequate to cope with the possible consequences of initiating conversation about sex. Given such parents, it is clear that the consequences of talking about sex might be different if one had parents without such informational and attitudinal hang-ups. In fact, I believe it is the partial realization of this situation that has made sex education in the public schools popular and that has made it of the poor quality that it is at present. Let me briefly explain what I mean.

Many parents may have decided that since they cannot handle sex discussions comfortably with their children, maybe the public school system can help them. It is difficult to say why this didn't happen a few generations ago, but I think one reason is the fact that there has been a shift in the premarital sex partners of middle- and upper-class males from prostitutes to the "girl next door," and so the parents of the girl next door are concerned. Also, many more children are in school now during their most sexually active years. There is increased awareness of the widespread nature of VD and premarital pregnancy even among middle- and upper-class groups. Although the changes are too gradual to be called revolutionary, there has been a noticeable removal of adult heads from the sand. The difficulties of hiding sex becomes greater when it is occurring nearby and when historical and cross-cultural studies point out further its pervasiveness. All our evidence suggests that no culture anywhere at any time on this planet has brought up even the majority of one generation of males to physical maturity as virgins. The major historical shifts have been predominantly in terms of the partners of men—are they prostitutes or are they the girl next door? Such a factual situation needn't affect one's moral values. One can favor for oneself or others goals that cannot be achieved by all, but even so one must realize that the universality of premarital sex of some kind in a child's life experiences makes it an important area to include in a child's education.

Most parents are, naturally, not very conversant with educational philosophies. Thus they haven't generally internalized the idea that teachers should not be moralistic in presenting their subject matter. When social changes make parents think of accepting sex education in the schools, they tend to project their own parental roles on the teacher and feel that she should be moralistic. By this they mean, of course, moralistic in their own way; for they would object violently if the teacher's moralism were in accord with some other group of parents and not with their own.

Public school teachers do not have as highly developed a sense of academic freedom as do college teachers; thus they are more easily intimidated by these parental pressures. In fact, many of them have become so accustomed to pressures from parents, school boards, and principals that they have only retained a very watered down version of the educational philosophy they were taught in college. Therefore, if one wants to obtain an academically respectable approach to sex in the public schools, it is essential to educate the parents and to strengthen the academic freedom of our public school teachers. They may then abide more closely with their original educational philosophy.

Such a closer adherence to accepted educational philosophy would force some parents into an uncomfortable situation. For if they accept the fact that the school is not going to teach their personal morals to all its children, then they cannot thereby escape from teaching sexual morals themselves. That means they will still have to transmit, directly or indirectly, their own moral values regarding sex to their children. Perhaps an adult education program on sex can help. It can aid the parents to understand their own values and the place of sex in their lives, to think through what they want to teach their youngsters and how.

Many practical problems are associated with any attempt to instigate a sound educational approach to sexuality in the public schools. As a sociologist, I realize that the social and cultural setting of the school cannot be fully excluded. It is obvious, for example, that Christmas and Easter and many other religious holidays permeate the school program and very often in obviously religious ways. Perhaps the best one can hope for is that at least films asserting the divinity of Christ will not be used in the schools. But if one does not aim at some objectivity, then such films and similar religious elements would surely permeate our school systems. Accordingly, perhaps certain widely shared values such as the vague notions of the value of love, respect, and responsibility will be endorsed in most all sex education classes. But this is still closer to our ideal of impartiality than would be the teaching of abstinence or permissiveness as the only moral way to behave. Sometimes we overestimate the public opposition to various educational endeavors. For example, I have seen reports that Catholic schools in some cities include more birth control information than do public schools in the same cities. While we cannot totally ignore social pressures, we can avoid exaggerating their potency.

It is also clear that different school settings will affect the emphasis on many school subjects, including sex. In a lower-class neighborhood with high VD and illegitimacy rates one can expect these factors to loom larger in the program. In an upper-class setting the psychological subtleties may well gain more attention. In both cases the approach could be objective. The question of whether to require sex education for all students becomes irrelevant in any school system that incorporates sex into its natural context in a wide variety of fields. Requirement is only an issue when one has but a single isolated course on sex education. The U. S. Office of Education announced in August, 1966, that funds were available to assist communities in the integration of sex into their public school programs and in the training of teachers. The specifics of the program are left up to the judgment of the communities.

One major point to bear in mind is that at least in recent American history the attempt to keep children ignorant of sex has rarely succeeded except in correlating highly with premarital pregnancy rates. The attempt to moralize about sex in public institutions has also not succeeded in changing major patterns of behavior. If we feel that sex is an important aspect of life, then it is important to enable people to think clearly about it. This the public school systems can do if the parents of America will let them. Sex education will not necessarily reduce to nothing our VD and premarital pregnancy rates, but it can, if taught in accord with accepted educational principles, make the sexual choices of our children less psychologically costly. A sound sex education can aid the individual student to choose his or her sex ethic in a more calm and less compulsive fashion. The choice of sex ethics is already an accepted part of youth culture. Young people feel that they have just as much right to choose their sex ethic as to choose their political party or their religion. They feel there are different ways suited best for different people. This is what is often called the "new morality." Parents may well favor one type of choice but ignorance or public moralizing will not achieve that goal. The parents have their chance to influence their child's choices by the values and attitudes they pass on. If they miss out there, they are not likely to change things by preventing a public discussion in a reasonably impartial manner of this area in the publis schools. At least by having a sound sex educational system parents can assure a less compulsive basis for choice. Given the free courtship system we have, we cannot control sexuality directly, nor can we stop the flow of information and attitudes about sex. But we can add an element of enlightenment and control to our youngsters' sexual life by supporting an unbiased approach to it throughout the educational system.

As an educator I feel that we should adopt sound educational approaches to sex in the public schools. As a sociologist I feel that we should not distort by our moralizing the research findings that are available. As a father, I feel that I and not the public schools should do the moral teaching of my children in my own way. If we do not realize the distinct qualities of these various roles we play, we will have sex education in our public schools in a form that will not prepare our children for the sexual aspects of the lives they lead. We will have missed the opportunity to make the best case for our private moral positions.

School Grounds Provide Opportunities for Outdoor Teaching

Thomas J. Rillo

Just outside the classroom walls abound opportunities to enrich the ongoing curriculum if only the teacher would open the door and step outside with the

Reprinted by permission of Ray Page, Superintendent of Public Instruction, State of Illinois, Springfield, Illinois; the *Illinois Journal of Education;* and Thomas J. Rillo, from *Illinois Journal of Education* 58:23-25, September, 1967.

class. Teachers with imagination, ingenuity, and the desire to help young people learn the art of observation can open up new areas of interest and understanding by taking their pupils into the out-of-doors.

Children, wherever they live and whatever they do, in and out of school, meet problems that involve both experiences and understandings. They achieve these understandings best through firsthand experiences and actual, purposeful contacts with materials, forces, and processes that affect their own lives.

To be effective, teaching must be closely related to circumstances that will arise outside the classroom. Young or old, we all learn best by doing. The more realistic the learning activity is, the more meaningful and lasting will be the lesson. There is little justification for merely looking at something which can be touched, handled, and used, or for just textbook presentations when the real-life situations are at hand. On the school grounds the student can do more than merely look. Experimentation and manipulation, practice and discussion characterize this outdoor laboratory.

In the outdoor laboratory the pupil may, through observation and direct experience, develop appreciations, skills, and understandings that will supplement the indoor curriculum of the school.

Outdoor education then becomes a practical approach to aspects of those subjects which are normally taught only in the indoor classroom. Outdoor education is the effective utilization of the natural environment to help promote the growth, welfare, and total education of the student.

The outdoor experience should have clear-cut, definite relationship to the regular school curriculum if it is to find acceptance on the part of parents and educators. A thorough examination of the curriculum must first be made and those concepts and learnings which can best be assimilated indoors should be developed there. However, those concepts and learnings which can be developed more effectively in the natural environment of the school grounds should be accomplished there. The school site is an excellent laboratory for learning, for it is near at hand and the teacher and the class can move in or out whenever it is feasible and right to do so.

Two of the major problems confronting the teacher without a background in outdoor teaching is that of finding an area suitable for study and that of supervising and organizing the class while out-of-doors. The preparation for outdoor teaching need not be extensive; however, it should be sufficient enough to act as a catalyst in the inspiration of teachers to utilize the outdoor environment whenever it is appropriate. The school grounds then become an excellent place for the beginning of outdoor experiences for pupils as well as teachers.

The late Dr. Lloyd B. Sharp contended that if outdoor education is to become an integral part of the total school curriculum it should start when a youngster first begins his schooling and continue in each grade level and in any curriculum area. In order for this concept to be implemented, utilization of the school grounds for outdoor experiences becomes imperative.

The school with the greatest variety in the outdoor environment will teach the most about man's relationship to his natural environment provided it is utilized effectively by teachers. However, even an apparently barren school ground can offer a great deal in terms of curriculum potential for outdoor teaching and learning.

The following school site survey is offered as an aid to teachers and administrators who are interested in the utilization of the school grounds for outdoor experiences correlated with the indoor curriculum. To use this survey, it is suggested that teachers examine the curriculum potential of the school grounds and check the available areas.

A Preliminary School Site Survey
for Outdoor Education

School Building
— Wood Frame
— Stucco
— Brick
— Other

Trees
— Shade Trees (native or planted)
— Plantations (deciduous or coniferous)
— School Forest (arboretum or experimental)

Shrubs
— Foundation Plantings
— Hedges (windbreaks, dust filters, erosion checks, etc.)
— Bushes (native species usually growing over grasses)

Grass Areas
— Lawn (soil stabilization, flowers)
— Playfields (soil stabilization)
— Wild grass

Forb Areas (Forbs are nonwoody, herbaceous plants, e.g., golden rod, bull thistle, etc.)

— Annual Plants
— Perennial Plants

Barren Areas
— Paved Areas (playgrounds, streets, parking lots, sidewalks)
— Eroded Areas (drainage ditches, drain pipes, exposed hills, etc.)
— Graveled Areas (driveways, parking areas, walks, etc.)

Water Areas
— Streams (drain pipes are a good substitute)
— Ponds
— Puddles
— Ditches (water runoff)
— Storm Sewers and Gutters

Elevations
— Hill Slope (gradual or steep)
— Hilltops (plateaus or pinnacles)

Animal Signs
— Homes (in trees, under roots, holes in the ground, on tree branches, etc.)

——Droppings (on stumps, side-walks, grass, side of build-ings, fences, etc.)

——Tracks (in mud, dust, etc.)

Wetland Areas

——Swamps (forested or in shrubs and bushes)

——Bog

——Marsh (cattails, grasses, reeds, etc.)

—— Flood Areas (sedimentation, debris, etc.)

Rocks and Mineral Areas

—— Stone walls

——Sidewalks

——Driveways and Parking Lots (graveled)

—— Curb Stones

—— Eroded Areas (exposed rocks)

Outlying Areas (near school grounds)

—— Open Fields

—— Croplands

—— Orchards

—— Deserted Farms

—— Old Graveyards

—— Old Building Foundations

—— Tree Stumps

—— Fence Rows

—— Nurseries (trees, shrubs, etc.)

—— Local Parks

—— State Parks

—— Vacant lots

—— Excavations

The Handicapped in the Regular Classroom

Samuel C. Ashcroft

Many educators agree that the regular classroom is the best place for most children with physical impairments to receive their schooling. Advances in medicine and changes in the schools are making it increasingly feasible for them to be enrolled in such classrooms. Experts are developing new skills for the educational management and remediation of children who have the kind of learning disabilities frequently associated with physical impairment. Modern building methods, particularly those used in school construction, are removing architectural barriers.

This article is designed to set the stage for the special feature which follows and to help give teachers the general understanding they need to deal with the increasing number of physically handicapped children who will take their places in regular classrooms.

Reprinted by permission of the National Education Association, Washington, D.C., and Samuel C. Ashcroft from *NEA Journal* 56:33-34, November, 1967.

Some physically handicapped children have muscular and/or skeletal difficulties which result in obvious motor disabilities (impaired ambulation, hand use, speech). Others may have impairments not immediately apparent: chronic or special health conditions, lowered vitality, or poor general health. All such children may have significant problems in school learning and adjustment.

Fortunately, we know many things about the children who are physically impaired, and most of what we know suggests that classroom teachers can usually do a great deal not only to educate such children but to promote their acceptance and to foster their general welfare.

The physically handicapped have a wide range of individual differences: They vary greatly in the nature, extent, and severity of their physical impairments and related disabilities and handicaps. Their scholastic aptitude, intellectual ability, and learning characteristics range from superior to very inferior. Their personal-social characteristics range from excellent to poor. (Much of the variation in personal-social characteristics among children who are physically handicapped, as well as that between such children and their nonhandicapped age, grade, or ability peers, can be attributed to environmental factors rather than to the physical impairment or to other stable characteristics, such as those which are genetic and/or physiological.)

Children with physical impairments frequently have specific learning disabilities. Such disabilities may be related to cognitive, perceptual, motoric, or environmental factors which complicate or prevent the children's development of skills in spoken or written language, reading, arithmetic, and other scholastic areas.

Because of their great heterogeneity, no universal characteristic of these children as a group provides a meaningful guide to understanding the individual child who is physically handicapped. Teachers should not rely on stereotypes as a guide to reacting to and working with the child who has physical handicaps.

A large proportion of handicapped children will have some type of neurological involvement, ranging from very mild neuromuscular and/or orthopedic impairment to severe central nervous system and motor complications. The medical diagnostic labels of most such impairments will be related to their causes: cerebral palsied (or, more specifically, spastic, athetoid, ataxic), brain-damaged, or post-encephalitic. Although these labels and related classifications are important for medical, physical, and occupational therapy, they neither prescribe, require, nor guide specific related educational treatment.

Even though intellectual retardation frequently accompanies physical impairment, the teacher must be aware that many children with severe physical handicaps are quite able intellectually. The uncritical use or faulty interpretation of conventional psychological and educational tests and testing procedures can vastly complicate the assessment of intellectual ability. Many children with physical handicaps have been misdiagnosed as retarded individuals because of motor and/or communication or learning problems which interfere with test performance.

An unnecessary amount of experiential deprivation may accompany physical impairment. Parents and teachers, by overprotecting, can contribute to such deprivation. Loss of motor coordination or mobility complicates, but need not prevent, the acquisition of many valuable experiences. All the child's potential for mobility needs to be exploited so that the child is able to get to and be involved in important childhood learning experiences. While some experiences must be brought to the child, overdoing this can prevent him from developing the motivation, curiosity, and mobility he needs to engage in significant experiences.

Educational retardation frequently accompanies physical impairment. Both intellectual retardation and experiential deprivation contribute to educational retardation, as do loss of school time for medical treatment, absence for recuperation and rest, and inappropriate or inadequate school placement or programing. Cooperation on the part of the school, physician, and child will keep such lost time at a minimum.

Setting realistic goals is one of the major problems in the educational management of children with physical impairments. The tendency is to expect either too little or too much from such children. Evidence indicates that children learn to set unrealistic levels of aspiration for themselves as a result of inappropriate expectations by others. The best objective for the teacher would seem to be to arrange assignments of just manageable difficulty. The goal should be ever-increasing independence in functioning through success experiences.

Below are several suggestions for the classroom teacher with physically impaired students:

● Be guided by behavioral and functional evidence of abilities and disabilities instead of making educational decisions solely in terms of medical diagnoses or stereotyped thinking about categories of physical impairment.

● View the physical impairment as only one of many important attributes of the child rather than as if it were his most significant characteristic.

● Provide a setting for, and expect achievement of, the pupil in terms of his aptitudes, abilities, and other attributes, not in terms of his physical impairment alone. Differentiate the effects of physical limitations from effects that have their source in other environmental causes, such as experiential deprivation, educational retardation, and attitudes.

● Obtain assistance in the form of constructive consultation and specialized equipment or materials from those who assume special responsibilities for children with physical impairment. However, consider the child one of *your* students rather than "one of theirs" (the special educators').

● Remember that the child with physical impairment probably needs as many firsthand experiences as possible. Help the child to develop concepts meaningful to him and in line with his own reality. Do not impose upon him artificial concepts he cannot understand or appreciate because of his lack of mobility or experience.

● Do not thoughtlessly exploit the child with physical impairment by showing him off to other children, to teachers, or to visitors.

How to Teach in a Ghetto School

Sidney Trubowitz

Current communication media focus on the failure of teachers to reach slum children. The fact remains, however, that some teachers in deprived areas do achieve success. How do they manage to create an educational environment in which children adhere to standards and apply themselves academically? The following discussion is based on interviews with some successful Harlem teachers and reports from their students and supervisors.

The teacher who succeeds in a ghetto school either has no abnormal expectations to start with or has found that bizarre behavior is just that—unusual rather than typical. By walking through the neighborhood, shopping in the stores, visiting in the homes, and talking to people in the community, he has gained some awareness of the backgrounds, the values, and the aspirations of the children and their parents. He has gained perspective through reading Negro magazines and newspapers, sociological treatises (those of Myrdal, Frazier, and Handlin), and the personal reminiscences of people like Roi Ottley, Claude Brown, and James Baldwin.

This kind of background helps a teacher gain insight into children's lives. It helps him to relate to the children and their parents in a way that commands their respect and convinces them that success in school is possible. It helps him to see Negroes as people like himself, desiring acceptance, wanting to believe in the possible fulfillment of aspirations.

The successful ghetto teacher clearly defines limits and shows his respect and liking for the children by insisting that they maintain standards. Teacher after teacher has stressed the importance of this.

Reprinted by permission of the National Education Association, Washington, D.C., and Sidney Trubowitz from *Today's Education* 57:26-29, October, 1968.

"Set up routines carefully," they say. "Let the children know what's expected."

"If you insist on regulations, the children will live up to them," another says.

These teachers, recognizing the value of firm structure, work with children on routines for entering the room, using the pencil sharpener, walking through corridors, distributing materials, checking homework, and changing seats for small group instruction.

Successful teachers have discovered that the classroom itself provides a means of talking to children without words. By providing an ordered, pleasant environment, the teacher gives children experience with a place that encourages respect and care. The enjoyment that children show as they guide visitors around the room indicates the pride they take in the appearance of their classroom. The use of colorful pictures, particularly of minority group children, can help give pupils a personal identification with their surroundings. Periodic changes of displays keep the children curious. Exhibits of the children's own work give recognition to their accomplishments. An attractive room is an offering by the teacher to the children.

Many children in depressed-area schools have had repeated experience with failure. The successful teacher knows that he must convince children of their ability to achieve. Rather than allowing himself to be overwhelmed by a child's apparent weakness, whether in academic achievement or emotional growth, the successful teacher learns to recognize, value, and develop the individual strengths possessed by each child.

One teacher described her approach this way: "I know that for many children school has been one big flop. I look for chances for children to contribute. If a child knows a song or a poem or a story, I let him present it. If a child just seems to have something to say, I let him say it. I try to make them feel good about themselves."

Another teacher explained her method of dealing with children who have failed academically. "These are kids who are deathly afraid of schoolwork. They feel they can't do it, that they'll be laughed at, or that they'll be marked as dumb. It helps when you encourage them and when you accept what they have to offer. For example, when they write or tell stories, I emphasize their ideas and not their grammar. After a while the ideas begin to flow, and they've got some good ones."

Other teachers planned opportunities for individual contact. One teacher said, "I try to give each child a few minutes every day." The teacher who gives individual attention to a child who is having learning difficulty is telling the child that when he makes a mistake adults don't necessarily punish or reject but stand by to help. By spending time with a child, the teacher says to him, "You are important to me." And the teacher who helps a child to find the answer himself is expressing confidence and declaring to the child that he has a basis for respecting his own ability.

The new teacher in the ghetto needs to realize that he may sometimes be defied, he may see fighting, and he may hear profanity. The successful teachers do not condone any and all actions, but instead of dealing with deviations from acceptable school behavior in a single, stereotyped manner, they examine the reasons underlying the deviant act. They ask such questions as:

Does the defiant child say, "I won't take my sweater off," because his shirt is torn or because the sweater is new? Does a boy fight because he is accustomed to protecting himself in this way or because he has seen adults frequently use this method to solve problems? Does a child use profanity to test authority or is it to express anger?

Determining the answers to questions like these guides teachers toward intelligent and effective ways of dealing with deviant behavior.

Louis E. Harper and Benjamin Wright in *The Exceptional Child* indicate the special importance of the teacher's managing his feelings in times of stress, so that he does not require all his emotional energy himself. Only if he is free from a preoccupation with his own needs will the teacher be able to remain sensitive to the child's needs and to help him.

Successful teachers are open with the children regarding their own feelings. As one teacher said, "A teacher in a ghetto neighborhood has to develop the capacity to accept his own human feelings and to express them if need be. The children don't expect you to be godlike."

These teachers communicate a sense of being close to the children and the community. They stop to buy sodas at the corner candy store, telephone or visit children who are ill, have friends visit the school, and bring personal possessions—family snapshots or souvenirs, for example—to show to the class.

The children identify with people who identify with them. Describing his teacher, one child said, "She knows how we feel inside. She lets us write about how we feel. She tells us she feels the same things sometimes."

Successful teachers in ghetto schools reach beyond the normal, everyday routine of teaching. One took the children to the library after three o'clock. Another escorted children to a puppet show. A group of teachers in a Harlem school met with some of the parents during the summer at the home of one of the teachers to work out a cooperative approach to school problems.

Successful teachers in the ghetto use a knowledge of the past experiences of children as a guide to help them acquire new skills, new knowledges, and new attitudes. They try to help children discover the relationships that exist between their past experiences and present classroom activities. They let the deep, lasting interests of the children guide them in approaching and choosing the curriculum. For example, teachers might use the question, "What caused your family to move to this neighborhood?" as a means of introducing these children, many of whom are from transient families, to a study of the westward movement of the pioneers.

Many of the children do the family marketing, and this experience can motivate lessons about spending money wisely and planning meals carefully. Children's experience in handling money can be used to develop their arithmetic skills.

Children's academic weaknesses are sometimes the result of negative environmental factors or unfortunate earlier school experiences. Many children, for instance, have developed poor listening habits. Perhaps a child learns in a home that is a maelstrom of different sounds (of television, of other children, of the street, and of strangers) to eliminate sound from his consciousness in order to develop an inner life of his own. Maybe they haven't learned to listen because, as Martin Deutsch indicates in his research, the most impoverished area activity for low socioeconomic children is that of language feedback in adult-child interactions. Sometimes past schoolwork has been so irrelevant to their experience that lack of interest blocks listening.

Teachers get good results by planning experiences designed to improve the children's listening ability. Some of these are: listening to dramatizations of such narrative poems as "The Creation" by James Weldon Johnson; involving children in informal conversations; using the telephone to act out imaginary conversations; and using the tape recorder to rehearse for assembly programs.

Many ghetto children read below grade level. For them, reading means failure, distasteful labor, joyless exposure to unintelligible concepts. In *Teacher,* Sylvia Ashton-Warner gives a clue to an approach that can change this when she says that books "must be made of the stuff of the child himself, whatever and wherever the child."

Books that are painfully white, nonurban, insipid in content, with pictures completely foreign to the child will very likely produce mechanical, sterile reading. Other books do interest the children—tales of fantasy, for example, or science fiction stories. One teacher, referring to the children's ability to relate to the world of fantasy, said, "They have to have vivid imaginations to get away from their everyday world of dreariness."

To some children, all books seem synonymous with failure. In these cases, inventive teachers utilize other reading materials. One teacher made summaries of stories and had them copied for the children. Another took the developmental vocabulary contained in the basal reader and made up realistic stories using this vocabulary. Other teachers have used filmstrips as a source of reading material. One teacher projected the words of songs on a screen, and the children read them together; another used "story" arithmetic problems. All the teachers who were interviewed used experience charts that dealt with such matters as walks through the park, rides on the subway, and ways to improve the neighborhood.

Successful ghetto teachers concentrate on and use the strengths the youngsters bring into the classroom. For example, many ghetto children display a knack for expressive language. One child calls a hole in his sock a potato in his shoe; another says that a cloud is the color of ham fat. There are children who can insult each other in neatly turned phrases.

Creative teachers find opportunities for children to use this verbal strength. Some permit children to express their gripes orally or in writing. Others arrange for small groups to discuss the things in school that help them to learn and the things that keep them from learning. The fact that the teacher listens closely to these discussions is a stimulus to further expression and a sign of respect for the worth of what the children say. When the children notice this respect for their efforts, they begin to see the value of language and to develop a desire to use it more effectively and more grammatically.

Children's curiosity is another strength that teachers can put to use. When teachers bring flowers from their gardens or shells from the shore, they find that children move easily and enthusiastically into a study of these things. Setting up and caring for aquariums and terrariums leads children to look in books for information about them, to write up results, and to develop a sense of pride and possession in their room.

Successful teachers realize that children's feelings are a facet of all curriculum content. They encourage communication and cooperation by showing children that their vital needs, as represented by their inner emotions, are understood. Children will not become involved with subject matter that does not take their feelings into account.

For example, class trips represent a situation that arouses the fears of some children. One child, with total seriousness, remarked as his class discussed a forthcoming trip to Chinatown: "We've got to be careful down there. They're liable to poison us." Some children always choose to remain behind when their classes go on trips. Others stay close to the teacher as they walk around in strange surroundings. If trips are to have optimum value, teachers need to deal with fears of this sort.

A teacher who is truly familiar with the lives of ghetto children, who learns about their experiences, their interests, their feelings, their needs, their strengths, and their weaknesses, is more likely to use the subject matter and approach that have meaning for his pupils.

Joe Doesn't Pledge Allegiance

Ruth Stephens MacGorman

"Please excuse Joe from pledging allegiance to the flag because of religious beliefs," read the note handed to me by one of my sixth grade pupils on the first day of school, some years ago.

I looked at the boy, but he kept his eyes on the floor. Obviously painfully shy and retiring and seeming by his very manner to apologize for being present at all, Joe, I sensed, had been bearing the brunt of his parents' convictions before he was old enough to accept or reject them for himself.

What would be the kindest way to handle the matter? Rather than risk embarrassing Joe by speaking of it publicly in his presence, I decided for the time being to accept without comment his not saluting the flag, hoping that my attitude toward him would rub off on the rest of the class.

But in spite of my example, most of the class reacted to Joe with indignation and disdain, and he became even more withdrawn.

In an effort to improve Joe's status, I often put his papers on our "Good Work" bulletin board; called attention to his writing achievements, which were better than average; and did a little underhanded campaigning to get him elected to one of our class committees. Then I bided my time until the day of his first absence.

At last that day arrived, and I began our social studies lesson with these words: "I am sure all of you have noticed that Joe does not stand and say the Pledge of Allegiance to the flag each morning. This makes him different from the rest of us. And because he is different in this way, I am afraid some of you have treated him as though he were bad.

"Usually if we understand why people act as they do, we can learn to appreciate them. That is why I am taking this time when Joe is absent to explain his behavior to you.

"The religious group to which he belongs believes in pledging allegiance only to God. Joe's parents have told him that this is what he must do, and each morning he is obeying them. He and his parents know that many people are strongly in favor of pledging allegiance to the flag and therefore will not like their actions. But part of the greatness of our country lies in our Constitution, which guarantees to every American citizen the right to exercise freely his religion without fear of persecution.

Reprinted by permission of the National Education Association, Washington, D.C., and Ruth Stephens MacGorman from *Today's Education* 57:63, November, 1968.

"We have studied about several communist countries. Do you imagine that in any of them a boy or girl in public school would be allowed to refuse to pledge allegiance to his country?"

Several hands went up. "I don't think so, Teacher, because I remember that all the schools are controlled by the government."

"Yeah, and think of all those people who have been killed or sent off to labor camps because they disagreed with the government!"

"Then why," I asked, "in our country can Joe and others like him disagree with the government?"

"Because our country is better."

"We have freedom of religion."

"And freedom of speech, too."

Finally I suggested that one good way to show that we love our country and believe in our Constitution is by trying to appreciate people who differ from us.

On Joe's return to school, it seemed as though the collective arms of the class opened to embrace a fellow human being who needed them and to whom they owed a back debt of kindness.

As each child tried to outdo the others, shy unassuming Joe blossomed in the warmth of this unexpected attention. He even began contributing to class discussions. When at last he started participating in an occasional sixth grade misbehavior, I knew he had become a true member of the group.

Final proof that the message of democracy had gotten through to the class came some time later. In my absence from school one day, the substitute scolded Joe for his refusal to stand and say the Pledge.

When I returned, each of my 28 little reporters began his recital of the previous day's events with an account of the teacher's rebuke to Joe. And each felt affronted because a fellow classmate had not been treated with the proper respect due him as an American citizen and as a valuable human being. The social studies lesson had indeed been learned!

Christmas in the Classroom

David L. Barr

"Tis the season to be jolly..." unless you are a teacher. For many a teacher, it is the season to be wary. Today's parents listen with care to their children's accounts of Christmas activities at school. The community observes with more than passing interest the seasonal lawn displays, and question marks appear in the eyes of many adults observing the school pageant.

Yet the Supreme Court decisions which aroused public concern over the practice of religion in the public schools in no way prohibit the study of the Bible or religion in the classroom. In both the 1962 N. Y. State Regents prayer case (Engle vs. Vitale) and the 1963 Bible-reading decision (Abington vs. Schempp), the Court was dealing with the *practice* of religion. In both cases, the Court ruled that *any* establishment of a practice of religion violates the First Amendment. Yet in the same decision the Court stated, "Nothing we have said here indicates that such study of the Bible or of religion, when presented objectively as part of a secular program of education, may not be effected consistent with the First Amendment."

The rulings affect the public schools' treatment of Christmas in two ways. First, the schools can no longer deal with Christmas as if its entire constituency were Christian. Secondly, those aspects of Christmas in the schools which take on the nature of a *practice* of religion must be eliminated.

What must be prevented is the school's taking sides in matters of belief. The school must not celebrate Christmas as if it believed the Christians were right, nor—and this is imperative—can it celebrate Christmas as if the Christians were wrong. The school must be neutral.

Neutrality is an elusive concept to define and perhaps even more elusive to implement, but it is the Constitutional standard. Blaine Fister, head of the National Council of Churches' public school division, declares: "The limits imposed, then, by the neutrality concept are indoctrination into specific religious beliefs or indoctrination into disbeliefs." To be neutral, the school neither celebrates Christmas nor ignores it.

Schools must do *something* with Christmas. In fact, this is the recommendation of the American Association of School Administrators' special commission on religion in the public school: "The commission recommends the policy that encourages reasonable recognition of Christmas in the schools in the spirit of exposition...." (*Religion in the Public Schools,* Harper.)

Reprinted by permission from *Scholastic Teacher,* Elementary Edition 17:11, 14, December 6, 1968. ©1968 by Scholastic Magazines, Inc., Englewood Cliffs, N.J.

This brings us to the heart of the matter. Although the public school cannot sponsor a *practice* of religion, it may sponsor a *study* of religion. The public school may deal with Christmas as it deals with many other controversial topics. It may study Christmas, what people believe about it, why they believe these things, and how those beliefs have affected our history, literature, and art.

Beyond this, the school must be sensitive to the student's beliefs and convictions and try to encourage him to develop those beliefs in a spirit of free inquiry. This cannot be done either by establishing a "right" approach to Christmas, or by ignoring Christmas, and thus teach by inference that it is not important.

The general principle may be formulated thus: The public school should approach Christmas in an attempt to educate the student, not to convert him. Its purpose is to study, not to worship.

This does not mean that the individual student may not worship—he may. The free exercise of his religion is guaranteed. If he chooses to worship while singing a carol the school is teaching him for some educational purpose, the school may not stop him. The point is that the school teaches him to sing as a learner, not as a worshiper.

The validity of an activity or procedure will be found not in the procedure itself but in the use made of it. An example of this comes from Ohio. One of the selections for the state's 1968 music contest was "Ave Maria." Many irate parents objected to this song as a prayer and asked POAU (Protestants and Other Americans United for the Separation of Church and State) to take the case to court. POAU refused. Commenting on the schools' right to use religious material in a nonreligious way, they said the case had "no merit."

In Hudson, Calif., a controversy over what could constitute a Christmas program produced this administrative ruling: "It is permissible and in keeping with the educational code (Section 8453) to present at the Christmas season any program depicting the Christmas story if the program is historical, cultural, or educational in nature."

Twice in New York, questions about nativity scenes on public school property have reached sufficient proportions to result in court cases (1958, 1963). In both cases the courts ruled nativity scenes permissible, but questions remain. Most legal experts seem to agree that such questions as the propriety of a nativity scene cannot be determined in advance, that this and many related questions can be answered only on the basis of the *use* made of the object in question: this use must not constitute a religious ceremony or activity. There seems to be some difference between the use of nativity scenes in an elementary classroom to explain the historical origin of Christmas and the public display of such scenes without comment.

Justice Tom Clark, who wrote the majority opinion in the 1963 Bible-reading case, attempted to explain the test the Court used when he said: "The test laid down in our cases seems to be that the purpose of a required exercise must be secular with a primary effect that neither advances nor inhibits religion. It, therefore, depends on the circumstances."

"Depends on the circumstances" was much the same kind of guideline that former Attorney General Edward Brooke of Massachusetts was using when he indicated in an official opinion that religious items, such as trees and nativity scenes, could be used if the purpose is "to promote understanding and tolerance. . . ."

The policy for the school to follow with respect to Christmas—and to every other area in which religious ideas, persons, or events touch the curriculum—is to study various beliefs and practices without attempting to indoctrinate the student or to infringe upon his freedom of conscience. The school must approach this in the spirit of neutrality and from a position of objectivity.

This, then, is what we are saying: The school may handle religious material at Christmas (the Bible, carols, religious symbols, and pageants). It may even do things other people do for worship (such as singing carols), but it must always do so for the purposes of education and not for the purposes of religion. It must do so in an open spirit of exposition, not attempting to impose certain attitudes or beliefs.

The school may not offend the religious beliefs of any group, nor may it endorse those beliefs. But it may study them, examine them, and understand them. For the teacher, Christmas can, after all, be a "season to be jolly."

The Best Start is an Early Start

Annette Grubman

Right from the very first day in school is the time to begin teaching about the Afro-American's contribution to our history.

Attitude formation is everything in the primary grades. What attitudes are your youngsters forming about themselves and others?

Do you still take out a peach-colored crayon to tell your primary graders which crayon to use to color skin? That's attitude formation. Do you only talk

Reprinted from *Grade Teacher* Magazine 86:107-110, April, 1969, by permission of the publishers. Copyright April, 1969 by *Teachers Publishing Corporation,* Darien, Connecticut.

about the "normal" family structure of mother, father, son and daughter, ignoring the possibility that some of your youngsters may live in broken homes, or with aunts, uncles or grandparents? That's attitude formation, too.

It's immaterial whether you teach an all-white class in an all-white suburb, an integrated group in an integrated neighborhood or an all-black class in a ghetto. *All* children need to have a strong self-image. All children must learn to respect and value individual differences.

Let's go back to that peach-colored crayon. Next time your children are coloring skin, use the situation as a teachable moment. Talk about different shades and colors of skin. Langston Hughes' poem, "Harlem Sweetie," can be read to the children. Discuss the various shades of skin—white, yellow, brown. Read *Your Skin and Mine* by Paul Showers (Crowell, New York). Now you're working towards creating "multi-ethnic attitudes" for an multi-ethnic society.

Start in Kindergarten

Most kindergartners generally study the family, the school and various groups. A kindergarten where positive multi-ethnic attitudes are being shaped studies these same subjects. Only the teaching tools differ:

The bulletin board contains pictures of black and white families. The doll corner has Negro dolls as well as white dolls in it. The pictures of play groups and school groups are multi-ethnic. Multi-ethnic picture books are available in the library corner. Discussion pictures—many are produced commercially—serve as excellent sources for encouraging the study of how groups live together comfortably. *Pictures for Beginning Social Studies* by Raymond H. Muessig (Harper & Row, New York) is an excellent multi-ethnic approach which introduces basic social studies concepts and puts strong emphasis on human relations. Other discussion pictures are published by Holt, Rinehart and Winston (New York) and Silver Burdett (Morristown, N.J.). The latter's pictures (in *Families and Their Need* series) relating to African countries will be helpful when discussing the culture of Africa. Pictures from magazines and newspapers can also be used for display and discussion purposes. These devices help you convey the idea that all black families and white families have similar needs and wants. Books such as *Evan's Corner* by Elizabeth Hill (Holt, Rinehart and Winston, New York) and *Sam* by Ann Scott (McGraw-Hill, New York) will reinforce this concept.

Introduce your children to the names and lives of famous Afro-Americans at the same time you begin to name other famous Americans—e.g. Frederick Douglass, Harriet Tubman, Martin Luther King, Jr. For example, when celebrating Lincoln's and Washington's birthdays in February, add that of Douglass. There are many good books about Harriet Tubman for primary grades. *The Story of Harriet Tubman, The Runaway Slave,* by Ann McGovern (Four Winds, New York) is one that primary children can read themselves, or you can read the beautifully illustrated storybook *Harriet and the Promised Land* by Jacob Lawrence (Simon and Schuster, New York) to them. There are several books on Dr. King. One of the newest is *Martin Luther King, Jr.* by Margaret Boone-Jones (Children's Press, Chicago).

The world of children's literature contains innumerable books that fit into an integrated teaching program. The themes often are universal without reference to race, but pictures are of black children or involve both black and white children. The widespread use of these books helps destroy the stereotyped view of the black. The Ezra Jack Keats books, the books by Beth Horvath, Crosby N. Bonsall and others treat black characters as one should treat children anywhere.

The Two Friends by Grete Mannheim (Knopf, New York) tells about a child's first day at school, making friends, etc. Many kindergarten children will find the experiences expressed in this book familiar. After reading the book encourage the children to talk about their first day in school. Have them draw pictures of the friends they made.

First-grade Reading

As one moves into the first-grade program, reading, of course, is the predominant curriculum area. Of many basic texts I think the *Bank Street Readers* (Macmillan, New York) and the *City Schools Program* (Follett, Chicago) best support a multi-ethnic approach to such subjects as the neighborhood, the farm and the local community. In introducing neighborhood schools or families around the world, the teacher can discuss various ways of life in African countries, showing that groups all have similar wants and needs—economic security, housing, clothing, success in their roles in the family.

A number of books and other materials are helpful in showing the inter-relatedness of family and economic roles—for example, *Father Is Big* by Ruth and Edward Radlauer (Bowmar, Glendale, Calif.) and *Hush Jon* by Joan Gill (Doubleday, New York). The filmstrip, *Robert and His Family* (Society for Visual Education, Chicago) can also be used in a family unit.

The pride a child feels for his or her father is expressed in *What Mary Jo Shared* by Janice M. Udry (Whitman, Chicago). *Father Is Big* expresses the same feelings of pride at a younger reading level. *Do You Know What* (Early Childhood Series), edited by Nancy Curry (Bowmar, Glendale, Calif.) is a book in which a child talks about the different names by which she is known. The story provides a splendid jumping off place for group discussion of the various nicknames parents, grandparents and other older friends have for children.

The variety of city life can be illustrated by using a number of books. *Evan's Corner* gives one view of community life, while *Hush Jon* gives another. So does Gwendolyn Brooks' poem "Rudolph Is Tired of the City."

As one moves into the first grade, the "I Can Read" books by Bonsall, *The Case of the Hungry Stranger, Case of the Cat's Meow* (Harper & Row, New

York) show how children play successfully together irrespective of color. Lorrain and Jerold Beim's *Two Is A Team* (Harcourt, Brace and World, New York) shows how children can work together for the same goals. The universal concern of children for animals is illustrated in Stan Williamson's *No Bark Dog* (Follett, Chicago).

In many second grades, the social studies program includes a unit on community helpers. Certainly, this unit should help children realize that people of all races contribute to the community. If you live in an integrated community, fine—buttonhole black teachers, lawyers, policemen, firemen and nurses and ask them to speak to the class about their contributions to the life of the community.

If your community is predominantly white, show how we are part of a world community and how many black Americans contribute to a better life for all of us. Point to contributions being made today by such men as Dr. Ralph Bunche, Supreme Court Justice Thurgood Marshall, Robert Weaver, Senator Edward Brooke, Julian Bond and others.

Many third-grade classes learn about the branches of our federal government. It would be appropriate to indicate that although Senator Brooke is the only Negro sitting in the U.S. Senate, he is not the first. Children can research and find that there were Negro Senators and Congressmen during Reconstruction.

In third grade a large map can be used to show the origin of our ancestors. Whether or not black children are in the room, you can indicate that a large group of Americans originally came from Africa. At this point, teachers could read some African folk tales. For second- and third-graders use *Why The Stones Were Soft* by Verna Aardema (Coward-McCann, New York). Proverbs of Africa and America can be used to show how people all over the world have similar thoughts and express them in a similar manner. Use *A Crocodile Has Me by the Leg*, edited by Leonard W. Doob (Walker, New York). Provide African proverbs and let the children provide the American counterpart. An example: African—*He was born with a full set of teeth;* American—*He was born with a silver spoon in his mouth.* (See *Grade Teacher's* special report on "Teaching About Africa," Oct. '68.)

Language, Music and Art

The primary-grade child should be introduced to poetry and literature as soon as possible. This provides an opportunity to introduce Afro-American authors and some of America's most beautiful literature. As an example, *Bronzeville Boys and Girls* by Gwendolyn Brooks (Harper & Row, New York) is the kind of poetry that children can enjoy and understand and is appropriate for all grade levels. Miss Brooks' poems such as "Charles," "Keziah," "Cynthia in the Snow" and "Eppie" express feelings all children experience. The universality of her poetry reminds us that when it comes to feeling all people are similar.

African art as compiled by Shirley Glubok in *The Art Of Africa* (Harper & Row, New York) can lead to some excellent art experiences. After studying masks, children can design their own. They may also want to design musical instruments after the African fashion. *The Africans Knew* by Tillie Pine and Joseph Levine (McGraw-Hill, New York) gives many examples of how early Africans lived and suggests ways children can construct items similar to those used in Africa long ago.

The Negro spiritual is very much a part of American music. However, it is important for the children to understand that these beautiful, poignant songs often served as protest music, expressing human anguish and dissatisfaction. The words cannot just be taken at face value.

There are innumerable books worth utilizing in an integrated school curriculum. Keats' *John Henry* (Pantheon, New York) is a tremendous contribution to American folklore. There is a record and filmstrip by Harcourt, Brace and World (New York) which follows Keats' text. The "I Can Read" books by Leonard Kessler (Harper & Row, New York) for beginning readers are excellent. *Big Cowboy Western* by Ann Scott (Lothrop, Lee and Shepard, New York), *A Ride on High* by Candida Palmer (Lippincott, Philadelphia) and *Hooray for Jasper* by Beth Horvath (Watts, New York) are just plain fun. *The Valentine Box* by Maud Lovelace (Crowell, New York), *The Halloween Kangaroo* by Mary Lewis (Ives Washburn, New York), and *Christmas Gif'* by Charlemae Rollins (Follet, Chicago) are good to add to holiday reading lists. One of the loveliest picture books demonstrating the hardship of life for the Negro working in the cotton fields is *Oh Lord, I Wish I Was a Buzzard* by Polly Greenberg (Macmillan, New York).

Older primaries might enjoy *The Empty Schoolhouse* by Natalie Carlson (Harper & Row, New York). This book will fit in with some of the current events items children bring to school for news time. Books on athletic figures will appeal to all children interested in sports.

Does all this seem like an overemphasis of black history and literature? Perhaps it is. But there are 300 years of "catching up" to be done if our classrooms are to reflect the needs and aspirations of all our nation's boys and girls. And by filling in the gaps the classroom teacher can add an exciting dimension to the school program.

Chapter 8

Evaluating Learning

Authorities on the topic of evaluation of learning generally define educational evaluation as a systematic, continuing process of determining the extent of achievement of educational objectives. It is an integral part of the teaching-learning process necessitating the use of a variety of activities. Fleming in "Evaluation Takes Many Forms" lists a number of procedures and their purposes, commenting briefly on each one.

It is the teacher's responsibility to appraise continuously his program of evaluation and to endeavor constantly to improve his methods of evaluating his pupils' achievement. In his article, "On School Marks," Williams speaks to this topic, deploring the persistent use of competitive evaluation policies in most school systems and offering, as an alternative, an individualized approach based on ability and previous achievement.

Evaluation Takes Many Forms

Robert S. Fleming

Skill in teaching requires resourcefulness. Today's effective teacher is constantly on the alert for techniques which yield needed information from which evaluative judgments can be made. There is great need for diversity, for appropriateness, for consistency, for comprehensiveness, and for the periodic accumulation of needed data.

Reprinted by permission of the publisher from *Curriculum for Today's Boys and Girls,* edited by Robert S. Fleming, pp. 507-516. © 1963 by Charles E. Merrill Books, Inc., Columbus, Ohio.

Perhaps no factor in the evaluative process is more important than to emphasize the necessity of accumulating a wide variety of data *early* in the year to serve as a basis from which judgments can be made at later times. In other words, what was the status of the student (or group) at the beginning of a period of time? Such an estimate serves as the point from which future comparisons can be made as progress is described. Hence, it is essential that each evaluation experience be dated and recorded. Statements should be made as to the conditions under which it was accumulated. If one assumes that growth is occurring in many areas, and if one concerns himself as to the extent, direction, and nature of growth, then evaluation procedures must of necessity take numerous forms.

Perhaps all evaluation activities cannot consist of highly "objective" devices. But taken in its totality the evaluation program can become objective, reasonable, and efficient. The teacher obviously assumes a leading role as an evaluator; however, she must share it with administrators, teachers, colleagues, parents, and children.

As one examines the variety of complex purposes being sought in our schools, it becomes evident that many procedures, instruments, and techniques are needed to assess them. No longer do we think of evaluation as being limited to tests. Rather, we recognize the need for extensive procedures.

Evaluation activities begin on the first day of school. The very minute children appear initiates the process for teachers to begin immediately to know children—how they are alike, how they differ, what they do, who they are with, how they respond to each other, and countless other valuable observations. Such a comprehensive "getting to know the group" cannot comprise a total evaluation program, yet it does give vital, alive, and helpful data from which a teacher begins to make judgments. These judgments reflect values purposes, and human qualities.

Numerous techniques are described in the literature of this field. Illustrative of these are *The Fifth Mental Measurements Yearbook,*[1] *The Measurement of Understanding,*[2] *Appraising and Recording Student Progress,*[3] *Judging Student Progress,*[4] *Measurement and Evaluation in Education,*[5] and *Evaluating Pupil*

---

[1] Oscar Krisen Burros, *The Fifth Mental Measurements Yearbook.* (Highland Park, New Jersey: The Gryphon Press, 1959).

[2] National Society for the Study of Education. Forty-Fifth Yearbook. 1946, Part I—*The Measurement of Understanding.* (Chicago: University of Chicago Press).

[3] Eugene R. Smith, Ralph W. Tyler, and staff, *Appraising and Recording Student Progress.* (New York: Harper Brothers, 1952).

[4] R. Murray Thomas, *Judging Student Progress.* (New York: Longmans, Green and Company, 1954).

[5] James M. Bradfield, and H. Stewart Moredock, *Measurement and Evaluation in Education.* (New York: The Macmillan Company, 1957).

Growth.[6] These and a variety of others describe techniques, list tests and sources of information about tests. In addition to such sources are materials such as Wood's *Test Construction,*[7] which helps teachers with technical aspects of test construction and with the application of rudimentary statistical treatment to test scores.

There are an endless number of evaluative techniques. A major concern of many educators is to stimulate teachers to seek appropriate data to describe growth toward achievement of desired purposes. Diversity of procedures seems essential if one assumes that growth of children occurs in many ways. The following list of evaluative procedures illustrates the diversity of *sources* of evidence.

Evaluation Procedure	*Purpose*	*Comments*
1. Achievement Tests in any area of importance, such as: reading, arithmetic, and other subject areas.	—To describe status in specific areas assumed important for a particular group and individual as means of comparison with those in other schools.	—Tests should be used in manner consistent with *purposes* being sought. —Should be used early in year as a means of helping to diagnose student's status in specific academic areas. —Specific scores in various areas rather than as a composite score are helpful in diagnosing status of learning.
2. Teacher-made tests (any field).	—To determine understandings of content thus providing information for the teacher and learner. May be used as means of self-evaluation for both student and teacher.	—Tests are carefully prepared by teachers to cover basic content of a topic, unit, or learning experience. —Tests may take form of specific questions or problems. —Tests usually involve individuals working alone. —The test should provide another learning experience for the learner.
3. Observations of pupils by teachers in terms of specific purposes. May include qualities such as: a. Work habits b. Play c. Relationships with other children d. Relationships with adults e. Health status	—To collect specific information concerning behavior of pupils in various types of situations.	—Observations should be made systematically. —Specific purposes for observation need to be identified. —Records must be kept of specific factors observed. —Each observation should be dated. —At intervals observations should be summarized and analyzed.

[6] J. Stanley Ahamann, and Marvin D. Glock, *Evaluating Pupil Growth.* (Boston: Allyn and Bacon, 1958).

[7] Dorothy Adkins Wood, *Test Construction.* (Columbus: Charles E. Merrill Books, Inc., 1961).

f. Health practices
g. Reading habits
h. Handwriting
i. Use of time

—Development of an observational guide may be helpful.
—Observations may be made by teacher, principal, parent, or supervisor.

4. Collection of products of student's work. These may take form of writing, art work, creative work, special assignments, news, exhibits.

—To analyze status of learning, find evidences of improvement in specific areas, discover needs, misconceptions, strengths and weaknesses, discover interests, identify values.

—Provide each student with folder.
—Each item included must be dated.
—At intervals materials in a given subject field should be examined chronologically, analyzed and summarized.
—Selection of "typical" samples may be helpful.
—Emphasis given to help learner raise *his* standards for *his* work.
—In some cases the "product" is in the form of a project, dance, or group activity which might well be recorded and described.

5. Record of the results of listening to children's discussions, conversations, comments.

—To identify speech and discussion needs.
—To collect leads which enables the teacher to better understand a child's interests, attitudes, anxieties, concerns.

—As one hears evidence of growth, expanding interests, improvement in discussion techniques, major growth in understanding of concept and relationships, records should be made.
—Teachers may listen for a specific purpose such as vocabulary, pronunciation, misconceptions.
—Teachers may listen to determine concerns, anxieties, fears.
—Teachers should record major items heard. Often they are taken as questions or hypotheses to be followed up in discussions with individuals or groups.
—Each record should be dated.

6. Analysis of reading bibliography.

—To describe status of reading activity.
—To be used in assessing interests.
—To provide a means of communication with the individual.

—Each student might well keep a bibliography of books, magazine articles, papers read.
—Each item should be dated as recorded.
—Provides a basis for questioning, conferences, discussions with parents.

7. Provide for free response writing.

—To provide an opportunity for a child to express his

—As students have opportunities to write about their ideas and feelings, beliefs, understandings.

understandings they often reveal interests, values, concerns.

—Free response writing may portray one's skill in communication and in expression, in handwriting, in sentence construction, in critical thinking.

8. Word lists.

—To develop and extend vocabulary.
—To serve as an indication of understandings and interests.

—Individuals may keep lists of new words learned in certain fields.
—May serve as incentive for new learnings.
—Provides basis for communication with the teacher. Teacher may find list an index to problems, interests, difficulties.

9. Sociometric data.

—To provide a picture of an individual's place in a group and a group's acceptance or rejection of the individual.

—Development of a series of sociograms may be helpful.
—Sociograms must be made in a series of different situations.
—Each sociogram must be dated.
—Group relationships may change.

10. Student's summary of work in a given study, unit, topic.

—To provide an opportunity for an individual (or group) to prepare a record of work carried out in given period of time.
—To assist the student in organizing, summarizing, and reporting.

—Time interval may vary from a single class period to several weeks.
—Individual (or group) describes such items as what was done, purposes, method of work, summary of findings, conclusions, etc.
—Ability of an individual (or group) to summarize major findings may reflect growth.

11. Record of an interview with a student (or group).

—To provide evidence of major understanding, maturity of insight, growth.

—An interview guide may be helpful in identifying major emphasis of interview.
—Record (summary) should be made and dated.
—Teacher must take findings at face value.
—Teacher's role is to ask few probing questions and to create a situation for student to talk and to reveal himself.

12. Record of an interview with a parent.

—To determine parents' perceptions of work of the child.
—To secure information about the child's activities, attitudes, concerns.
—To interpret work underway and to clarify purposes and next steps.

—An interview guide may be helpful in identifying major emphasis of interview.
—Record (summary) should be made and dated.
—To provide evidence of major understanding and growth.
—Teacher must take findings at face value.

13. Preparation of a series of newspaper articles on work of school (or group).	—To interpret work underway. —To provide information of activities and procedures.	—Articles on variety of topics may be helpful. —Display of articles dated and arranged in systematic means enables one to study balance, variety, participation.
14. Record of assembly program.	—To provide information of progress of children toward certain purposes assumed to be important (assuming responsibility, leadership, creativity expression).	—Summary of planning that went into program. Role of individuals in assuming responsibility, creating scenery, improvising, composing music. —Degree to which individual became more responsive.
15. Record of exhibits, displays or demonstration.	—To describe evidence of student's accomplishments, understandings, and creative work. —To communicate work of the school.	—As students become more active in communicating ideas, growth is occurring. Subtle accomplishments may be evident—growth in harmony, resourcefulness. —A series of photographs, or descriptions of an exhibit or demonstration of a student or group may provide evidence of cooperation, understandings, knowledge of relationships, creative work, etc.
16. Responses of boys and girls to particular problem situations (emergency, seasonal, etc.)	—To study student's behavior in variety of problem situations, as means of describing maturity, balance, poise, ingenuity, resourcefulness. —To provide for an application of knowledge and attitudes.	—As students can express feelings and attitudes, their growth in human qualities may be described. —Observations of reactions of students to a fire, theft, death; to new student, to routine tasks, may reveal values, attitudes, understandings. —Learning outcomes are numerous and varied.

17. Tape recordings of work of an individual (or group) in such activities as
    poetry
    reading
    piano
    chant
    singing
	—To record actual experiences of children as a source of data from which value judgments can be made.	—Tapes recording specific work of individuals can be developed.
		—Dates must be established and conditions under which the tape was developed should be described.
		—Opportunity should be provided for an individual to listen to his tapes and analyze progress, problems, next steps.

18. The development of a film, filmstrip, or series of slides.	—To serve as a source of data describing progress. —To provide a specific re-	—Planning for a pictorial summary of a project provides a variety of learnings.

	cord of work over a period of time.	−Useful in interpreting work to parents and community.
19. Record of group discussions of faculty members concerning an individual child and/or class group.	−To summarize existing information in a school. To be used in assessing status, needs and progress.	−Several teachers in a given school have extensive knowledge about a group (or individual). −The pooled information of the faculty group provides extensive information. −Progress and problems become evident.
20. Use a variety of commercial tests other than "subject matter" tests.	−To be used in studying a group quietly in terms of a general purpose (interest). −To establish some general characteristics of the group. −To learn more about an individual child.	−A variety of tests are available which help teachers better know groups and/or individuals.* −Results used in planning. −Results may help individuals know themselves better. −Results aid in communication with parents. −Results may be taken as hypotheses to be tested.

Illustrative Tests

A. SRA Junior Inventory[8]	Grades 4 - 8	−To identify student problems.
B. What I Like To Do[9]	Grades 4 - 7	−To identify interests.
C. A Book About Me[10]	Ages 5 - 7	−To better understand a child's home background and maturity.
D. Davis-Eells − Test of General Intelligence or Problem-Solving Skills[11]	Primary Test, Grades 1 - 2 Elementary Test, Grades 3 - 6	−Tolerate intelligence to problem-solving ability. Test items deal with realistic problem areas and child responds to variety of verbal material.
E. Ohio Social Acceptance Scale[12]	Ages 4 - 8	−To study social acceptance and relate it to behavior.
F. Van Pit Series− Wishes[13]	Grades 4 - 8	−To aid in identifying unfulfilled emotional needs.

No effort is made to suggest specific techniques for a given teacher or school to use. It is not proposed that any teacher would necessarily use every evaluative procedure listed above. Rather, it is felt that individual teachers must make decisions in terms of their purposes, their facilities and their situation. Many teachers use some informal, casual and subjective procedures. Such informal procedures can be used in a manner which increases their realiability. When the total evaluation program is considered, its validity and appropriateness seem

[8] Science Research Associates, Inc., 259 East Erie Street, Chicago 11, Illinois.
[9] *Ibid.*
[10] Science Research Associates, Inc., 259 East Erie Street, Chicago 11, Illinois.
[11] Harcourt, Brace and World, Inc., Tarrytown-On-Hudson, New York.
[12] Bureau Educational Research, Ohio State University, Columbus, Ohio.
[13] Modern Education Service, Box 26, Bronxville, New York.

evident. The criterion of "comprehensiveness" must be employed locally in terms of local purposes. The teacher is constantly on the alert for ways of increasing the reliability of procedures used.

On School Marks

Robert L. Williams

What is the most appropriate way for teachers to evaluate pupils' academic achievement? This question is one of the genuinely important issues in education. Despite many vociferous arguments to the contrary, competitive evaluation policies have persisted in most school systems. Typically, pupils of varying abilities and sociological backgrounds compete for academic marks.

Children of low ability perceive early in their academic experiences that they have little chance for success. However hard they try, they simply cannot compete with brighter pupils. Consequently, school becomes a succession of experiences in failure.

Several school systems, having an uneasy conscience about competitive evaluation, have tried to work out policies that provide positive appraisal for all pupils, including slow learners. Yet most of these systems have retained certain components of competitive appraisal.

Ability grouping is one such attempt. With this arrangement, the pupil is evaluated according to his ability level. On the surface it might seem that homogenous grouping would be effective, but in actuality it is often a miserable failure. After reviewing relevant studies, Johnson concluded that retarded children in regular classes achieve at a significantly higher level than retarded children in special classes (1). According to Johnson, placement in special classes does not enhance the school achievement of retarded children. Other researchers have found that placement in special classes is also ineffective in enhancing personal adjustment (2, 3). Slow learning groups often have a stigma that seriously undermines achievement and adjustment. One must admit, too, that a child is graded by the very act of being placed in an ability group. Assignment to a low group may give a pupil a more humiliating and lasting sense of failure than low marks in the regular classroom setting.

Reprinted by permission of the University of Chicago Press, publisher, and Robert L. Williams from *The Elementary School Journal* 69:1-5, October, 1968. Copyright 1968 by the University of Chicago.

Some educators have explored the efficacy of a dual grading policy. With this arrangement, each pupil gets two school marks. One mark is based on achievement in relationship to individual ability; the second mark is based on competitive standing (4, 5). In the main, educators seem unwilling to eliminate competitive appraisal and the practice of assigning marks.

Assessing an Evaluation Policy

Three considerations are of paramount importance in assessing the efficacy of an evaluation policy. They are the effect of the grading system on the pupil's self-respect, on his achievement, and on his attitude toward schoolwork.

Specialists on theory about the self-concept believe that the perpetual negative feedback that low ability pupils characteristically receive produces pernicious feelings of self-abasement (6, 7). Research indicates that indices of self-esteem in a competitive milieu correspond closely to assigned school marks and standardized measures of ability and achievement (8, 9, 10, 11).

Proponents of competitive school marking often contend that while pupils of lower ability may suffer emotionally in a competitive milieu, the total result of competitive appraisal is higher academic achievement. Negative evaluation is said to motivate pupils by causing them to work harder to raise their standing.

This argument is based on the erroneous assumption that all pupils have the capacity to work at the same level. Pupils of low ability, however hard they try, cannot compete successfully with much brighter pupils. Therefore, increased efforts to compete only confirm and intensify the pupil's sense of failure and inadequacy. Feelings of inadequacy produced by competitive appraisal typically lead to diminished academic achievement (12, 13, 14). Consequently, competitive evaluation may cause the slow learner to perform far below his potential (15). In a competitive milieu the only way a slow learner can maintain a modicum of self-respect is not to try at all. He can at least tell himself and others that he could do better if he chose to expend the effort. Furthermore, since the child of high ability can with very little effort compete successfully, he may produce far less in a competitive milieu than his capacity would permit.

A competitive atmosphere often creates the impression that school marks are all important. If a pupil does not get acceptable marks, he is likely to feel that all is lost. Conversely, if a pupil gets high marks, he automatically assumes that the academic venture has been successful. Strom has reasoned that if grades become the primary goal of learning, the individual, once outside the educational setting, is likely to make little effort to continue learning (16).

In a competitive situation, defeating others may be construed as far more important than learning itself. In one extensive survey of adults enrolled in organized classes, an overwhelming majority of the students wanted grades as well as examinations (17). Students who preferred grades generally thought that a grade indicates "who is better or worse than someone else." The attitude of attaining success at the expense of others is not the kind of orientation needed to deal effectively with the excruciating social and international problems of our time. A cooperative, not a competitive, spirit is necessary to resolve the human conflicts of the day. Also, by emphasizing the glory of successful competition, we often discourage the bright pupil from developing his lesser capacities.

Competitive marking may be a major cause of behavioral problems in academic settings. Briggs contends that cheating, extreme anxiety, and student irresponsibility typically accrue from an overemphasis on school marks (18). Many pupils feel that if acceptable marks are the only means of maintaining the approval of teachers, parents, and, in some instances, peers, then appropriate marks must be attained at all cost. The cost sometimes includes cheating. Counselors in academic settings recognize that many emotional problems pupils have may result primarily from the pressure of marks. Furthermore, if the teacher's appraisal is all that matters, pupils refrain from pursuing projects and ideas that run counter to the teacher's bias. Consequently, pupils become increasingly dependent on the teacher for direction in the learning process (19).

What effect does competitive evaluation have on the pupil's attitude toward school? Apathy and outright antipathy toward school are among the more serious problems in public education. Research in learning has demonstrated that if Stimulus A, a neutral stimulus, is frequently paired with Stimulus B, an aversive stimulus, Stimulus A also acquires aversive qualities. If academic experiences are repeatedly paired with derogatory feedback on the competence and the achievement of a particular child, such experiences soon acquire highly aversive connotations for that child. The present author, studying pupils in competitive settings, has found a highly significant relationship between attitude toward school and grade point average. Undoubtedly, schools that have stringent competitive marking policies produce in many pupils irreparable despair concerning education (20).

A Feasible Alternative

To deplore the evils of competitive marking is not enough. One major reason why school systems have continued to use competitive evaluation may be the lack of a feasible alternative. It is the author's belief that the most equitable, efficacious policy for enhancing self-esteem, achievement, and affinity for school is to appraise a pupil's work primarily on the basis of his ability and previous achievement. As long as a pupil is trying to surpass his previous performance, he has ample opportunities for experiences in success. This individualized evaluation should not be couched in the form of school marks. To be of optimal value, appraisal ought to be frequent and specific. A mark of C in a content area after six weeks of work provides little information that would facilitate subsequent learning (21). A more productive approach would be to provide frequent feedback—daily or weekly—that would indicate the areas of a subject in which the child is making suitable improvement and the areas that need special attention. One major virtue of automated instructional devices is that they provide specific and frequent feedback for pupils.

What would be the repercussions of eliminating competitive marking in the public schools and using instead individualized, specific, and frequent appraisal of pupils' achievement? School systems that have tried to use the individualized appraisals described have encountered considerable resistance from teachers, pupils, and parents (22, 23, 24). Most of us have been conditioned to think that school marks are indispensable and consequently feel shortchanged if no marks are given. Resistance to change, however, is hardly an adequate index of the soundness of existing policies.

Another reservation often voiced with respect to individualized evaluation is the difficulty of assessing a pupil's preparation for a certain academic level without some type of competitive appraisal of his previous work. For example, how do we know that a high-school graduate is prepared for college work if we have no index of his high-school rank? If employers, colleges, or parents demand information about a student's competitive rank, scores on standardized ability, aptitude, and achievement tests would provide more complete and objective evaluations than assigned marks (25). Certainly, specific assessment of a pupil's strengths and weaknesses in a content area tells more about his readiness for subsequent work in that area than one global mark in a course. In an individualized evaluation the question of preparation would not be "Can the student pass the course?" but "Does the student have the knowledge that would enable him to profit from the course?"

Proponents of competitive marking often declare that anything less would create in the thinking of the child of low ability unrealistic expectations of success in adult life. These advocates of competitive marking contend that the adult world is highly competitive. In contrast, the individualized approach tells the child that what matters most is not his competitive standing, but the use he makes of his capacity. Whatever the nature of the adult world, would several years of bitter frustration in a competitive academic setting adequately prepare one to deal with the demands of adult life? The individualized approach does not purport to convey to the child the idea that he is as bright as someone else or that he can expect to be the president of a large corporation some day. The individualized approach simply sets forth the proposition that the primary test of human success is the use of one's capacities and opportunities, be they great or small. Individualized appraisal does not camouflage a child's limitations, but rather allows him to accept his limitations without losing self-respect. The individual most adequately prepared to deal with the realities of an adult world is the one who has used his intellectual potentialities appropriately. A completely individualized appraisal would be far more effective in producing this kind of person than a highly competitive atmosphere.

REFERENCES

1. M. Johnson. "Solving the Mess in Marks," *Education Digest,* 27 (February, 1962), 12-14.
2. H. Goldstein, J. W. Moss, and L. J. Jordan. "The Efficacy of Special Class Training on the Development of Mentally Retarded Children." U.S. Department of Health, Education and Welfare; Office of Education; Cooperative Research Project No. 619. Urbana: Institute for Research on Exceptional Children, University of Illinois, 1965.
3. J. H. Meyerowitz. "Self-Derogations in Young Retardates and Special Class Placement," *Child Development,* 33 (June, 1962), 443-51.
4. M. Alpren. "Fair Grading System," *Clearing House,* 35 (October, 1960), 113-14.
5. E. D. Doak. "Grading: A Deterrent to Learning," *Clearing House,* 37 (December, 1962), 245-48.
6. A. W. Combs and D. Snygg. *Individual Behavior: A Perceptual Approach to Behavior.* New York: Harper and Brothers, 1959.
7. E. C. Kelly and M. I. Rasey. *Education and the Nature of Man.* New York: Harper and Brothers, 1952.
8. S. Coopersmith. "A Method for Determining Types of Self-Esteem," *Journal of Abnormal and Social Psychology,* 59 (July, 1959), 87-94.
9. P. H. Stevens. "An Investigation of the Relationship between Certain Aspects of Self-Concept Behavior and Students' Academic Achievement," *Dissertation Abstracts,* 16 (1956), 2531-32.
10. R. L. Williams and S. Cole. "Self-Concept and School Adjustment," *Personnel and Guidance Journal,* 46 (January, 1968), 478-81.
11. R. L. Williams. "Personality, Ability, and Achievement Correlates of Scholastic Attitudes." In preparation.
12. E. D. Alexander. "The Marking System and Poor Achievement," *Teachers College Journal,* 36 (December, 1964), 110-13.
13. E. Drews. "Evaluation of Achievement," *Instructor,* 75 (April, 1966), 20.
14. A. M. Walsh. *Self-Concepts of Bright Boys with Learning Difficulties.* New York: Bureau of Publications, Teachers College, Columbia University, 1964.
15. L. E. Peterman. "Let's Junk Our Grading System," *Michigan Education Journal,* 35 (February, 1958), 223.
16. R. D. Strom. "Academic Achievement and Mental Health," *Journal of Secondary Education,* 39 (December, 1964), 348-55.
17. E. E. McMahon. "Report Cards for Adults?" *Adult Leadership,* 13 (December, 1964), 169-70.
18. F. M. Briggs. "Grades: Tool or Tyrant? A Commentary on High-School Grades," *High School Journal,* 47 (April, 1964), 280-84.
19. R. N. Bostrom. "Grades as Reinforcing Contingencies and Attitude Change," *Journal of Educational Psychology,* 52 (April, 1961), 112-15.
20. L. F. Malpass. "Some Relationships between Students' Perception of School and Achievement," *Journal of Educational Psychology,* 44 (December, 1953), 475-82.
21. R. H. Muessig. "How Do I Grade Thee? Let Me Count the Ways," *Clearing House,* 36 (March, 1962), 414-16.
22. G. Bloom. "There Should Be No F's—Students Should Be Judged on the Basis of Whether or Not They Are Achieving Their Potential," *Business Education World,* 46 (March, 1966), 13-14.

23. J. W. Halliwell. "The Relationship of Certain Factors to Marking Practices in Individual Reporting Programs," *Journal of Educational Research,* 54 (October, 1960), 76-78.
24. I. F. Johnson. "Injustice of Grades," *School ana Community,* 54 (October, 1967), 24-25.
25. W. A. Yauch. "School Marks and Their Reporting," *NEA Journal,* 50 (May, 1961), 50.

Suggested Additional Readings

Allen, Evelyn Young. "What the Classroom Teacher Can Do For the Child with Speech Defects," *NEA Journal* 56:35-36, November, 1967.

Allen, Paul E. "Teaching for Commitment." *Educational Leadership* 22:170-172, December, 1964.

Allen, R. V. "Grouping Through Learning Centers." *Childhood Education* 45:200-203, December, 1968.

Alonso, Lou. "What the Classroom Teacher Can Do for the Child with Impaired Vision." *NEA Journal* 56:42-43, November, 1967.

Barnes, Donald L., and Arlene B. Burgdorf. *New Approaches to Teaching Elementary Social Studies.* Minneapolis: Burgess Publishing Co., 1969.

Beauchamp, George A. "Teacher-Pupil Planning," pp. 157-160 in *Basic Dimensions of Elementary Method.* Boston: Allyn and Bacon, Inc., 1965.

Bender, Kenneth R. "Using Brighter Students in a Tutorial Approach to Individualization." *Peabody Journal of Education* 45:156-157, November, 1967.

Bettelheim, Bruno. "Teaching the Disadvantaged." *NEA Journal* 54:8-12, September, 1965.

Bothwell, Hazel. "What the Classroom Teacher Can Do for the Child with Impaired Hearing." *NEA Journal* 56:44-46, November, 1967.

Burns, Paul C. *Improving Handwriting Instruction in Elementary Schools,* Second Edition. Minneapolis: Burgess Publishing Co., 1968.

Connor, Frances P. "What the Classroom Teacher Can Do for Crippled and Health-impaired Children." *NEA Journal* 56:37-39, November, 1967.

Dawson, Mildred Agnes, and Frieda Hayes Dingee. *Children Learn the Language Arts,* Second Edition. Minneapolis: Burgess Publishing Co., 1966.

Durkin, Dorothy, Hubert Kirkland, and Janet Purnell. "When the Books Don't Tell. . ." *Grade Teacher* 86:111-114, April, 1969.

English, Raymond. "Focus on Religious Ideas." *Scholastic Teacher,* Elementary Edition 17:12-13, December 6, 1968.

Estvan, Frank J. "Teaching the Very Young: Procedures for Developing Inquiry Skills." *Phi Delta Kappan* 50:389-393, March, 1969.

Frances, Sister Marian. "Discipline Is. . ." *NEA Journal* 54:26-28, September, 1965.

Franseth, Jane. "Does Grouping Make a Difference in Pupil Learning?" pp. 25-33 in *Toward Effective Grouping.* Bulletin No. 5-A, Association for Childhood Education International, 3615 Wisconsin Avenue, N.W., Washington, D.C., 1962.

Gans, Roma. "How to Put a Happy Ending on Those Hectic Final Weeks." *Grade Teacher* 83:55-56, May/June, 1966.

Garrett, Henry E. "Discipline," pp. 57-64 in *The Art of Good Teaching.* New York: David McKay Co., 1964.

Gerhard, Muriel. "How to Write a Unit." *Grade Teacher* 84:123-124, April, 1967.

Grade Teacher. "How to Teach the Hard to Reach." *Grade Teacher* 84:97-101, May/June, 1967.

_____. "Sex Education." *Grade Teacher* 86:60-63, November, 1968.

_____. "Sex Education: How It Is Being Taught in Elementary Classrooms." *Grade Teacher* 84:122-125, 172-173, May/June, 1967.

_____. "Teach Them How to Study." *Grade Teacher* 84:123, 172, 174-181, February, 1967.

Hammerman, Donald R., and Wm. M. Hammerman (Editors). *Outdoor Education: A Book of Readings.* Minneapolis: Burgess Publishing Co., 1968.

Hanson, Earl H. "What About Homework?" *NEA Journal* 57:32-34, January, 1968.

Hart, Leslie A. "Learning at Random." *Saturday Review* 52:62-63, April 19, 1969.

Herman, Barry E. "To Help a Deprived Child You Have to Talk His Language." *Grade Teacher* 84:12, October, 1966.

Jordan, Susan B. "Teaching in the Inner-city School: What It's Really Like." *Grade Teacher* 85:86-87, 128-133, September, 1967.

Kapfer, Philip G. "An Instructional Management Strategy for Individualized Learning." *Phi Delta Kappan* 49:260-263, January, 1968.

Kirkendall, Lester A., and Helen M. Cox. "Starting a Sex Education Program." *Children* 14:136-140, July/August, 1967.

Larson, Karen, and Jeanne Swan. "Spelling the Words They Need Today—an Individualized Approach." *NEA Journal* 55:51-52, February, 1966.

McCall, Margaret. "An Experienced Teacher Speaks." *Childhood Education* 42:407-410, March, 1966.

McMillan, Gene, and Evelyn Stryker. "How to Survive a Field Trip." *NEA Journal* 56:58, October, 1967.

Magoon, Thomas. "Confidentiality of Student Records." *NEA Journal* 51:29-30, December, 1962.

Milander, Henry M., and Elwood F. Egelston. "Utilizing Police in the Classroom." *Illinois Education* 56:175, December, 1967.

Nerbovig, Marcella, and Herbert J. Klausmeier. "Reporting Pupil Progress," pp.

571-601 in *Teaching in the Elementary School,* Third Edition. New York: Harper and Row, Publishers, 1969.

Norton, M. Scott. "Helping Pupils Help Themselves Through Self-evaluation." *The Arithmetic Teacher* 7:203-204, April, 1960.

Olsen, James. "How to Help Your Pupils Pay Attention." *Grade Teacher* 84:148-150, September, 1966.

Olson, Waldemar. *Methods of Teaching Elementary School Mathematics.* Minneapolis: Burgess Publishing Co., 1968.

Paine, Irma Littler. *Art Aids for Elementary Teaching,* Fifth Edition. Minneapolis: Burgess Publishing Co., 1965.

Pines, Maya, Catherine Brunner, and Bernard Spodek. "How and What to Teach the Very Young Child." *NEA Journal* 57:43-46, 71, February, 1968.

Reynolds, Robert W. "Developing Concepts." *Childhood Education* 43:133-136, November, 1966.

Roach, Jack L. "We Found Better Ways to Improve Pupil Behavior." *The Instructor* 76:29, February, 1967.

Rogers, Helen E. "How's Your Classroom Climate?" *The Instructor* 78:96, 140, October, 1968.

Sagl, Helen. "Problem Solving, Inquiry, Discovery?" *Childhood Education* 43:137-141, November, 1966.

Salot, Lorraine, and Jerome E. Leavitt. *The Beginning Kindergarten Teacher.* Minneapolis: Burgess Publishing Co., 1965.

Senn, Milton J. E. "Early Childhood Education—For What Goals?" *Children* 16: 8-13, January/February, 1969.

Smith, Mildred Beatty. "Reading for the Culturally Disadvantaged." *Educational Leadership* 22:398-403, March, 1965.

Stephens, Robert. "Charlie vs. the Teacher." *California Teachers Association Journal* 61:21-22, January, 1965.

Toler, Lola. "Asking Questions." *Childhood Education* 43:279-280, January, 1967.

Trow, William Clark. "On Marks, Norms, and Proficiency Scores." *Phi Delta Kappan* 48:171-173, December, 1966.

Waskin, Yvonne, and Louise Parrish. "The Role of the Teacher," pp. 91-97 in *Teacher-Pupil Planning for Better Classroom Learning.* New York: Pitman Publishing Corporation, 1967.

Werry, John S., and Herbert C. Quay. "Observing the Classroom Behavior of Elementary School Children." *Exceptional Children* 35:461-470, February, 1969.

Wheeler, Wallace, and Donald Hammerman. "What Is the Educational Potential in the Outdoor Setting?" *Illinois Journal of Education* 55:2-4, December, 1965.

Part III

BECOMING A
TRUE PROFESSIONAL

Introduction

During the early part of his first year of teaching, the neophyte to the profession usually is so occupied that he has little time or thought for other than immediate tasks and problems. But as the months go by, and as he gains skill and confidence in accomplishing his teaching assignment, there develops within the first-year teacher an ever-increasing awareness of the differences that exist between the person who has just begun to teach and the teacher who is a true professional.

As he talks with other teachers, as he confers with parents, as he mingles with the members of the community, and, especially, as he works with his pupils, he perceives the necessity of his taking the initiative in planning and pursuing a program for his own professional growth and development.

What are the areas in which the beginning teacher will want to concentrate his efforts as he works toward becoming a true professional? His major concerns will be with improving himself and with advancing the profession. Certainly, as he plans for self-improvement, he will want to give primary consideration to his instructional practices; and, as he begins to develop a program for making his instruction more effective, he will find it necessary to plan for increasing his competency in working with other members of the faculty and staff and with parents.

Experience alone cannot assure professional growth; experience must be examined, evaluated, and directed. A good program of in-service education consisting of organized classes and independent reading and study will help the beginner evaluate, direct, and improve his professional endeavors.

The true professional feels a personal responsibility for the welfare of his vocational field and recognizes the importance of working for its advancement. He is concerned with discovering the meaning of professionalism in teaching, with determining the role of various teachers' groups, and with supporting actively the organizations that he believes will do the most to help improve him and his profession. Likewise, he is aware of his obligations as a citizen of the community and welcomes and seeks opportunities to work for its betterment.

The selections included in this portion of the book are focused on the problems and concerns of the teacher who is striving to move from the beginning stages of teaching to true professionalism in all facets of his educational pursuit.

Chapter 9

Working With Parents

The successful teacher is aware of the importance of working closely with parents, and he is knowledgeable and skillful in teacher-parent relationships. He knows the value of communicating effectively, of acquiring as much information as possible about the out-of-school life of the child, of involving parents in the school program, and of using a variety of procedures in working with parents.

The role of the teacher as an interpreter of the school to the community is the theme of Hubbell's selection, "It Still Starts in the Classroom." Hubbell says that the secret of effective school-community relations is fundamentally good classroom teaching and the attitudes that children develop as a result.

If parents are going to understand and support their schools, they need to know the principles of learning and of child growth and development upon which teachers base their practices. Dunfee discusses some of these principles, then suggests three means which schools can use to help parents understand their importance and meaning: evidence through research and observation; communication through such activities as demonstration lessons; and involvement through participation in school processes.

One highly effective way of working with parents is through the use of individual parent-teacher conferences. Primary purposes of such conferences include the reporting of pupil progress, discussion of problems, exchange of information, and the planning of a course of action. Cholden believes that the parent-teacher conference offers valuable opportunities for the parents and the teacher to help the child by sharing their knowledge and understanding of him. She suggests a number of guidelines for making conferences meaningful and successful.

The chapter concludes with an article titled "A Beginning Teacher Works with Parents" in which a teacher of young children shares some of her concerns, problems, and procedures in involving parents in the education of their children.

It Still Starts in the Classroom

Ned S. Hubbell

• Once upon a time in a third grade classroom, a group of elementary school youngsters defined school-community relations.

That wasn't their original assignment. In fact, all that their teacher had told them to do was to try out their new skills in cursive writing by preparing a one-sentence written answer to the question: "What is a school?"

Replied the handwriting hopefuls:

"A school is Mrs. Swanson [she was the first grade teacher], who taught me how to read."

"A school is Mr. Schaefer [he was the principal], who took me home when I was sick."

"A school is Mr. Wood, who fixed my galoshes." [Mr. Wood was the custodian.]

"A school is Mrs. Ross [she's the school bus driver], who picks me up every day on the corner."

One third grader summarized much of this by writing, "A school is kids and teachers." (But that leaves out parents, custodians, clerks, principals, and many others.)

Probably the best of the lot was offered by one youngster who simply wrote, "A school is people."

What's all this got to do with school public relations, you ask?

Everything.

People who work in a school, especially classroom teachers, are "the school" in the eyes of those who have the most personal contact with the schools.

Gloria Dapper points this out in her book, *Public Relations for Educators,* when she says: "Unavoidably, the public holds certain convictions about the schools, believes certain things to be true, and, when the word *school* is pronounced, conjures up a particular mental picture. These convictions, opinions, and mental images are the product of public relations, planned or otherwise."

And Benjamin Fine agrees. The former education editor of the *New York Times* has defined *public relations* as the entire body of relationships that go to make up our impressions of an organization or individual. The keys, then, in

Reprinted by permission of the National Education Association, Washington, D.C., and Ned S. Hubbell from *Today's Education* 57:53-55, December, 1968.

school-community relations, are the personal relationships among children, their parents, and others in the community who come in contact with school personnel.

It's this personal interaction that forms the image people have about their schools. An image, we're told, is a reflection of reality, as viewed by the beholder. And these images are based on attitudes formed through experiences and information. The secret to effective school-community relations, and thus the chief determinant of the school's image by parents, is fundamentally just good classroom teaching.

Of course, it may be more than that. But the things that happen after a teacher closes the door and begins to teach are more effective in developing positive school-community relationships—"good public relations"—than anything else the school can do to build understanding and support. Good teaching not only helps children, it helps earn the goodwill, respect, and confidence of the public in the school's professional personnel and services.

Unfortunately, good teaching alone may not be enough to help parents understand and appreciate all of the things the schools are doing, day after day, to provide a good educational program for their youngsters. The primary communications channel to convey this information is the children themselves, and they are often not the most reliable of reporters. For instance, when a parent asks his youngster, "What did you learn today?" the usual answer is likely to be "Nothing!"

In spite of this, much of the communication research into school-community relations indicates that parents report "my children" are their primary source of information about school. Notes sent home with students don't help. The older the student, the greater the throw-away rate. Children in the early elementary grades almost always bring home every single message distributed by the school; junior high boys usually stuff such messages into the pockets of their blue jeans, and mothers discover them on (or after) washday; high school students frequently find some other resting place for a message from the school, such as on the floor of the school bus or on the bottom of a locker, or they use the back of the paper to write a note to a classmate.

But youngsters do take one thing home with them—an *attitude* about school, about teachers in general and some in particular, and about learning. That's the framework on which good teachers build the structure of good school-community relations.

In addition, teachers and their school districts have taken a big step in the improvement of school-community relationships by establishing parent-teacher conferences. Designed to supplement the report card, these conferences do something else: They bring classroom teacher and parent together for a face-to-face discussion of the only thing they really have in common—the parent's child. They offer parents a chance to experience firsthand the professional skills and competence of teachers. They give the teacher a chance to learn something of a particular parent's attitude toward education.

One of the best public relations tools available to a school is what happens to parental values and attitudes as a result of a conference with a teacher. This was evident, for example, after a young mother raced home from her first conference with her first grader's teacher and couldn't wait to call her friends. She was positively thrilled. Why? Because she had innocently and in all seriousness asked the teacher, "How in the world can you teach a child how to read, when my husband and I have been trying to do that for months, but with no results?"

Our good public relations agent, the teacher, spent the next half hour describing the process of teaching children to read, showing the mother materials, and demonstrating and explaining the fascinating adventure a child has when he first learns to read. The moral of the story? When asked what she thought of the school system that young mother replied, "I think it's the greatest!" All because of one teacher, one darn good teacher, that conference did more to develop a positive image of the schools than all of the news releases, radio programs, TV shows, publications, and speeches combined—at least for one parent, to say nothing of her husband, and the people they told about that illuminating conference.

This is not to say that press releases and television programs and other communication tools aren't important in interpreting the schools to the community. These techniques help, but they're *supportive,* and reenforce the real image-making element in a school public relations program—the contributions of classroom teachers and all other school personnel.

Look, for example, at Mrs. Rodriguez (a fictitious name but a true illustration). She proudly carries in her purse a note she received months ago from her child's teacher. Jimmy is twelve years old and in a third grade special education class. His teacher sent home a note to Mrs. Rodriguez one day that said: "I just wanted you to know how thrilled I was today when Jimmy learned the words of a song and sang with the rest of the class!" Much ado about nothing? Not in Jimmy's case. Memorizing the song was a major achievement; joining in a class activity was an exciting "first." That note has done more to convince Mrs. Rodriguez of the skills and concerns of teachers than any other efforts the school system could make.

Want more examples of good school public relations?

• Teachers visit the home of a youngster, either as part of a planned visitation program of the school or on their own;

• Teachers join with parents and other residents of the community in informal advisory councils to search for ways to improve the communication of their neighborhood school with people who live in the attendance areas the school serves;

● Teachers serve on a Speakers' Bureau organized and directed by their professional association or the school district to tell their part of the curriculum story to community groups;

● Teachers who don't know the answer to a citizen's question about a school policy or program obtain the questioner's telephone number and see to it that someone who does know calls to provide the answer.

These are only a few of dozens of ways in which classroom teachers contribute to positive school-community relations. The National School Public Relations Association, a department of the NEA, focused on just this type of "PR" when it produced its first publication, *It Starts in the Classroom*, many years ago. This excellent newsletter for classroom teachers is still being published throughout the year, and is crammed with examples of how teachers practice effective school public relations.

We're not trying to imply that telling the school story to the community is strictly up to teachers. They're most important. But helping to organize and maintain a program of two-way communication (sending and receiving messages) in the community served by the schools is the responsibility of the school district.

Ideally, the board of education has formulated policies toward improving communication (both within the school district organization and with the community) and has drafted a priority commitment to organize a continuing school-community relations program. The superintendent of schools is the public relations director of the school system and, as such, has the responsibility to formulate an organized plan for carrying out improved communication. The real "PR agents" of the school system, though, working within an organized communication program, are the employees of the school district.

In effect, more people, spread over larger territories, need to communicate more about educational subjects. Communication (and that includes listening) is a key area of school district operation. To be successful, and thus to improve the quality of education in a community, demands a collaborative effort involving the board of education, the superintendent, the director of school-community relations, teachers, all noncertificated personnel, pupils, and parents.

The job is too big for any one person, or even a small team. This is the "everybody works at our house" theory, based on the belief that an ounce of participation is better than a ton of pamphlets. In order to compete with the shouts, warnings, and the blandishments by means of which the mass media and a host of public and private organizations compete for the public's attention and support, a school district needs and is entitled to the cooperative efforts of everyone who is affected by the services of that district.

One of the untapped resources available to a school district's public relations program is the local professional education association. And it's high time this valuable resource is tapped!

Public relations offers a real opportunity for the local association to take an active part in improving the quality of education and the degree of understanding and support held by citizens of the school district. Teachers have demonstrated their organizational skills time and time again through the action programs of their local professional organizations.

Many local education associations are displaying that organizational skill by developing school-community relations programs that coordinate and demonstrate the professional skills and competence of their members. A number of local associations have taken the initiative in organizing a school news-reporting network to provide the public with regular curriculum-based classroom news from the school district via the local newspaper.

Associations have organized speakers' bureaus to provide teachers as speakers for clubs and organizations in the community. Some teachers' associations have inaugurated scholarship programs, after-school enrichment programs, tutoring services, and other special services for students. These action programs by the local association offer continued evidence that teachers still are what they have always been—the heart of a school system's educational program and the key to community understanding and support.

If communication is to become really effective, if it is to serve as the information vehicle so necessary to formulate public understanding, teachers need to help *interpret* the goals, problems, and progress of the community's public school system. People just don't like what they don't understand, nor approve of that which they know very little about. The image of the school is based on how well people know and understand what their schools are doing.

It isn't a matter of trying to sell the school to the community; the public already "owns" its school system. It's chiefly a matter of trying to find better ways of interpreting those schools to citizens, through every known channel of communication available. And people who know what's really going on in the community's school system—those who teach—constitute the most important of these interpreters.

So welcome to the land of the "image makers," because, like it or not, as a teacher that's what you are.

What Do Parents Need to Know?

Maxine Dunfee

Parents have always been interested in the schools their children attend. They have always welcomed assurance that their offspring were learning happily and successfully, and that they were participating in a variety of school activities. Only rarely, however, have they shown concern for such professional matters as school organization, curriculum or methods. Having gone to school themselves, parents felt they knew it well and were content. Although the school may have been changing more than they realized, these changes passed unnoticed or were accepted almost without comment.

In recent years, however, parents' awareness of their schools has been considerably sharpened. In the wake of Russian successes in space exploration, widespread criticism of education has become the order of the day. Modern journalism has turned its penetrating analysis upon American schools, and parents have read the results in newspapers and in a score of popular magazines. Interest-catching headlines—*Can Ivan Read Better Than Johnny?*—*Big Troubles in Our City Schools*—*Coming Boom in Ignorance*—*Harder Work for Students*—*U.S. Education Too Slow?*—have stimulated parents to ask questions—questions about aspects of education they have seldom before considered their domain. Should children be learning more at an earlier age? Should more time be given to the 3 R's? Should children be grouped according to IQ? Should pupils be compelled to meet grade standards before promotion? Are new science and mathematics programs better than the old? Are our schools out-of-date?Why are we not taking steps to improve them? Questions and more questions have become the subject of community speculation and discussion.

Such unprecedented interest on the part of parents and others has generated a variety of pressures on the schools. Pressures to begin formal learning at earlier levels, to eliminate subjects not considered "fundamental," to group children according to ability, to departmentalize the elementary school, to restore fixed promotion standards, to apply external incentives to improve achievement—all these, for various reasons, have appeal for many parents. If pupils are not learning all they can in the primary grades, it seems logical to parents to insist that instruction in certain subjects be undertaken at an earlier age. If the fundamentals are being neglected, the solution, of course, is to give them more time in every school day. Convinced that special teachers can teach mathematics

Reprinted with permission of the Association for Supervision and Curriculum Development and Maxine Dunfee from *Educational Leadership* 22:160-163, December, 1964. Copyright © 1964 by the Association for Supervision and Curriculum Development, Washington, D.C.

better than the usual classroom teacher, parents naturally add their voices to the demand for specialists in various subjects. And so on. Parents want the best for their children. They want to conform to that which is being thought of as "moving in the right direction." It is to be expected that they may be caught up in pressures for change and may actually contribute to their realization.

How can patrons of the school understand and interpret changes and pressures for changes which are bound to come to their attention through various communication media and through their own contacts with the school? Will statistics about school finances, data about needs for new facilities, outlines of curriculum content, and descriptions of special services, all of which are commonly communicated to school patrons through various avenues of information, adequately prepare parents to evaluate proposals for change in terms of the needs and well-being of their own children? What, then, do parents need to know?

Children Are Different

Parents need to know, first of all, that children are different. To be sure, parents know this fact in a certain way. They buy clothes of different sizes for children of similar age; they do not expect all children to learn to walk or talk at the same age; they have daily evidence that children do not react emotionally or intellectually to problems in just the same way. Yet frequently they regard school achievement as though all children are the same and should be expected to act uniformly.

Furthermore, parents need to know that how and when a child learns are individual matters and that rules cannot be laid down for all children to follow. Understanding this principle is an important step toward helping parents consider whether or not beginning formal instruction in certain subjects at lower levels of the elementary school is desirable for all children and for their children in particular. Even though embarkation upon such stepped-up programs may enhance the prestige of the school, parents need to be well-enough informed to think clearly about the advantages and disadvantages of certain new programs so enthusiastically reported in the press.

Parents need to know that children, not subjects, are the focus of the school curriculum. Since their own school experience emphasized the learning of content and the development of skills in the 3 R's, parents find it difficult to understand the modern school's concern for process, for functional use of knowledge, and for the acquisition of behaviors and skills consistent with the social setting of the school. Many and varied opportunities for experience, extensive resource materials, and experimentation with new teaching techniques make sense when parents understand that the curriculum must serve the needs of children.

Parents need to know that learning to learn has come to be an imperative in becoming an educated person. Many parents are aware of the explosion of knowledge, the difficulty of keeping up with what is happening in the world, and the multiplication of sources of information available to those who want to learn. Because it is impossible for children to deal specifically with all existing knowledge about their world, parents need to know that the emphasis must be upon acquiring habits of inquiry and upon learning principles and ideas that can be used to organize information needed in solving problems today and in the future.

Learning and Evaluation

Parents need to know that seeing a purpose in learning produces more effective and lasting motivation than do the external incentives commonly employed by many schools. This knowledge is basic to understanding why the problem-solving approach to learning secures more active pupil participation than the traditional textbook emphasis. This knowledge also helps parents understand why pupil planning plays such an important part in their children's learning.

Parents need to know that evaluation of progress through school goes far beyond interpretation of test scores and the awarding of grades. Properly impressed with the many aspects of child growth and development with which the school is concerned, parents can readily see the inadequacy of these techniques in describing the child's total performance in school. The current interest in parent-teacher conferences to supplement or even to replace the report card is contributing much to parents' understanding of evaluation in its broader sense.

These, then, are some of the things parents need to know. A real understanding of such imperatives will do much to encourage the reasoning parent to support many of the improvement projects in which school patrons are frequently involved—pleas for space and equipment, for expanded libraries, for new forms of reporting, for extended school experiences, or for special services. All these are practical concerns too little understood by patrons in terms of children's learning. Parents need to know the principles on which educators base these calls for help.

How can parents be brought into partnership with the schools in a helpful way? How can they acquire a background of understanding about their children's school progress that will make their participation in school affairs meaningful? To achieve this partnership, dozens of handbooks and bulletins have been written; just turning through them produces an impression that every conceivable technique for improving home-school relationships already has been invented and tried. This article does not need to summarize this long list of ideas. It is important, however, to emphasize three keys to the problem which may help parents unlock the door to some of the ideas mentioned earlier.

Keys to Understanding

The first essential key is *evidence.* Intelligent parents can be impressed with evidence, and there is evidence to support most of the ideas parents need to understand. The evidence is available from at least two sources—research and observation. Research evidence, unfortunately, seldom leaves the office of the professional; yet why would it not be possible to muster the evidence on any given point, present it simply and effectively in terms that parents can understand, and make it available in a variety of striking ways? If research evidence has convinced educators, why would such evidence not convince parents who really care about their schools?

Observation offers another avenue for gathering evidence. Why not a series of directed observations for interested parents? Guide sheets could be made available to them, calling attention to individual differences, to improvements in methods of teaching, or to changes in emphasis in the school's program. Directed observation is a dependable technique for the education of teachers; would it not be effective in the education of parents?

A second key to the problem of helping parents to know is *communication.* Communication is essential if evidence gathered through research and observation is to be interpreted successfully. It thrives best when parents feel comfortable at school and in the presence of school people, when the school is a real part of the local community, and when parents and teachers can speak the same language. There are no substitutes for these conditions, and schools would do well to achieve them as a prerequisite to improved understanding.

Demonstration lessons illustrating new methods and techniques, emphasizing ways of meeting individual differences, problem-solving approaches to study, and the use of varied resources for learning—all followed by discussion, questions and answers—can promote a sense of partnership and sharpen parents' appreciation of the educational process. Study groups which explore further how knowledge of children gives guidance to the school program can be a challenge to both professional and lay participants. Mass media, of course, have a significant role to play in this communication between home and school. Graphically and accurately, with eye- and ear-catching accoutrements to attract the most casual reader or viewer, these resources can tell the story of the school—not only what it is but what it ought to be and why.

A third key to helping parents learn what they need to know is *involvement.* In building understanding there is nothing more effective than participation in a process.

Parents, like their children, learn best when they are personally concerned about a problem and when they take part in searching for a solution. Parents can be involved in gathering evidence needed to illustrate any one of the ideas important for them to grasp. In informal conversation groups they can analyze and interpret such evidence and consider its implications for school practice. Assisting in classroom and school activities clarifies problems of teaching and administration, especially if professional people in charge seize the opportunity to emphasize the philosophy and point of view of the school about children and their learning experiences.

Acting in advisory capacities in curriculum study groups is an experience for parents so rewarding in real insight into the educational process that there is no acceptable substitute. Participation in community projects from which all children will benefit—the building of a museum, the improvement of recreational facilities, the sponsoring of out-of-school activities for youth, or the establishment of educational television—these also lead to better parent understanding of the central concern of the school—the growth and development of the child within the social setting.

Parents need to know, and in the knowing they become more effective participants in the educational effort, more confident and supportive patrons of the school, and better interpreters of its program to segments of the community not touched by school activities. The headlines will continue to attract parents interested in children and schools. Yet some fortunate parents who have been accepted as real partners in the educational process will understand, interpret and evaluate wisely what they read and hear about their schools because what they need to know at a critical time, they will know.

Making the Most of a Parent Conference

Harriett B. Cholden

When a parent-teacher conference is merely a routine progress report, a valuable opportunity has been lost to make it a significant step in a cooperative venture. By sharing their understanding of the child, parents and teacher can help each other to help him. It is well worth your time to plan the meeting carefully.

List the points you want to make. Brief but specific notes on the child's day-to-day performance, his performance in relation to his capabilities, his work

Reprinted by permission of The Instructor Publications, Inc., Dansville, N.Y., from *The Instructor* 77:87-88, March, 1968. ©The Instructor Publications, Inc.

habits, and his social and emotional adjustment provide the conference with structure and substance.

Start with a favorable remark. Your opening comment should reveal not only that you know the child well but that you like him. A teacher who intends to discuss a child's problems may be so anxious to get this difficult part of the meeting over that he immediately launches into a critical remark. A favorable comment better sets the tone of the conference.

Use examples of academic performance. Use examples to present the child's strengths, his weaknesses, and a means of improvement. For example, the pupil is able to add and subtract fractions with like denominators (strength) but not unlike denominators (weakness). This is because of his lack of familiarity with the multiplication tables. Temporarily he can use a list of the tables at his desk, but he should drill at home so that eventually he will not need this aid.

Generalize about class standings. Give parents an understanding of how the child performs in relation to his class in each academic area. Attempting to evaluate how he would do in another school or in another class is largely conjecture and usually irrelevant. Also, it is unnecessary and undesirable to state the child's exact position in the group; just indicate what quarter he is in.

Be specific about standards. Be definite about how you have determined the child's capabilities. If you are talking about how the child performed on an achievement or intelligence test, say so. When you use a standardized test, remind parents that a multitude of factors help to determine the results of such a test, and that it may be an unreliable indicator of the child's true ability.

Cite specific incidents of classroom work which exemplify the level of his thinking.

Avoid misleading or professional terms. Don't use such misleading terms as *overachiever.* If the student is working at a certain level, then he is capable of it and certainly not achieving beyond his ability. Also avoid labels like *low normal, genius, borderline, gifted.* They are professional terms difficult for parents to interpret and translate into reasonable expectations.

Don't make predictions. Some parents do not realize that a teacher may be wrong. Expressing your opinion about the child's future achievements or limitations can do lasting damage. Always remember that you should be describing the child as you see him in the *current school year.*

Relate work habits to attitudes. Using examples of work habits, show how they are representative of the child's total mode of behavior. Is he able to settle down to study? Does he listen to instruction? Does he assume responsibility for his assignments? Parents will be better able to see and evaluate the work patterns their child is developing.

Stay away from psychological terms. In discussing social and emotional adjustment, replace terms such as *regression, inner controls,* and *anxiety* with a description of specific behavior. For example, the child frequently sulks when he does not know an answer; he asks for help before he needs it; or he blurts out answers without thinking.

Illustrate adjustment by examples. In preparing for a discussion of the child's adjustment, attempt to answer questions like this: Does the child have friendships he enjoys? Can he see how his own behavior is related to his friendships and fights, rewards and punishments? Does he seek attention with constructive or destructive techniques? Prepared, you avoid the ambiguity of generalizations in illustrating the child's level of maturity.

Ask about home routines. Encourage parents to discuss the child's adjustment by asking about work and play routines at home. When parents describe effective arrangements such as a new desk or a regular study schedule, comment favorably.

Present suggestions as techniques you have used. Telling parents what to do can arouse resentment. A better way is to present your suggestions as techniques you have used successfully in your own classroom. This permits you to talk in detail about your proposals.

Parents must agree there's a problem. If parents do not acknowledge a difficulty, it is futile to force a discussion of corrective measures. Rather, give further illustrations of the child's poor behavior or academic performance. When parents admit they have noticed the problem or have heard something similar from other teachers, you can proceed to search for solutions.

If the child has many problems, you may choose to focus now on only one difficulty. A clear understanding of one problem is more valuable than a superficial summary of many.

Refuse to discuss certain matters. When parents keep returning to a subject, allow time for it even if you consider it insignificant. However, avoid topics that do not contribute to or that mislead the interview: (1) a psychological interpretation of the family constellation; (2) comments placing the blame for a problem on the other parent's behavior; (3) the child's specific test scores or ratings, especially IQ; (4) another teacher's handling of the child; (5) a discussion of other children, either siblings or classmates.

If parents insist on asking about these "taboo topics," remind them that the conference is about *their* child and he would not benefit from exploring the subject further. Point out that a policy of confidentiality also protects their child.

Invite questions from parents. To be sure all aspects of the child's work and behavior have been discussed to the parents' satisfaction, inquire directly, "Is there anything else you'd like to ask me about? Is there anything else about Johnny's life at school or at home you feel I should know about?"

Recapitulate the entire conference. Conclude by reiterating the parents' ideas, summarizing your own remarks, restating your suggestions, and reaffirming the ways you and the parents expect to follow through. (It is well to keep a written record of these plans.) Finally, thank them for their help and extend an invitation to call or return for another conference.

A Beginning Teacher Works With Parents

Susan L. Bromberg

One of the chief aims of many preschool programs, especially those for lower-class children, is to involve parents in the education of their children. Although little has been written specifically about working with low-income parents, there is much in the literature of teacher-parent relations which can be applied to any setting. However, the application of these general principles can be particularly difficult for the beginning teacher, as I have discovered in learning to work with parents at the Bank Street College Early Childhood and Family Resource Center. This Center, located in the area of Manhattan known as Hell's Kitchen, serves low-income families from a wide variety of ethnic backgrounds through a preschool educational program, after-school programs for older siblings, and health, recreational, social and guidance services for the whole family.

When I began teaching, I knew that I was expected to hold parent conferences and parent meetings but I was reluctant to begin. I had started to teach in the middle of the school year, and I had met very few of the parents since most of the children were bussed to and from school. Also, I had little experience in working with parents and lacked confidence in setting forth.

I knew generally that the conference could be used as an opportunity to obtain information about the child from the mother, mentioning areas of interest and success, but also bringing up areas of difficulty. However, I was afraid of bringing up negatives in a conference, because I feared that this might alienate the parents and I felt I might do it clumsily. After I had been teaching a couple of months, it was suggested that I begin my conferences, but I kept putting them off. Finally, I was advised to select a few children who presented the least problems, and to make appointments with their parents first. It was recommended that I observe the child carefully before the conference so that I

Reprinted by permission of *Young Children,* official journal of the National Association for the Education of Young Children, Washington, D.C., and Susan L. Bromberg, from *Young Children* 24:75-80, December, 1968.

could relate current, specific details about the child's interests, talents and activities to the parent.

Thus prodded and encouraged, I finally called one parent to set up a conference. The conference had to be cancelled because the child was hospitalized for pneumonia. A couple of days later, I called to find out how the child was and to set up another time. When the mother answered the phone, she was crying. I offered to call back later but she wanted to talk. She had just come home from the hospital, where she had become extremely frightened by her son's condition. I sympathized with her about her feelings, and we continued to talk about her son. Gradually she stopped crying, and at the end of the conversation, she told me how helpful it had been for her to talk with me.

When I hung up, I felt a tremendous sense of relief, for it had been a very emotionally demanding situation. But I also had a wonderful feeling of success. I had faced an emotionally-laden situation and had managed; therefore, I might be able to handle others. This also put my role in relation to parents into some perspective, and I saw that parents were not so frightening as I had thought. I also suddenly realized what an important thing it was to the mothers for me to demonstrate my interest and care for the children by calling when a child was ill. Thereafter I made a concerted effort to call parents when their children were out of school. This afforded an occasion for that casual contact which was missing because the mothers did not take their children to and from school.

Around this same time, a mother, whom I had never met, called me at school and asked me for the names of some of the children that her son played with, so that she might invite them to his birthday party. During the two weeks before the party we talked together on the phone at least three times. Each time, we covered a number of subjects aside from that of the party. I found myself dealing with such topics as her concerns about home discipline and racial prejudice (she was Negro). I also got involved in helping her to invite people and in helping other mothers to bring their children to the party. This mother was very shy and told me during our phone conversation that it was easier for her to talk over the phone than in person. We established a relationship over the phone which enabled us to talk more easily when we met for our first conference.

Encouraged by these successful telephone conversations, I finally plunged into the conferences. I read *Individual Parent-Teacher Conferences* by Katherine E. D'Evelyn, which gives a thorough analysis of actual conferences. D'Evelyn suggests ideas which I felt I should try to incorporate: that in approaching a problem about a child, the teacher should attempt to give the parent a role of sharing with the teacher the responsibility for working out a solution; that the teacher, rather than giving advice or answers, should guide the parent into finding some answers herself; that the teacher should give the parent as much chance as is possible and reasonable to express herself; and that the teacher should take her cues for what she says from what the parent has said.

I went into my conferences with these good intentions and managed the first two fairly well. But the third conference was with one of the most difficult mothers. It was arranged because the mother had been complaining about fights between her son and another child. However, during the conference, she never brought up the subject. On the theory that one should allow the parent to talk about whatever was foremost on her mind, I did not bring it up. She used the time to talk about the difficulty she was having in disciplining her son. I tried to get her to share in searching for solutions, but she seemed almost to not want to find any. She said she could not do anything, because her husband interfered. She then began to complain about her husband. I finally suggested some possible approaches for effective discipline for the child. These she rejected.

At last I broke all the rules (of what I thought was proper conferencing), tried becoming more authoritarian, and told her how necessary limits were for her son and that she needed to find ways to give him these limits, no matter what. This much firmer approach seemed in some way, more effective. In looking back now, I wonder whether she was really avoiding the original issue of her son's fights and therefore should have been guided into discussing that. The teacher needs to assess the situation in terms of her knowledge of the family and the child, and, if she feels the parent is uncomfortable, she should bring it up herself. She thus can demonstrate to the parent that she is not afraid to deal with difficult subjects and help the parent to face them.

I came out of that conference feeling I had accomplished practically nothing. The only thing I could do was to refer the mother to our guidance director, who would be better equipped to deal with her problems. I know now that the beginning teacher must be willing to recognize her own limitations and realize that she cannot be expected to solve all of the problems of the parents. She needs in such cases to refer the parent on to another professional. The teacher is fortunate if she has such auxiliary personnel on the staff of her school, but if she does not, she should acquaint herself with the agencies in the community.

Teachers Aren't All-Wise

One of the hardest things about conferencing is the feeling of being put on the spot. It is natural to feel this way, but I have begun to realize that the teacher should not expect to have an answer to every problem. What is most important is that the teacher and the parent together work toward the answers. Sometimes the teacher just doesn't have enough information at her disposal; at other times she feels the subject is so important that she needs more time to carefully prepare for a discussion. She should explain this honestly to the parent and arrange for a future appointment. Parents, too, should be helped to know that teachers do not have all the answers.

A delaying technique is essential in dealing with the parent who in a casual contact suddenly catches the teacher off guard and asks questions such as,

"Doesn't Billy ever play with blocks?" or "Has Judy been eating her lunch at school?" I have learned that these are often "loaded questions," which should not be taken at face value and answered directly. The teacher needs time not only to find out the answer and to think what she might say, but she especially needs to provide a situation where she can let the parent talk and perhaps get to what might really be behind such a question. She needs to do this also as a means of protecting herself. For when a teacher is caught in such a situation, she might impulsively say things which she later may regret. There are also those parents who do this as a means of getting attention for themselves. Such parents have shown up in my classroom (often at the most inopportune times) and attempted to draw me into conversation. Sometimes, by asking these seemingly simple questions, they have managed to draw me in before I realized what was happening. When I learned who these parents were, I became able to anticipate when this might happen, and I became more adept at understanding the underlying dynamics of these conversations and thus handling them more effectively.

It happens that parents sometimes involve teachers in real crisis situations, where the teacher cannot postpone dealing with them. For example, a father once appeared on our roof play area and unleashed his anger against a child (whom I happened to be carrying in my arms at the time) who had hurt his son, and yelled about "those dirty black niggers" who "are no better than apes." To maintain one's calm, professional manner in such situations can be extremely difficult. I cannot recall what I said in response, but I remember pressing the child closer to me and somehow managing to move the father toward the door, as I tried to calm him down.

The inexperienced teacher often becomes the target for the manipulating parents. In the case of some of the parents, it seems that when they have developed a sense of trust in the professionals as people who can help them, they begin to bring us all of their problems. It is important for the teacher to distinguish when and how she can be effective in helping parents. She must decide which situations are within her domain. She should also avoid the feeling of being taken advantage of. For example, teachers have found themselves agreeing to do things for parents, such as babysitting, without realizing how they got themselves into it. When confronted with such situations, the teacher needs to ask herself, is this a real emergency; are other solutions possible; and what is her role in helping the parent to find an appropriate solution?

Importance of Home-Visits

Towards the end of the year I suddenly became involved in home-visits. I had made only one home-visit earlier in the year, the purpose of which was to try to re-enroll a child who had dropped out before I took over the class. The visit was a success, but I did not think to go on and make more home-visits. I had thought of home-visits as another means of talking with parents. Therefore, I thought a conference at school would be more effective, since one could not talk very well in front of the child, and I was afraid that would happen at home.

I also thought the parents might consider my visit an intrusion or, because they were used to visits from welfare inspectors and the like, might view my desire to visit with suspicion. Thus, I could never see enough reason to make home-visits. It was really by chance that I finally tried it. I had taken one of the girls in my class home once in an emergency, and we were talking about it one day at school. A boy heard us talking and asked me to come to his house. I told him he would need to ask his mother. She seemed eager to have me come; so we arranged a time. I had a most delightful visit. I felt the mother was not threatened, because she knew that the purpose was primarily to visit her son. However, she also made it into a social occasion for herself, which she seemed to enjoy, for she had refreshments prepared, engaged me in conversation about things unrelated to school, and said she would like to invite my assistant teacher another day.

First-Hand Information

When the other children found out about the visit, they all began to beg me to come to their homes, too. So I realized what should have been obvious all along, that the home-visit should be chiefly for the child, and that what could be conveyed to the parents is that the teacher likes and is interested in their child, and therefore would like to see his toys, his cat, where he lives, etc., or to meet other members of his family. Of course the home-visit is important to a teacher also, because it provides her with first-hand information about the child's physical environment. It is important to know the home setting when talking with the mother about activities she can provide for the child at home.

In conclusion, I should like to set forth some of my present thoughts on working with parents at our Center. The first has to do with how to establish a warm, casual, communicating relationship with parents when the children are bussed to school. I believe the most important ways are through periodic telephone calls or notes, which keep the parents informed and provide a link between contacts made in person. Home-visits provide a more informal setting, if the emphasis is on visiting the child and it is understood that the teacher is not there to discuss the child. Another important way is to extend an open invitation to come and visit in the classroom or perhaps special invitations to lunch. Another idea, which is more successful in the summer, is to invite parents to accompany their children on trips. These contacts are most helpful to the teacher who does not yet feel ready for conferences and meetings. Relationships established in these ways make confrontations over more serious matters much easier.

At this point I feel fairly comfortable about working with the parents. However, I still have some tendency to want to put off contacts, for they are so often difficult to handle. Working with parents at our Center is made more difficult for me because of my personal feelings about working with parents who are older than I am even though they tend to see me, a professional, as an authority figure. Then there are cultural and class differences. In talking with many of the parents, I have to make a conscious effort to change my normal vocabulary and to translate my ideas into more concrete images in order for them to understand me. Some of the cultural differences also arouse in me strong feelings with which I have to cope. For example, I can never hear about or see a parent beating a child without becoming upset. Sometimes my reactions are anger or disapproval, and I have to keep these feelings from interfering with the effectiveness of my relationship with the parent. It is necessary to have an understanding of the cultures from which these parents come, and I need to be aware of my own cultural background and values, in order to avoid unnecessary imposition of my values upon them, and in order to try to control negative or disapproving responses to differences.

I have also learned that the teacher cannot be expected or expect herself to have an answer to every question. When a parent brings up a problem, and the teacher is uncertain how to proceed, it is wise to arrange for a future conference, thus allowing the teacher more time to evaluate the problem and gather relevant information. Most important to remember is that successful parent-conferencing depends on teachers and parents working together toward what is best for the children.

Chapter 10

Working With School Personnel

For the beginning teacher the necessity of establishing a sound relationship with those with whom he works is vital. In the first article in this chapter, Harrison and Gowin emphasize the importance of a cooperative and harmonious relationship with other teachers, with supervisors, administrators and the board of education, and with noncertificated personnel. They suggest attitudes, understandings, and procedures for accomplishing this goal. Cruickshank, in "Teacher v. Teacher," notes various factors that contribute to discord among faculty members and then proposes some solutions for increasing positive teacher-to-teacher relationships.

Use of teacher aides and other auxiliary personnel to assist teachers is increasing rapidly. In "Volunteers in the Classroom" Schrag describes briefly the growth of the volunteer movement and discusses ways that members of the community can help teachers. In the final article, Herman lists a number of suggestions for using aides in noninstructional and semi-instructional tasks.

The Teacher and Human Relations

Raymond H. Harrison and Lawrence E. Gowin

Much has been said and written during the past several years concerning teacher-teacher relationships. In many respects these relationships are probably better than they have ever been, but there is still much room for improvement. The importance of effective teacher-teacher relationships can be understood best

Reprinted by permission of the publisher from *The Elementary Teacher in Action* by Raymond H. Harrison and Lawrence E. Gowin, pp. 88-99. ©1958 by Wadsworth Publishing Company, Inc., Belmont, California.

when we realize that the complexity of the school situation demands cooperation and harmony. Perhaps one of the penalties that we must pay for our
modern educational system is the difficulty involved in securing the teamwork
necessary for effective working conditions. Certainly the job to be done is a
monumental one, and the great number of people involved makes it mandatory
that we work well together.

Professional jealousies have been known to play havoc with staff relationships. The teacher who recognizes the dangers involved in petty jealousies will
refrain from harboring or encouraging them; he will also refrain from belittling
or "undercutting" others by any means. Instead, it should be recognized
throughout the profession that one of the surest ways to enhance one's position
is to strengthen and build up that of one's fellows in any way that is in keeping
with good judgment and professional ethics. Opportunities to be of assistance to
fellow teachers should be looked upon as opportunities to exercise a privilege
rather than perform a duty.

Teachers know perfectly well that much of the sustaining force in their
profession is the satisfaction of a job well done. Call it "prestige" or whatever we
will, it is pleasant once in a while to realize that the job we are doing is
important and that we are appreciated for it. However, it might be surprising to
a great number of people to know how little encouragement and praise come
into the lives of a great number of teachers. Too many teachers are taken too
much for granted. This seems to be more true for the good ones, since it is
usually the teacher whose work is questioned who gets the attention. Perhaps
the general public can be excused for some of its inattention to the work of the
teacher; possibly this can be traced to the confidence that it has in the ability of
the teacher to do a good job. But what about the members of the teaching
profession? Surely teachers can find time to recognize some of the good work
that their colleagues are doing. A little praise now and then for a job well done
can go a long way in contributing to job satisfaction and a sense of personal
well-being and professional worth.

Additional encouragement and assistance could be given by teachers to their
fellows by sharing educational materials and techniques with them. This is
especially fruitful where experienced teachers are working with beginners, or
teachers new to a system or building. Experienced teachers may contribute from
the richness of their experience and their familiarity with the situation; new or
beginning teachers may contribute new techniques and some of their vigor and
enthusiasm. Some teachers guard too closely their materials and techniques, not
realizing that a good educational technique if shared will benefit the entire
profession, and what is more important, many more children. This is generally
understood by most teachers, and good teachers everywhere are sharing with
their fellows to the extent that all are growing and becoming more effective.
This cooperation is to be encouraged by every means possible.

In most cases, the good teacher has chosen his profession because there was something in his nature that made him want to work with people. Much evidence points to the possibility that most teachers really want to be of service to mankind; that the service motive is what prompted them to go into teaching in the first place. It is commonly accepted that one of the highest compliments that can be paid a fellow teacher is to ask him for advice or assistance. No teacher should be reluctant to make such a request from his fellows. The teacher who is new to the profession or to a faculty should not hesitate to seek the counsel of more experienced members of the faculty. Care should be exercised not to get too "thick" with any of them, but he should try to establish good relationships with all of them. Most teachers will be glad to welcome the newcomer to their professional family. Few of them will expect the new teacher to be "onto the ropes" and most will be ready and willing to meet the newcomer more than halfway if he is friendly, courteous, willing to learn, and appreciative of assistance.

Considering the Rights of Other Staff Members

Consideration should be given to the rights of others on the staff in every situation that involves them directly or indirectly. For every teacher—veteran or neophyte—*caution* should be the watchword in all new situations. He must learn to avoid hasty decisions and hasty actions at all times. More than this, activities or decisions that may affect others of the staff should be carefully appraised in the light of consequent results to human relationships. Areas that frequently cause dissension include:

> Holding pupils who rightfully belong under another's supervision (in shops, playgrounds, gymnasiums, music rooms)
> Sympathizing with pupils who have been disciplined by another teacher
> Commenting unfavorably about another teacher or his work
> Grading too highly (so as to reflect unfavorably upon another teacher's evaluation)
> Carrying tales of school out of school
> Laxness in discipline (making discipline more difficult for others)
> Cliquishness
> Being a chronic griper

The teacher owes it to himself to develop the kind of human relationships which will render his work most effective, for it is in these relationships that the greatest satisfaction is found. Since a large part of the reward for teaching is to be found in the satisfaction that comes from being of service to one's associates, it follows that attention given to personal and professional relationships with others is a pretty important matter to the teacher.

Many of the interrelationships in and around the school are so complex that the course of action is not always clear, even to the experienced teacher. The teacher who makes it a common practice to consider the effect of his actions upon others with whom he is working will be alright most of the time. State and national educational associations have published codes of ethics for teachers that cover in a general way all of the areas of human relationships that most commonly cause trouble. Every teacher should be familiar with the code of ethics of his particular state association as well as that of the National Education Association.[1]

RELATIONSHIPS WITH ADMINISTRATORS AND SUPERVISORS

There is every indication that many new demands will be made upon the school in the future and that its program and organization will become more and more complex. Certainly, division of labor and specialization have made it possible in the past to provide many new services. The provision of these services has brought about new problems in human relationships. Not the least of these problems are those involving teacher-administrator relationships. Many of these problems have been aggravated, if not actually caused, by the lack of understanding of the nature and function of administration by both administrators and teachers. Since the field of school administration is a relatively new one, it is not surprising that there is still a lack of understanding of the nature and function of good administration.

Administration is not an end in itself, but rather a service function necessary to the fulfillment of other needs or obligations. [Reeder, 6] Generally speaking, the function of administration in education is the coordination of material and human resources to provide learning experiences for pupils. Such coordination must be effective enough to bring about harmony and unity of action if there is to be a good school. Though the administrative staff is charged with the major responsibility for setting the stage, the job cannot be done by administrators alone. Teachers have a responsibility for the promotion of harmony and wholesome cooperation wherever and whenever possible.

Teacher Participation in Administration and Supervision

Though much has been written and said concerning the role of the teacher in the administration of schools, the nature of such participation has not been clearly defined. Most writers on the subject are agreed that democratic administration has its advantages, but few go so far as to describe in detail how it is to be brought about or the exact nature of it. Pointing to the nature of the problem, Moore and Walters conclude that no *clearly defined pattern* of acceptable teacher-administrator relationships is in existence. [Moore and Walters, 91]

[1] See the *NEA Handbook*. Washington: The NEA, 1955, pp. 362-364.

The history of educational administration and supervision has been one of autocratic domination over, and a paternalistic attitude toward, teachers. Teachers have responded by looking upon administrators as bosses, and supervisors as inspectors, both of whom they fear. Efforts to achieve any appreciable degree of democracy in school administration have been difficult because of the old "power over" rather than "power with" attitude on the part of administrators and supervisors. Sometimes teachers have not responded too well to efforts to involve them in formulating administrative policy, often interpreting such actions as expressions of weakness or indecision on the part of the administrator. Where such attitudes exist there is a need for a new perspective which can only be attained by thorough study.

The American Association of School Administrators has suggested areas of administrative concern in which teachers are being involved as follows:

The development of a strong professional staff and the maintenance of high morale among school employees require hard work, good judgment, and skill in human relations.   The task of finding the right persons to fill vacancies, of determining assignments and service loads, of orienting newly appointed teachers to the school system in a highly efficient fashion, of establishing salary policies and wage scales that encourage employees to put forth their best efforts, of evaluating staff achievements, of recommending for promotion to leadership positions staff members who are best qualified— these are some of the major responsibilities of the superintendent of schools. And . . . . he shares the responsibilities with various members of his staff. [AASA, Staff Relations, 31]

It is the concern of many educators that effective ways be found to involve teachers in the many activities of administering a school. Efforts toward this goal have in many instances brought about better teacher-administrator relationships. However, if teachers are to be involved they must have some knowledge of the more general areas of administrative concern. Where students who are preparing to teach are permitted to do so, at least one course in general school administration should be taken as an elective in the preparation course.

Regardless of whether or not provisions are made to involve teachers officially in policy formulation, all teachers are involved in the administration of the schools in which they work. No single factor influences the scope and quality of education in a community as much as the teachers of its schools. If teachers are not effective in their work it is impossible to have a good educational program. If the greater part of them are effective there will be a good school. There has never been, nor is there likely to be a school administrator proficient enough to have a good school without good teachers. Since it is expected that he bring about those conditions that contribute to a good school, his success or failure is directly and positively related to the success of his teachers. The administration succeeds to the degree that teachers succeed, and fails to the extent that any of them fail. Likewise, the successes and failures of administrators are those of the teaching staff as well as others employed by the school. [Hansen, 330-354] Teachers should remind themselves over and over that they have an obligation to do everything possible to help administrators and supervisors succeed in their work. New concepts and new understandings of the teamwork aspect of school administration must be gained by teachers and administrators if we are to make the necessary progress in school management.

Because human beings tend to be suspicious of things they do not understand, it follows that more understanding of the nature and function of school administration is necessary to allay the fears and suspicions that teachers have of administrators and supervisors. [Reavis, *et al.,* 291-333] Both teachers and administrators must look upon administration as a service function which has no reason for being except to facilitate instruction. Supervision of instruction is only a facet of the total job of administration. Supervision of instruction is an *administrative job* accomplished in part through the efforts of supervisors where provision is made for them; where one person is charged with administration and supervision, as is the elementary principal, he performs both the administrative function and the supervisory. There is something of the one in the other.

Working Effectively Together

Both teachers and administrators must work hard at the job of establishing effective working relationships. [Anderson and Davies, 1-27] The effective administrator will constantly be on the lookout for ways of improving staff relationships, and the good teacher will strive to understand the problems of his administrators and supervisors. He will not allow his perspective to be limited to the four walls of his classroom, but will strive for more understanding of school policies, problems, procedures, and concerns. He will endeavor to become a student of education in the broadest sense as well as a good and effective teacher in the classroom. His study will not be confined to his own particular area of interest, but he will seek more understanding of the many specialized jobs to be done about the school and the difficulties encountered by those who are responsible for doing them. Such knowledge and understanding is necessary to good staff relations and morale. Certainly more tolerance for administrators might be shown by teachers if they were more aware of the pressures upon them and the dilemmas they face.

Administrators and supervisors have a right to expect: (1) that teachers will fit into the accepted pattern of the school and community; (2) that all criticism of administrative policy and procedure will be directed through the proper channels; (3) that ethical practices will be followed in dealing with colleagues; (4) that teachers will be loyal to administrators and supervisors; and (5) that in instances where a teacher finds that he cannot work effectively within the pattern or framework prescribed by the community, the board of education, and the administrative staff, he will seek employment elsewhere. No teacher has the right to disrupt an entire school program because he finds it uncomfortable to work in the existing framework. Though the matter of securing employment will be discussed later, it seems well to point out here that the teacher in search of employment should appraise the quality of administration, the general framework of school organization, the philosophy of the school and community as exemplified by their programs, and other pertinent aspects of the position before accepting employment. Many problems of staff relationships could be averted by this course of action on the part of teachers.

Much of the best—as well as the worst—in education hinges upon a point of view. Administrator-teacher relationships are influenced greatly by the point of view that each has toward the other's responsibilities. The effective teacher will look upon his administrator as a co-worker and a source of power. He should expect to give assistance in: (1) solving pupil personnel problems; (2) clarification and interpretation of policies; (3) working out satisfactory relationships with others; and (4) the selection of things to be taught and how they are to be taught. He may rightfully expect his administrator to be impartially loyal to him, right or wrong, and to help him back on the right track when necessary. In return he should cooperate to the fullest extent with the administrative staff, deal directly and openly, and evidence a strong sense of loyalty to and support of his administrator. Many fine schools throughout the country attest to the fact that this can be done with good results.

The teacher who is really concerned with effective human relations in his school will do everything in his power to work so that others can work with him. To be most effective at this requires that he have a genuine concern and high regard for those with whom he works. If he does he will do a little more than is required of him in most instances. In order to fulfill his obligation to his pupils and the school he will give attention to many duties and obligations not directly connected with instruction, such as:

> Keeping accurate, complete, legible records
> Making all required reports (on time)
> Handling minor discipline cases
> Contributing service outside the classroom
> Maintenance of wholesome relations with the community
> Maintenance of a classroom atmosphere conducive to learning

The teacher who sincerely tries to do a good job, who is friendly and courteous to others, willing to accept constructive criticism, amenable to suggestions, and interested in getting along with others will have little trouble getting along well with administrators.

RELATIONSHIPS WITH NONCERTIFICATED PERSONNEL

It cannot be too strongly emphasized that the provision of adequate educational opportunities for boys and girls is a complicated enterprise, but often overlooked or underestimated is the influence that noncertificated people exercise in the determination of school atmosphere or climate. The necessity for the teacher to recognize the importance of nonteaching personnel has been pointed out by Kyte as follows:

> *The teacher must recognize nonteaching personnel, such as the custodians, the school secretary, the school nurse, and other employees, as members of the school staff with specific and important responsibilities. Their services must be appreciated and acknowledged and the working time of each respected. All of them are employed to contribute to the welfare of both pupils and teachers and to relieve the teacher of duties these specialists can perform better than he. [Kyte, 148]*

Noncertificated personnel are so essential to the welfare of the school that many educators count class custodians, clerks, cooks, bus drivers, and others among the most important personnel about the school.

Working for Harmony

The conscientious teacher will apply the principles of sound human relations to his dealing with noncertificated personnel and will respect the dignity and worth of each as an individual. Since most of the work that the teacher does overlaps that of others about the school, he will see to it that he does not make the work of others more difficult, either by omissions or commissions. In addition, there are many ways that a teacher can deliberately make the work of these persons less difficult. He can help the custodian by keeping litter off the floors, keeping chalk picked up, erasing boards, adjusting or closing windows, turning off lights, and arranging things so that the room can be easily cleaned and dusted. Most of this work can be done by pupils, and serves to present situations wherein a pupil can be accepted. He can teach his pupils to respect the work of the custodian and to care for other aspects of the building outside of the classroom also. The instruction of pupils in social behavior and in routine self-management practices should make life at school easier and more pleasant for all persons who work around it. Clerks, cooks, bus drivers, and all others benefit when pupils can also be taught to refrain from making unnecessary demands upon them. Perhaps parents may pick up after their children a bit too much; perhaps children are allowed to make many demands upon parents in the home. But from the very fact that the schools deal with such large numbers springs the necessity for closer cooperation than may be expected in smaller groups. For this reason, training in the everyday business of living and working together is necessary to good relationships. Some teachers have been accused of taking a "holier than thou" attitude toward noncertificated personnel. Occasionally a teacher will make the mistake of bossing a custodian or other nonteaching colleague. What usually follows is illustrated in the following situation:

Mrs. ——— was in charge of a student activity which required the use of a stage. She wanted some changes made in the backdrops that could not easily be managed by her and her pupils. In spite of the fact that it was not common practice to do so, she ordered the custodian to make these changes. When it was not done promptly, she proceeded to give him a piece of her mind. The custodian became upset and appealed to the building principal, asking, "How many bosses do I have anyway?" thus involving the principal only after emotions were stirred.

Anyone can see the difficulties in such a case. By going through the proper channels to make similar requests incidents of this sort can be prevented. By placing himself in the position of the custodian, any teacher can see that he would not want a score or more of bosses. The application of the Golden Rule is the simplest, most practical solution.

Every teacher should remind himself that friction with noncertificated personnel is often more disastrous to school morale than any other kind of difficulty. For one thing, laymen are likely to be more sympathetic toward the noncertificated person's side of the story. This must be remembered, not because the teacher needs to be on the defensive, but because of the harm that can be done the pupils and the school.

Aside from the work that noncertificated personnel do, they are often the second most important link with the community—second only to the children. It is generally recognized that they are potent forces on the side of the school, and that is the side they must be on if they are to be successful in their work. They must be recognized as peers and colleagues of teachers and not as second-class citizens around the school. The welfare of children and youth can be greatly promoted by the establishment of sound relationships between certificated and noncertificated personnel.

RELATIONSHIPS WITH THE BOARD OF EDUCATION

The legal responsibility for education rests with the state. In every instance the state has delegated to the local unit or school district certain responsibilities, which are, in most cases, clearly defined in the education code. Generally speaking, the responsibility for education rests with the board of education. Through common practice, many of the duties and obligations of the local board of education have been delegated to an executive officer of the board, the superintendent of schools. He is responsible to the board, and finally to the people.

The teacher's relationships with board members is dual in nature: first, he must deal with board members as parents and patrons. In this sort of relationship, board members should be treated as any other patron of the school district and their children the same as any other children. Second, the teacher has some professional relationships with board members that he does not have with other citizens of the community. Proper professional relationships would be easier if all board members understood that they are in reality officials only when the board is in session. At no other time can a board member speak as an official.

Following Proper Channels

The teacher, most especially of all persons, should be aware of this, and if the need arises to go before the board he should do it through proper channels. Ethical procedures dictate that the teacher present his case or seek redress for grievances through his immediate administrative officer. It is not good practice to go directly to the board of education without the blessings of the administration. As a matter of ethics the teacher will do so only when his rights have been denied. This is a ticklish proposition, and every teacher should think twice before appealing to the board, even with the blessings of the administration. It is almost certain that if the administration has the backing of the board of education, the administrative officers have good reason to know how the board is likely to react to a given situation, and they might well be in a position to render the final decision themselves. In few instances is it wise to appeal to a board of education over the wishes of the administration. At no time is it wise for a teacher to contact individual board members and pressure them for opinions or decisions. It is not good for anyone to do this, especially persons who ought to have some knowledge of professional ethics in education.

SUMMARY

It is not enough that the teacher have competence in the mechanical aspects of teaching. The teacher cannot do his job well if he is unsuccessful in his relationships with others.

Many teachers fail each year because of poor relationships with pupils. Many such failures can be traced to poor planning and poor organizational procedures. It goes without saying that there are certain personal traits that must be cultivated by the successful teacher. Teachers must realize that skill in the art of communication is a two-way affair. It is also important for the teacher to realize that much is communicated through actions, and that pupils will be watching for signs that might tip them off as to the teacher's weaknesses. Firmness and fairness have always been appreciated by pupils, and the wise teacher will make sure that this is what his pupils will see when they "size him up."

The teacher's relationships with parents should be of such a nature as to insure a maximum of wholesome growth and development for the children. Out of mutual respect for children should come a sound relationship between parent and teacher.

Every teacher has a responsibility to work so that others can work with him, to encourage his fellow teachers in every way possible, and to refrain from belittling them or their work. Through the sharing of materials and techniques and the giving of assistance where needed, the teacher can make the work of his fellow teachers as well as his own more effective. In matters where others are concerned, their rights should be considered. All situations involving others should be carefully appraised for the possible effect on them. Every teacher should be acquainted with the code of ethics of his state education association as well as that of the National Education Association.

A lack of understanding of and appreciation for the nature of supervision and administration has contributed a great deal to misunderstanding in the relationships of teachers and administrators. The use of the democratic process in administration is becoming more and more prevalent, but the nature of the most desirable form of democratic participation has not always been clear. Both teacher and administrator must realize that they have a mutual obligation to see that the other succeeds. Failure in either case results in harm to children. The teacher who is new to a school must fit into the existing framework of organization as he finds it. It is wise to find out whether this framework is compatible with his philosophy of education and methods of operation before he accepts employment.

Very often the second most important link between school and the rest of the community is the noncertificated staff. Such personnel must be looked upon with respect and treated as peers. The welfare of children can be promoted further by sound relationships between certificated and noncertificated personnel.

Though the responsibility for education in a community rests with the board of education and finally the people, it does not follow that the teacher has any inherent right to go directly to the board with educational problems. Operating as a policy-making body, the board of education establishes policies to guide persons to whom it has delegated responsibilities. The teacher needs enough knowledge of the organizational pattern of his school to know where to go with his problems. It is never wise to go to one member of a board of education at a time. It is seldom wise to go directly to the board in session unless all other avenues have been tried first.

REFERENCES

American Association of School Administrators, *Public Relations for America's Schools,* 1950 Yearbook. Washington: The NEA, 1950.

————, *Staff Relations,* 1955 Yearbook. Washington: The NEA, 1955.

American Education Research Association, "Teacher Personnel," *Review of Educational Research,* vol. 25, 1955, 193.

Anderson, Viviene, and Daniel R. Davies, *Patterns of Educational Leadership.* Englewood Cliffs, N.J.: Prentice-Hall, 1956.

Bartky, John A., *Supervision as Human Relations.* Boston: D.C. Heath, 1953.

Elder, Franklin Lester, *Explorations in Parent-School Relations.* Austin: The University of Texas, 1954.

Elsbree, Willard S., and Edmund Reutter, *Staff Personnel in the Public School.* Englewood Cliffs, N.J.: Prentice-Hall, 1954.

Hansen, Kenneth H., *Public Education in American Society.* Englewood Cliffs, N.J.: Prentice-Hall, 1956.

Herrick, Virgil E., John I. Goodlad, Frank J. Estvan, and Paul W. Eberman, *The Elementary School,* Englewood Cliffs, N.J.: Prentice-Hall, 1956.

Kyte, George C., *The Elementary School Teacher at Work.* New York: Dryden, 1957.

Lawson, Douglas E., *School Administration: Procedures and Policies.* New York: Odyssey Press, 1953.

Moore, Harold E., and Newell B. Walters, *Personnel Administration in Education.* New York: Harper, 1955.

Otto, Henry J., Hazel Floyd, and Margaret Rouse, *Principles of Elementary Education.* New York: Rinehart, 1955.

The Preparation of Teachers for Home-School Community Relations. Sacramento: California State Department of Education, 1953.

Reavis, William C., Paul R. Pierce, Edward H. Stullken, and Bertrand L. Smith, *Administering the Elementary School.* Englewood Cliffs, N.J.: Prentice-Hall, 1953.

Reeder, Ward G., *The Fundamentals of Public School Administration,* Third Edition. New York: Macmillan, 1951.

Richey, Robert W., *Planning for Teaching.* New York: McGraw-Hill, 1952.

Saucier, W. A., *Theory and Practice in the Elementary School.* New York: Macmillan, 1951.

Stearns, Harry L., *Community Relations and the Public School.* Englewood Cliffs, N.J.: Prentice-Hall, 1955.

Teacher v. Teacher:
A Proposal for Improving Relationships

Donald R. Cruickshank

"Now all the evidence of psychiatry . . . shows that membership in a group sustains a man, enables him to maintain his equilibrium under the ordinary shocks of life . . . If his group is shattered around him, if he leaves a group . . . and finds no new group to which he can relate himself, he will, under stress, develop disorders of thought, feeling, and behavior."

George C. Homans
Harvard University

Reprinted by permission of *The Clearing House,* Teaneck, New Jersey, from *The Clearing House* 41:304-307, January, 1967.

The Problems

Each year, approximately 150,000 teachers enter classroom for the first time. At the same time, countless experienced teachers are moving from one teaching position to another. Both groups share the problem of adjusting to environments which are strange and, at times, even hostile. In each case, new and satisfying relationships must be formed if the individual teacher is to function as a mature human being and an effective teacher. Unfortunately, little time or conscious effort is given to helping teachers, both newcomers and old-timers, to know, understand and work with each other.

As the recent arrival strives to meet his new needs, he sometimes unintentionally manifests behavior which has unanticipated consequences. For example, because a new teacher seeks the acceptance of his students, he may indulge them in ways which disturb old-timers. Again seeking professional recognition, he may appear too eager in his relationship with superiors. In both cases, personal needs and lack of understanding of the norms of "acceptable teacher behavior" in the new setting place the newcomer in jeopardy. In short, his behavior is incompatible with that which would be accepted by his peers.

Self-Evaluation

Some of the more common "mistakes" made which disturb relationships with other teachers are cited in a study by Allen.[1] Teachers were asked to report behavior they found unacceptable in their colleagues. The kinds of behavior mentioned most frequently as being undesirable in a classroom teacher are arranged below in checklist form. Each item requires a yes or no response.

(1) Do I criticize or report fellow teachers to the principal?
(2) Am I inconsiderate of pupils?
(3) Am I inconsiderate of my colleagues?
(4) Do I gossip about other teachers?
(5) Do I interfere in another teacher's work?
(6) Do I complain constantly about students?
(7) Do I complain constantly about school conditions?
(8) Do I complain constantly about school duties?
(9) Do I engage in petty arguments?
(10) Am I intolerant of others?
(11) Do I criticize the former teacher's achievement with children?
(12) Am I unsympathetic with other teacher's problems?
(13) Am I jealous of other teacher's success?
(14) Do I expect special privileges?

[1] Ruth A. Allen, "And How About You," *National Elementary Principal* (February 1959), pp. 37-40.

(15) Am I *constantly* talking shop?

(16) Do I take out personal feelings on children?

(17) Do I criticize or gossip about children in front of others?

(18) Do I belittle my co-workers?

(19) Do I belittle my supervisors?

(20) Am I sarcastic with my pupils?

(21) Do I fail to settle complaints in a professional manner?

(22) Am I "cliquish" with other teachers in the building?

(23) Do I go to the principal with petty problems?

(24) Do I spread rumors?

(25) Do I borrow materials and not return them?

(26) Do I borrow without asking?

(27) Am I unable to take criticism or suggestions?

(28) Do I discipline other teacher's pupils without informing him?

(29) Do I snoop?

(30) Do I dwell on personal troubles?

Obviously the affirmative responses are seen as least desirable by fellow teachers.

A self rating might tell us, to some extent, how our colleagues look upon our behavior which affects our acceptance and effectiveness in the faculty group.

Another way we might look at "acceptable v. unacceptable teacher behavior" is by noting *how* teachers react when they are in conflict situations with fellow staff members. Spector[2] has provided us with a continuum of courses of action a teacher may take in a conflict situation. They are arranged from the immature physical exchange of blows to the objective attempt to determine the cause of the irritation as follows:

(1) a. Exchange blows
   b. Threaten with fists
   c. Curse vocally

(2) a. Talk back
   b. Bluster
   c. Threaten or curse under the breath

(3) a. Laugh it off
   b. Placate by smiling
   c. Be coldly polite

(4) a. Remain calm and silent
   b. Ignore
   c. Walk away

[2] Samuel I. Spector, "Teacher Reactions to Conflict Situations," *Journal of Education Psychology* (November 1955), pp. 437-45.

(5) a. Feel annoyed
   b. Feel resentful
   c. Feel hurt

(6) a. Discuss calmly
   b. Stick to the facts of the situation
   c. Try to determine the cause of irritation

The subjects in Spector's study were asked to react to school conflict situations by selecting a course of action from the possibilities above. One conflict situation to which an action was requested was, "You have been accused of spreading gossip about another teacher. You are entirely innocent. The teacher confronts you and berates you. What would you do?"

Some Causes of Friction

It has been noted that, among other things, our degree of acceptance by other teachers is affected by our behavior in relatively unstructured situations and by our reactions in the face of conflict. Since behavior is symptomatic, it is incumbent upon us to understand better the causes of any behavior. Since behavior is dynamic, it is possible that this increased understanding of the causes of behavior may lead to increased personal effectiveness and provide better understanding of others.

Initially, it was noted that the growth of the teaching force and its increasing mobility cause a teaching faculty to be composed of newcomers and old-timers. Empirically it could be argued that age differences among staff members might affect teacher relationships. Some support for this supposition is found in the work of Havighurst.[3] According to his classification, members of each age group have different needs. For example, the new teacher—as a young adult—generally is occupied with selecting a mate, learning to live with a marriage partner, starting a family, rearing children, managing a home, getting started in an occupation, taking on civic responsibility, and finding a congenial social group.

In contrast the old-timer, having accomplished these tasks to some extent, is confronted with a different array of needs such as achieving adult civic and social responsibility, establishing and maintaining an economic standard of living, assisting teen-age children to become responsible and happy adults, developing leisure time activities, relating one's self to one's spouse as a person, accepting and adjusting to the psychological changes of middle age, and adjusting to aging parents.

Lack of understanding of the needs and behavior of those of a different age group well may contribute to discord among faculty. At the same time the very nature of the differences sometimes are difficult to accept. For example, while

---

[3] R. J. Havighurst, *Developmental Tasks and Education* (New York: Longmans, Green), 1952.

the newcomer is at her aesthetic best, the old-timer may increasingly be aware of and concerned with her vanishing youth.

Beside the differences in needs which may contribute to poor teacher to teacher relationships, at least one other cause may be speculated here. Perception of the role of the teacher varies widely, as shown in studies of teacher effectiveness. We all are convinced we can tell a good teacher when we see one. Thus, we judge our colleagues on the basis of *our* perception of what *they should do* as professionals. When they behave as we would wish, they are "good teachers." Good teaching, then, is value loaded. Our failure to recognize this leads us all to set up personal models to which we expect others to conform. Seeking a common denominator for the teaching behavior of our colleagues is a mistake we cannot afford.

Possible Solutions

After noting the problems and discussing some possible causative factors, our attention must focus on alternative solutions.

It has been illustrated that knowledge of the causes of ineffective teacher to teacher relationships is imperative. Such diagnosis makes progress possible, for the causes and not the symptoms must be treated. It is only a first step albeit an important one, to recognize that one "gossips about other teachers" or "is cliquish." The fundamental question is *why* one behaves so. This question is indicative of a desire to understand the forces that shape our behavior. Unfortunately, few of us are willing to commit our personal behavior to discussion or inspection by others. Opportunities to discuss the problems collected by Allen as problems of a "third person" might prove fruitful. Case studies have an advantage for this purpose.

Awareness of our reactions to conflict situations is commendable, but achieving better self control or more objective behavior is a more difficult task.

Possibly the most fruitful avenue for increasing positive teacher to teacher relationships is suggested by Homans,[4] who hypothesizes that the oftener people do things together the more they will tend to like each other; the more they like each other, the oftener they will tend to do things together. If this is true, it is incumbent upon the school leader to provide satisfying opportunities for staff members to relate to one another. Efforts might be worthwhile which would enable teacher isolates and stars, newcomers and old-timers, to work together.

Interclass visitations are one way in which teachers can better get to know and understand each other. Several studies report this as a successful technique for improving teacher interrelationships.

---

[4] George C. Homans, *The Human Group* (New York: Harcourt, Brace and World, Inc), 1950.

In the final analysis, however, our ability to relate successfully within our professional peer group seems to be in direct proportion to our ability to accept ourselves and others. The ability to do this may come only late in life, if at all, for some. However, we must be diligent in our efforts for our happiness and effectiveness depend a great deal upon whether we can say, "I like myself, I like others, and others like me."

Volunteers in the Classroom

Peter Schrag

In San Francisco, 250 women, most of them housewives, are working in 21 schools, helping children with mathematics, spelling, and music.

In Seattle, 23 volunteers are working in a high school to help sub-par students.

In New York City, 130 volunteers, who work in a conversational-English program for youngsters new to the language, have helped 3,000 children in the past five years.

In Detroit, an eighty-two-year-old arborist—one of 1,400 volunteers in that city—gives lectures in the elementary schools on the trees found in the city's parks. In the same city, an experienced labor arbitrator goes into high-school classes and participates in mock negotiation sessions with the students.

In city after city today throughout the United States, women go to the schools on a weekly basis to assist teachers in keeping records, monitoring lunchrooms, and correcting children's work.

No one is certain how many volunteers are now working in American schools, but the figure may well be as high as two million. Some receive nominal sums, usually under federal grants; most work for nothing. Among them are college and high-school students (including 250,000 after-school tutors), retired men and women, and hundreds of thousands of parents. The volunteers range from school dropouts to men and women with doctorate degrees, who go into classrooms periodically to talk with children about physics or poetry or the currents of the ocean.

Reprinted by permission of McCall Corporation, New York, from *McCall's* 95:4-5, March, 1968.

In a survey of some forty American communities, conducted by the National School Volunteer Program, projects that involved a total of 1,700 volunteers four years ago are now staffed by more than 19,000. Volunteers have been the backbone of the Head Start program, and they comprise almost the entire after-school tutoring force in America. At the same time, their most important function may still be in relieving hardpressed classroom teachers from routine duties, so that they can concentrate on the central job of teaching children.

For the past two years, while the interest and glamour associated with American education have been directed primarily to the development of new technological devices for relieving the teacher shortage, the real action is taking place on an entirely different front. It is not the machine and the technician that are moving into classrooms, but the volunteer—the interested amateur, the tutor, and the "paraprofessional."

Although some volunteer programs have been in existence for more than a generation, apathy as well as the hostility of professionals blocked any large-scale introduction of such programs. It was not until two or three years ago, when major federal funds became available to support programs for disadvantaged children and when large staffs were created for new projects, that the volunteer movement started its dramatic growth. Although the Ford Foundation and other agencies have been promoting the use of teacher aides and other paraprofessionals for some time, it was probably sheer necessity—the pressing shortage of personnel—that gave volunteer work its greatest impetus. In the long run, the acceptance of volunteers in the schools may be one of the most permanent (though unexpected) benefits of federal aid to education.

Clearly, the presence of hundreds of thousands of amateurs is not an unmixed blessing: Good intentions alone are not sufficient. Children can quickly spot condescension and pretentiousness, while some teachers have the feeling that volunteers sometimes create more problems and work than they eliminate. Some, moreover, antagonize the professionals by trying to take over the classes or the programs, in which they are presumably only helpers. Conversely, oversensitive teachers still feel easily threatened by outsiders, who, they fear, will upset established routines.

Nevertheless, no one doubts that ultimately the volunteer programs will be one of the most significant new assets for American schools. For years we have talked piously about the need for greater community participation and increased parental involvement in the schools. Now we are beginning to get them.

Our American classrooms are better because the volunteers are there. New ideas and faces are making an impact on school systems that had been isolated not only from the communities they served, but from the larger world, as well. As a consequence, the children and the teachers are learning more—and so, needless to say, are the volunteers.

Teacher Aides: How They Can Be of Real Help

Wayne L. Herman

Using a helper effectively is not as simple as it may seem. Here are suggestions for tasks that can ease the teacher's load without conflicting with basic instruction.

One of the problems that increasing numbers of teachers and principals have to face when funds become available for teacher aides is: "Now that we have the aides, what are we going to do with them?"

This isn't as humorous as it may seem. The fact is, there is very little advice available on just how teacher aides can be worked into an efficient and productive classroom routine. I know because I have been asked the question many times and have attempted to find sources of helpful information without much luck. As a result, I have done considerable research on my own and have come up with a list of possible duties that may be useful to those blessed with an aide for the first time.

Because every school system has its own policy regarding the functions of aides, and because personnel qualifications vary widely, the following list is intended only to offer suggestions. No one school will employ aides in all of the capacities mentioned, but all of them are functions that have been tried and found successful at one school or another around the country. For convenience in separating basic duties, the list is divided into two parts—one for routine jobs requiring no instructional skills, and one for more advanced duties involving some instructional responsibility.

Non-instructional functions

1. Collecting lunch and milk money.
2. Collecting supplementary books and materials for instruction.
3. Collecting and displaying pictures, objects, realia, and models.
4. Collecting money for charity drives, pupil pictures, trips, etc.
5. Correcting standardized and informal tests and preparing pupil profiles and scattergrams.
6. Correcting homework and workbooks; noting and reporting weak areas.
7. Proofreading class newspaper.
8. Ordering and returning films, filmstrips, and other A-V materials.
9. Telephoning parents about routine matters.

Reprinted from *Grade Teacher* Magazine 84:102-103, 168-169, February, 1967, by permission of the publishers. Copyright February 1967 by *Teachers Publishing Corporation,* Darien, Connecticut.

10. Filing correspondence and other reports in children's records.

11. Distributing books and supplies to children.

12. Distributing and collecting specific materials for lessons, such as writing paper, art paper, and supplies.

13. Procuring, setting up, operating, and returning instructional equipment.

14. Requisitioning supplies.

15. Building up resource collections.

16. Sending for free and inexpensive materials.

17. Obtaining special materials for science or other projects.

18. Completing necessary records and bringing other information up to date for cumulative records.

19. Keeping attendance records.

20. Entering evaluative marks in the teacher's marking book.

21. Averaging academic marks and preparing report cards.

22. Completing school and county reports.

23. Keeping records of books children have read.

24. Supervising the playground, cafeteria, and loading and unloading of buses.

25. Supervising the classroom when the teacher has to leave it.

26. Arranging and supervising indoor games on rainy days.

27. Preparing and supervising work areas, such as mixing paints, putting drop-cloths down, arranging materials for accessibility, etc.

28. Supervising cleanup time.

29. Organizing and supervising the intramural athletic program.

30. Accounting for and inventorying non-consumable classroom stock: books, textbooks, dictionaries, reference books, athletic gear, etc.

31. Checking out books in central library and other supervisory duties.

32. Managing room libraries.

33. Supervising seatwork.

34. Typing teacher correspondence to parents.

35. Typing and duplicating mass communications.

36. Typing, duplicating, and collating instructional materials.

37. Typing and duplicating the class newspaper.

38. Typing and duplicating children's writings and other work.

39. Typing and duplicating scripts for plays and skits.

40. Making arrangements for field trips, collecting parental permission forms, etc.

41. Keeping and maintaining a folder of representative work for each pupil.

42. Telephoning and making arrangements for special classroom resource speakers.

43. Displaying pupil work.

44. Attending to housekeeping chores.

45. Helping with children's clothing.

46. Setting up and maintaining controls on seating arrangements.

47. Routine weighing, measuring, and eye testing (by chart).

48. Administering first aid and taking care of sick and hurt children, telephoning parents to pick up a sick or hurt child, taking home a child who does not have a telephone.

49. Taking an injured child to a doctor or hospital.

50. Telephoning parents of absent children.

51. Telephoning parents to verify notes requesting that children leave school early.

Semi-instructional functions

1. Conferring with other teachers and the principal about specific children.

2. Interviewing children with specific problems.

3. Observing child behavior and writing reports.

4. Preparing informal tests and other evaluative instruments.

5. Preparing instructional materials: cutouts, mastercopies, flannel board materials, science materials, social studies displays, concrete teaching aids for arithmetic, etc.

6. Arranging bulletin board displays for teaching purposes, such as flow charts.

7. Arranging interesting and inviting corners for learning: science or recreational reading areas, investigative areas.

8. Keeping bulletin boards current.

9. Preparing introductions to A-V materials that give children background for viewing them.

10. Developing techniques and materials to meet individual differences, such as rewriting reading materials down for less-able readers, developing study guides, taping reading assignments for less able readers.

11. Supervising club meetings.

12. Supervising seatwork calling for some judgment.

13. Supervising committees engaged in painting murals, constructing, researching, or experimenting.

14. Teaching a part of the class about a simple understanding, skill, or appreciation.

15. Teaching a small and temporary instructional group, such as on the use of the comma or overcoming slang.

16. Tutoring individual children: the bright or the less able.

17. Reviewing, summarizing, or evaluating learnings.

18. Teaching children who missed instruction because they were out of the room for remedial reading or speech therapy; repeating assignments.

19. Helping pupils who were absent to get caught up with the rest of the class in content, skills, appreciations.

20. Assisting children with their compositions and other writings: spelling, punctuation, and grammar assistance.

21. Listening to oral reading by children.

22. Instructing children on the proper use and safety of tools.

23. Settling pupil disputes and fights.

24. Teaching good manners.

25. Contributing one's talents in art, dramatics, music, crafts, etc.

26. Reading and storytelling.

27. Helping with the preparations of auditorium plays and programs.

28. Previewing films and other A-V materials.

Chapter 11

Developing Competency

The teacher who is really concerned with becoming a true professional is searching constantly for better ways of teaching boys and girls. He is aware that his education and growth have only begun as he commences to teach and that continual self-development is essential for effective teaching. He will need, therefore, to seek out and engage in programs for self-improvement, both in and out of the classroom.

The first article in this chapter describes three techniques that are used in one school system to help teachers evaluate and improve their teaching: the use of the tape recorder in the classroom, the practice of having pupils make written evaluations of the teacher, and the formation of discussion teams including the teacher, the principal, and students.

The teacher who expects to improve his teaching must utilize the techniques of research. Not only should he be aware of and use the findings of research specialists, but also he needs to experiment in the classroom, to conduct action research. The day-by-day interaction between the teacher and his pupils as they work together offers the greatest of opportunities for improvement of instruction and professional growth through experimentation and evaluation. How one teacher conducted classroom research with considerable success is the subject of Camp's article, "A Classroom Experiment."

Hanna and Geston believe that most teachers fail to obtain maximum benefit from professional periodicals. They suggest ways that educational publications can be used to increase the teacher's knowledge, improve his teaching, and provide information and insight for parents and patrons of the school.

Contending that it is possible to identify the qualities of excellence that distinguish the true professional, Garcia in "To Be a Very Good Teacher" proceeds to do so in terms of specific happenings that occur in establishing the environment, in instruction and evaluating, and in the teacher himself.

Nearly all teachers feel that their teaching is not as good as they would like it to be, and most of them believe that they could do better. Foster's article, "What Teachers Think of Their Teaching," reports the reasons that more than two hundred experienced teachers gave for not teaching to capacity and the suggestions they made for improving their own teaching.

The teacher who is endeavoring to grow in competency will be engaged in an ongoing process of self-evaluation. The concluding article of this chapter suggests some procedures and tools that are available to the teacher to help him evaluate his effectiveness in his professional activities.

Three Gimmicks That Help Teachers Grow

For a realistic appraisal of the Aurora West Side public schools, teachers and administrators have been tapping two productive and readily available sources: students . . . and each other.

The district's "self-assessment" programs have relied heavily upon the aid and cooperation of youngsters. And these novel inservice efforts haven't gone unnoticed—Aurora was the 1966 Illinois winner of an NEA Pacemaker award for an inservice workshop.

One technique used often in the district—tape recording class sessions—has opened some traditionally closed doors.

Another—written inventories of teachers by students—has helped teachers see their strengths and weaknesses.

And a third procedure—formation, in individual schools, of discussion teams comprising principal, teachers and students—has opened up (permanently, it is hoped) lines of communication that, too often, are clogged.

School Building Teams

Generally speaking, problems of human relationships within individual schools aren't difficult to solve—*if* you have the principal, teachers and students all working on them. But first, you have to get all three parties talking openly and honestly to each other. And *that* ain't easy, bub!

Aurora is keeping these doors of communication open through what it calls "cross-generational cross-status development teams." Translated into English, these are discussion teams, each consisting of a principal, three teachers and three students. One team is located in each school. The goal is to identify and solve such human problems within the school as youngsters who don't understand why they can't get through to teachers and teachers who are puzzled by lack of rapport with their classes.

But before participants in these teams even begin to talk about these problems, they must first break through the barriers to honest communication that exist between them. Consequently, in the inauguration of the program last December, participants from the district's eight schools (high school, two junior highs and five elementary) were brought together for a three-day training session.

Most student representatives had been elected by schoolmates on their grade level. Teachers in most buildings had elected their representatives from lists of those who had previously told principals they would be available for the three days. (Some students and teachers were appointed by principals.)

These three types of representatives first met separately during the first day of the training session and reviewed various impediments that might later hamper free discussions. All three groups, it turned out, faced essentially the *same* barriers! Students, principals and teachers felt that:

● The others didn't really care about their opinions and preferred to make decisions without their help.

● They might damage their status if they sought the opinions of the others.

● They didn't like pressure ("They try to force me to respect them").

● They couldn't always trust the others.

● They risked personal embarrassment in disclosing thoughts or ideas ("He might think less of me" "She'll think I'm stupid"). This personal insecurity was reflected in students' comments that they feared teachers might not like them if they spoke honestly; in teachers' admissions that concern over student reaction sometimes influenced classroom decisions; and in principals' disclosures that fear of possible teacher dislike sometimes caused them to soften administrative procedures.

After this opening session, the participants re-grouped into seven-person building teams. They were aided by five experts from the University of Michigan who were trained in group dynamics, interpersonal relationships and change processes. Also assisting were Aurora administrators who had some experience in these fields.

After some frank talk about the communication barriers that had been identified in the initial session, the teams got down to hardnosed consideration of problems. The technique used to unearth those problems: brainstorming. Among the many irrelevant thoughts tossed out by participants were, usually, a few genuine problems of human relationships within the school. Then, it was a step-by-step process of discovering contributing factors to the problems and finding ways to alleviate or solve them.

Sometimes, one group would watch another in action and then discuss the effectiveness of its approach.

Then and later, participants also played roles in impromptu dramas to seek solutions to such problems as, for example, the attitude of the traditional teacher who is adamant against innovation, or the impasse between a principal who is eager to try new things and guidance counselors who are not.

Throughout the school year, these teams continued to meet in their own schools. There was no overall pattern. Some met during school hours for two-hour periods, and others met before and after school hours. This same flexibility obtains today; building teams continue to meet when they can and sessions are still informally structured but geared to a definite problem-solving approach.

There have been problems, according to Charles Sweatman, director of the program. One has been a shortage of personnel trained in group discussion techniques. It has been suggested that the district have some of its teachers and principals trained specifically for this purpose.

As always, personality problems have developed. One youngster who was elated at the honor of being chosen as a team member, for example, translated this into displays of superiority at team meetings. He irritated fellow team members, who finally barred him from the meetings—after discussing it, face to face with him. They later relented and readmitted him.

The resignation of a teacher from another team led, ultimately, to the demise of the team. (This team, incidentally, had been *appointed* by a principal.)

But there have been positive, as well as negative, results.

Two examples:

1. Youngsters in one elementary school team said they felt the teachers didn't believe the students' ideas were important. "You're talking with us, but you don't *really* care," they said. Out of subsequent discussion came a plan whereby the teachers arranged for interested older elementary students to help out with teaching in the lower grades—coaching younger students on arithmetic problems, for example.

2. After the initial December meeting, Franklin junior high formed three additional building teams. They met several times a month. One team discovered that both teachers and students disliked the school's home-room procedures. (During the weekly home-room period, the teacher is expected to lead students in guidance or related activities. Example: a discussion of manners or dress for a prom, or elections of student body representatives.) Teachers felt they were doing a guidance counselor's job; students resented having so little voice in choosing activities. The building team then drew up a list of recommendations for change.

Generally speaking, teachers and students on building teams seem to have developed an ease in expressing their opinions. And teachers report that this freedom has spread to classrooms.

"We've got people talking to each other now," says Sweatman, "which is an accomplishment in itself. Many people are aware that problems of human relationships *do* exist and can be solved; formerly, there was often merely frustration and annoyance. Hopefully, the building teams, by providing us with more knowledge about ourselves and about those we come into contact with, are helping to build a basis for continuous growth by the entire staff."

Taping the Teacher

A teacher in the midst of a lesson doesn't have too much leisure to analyze her techniques. Mulling it over later, she may decide she might have done this or that a different way, or she might think of something to add the next time. One way to realistically "relive" a lesson is through a tape recording. And if several teachers listen to replays together, the potential gain—from the point of view of constructive criticism—is enormous.

This is just what Aurora teachers do. Staff members who are enrolled in self-assessment programs are urged to tape their lessons (using a standard tape recorder) regularly.

Recordings are made during regular class periods and revolve, usually, around a regular lesson.

For clarity, it has been found best to limit actively participating students to no more than 10—and those the more vocal ones. The recorder is usually placed right in their midst. The other students simply observe during the taping, joining in discussion only after it is over. Reason for excluding some youngsters: the recording is blurred if there are too many participants. Other than this practical arrangement, the aim is to have the tapings reflect, as truly as possible, the teacher's normal classroom behavior.

For analysis purposes, it has been found that taped lessons should run for at least a half hour.

Teachers are not forced to expose their teaching—good or poor—to colleagues. Nevertheless, of the 100 or so junior high teachers participating in one inservice program, well over half welcomed critiques of taped lessons, however potentially painful.

These critiques are part of the activities conducted during weekly inservice sessions of teachers, meeting in groups of 10 or 12. Aurora teachers analyze their taped classroom techniques by means of a system developed by Ned. A. Flanders of the University of Michigan. Ten categories of teacher-pupil relationships are explored. The tape is studied to see if the teacher accepts the youngsters' feelings, if she praises or encourages her pupils, if she accepts and uses their ideas. Does she ask questions? Does she lecture, give directions, criticize or justify her authority? All of this is noted. Students' recorded responses are separated into those that they initiate and those that are responses to the teacher. Even silence or confusion gets a rating!

Each category is assigned a number. At three-second intervals, the taped classroom action is classified by number and noted on paper. These results are then analyzed by formula.

Using this procedure, a teacher may discover she talks too much. Or that she's light on praise of students. Or that she's a bore.

Occasionally, at critique sessions, tactless comments have stung teachers whose tapes were being analyzed. And, not surprisingly, some teachers have reacted defensively to criticism. For the most part, however, a constructive atmosphere is maintained.

Results of the use of these tapes are not easily isolated or readily apparent.

But Aurora's superintendent, Harold G. Fearn, is convinced that the overall impact in improving teaching is considerable.

Teaching Inventory

No question about it: that youngster sitting in the third row sees his teacher in a certain way. His observations and conclusions may be accurate or false, immature or well-reasoned. But they do exist. And they can be extremely helpful to the teacher who wants to do a better job of teaching him.

In Aurora, a six-page "style of teaching" inventory is available to teachers who want to find out what their students think about them.

The principal section of the inventory is a list of 52 statements, describing various professional aspects of teachers. The student circles one of five numbers—1) always true, 2) true most of the time, 3) true about half of the time, 4) seldom true, and 5) not true—to indicate the degree to which each statement describes *his* teacher.

The idea is to find out what the student thinks of his teacher's relationship with the class, personal characteristics, professional ability and classroom techniques.

Sample statements: "my teacher . . . expects too much of us . . . makes the class work exciting . . . praises the students when they do a good job . . . is a happy teacher . . . keeps changing the rules for punishment . . . talks more than most teachers . . . has the class do individual or group projects . . . asks facts or memory questions on examinations . . . knows what students like best."

Two additional sections of the inventory help the teacher determine the ability and creativity of the student who is rating her. This information, together with students' answers to the evaluation section, helps teachers gauge whether they are teaching toward high or low ability, high or low creativity. These two additional sections are:

1. *Twelve statement choices,* in which the student compares himself to his classmates. Examples:

"My grades in this course are . . . much better than most students in this class, about average, lower than most students in this class."

"I like my teacher . . . more than most students in this class, about average, less than most students in this class."

2. *A creativity-testing exercise,* in which the youngster is asked to write down 10 or so unusual things a symbol (square with four lines extending from its corners) reminds him of.

To gain further insight into classroom performance, each teacher is urged to list—*before* seeing the inventory results—what he considers an ideal rating and also the rating he *predicts* the youngsters will give him. These projections are then compared with the *actual* overall ratings, which are usually computed *for* each teacher. (The district has used the services of both the University of Illinois and commercial computer firms. Individual teachers sometimes do tally their own scores, however; the creativity test must be hand-scored.)

While the inventory is primarily for the individual teacher's own information, the results—like the tapes made in classrooms—are also discussed in groups.

Problem? For one, teachers have questioned the validity of assigning too much weight to individual items on the inventory. And the "always true" category has also been criticized.

But there has been general agreement that these inventories do give a broad indication of the teacher's classroom "image."

And many teachers have found they can go *back* to their students to review with them the results of the inventory-taking, particularly to probe discrepancies between their views and the self-view of the teacher.

A Classroom Experiment

William L. Camp

The practices of a successful teacher of reading are sometimes the results of historical and traditional influences rather than of carefully conducted study. As Russell (1963) wrote, "In the United States, the teaching of reading dates back over 250 years. During that time, both skillful teachers and textbook writers

Reprinted with permission of William L. Camp and the International Reading Association, Newark, Delaware, from *The Reading Teacher* 22:145-147, 152, November, 1968.

have developed materials and methods which have greatly influenced reading instruction, usually without making a careful study . . . . in the modern sense of controlled experimental tryout. When teachers do not have justification for their teaching methods, they often have a precedent of successful practice to which they can point. Resourceful teachers sometimes use . . . . teaching methods which work well for them, before careful evaluation of these procedures has been made." In one sense, these persons are experimenting at a demonstration or action research level, and the initiative displayed by such highly motivated teachers is to be encouraged. However, such efforts can be advantageously combined with more carefully controlled classroom study of a sort which can promote individual teacher growth in teaching technique, knowledge of materials, and understanding of the dynamics of variables which can influence the teaching-learning process.

An example of this kind of do-it-yourself inservice training was conducted by a classroom teacher in Illinois school district U-46 between September 1960 and June 1964. The purpose of her study—in addition to the goal of increased personal growth—was to compare two widely discussed methods of teaching reading to first grade pupils.

During the 1960-61 school year this experienced first grade teacher taught reading to her class of nineteen students, emphasizing the whole-word method accompanied by appropriate materials obtained from a well-known publisher. The teaching involved asking the pupils to look at pictures and to associate words, learned by sight, with stories about the pictures seen. Words were taught first; sounds were taught later. These learned skills were then combined by teaching the pupils to group words into sentences and stories. Similar teaching methods have, in the past, been classified as part of the look and say or sight theory of teaching reading. During the last week of the school year a mastery type reading test (Monroe, 1954), obtained from a neutral publisher, was administered to the group. This was duplicated during the 1961-62 school year with a class of twenty-seven pupils and during the 1962-63 school year with a class of twenty-three pupils. The same teacher conducted each of the classes which had been made-up of pupils, matched, as closely as possible by class, for sex, for age in years and months, and for tested intelligence. Intelligence information was collected from the *Pintner General Ability Test* (Pintner, Cunningham, and Durost, 1939) data available in the school files.

Using this information as control data, a similar class of twenty-two pupils, again approximately matched with the other classes for sex, age, and intelligence, was formed for the 1963-64 school year. Reading was taught to this group by the same teacher, but in this case the phonics method, with appropriate materials, was used. In this group, students learned word sounds first and complete words later. Again the reading test (Monroe, 1954) was administered to the class during the last week of the school year.

With data thus available for one experimental and three control classes, the hypothesis that no significant achievement differences would be found between the experimental and control classes was tested. Means, standard deviations, and Student's "t" differences were computed, with scores appropriately weighted to compensate for differences in class size. Differences between mean raw scores computed for total class achievement, and differences between mean raw scores computed for class achievement on seven sub-tests were determined comparing the phonics class with each whole-word class.

No significant differences were found between the experimental and the control classes when total class achievement was compared or when sub-test achievement was compared. To further test the hypothesis, for differences within classes, differences were computed between percentages of pupils scoring in each sub-group of the experimental and the control classes. Class divisions were based upon percentile groupings suggested by the test publishing company (Monroe, 1954).

No significant differences were found between the experimental and the control groups when percentages of students achieving in the "low" (1st to 24th percentile) category, in the "high" (75th to 89th percentile) category and in the 1963 and 1961 groups of the "low average" (25th to 49th percentile) category were individually compared. Of the ten comparisons for which statistically significant differences were found, six were in favor of the experimental (phonics) group and four were in favor of a control (whole-word) group. Significantly higher percentages of experimental students were found to achieve in the "very high" (90th to 99th percentile) category and in the "mid average" (50th percentile) category than were found in any control group. For "high average" (51st to 74th percentile) category achievers in all groups and "low average" (25th to 49th percentile) category achievers in the 1962 group, however, the reverse was true. Significantly higher percentages of control pupils, than experimental pupils, were found to achieve at these percentile levels.

Significant differences were found at varying levels of confidence from .01 to .001. While use of a mastery test rather than a standardized reading test restricts use of the results of this study, many valuable understandings accrued to the teacher who conducted the program as well as to several other first grade teachers who became interested enough to take part in analysis of the data.

In addition to the objective study of data gathered during this experiment, many subjective observations were made and recorded, over the four years, by the teacher and by the school principal. In the whole-word groups, for example, grouping by slow, average, and superior learning ability seemed most productive, in terms of motivation. The phonics group, however, seemed to best lend itself to teaching the class as a whole, using grouping only for extra help and supplementary reading. Also, the phonetic method of learning new words seemed to present a consistent challenge to top students. Transfer of learned concepts and reading skills to other learning areas also seemed especially valuable for the phonics group. Finally, additional recorded observations reflected difficulty displayed by slow learning pupils in keeping up with the phonics groups unless large amounts of extra help were provided by the teacher.

A Final Comment

Studies, such as the one reported here, can be of immense personal value to the teachers who conduct them. Much more important than the contribution which studies of this sort may make to the body of literature which relates to teaching is the resulting personal growth and enthusiasm which can be carried over into the teaching practice of those participating.

Plans are now underway for other teachers to conduct a more refined variation of this experiment over the next several years, using more appropriate testing-instruments and a more carefully controlled research design. Although these teachers have had no formal training in educational research, they now believe that study of this type can yield understandings which will help them to become better teachers. Growing interest has lead to development of an informal seminar group which is made up of lower elementary teachers who have begun further study of the teaching of reading, using the director of research and several other central office administrators as research design and statistical consultants.

REFERENCES

Monroe, Marion. *New basic reading test* (grade one). Chicago: Scott, Foresman, 1954.

Monroe, Marion. *Norms, scoring key, and directions for scoring: new basic reading test.* Chicago: Scott, Foresman, 1954.

Pintner, R., Cunningham, B.V., and Durost, W. N. *Pintner general ability test.* New York: Harcourt, Brace and World, 1939.

Russell, D. H., and Fea, H. R. Research on teaching reading. In N. L. Gage (Ed.) *Handbook on research on teaching.* Chicago: Rand McNally, 1963. P. 865.

How to Use Professional Periodicals

Nancy W. Hanna and John M. Geston

Teachers use professional magazines in many ways—among them keeping up with new developments in education, finding ideas and materials to use in the classroom, obtaining information that can be used effectively in working for teacher welfare, and obtaining facts and figures that are more current than those in textbooks. Even so, many do not get maximum personal benefit from professional magazines, and most seem unaware of how valuable these publications could be in giving parents and other interested laymen insight into the teaching and learning processes.

First, we will discuss how the individual teacher can, and does, use professional periodicals.

Teachers probably tend to spend much of their reading time on special-interest magazines—*Music Educators Journal, Instructor, English Journal, Science Teacher,* and others. They rely on these magazines for such things as reviews of new books in their fields; ideas for composition topics, math puzzles, or science experiments; and illustrations or articles suitable for bulletin boards. Many teachers keep files of articles and special features clipped from these magazines or even file entire issues.

Few teachers, however, limit their professional reading to articles about the subjects they teach and ways to teach them. Other topics of special interest include research, educational philosophy, teacher welfare and status, child growth and development, and general education news. (See "Teachers' Reading and Recreational Interests," *NEA Journal,* November 1966.) For broad coverage on topics of this sort, the teacher must often read a number of publications.

Many administrators and supervisors read and clip several professional magazines. Some call to teachers' attention material of special relevance and keep an extensive file of articles on various teaching methods and ideas which may be of help to teachers, particularly the neophytes. If a school is introducing a new program, ungraded classes, for example, administrators report that a clipping file can be a valuable source of information to use in explaining such a program and building confidence in it.

In order to see how teachers can use professional magazines in general, let's consider how they use one in particular—the *NEA Journal*—which carries articles

Reprinted by permission of the National Education Association, Washington, D.C., and Nancy W. Hanna and John M. Geston from *NEA Journal* 56:63-64, February, 1967.

on a wide range of topics at all levels from preschool through higher and adult education.

In each issue, the *Journal* (like a number of other magazines) presents a special feature of several articles dealing with various aspects of some broad phase of education, such as learning, guidance, and individualizing instruction. Articles of this sort are of interest to teachers no matter what subject matter or grade level they teach, and many educators save them for ready reference.

The *Journal* also includes a wealth of material on such topics as teacher salaries, teacher load, negotiation practices, and interpretation of Association policy.

Other types of articles which cut across subject and level boundaries include general interest ones, such as "What's New in Urban School Buildings?" and varying viewpoints on controversial issues, such as the desirability of education for all four-year-olds.

The *Journal* serves the dual purpose of helping a teacher do a better job in his classroom work and of making him a well-informed member of the teaching profession. Keeping up-to-date on what's going on in education all over the country makes the teacher better qualified to participate in educational planning in his own school system and to answer questions posed by the school board, parents, and others interested in education.

Among the *Journal's* continuing features, one of the most regularly used, according to a recent readership survey, is the "Unfinished Story." Many elementary teachers (and some secondary ones) report that this feature stimulates helpful and thought-provoking classroom discussions of ethical values. Some teachers have pupils role play the stories, an approach particularly successful with disadvantaged youngsters. Teachers have also successfully used an "Unfinished Story" to launch a short story unit.

Even more popular—according to the most recent readership survey—is the monthly "Classroom Incident," in which a high school teacher describes how he handled a difficult situation, and consultants then evaluate the teacher's behavior. In some instances, teachers report having their students discuss what procedure they think should have been followed.

Many teachers not only read but make practical use of suggestions that appear in the *Journal's* "Idea Exchange" column, and those that appear in similar pages of other educational periodicals. For people who like to find humor in their professional magazines, there are cartoons and light-hearted columns, such as those labeled the "Light Touch" in the *Journal.* One teacher says she likes to put professional magazines containing humor on her free reading table because it shows the children that teachers are human too.

Because they *are* human, teachers sometimes need a chance to blow off steam. In addition to the traditional letters to the editor forum ("Our Readers Write") which may influence a magazine's tone or content, the *Journal* gives teachers a chance to speak out in "It Burns Me Up." The column not only allows teachers and administrators to express their frustrations but also, on occasion, undoubtedly gives them a new awareness of each other's feelings.

Though few magazines attempt to cover as much educational territory as the *Journal* does, most—including the state association publications—carry a wealth of useful material.

To be valuable, a magazine must not only be good but accessible. We believe every school should subscribe to a number of professional magazines and have a place, perhaps a teachers' corner in the library, where teachers can use them. Inasmuch as reading these publications can be a valuable aspect of in-service education, their expense is easily justified.

Since many teachers are too busy to go through numerous magazines to find and read articles of special interest, we suggest that either the school or the local association form a periodicals committee to review professional periodicals and call colleagues' attention to particularly good articles. (Merely listing titles is usually not enough; a sentence synopsis of each article, for example, would probably encourage much more readership.)

The committee might also keep an eye out for inaccurate or unfairly biased articles. Letters or even articles of rebuttal could then be prepared and signed by a group as a whole or by several individual members of the committee.

Since an effective committee will have much work to do, we strongly recommend that the already overworked building representative be freed of any responsibility in its formation or functioning. A local association president may appoint a committee on periodicals, or a principal may assign some teachers to such a committee just as he assigns others to sponsor various student extra-curricular activities.

Though the primary purpose of professional magazines is to help teachers do a better job and be knowledgeable about education in general, these magazines can also serve those outside the teaching profession. If laymen were better informed about what's going on in education, the teacher's burden would be lighter. One way to educate them is to put professional publications where the public is likely to see and read them—places such as beauty and barber shops, doctors' and dentists' offices.

Many associations have already discovered how feasible and effective this can be. For example, NEA makes copies of the *Journal* available at cost ($4 a year) for those associations who wish to distribute them. Many teachers give their local periodicals committee issues of educational magazines they have read but not clipped for distribution. Numerous families which contain more than one association member request that the additional *Journal* subscriptions be sent to a key nonmember, such as a school board member, PTA president, or mayor.

Even if every issue of the *Journal* is not made available for doctors' offices and the like, a local association can make a point of distributing special issues like the December *Journal* (which was designed for laymen as well as professionals), reprints from professional magazines, and items such as the NEA *Journal's* annual "Briefing for Parents" feature.

Others who could profit from greater familiarity with professional publications are those preparing for a career in education. Such individuals may begin collecting articles for their teaching file, becoming familiar with issues and trends in education, and finding material for research papers. The prospective teacher needs to know what the NEA is, what it is accomplishing, and what goals it has set. Members of Student NEA become familiar with the Association through the *Journal* and other NEA publications. In the case of institutions that do not as yet have such organizations, local associations from town and gown might join forces to increase the use of professional publications on college campuses.

For optimum benefits from professional publications, teachers must do more than read them and see that laymen have access to them; they also ought to have a sense of involvement in what is printed. They should send editors their reactions to articles and suggest topics for future ones—indeed, they may even write their own.

To Be a Very Good Teacher . . .

Elvira T. Garcia

Assuming that a teacher has a well-integrated personality and is adequately prepared for her position, what distinguishes her as a true professional? Can qualities of excellence be identified for further examination?

Qualities of excellence *can* be identified—in terms of specific happenings. Here are some highlights.

Instruction

In the area of instruction, a professional teacher's goal is to provide interesting lessons that will be meaningful to each child. To achieve this, she:
* Studies each child's social and cultural background.
* Notes the level of successful achievement he has reached in any given area.
* Discusses the child's needs with parents and school personnel.

Reprinted by permission of The Instructor Publications, Inc., Dansville, N.Y., from *The Instructor* 77:139, 150, August/September, 1967. ©The Instructor Publications, Inc.

● Plans individual and group projects that will meet the needs she has noted and will challenge him.

● Decides on a type of motivation she hopes will reach the individual and the group of which he is part. (If one approach fails, she tries another immediately.)

● Organizes her day to provide for work with individuals and with groups having common needs or interests.

Pupil Evaluation

Evaluation is done by the teacher with the help of other qualified persons. (At the same time, the effectiveness of her own approaches and teaching techniques is assessed.)

In evaluating a child's progress and growth, the perceptive teacher looks for:

a display of eagerness.

ability to think critically in new situations.

degree of reading comprehension.

ability to use mathematical concepts in solving problems.

skill in communicating through writing and speaking.

the kind of rapport the child has with others.

The Classroom

The classroom is the place where the child works. It must provide him with space and tools for working and as much physical comfort as possible. It should also be attractive—a place where the child looks forward to being.

To provide the proper room atmosphere, the teacher:

● Sees that it is well equipped with textbooks, library books, visual aids, and reference sets.

● Sets up centers of interest with educational games and other manipulative materials.

● Displays children's work.

● Keeps live plants and perhaps animals for the children to observe and care for.

● Arranges for bulletin boards to enhance instruction.

● Keeps track of heat, light, and ventilation.

● Supervises committees set up to keep the room neat and attractive.

● Arranges for the use of temporary supplementary teaching aids.

● Varies seating arrangements and sizes of instructional groups.

The Self-Governing Child

"Every child in command of himself" is the goal of the professional teacher. Since children learn best to discipline themselves in an orderly environment, to provide such an environment is the teacher's responsibility.

Then the teacher:

- Helps pupils define standards of behavior realistic to them.
- Guides them in analyzing the reasons for inevitable failures to live up to those standards.
- Avoids threatening punishment.
- Stresses the idea that in a free society the actions of one individual affect many others.
- Lets every child feel he is liked at all times even when what he does is not acceptable.

The Teacher Herself

The very good teacher constantly bears in mind that her actions and attitudes are the key to what happens in the classroom. She knows she must achieve self-realization if the children are to achieve it too. She *expects* to:

derive satisfaction as a personal consultant.

enjoy aiding children as they learn to think and to find positive solutions to their problems.

like guiding the development of their patterns of behavior.

feel good about showing them how they can contribute to their own group and to the larger group society of which they are a part.

As a true professional, a teacher is objective. She talks over her personal performance with other members of her team or with her principal, welcoming their comments and constructive criticism.

Above all, the very good teacher accepts each child as he is, particularly in terms of social and emotional maturity, and seeks to help him progress as far as he is able. When the child realizes that his teacher is both uncritical and realistic, he is ready to make the most of one of life's most rewarding experiences—the learning adventure!

What Teachers Think of Their Teaching

Walter S. Foster

Educational literature abounds with statements and inferences to the effect that teachers do not teach as well as they know how and that their instructional practices are not consistent with their beliefs and capabilities. The literature, however, has little to say relative to *teachers'* opinions of their teaching practices. To obtain teachers' perceptions of their methods of instruction, the author had 213 experienced elementary-school teachers complete an opinionnaire designed to obtain data related to the following questions:[1]

1. Do teachers believe that they are teaching as well as they know how?
2. What do teachers advance as reasons for not teaching better?
3. What instructional methods do teachers believe they should employ under current conditions?
4. What changes would teachers make in conditions to remove obstacles they perceive to better teaching?
5. What instructional methods do teachers feel they would employ if conditions were changed?

Do teachers believe that they are teaching as well as they know how? Apparently not, for not even one of the 213 respondents to the opinionnaire claimed that he was teaching to capacity. Furthermore, only 8 of the 213 felt that they were teaching as well as conditions permitted, whereas more than 95 percent stated definitely that they could improve their teaching within the confines of existing conditions.

When asked to explain their failure to teach to capacity, the teachers offered 144 reasons for not teaching better. Each of 8 of these reasons was mentioned by 10 percent or more of the study population (Table 1). Well over one-third of the teachers acknowledged spending insufficient time in planning and preparation, one-fourth recognized their failure to plan with pupils, one-fourth blamed fatigue for their failure, and one-fifth stated that they were not grouping pupils adequately for instruction. Lack of knowledge of subject matter to be taught was admitted by one of every eight teachers, and demands of home life were considered as being causes of inferior teaching by nearly as many. Awareness of their failure to make adequate provision for individual differences and to work with individual pupils was evidenced by more than one-tenth of the respondents.

Written for this volume.
[1] Walter S. Foster, "Teachers' Perceptions of Their Teaching Practices and Means for Improving Their Instruction" (Unpublished Doctoral Dissertation, University of Oregon, 1964).

Table 1
Most Frequently Given Reasons for
Not Teaching to Capacity

Reason	205 teachers f	%
1. Insufficient time spent in planning and preparing	78	38.0
2. Insufficient teacher-pupil planning	52	25.4
3. Fatigue and lack of energy	51	24.9
4. Insufficient grouping for instruction	40	19.5
5. Lack of knowledge of subject matter	26	12.7
6. Demands of home life	25	12.2
7. Failure to provide for individual differences	23	11.2
8. Insufficient time spent in working with individual pupils	22	10.7

In response to a question asking them what they could do to teach better under existing conditions, the teachers suggested 130 specific means they would employ. The seven most frequently volunteered (Table 2) show that, in part at least, the means suggested for improving instruction were directed at the more common reasons these teachers gave for not teaching better. Emphasized were teacher-pupil planning, planning and preparation by the teacher, grouping for instruction, providing for individual needs and differences, and use of audio-visual materials.

Table 2
Most Frequently Suggested Methods
for Improving Teaching

Method	205 teachers f	%
1. More teacher-pupil planning	66	32.2
2. Grouping and regrouping for instruction	63	30.7
3. More individualized instruction	51	24.9
4. More and better planning by the teacher	30	14.6
5. More use of audio-visual aids	28	13.7
6. Exploring, determining, and providing for individual needs	28	13.7
7. Better, more comprehensive lesson preparation	25	12.2

Every teacher who took part in the study asserted that he could improve his teaching if he could remove specific obstacles by changing certain conditions under which he worked. Of a total of 208 specific changes recommended, 9 of the 11 presented in Table 3 were advocated by 10 percent or more of the respondents and the other 2 by nearly that large a percentage.

Table 3

Most Frequently Advocated
Changes in Conditions

Change	213 teachers f	%
1. More planning and preparation time during the school day	52	24.4
2. Class size maximum of twenty-five pupils	40	18.8
3. Central, conveniently located supply storerooms with simple check-out systems	31	14.6
4. Release from playground supervision	28	13.1
5. Teacher aides to help with supervision, films, supplies, bulletin boards, art work, and grading of papers	25	11.7
6. Teacher aides or parents for playground and lunchroom supervision	24	11.3
7. More secretarial help for teachers	23	10.8
8. Full-time physical education teachers	23	10.8
9. Central, convenient locations for audio-visual mateirals with adequate check-out systems	22	10.3
10. Full-time music teachers	21	9.9
11. Full-time librarians	20	9.4

It appears that teachers would make changes to give them more planning and preparation time, smaller classes, greater convenience in obtaining and using instructional supplies and audio-visual materials, teacher aides and secretarial help to handle nonprofessional duties, assistance with physical education and music instruction, and better library services.

Assuming changed conditions, the teachers who completed the opinionnaire specified 116 methods they would use. Five instructional practices were designated by 10 percent or more of the participants, and a sixth practice by nearly that many (Table 4). Given the conditions they desire, the teachers would endeavor to individualize instruction, introduce more flexibility in grouping, have pupils do more experimenting and research, and use more audio-visual materials.

Table 4

Most Frequently Mentioned Methods
Teachers Said They Would Use

Method	213 teachers f	%
1. More individualized instruction	45	21.1
2. Individualized reading	41	19.2
3. Flexible grouping	29	13.6
4. Individualized help in mathematics	22	10.3
5. More research-type work and experimentation by pupils	22	10.3
6. More use of audio-visual aids	20	9.4

Teachers' perceptions of their teaching practices, as revealed in the expressed opinions of the 213 experienced elementary-school teachers who contributed to the findings of this study, indicate that they know that they are not performing to capacity, that they can identify obstacles that hinder their teaching, that they do want to teach better, and that they have ideas as to how improvements can be achieved.

Self-Evaluation: Procedures and Tools

Ray H. Simpson

The instructor who wants to go about the important task of improving his effectiveness almost always can get help from the great variety of tools and procedures that have been found useful by other teachers. Typically, it is desirable for the teacher periodically to conduct some type or types of self-diagnosis. Such diagnosis will likely show he is relatively strong in some areas of his professional activities. The diagnosis will also point out to the teacher some areas in which he is relatively weak and in which improvement is to be desired. For example, one teacher using Cosgrove's, "The Descriptive Ranking Form for Teachers,"[1] found she was particularly strong in (1) knowledge and organization of subject matter, and (2) adequacy of plans and procedures in class. She also found that she was relatively weak in (1) adequacy of relations with students in class, and (2) enthusiasm in working with students. One reasonable approach for this teacher is to do some careful and intensive study of some of the wealth of research studies in the general field of social psychology, including such subdivisions as leadership, development of peer- and self-leadership in classes, improving class climate, and use of groups and grouping. Such studies can result in improved interpersonal relations in the classroom.

In order to diagnose effectively it is very desirable that the teacher become acquainted with the great arsenal of tools and procedures available to him. The following paragraphs contain a picture of some of the types of tools and procedures that the teacher should at least be cognizant of so that he can select those which he believes are likely to be most helpful to him.

Reprinted with permission of The Macmillan Company from *Teacher Self-Evaluation* by Ray H. Simpson, pp. 12-23. Copyright ©by Ray H. Simpson, 1966.
[1] D. J. Cosgrove, "Diagnostic Rating of Teacher Performance," *Journal of Educational Psychology,* 50 (1959), pp. 200-204.

Instructor's Written Assessment of His Teaching

To set the stage for systematic change in activities that will result in improvement, it is desirable for the instructor continually to diagnose what he is doing, why he is doing it, and how it is succeeding.

One of the ways of collecting data that will encourage self-improvement involves framing and answering questions that will help the teacher view objectively his current inadequacies and so help him chart the directions in which he wants to grow professionally. Teachers, inveterate testers of their pupils, are invited by Simpson[2] to apply the testing processes to some of their own activities. For self-diagnostic purposes, the individual teacher is encouraged to evaluate himself on 33 questions. Questions relate to three main areas, and illustrative examples follow:

1. Provision for individual differences in academic ability.

   Examples: In the last year did I have as much concern for the very rapid learner as for the very slow learner? Did I help provide reading materials for daily use which had a spread in difficulty of at least five grades?

2. Provision for professional development.

   Examples: During the last year, did I participate *actively* in teachers' meetings? Did I read at least four professional magazines in the average month?

3. Provision for aiding youngsters in developing socially.

   Examples: During the last year, did I encourage pupils to study and work out many of their problems together? Did I discuss more than once with pupils the problems of how to work more effectively with others in a committee?

Another type of instructor self-evaluation involves writing down after each class period what the instructor himself feels were the strong points and weak points during the teaching-learning situation under consideration. While such an evaluation may take three to seven minutes of instructor time, it can be quite helpful, if it is done periodically, in showing the teacher places where he believes additional attention is needed in his instruction.

A third type of written assessment which many teachers have found helpful is one made at the end of each semester or each year. Such an assessment can include types of things the teacher feels went successfully during the year as well as areas where the teacher thinks improvement would be very desirable. Such lists, if done carefully, can provide the teacher with a basis for changing materials that are used, changing assignments, modifying class procedures, and other types of things which have been identified by the teacher as needing modifications.

[2] R. H. Simpson, "Teachers, Here Is Your Final," *The Clearing House,* 16 (September 1941), pp. 47-48.

Student Achievement

The acid test of teaching, of course, revolves around the achievements of learners. This suggests that it is important for the teacher to attempt systematic follow-up of former students, both those in school and those out of school, in order to get suggestions for improvement.

Some primary teachers have found it helpful to talk with pupils they have had who have moved into the intermediate level, and question them as to what difficulties they are currently having. In a similar fashion, intermediate teachers have interviewed high school students. And additionally, high school teachers have found it helpful to follow up, either on vacations or by means of correspondence, students who have gone to college or who have gone into jobs in the community. Some instructors have found it desirable to help *current* students interview a certain number of the teacher's past students. This not only can provide useful feedback to the teacher but sometimes improves current motivation among students and helps them to understand better the purposes and possible future uses of a course.

Another way of checking on student achievement is to list teaching objectives and then to use structured tests, either teacher-made or commercial, to see the extent to which objectives are being achieved. An important feature of this activity is to first list objectives specifically and then attempt to find tests that seem to measure these objectives. Oral testing of students' achievement should not be neglected. Interviewing a sampling of students may improve the teacher's perspective.

Some teachers have found it stimulating to make a comparative check of their own efficiency using one technique or approach as compared with efficiency in using another, different technique or approach either with different groups or in two semesters. For example, one junior high school teacher, concerned over poor mathematical growth in her students the preceding year, decided to make some changes and to measure the results. She recalled that when she had been an elementary teacher of reading she had learned to make adjustments to individual students' abilities in learning to read. She had used two, three, or four groups of pupils reading from different books and using different materials. She decided to try something similar in her junior high school mathematics classes in the following year.

In brief her plan, evolved largely the preceding summer, was characterized by the following: use of a pretest on the first day of classes to determine individual abilities in mathematics; use of three different texts, acquired with the help of her principal; varied assignments, the one for a particular child depending upon his stage of mathematical development; development of much self-responsibility in self-assignment making on the part of individual pupils; use of peer help and leadership; and finally a retest at the end of each semester. The results of retest were compared with pretest scores to obtain an indication of mathematical growth. When growth with the revised setup was compared with that of the preceding year, the teacher was very pleased, particularly with significantly greater gains in word and thought problems.

Work with Colleagues

The process whereby a teacher committee gets together in a workshop to discuss or to construct a teacher-evaluation instrument or questionnaire can be a very stimulating activity, particularly for those who are directly involved in the workshop or in the committee. Regardless of what subsequent use is made of the questionnaire or evaluation instrument that is discussed or produced, the actual process of developing it is in itself an excellent type of in-service activity.

Team teaching is a much-emphasized arrangement in recent years which offers great possibilities for teacher self-evaluation. Team teaching is, of course, a way of organizing the instructional program and may be used on either the elementary or the secondary level. Cooperating teaching groups may work vertically (that is, at all grade levels in a single subject or similar subjects); or they may work horizontally (that is, at one grade level but in several subjects). In any case, members of a team set up objectives together, plan together to achieve these objectives, talk freely with each other, and are constantly assisting and assessing each other. It is this latter feature which offers great promise in helping the teacher in self-diagnosis. As each teacher works with other members of his team he can gain stimulation through comparing his strengths and weaknesses with those of others on his team. The spirit of frankness that is characteristic of a well-functioning team permits the teacher to get direct and indirect reactions of colleagues to various aspects of his teaching.

Regularly planned meetings of all of those teaching at a certain grade level or in a particular course permit the teacher to obtain the suggestions of colleagues relative to his objectives, plans, and procedures. Such regular meetings or seminars should meet on school time, and a frank discussion of points of view relative to proposals is essential. One plan of operation involves having one teacher responsible at each meeting for presenting to colleagues something he is doing or is planning or has read about in a professional journal. A free exchange of ideas permits the teacher to make some evaluation of his ideas and procedures through the continuous verbal interchanges with colleagues. The exchanging of staff ideas is frequently facilitated by regular small group luncheons where the avowed purpose of the discussion is to evaluate the teaching proposals and practices of those involved.

In many schools such specialists as the administrator, the supervisor, or the guidance specialist have the time, knowhow, and willingness to help the teacher in his self-assessment. For this to happen in a beneficial way it is usually necessary for the teacher to request such help. When this is done, it is frequently taken as a sign of strength on the part of the teacher that he is willing to request aid in self-diagnosis. Such aid may involve conferences with the teacher, observations in the teacher's classroom, getting feedback from students, or other information about some aspects of the teaching-learning situation about which the teacher is concerned. The guidance specialist may, for example, help the teacher diagnose the social-emotional climate for learning in the teacher's classroom by suggesting tests, inventories, or other approaches. For best results, (1) the teacher should request the help, (2) the interaction between teacher and specialist should go on over a considerable period of time, and (3) the teacher should give ideas and insights a tryout which then should be followed by an assessment of effectiveness.

An exchange program of materials and observations can be mutually stimulating to the instructors concerned. In such a program, two or more instructors agree to supply the other cooperating person involved with the professional materials, diagnostic tests, and other materials that have been found particularly useful. Also, a reciprocal type of class observation is set up in which each teacher observes the other teaching and then offers suggestions on how the situation might be improved. Many administrators are willing to provide teacher substitutes or other arrangements to make such a plan for diagnosis and improvement possible.

For greatest value from shared materials and observation, those involved must desire this type of stimulating interaction; frankness and reciprocated confidence must be shown; and sufficient time must be provided not only for the observations but also for the conferences which should typically be held subsequent to each activity.

The possibility of setting up such reciprocal aid in diagnosis with teachers in other parts of the school system or even with teachers in neighboring systems should not be neglected. A local organization of classroom teachers can sometimes appropriately take the lead in sponsoring reciprocal observations and in getting necessary administrative arrangements made for them.

Professional Reading and Self-Evaluation

The well-trained teacher increasingly appreciates the wealth of help that professional reading can provide. A key area of help involves the discovery, analysis, and use of tools for self-evaluation. Descriptions and discussions of such tools regularly appear in such periodicals as *The School Review, Harvard Educational Review, The Clearing House, The Journal of Educational Psychology, Educational Leadership,* and the *Phi Delta Kappan.* The new experimental studies involving teacher-evaluation tools with potential implications for the teacher must be continuously assayed.

The tests and inventories for investigating teacher reading skills and practices, for example, have provided some interesting and thought-provoking conclusions.

Much has been written about reading disabilities, but educators sometimes forget that they themselves may suffer from such liabilities. For example, in a large urban school system it was found that 3 percent of the twelfth-grade pupils actually read better than 100 percent of the teachers.[3] The educators were found to be particularly low on these subtests of the Iowa Silent Reading Test: selection of key words, use of index, and directed reading.

The diagnosis further revealed that a reasonable amount of leisure-time, recreational reading was done by the teachers, but little or no professional reading to help solve school problems was engaged in by the typical teacher or administrator. Unfortunately, even those teachers who scored high on the reading test, which indicated that they knew how to read well, made little if any more professional use of this ability than did those who scored low. A study of 746 teachers and administrators indicated the following results related to professional reading for a particular month:

No magazine articles read 14%
One magazine article read 10%
Two magazine articles read 13%
Three to five magazine articles read 29%
More than five magazine articles read 34%
Had not even looked at one professional book 40%
Had sampled one book 17%
Had read parts of two books 24%
Had read parts of three to five books 15%
Had read parts of five or more books 4%

When the results of this type of diagnosis face the individual teacher or the group, it is likely that some decisions will be made to change the situation.

Analysis of Class Sessions

One way to set the stage for systematic change in activities that will result in improvement is to make tape recordings or even television recordings of regular class sessions and then make a feedback analysis. Modern recording devices that are relatively inexpensive permit a fairly accurate pickup in classroom situations. This permits the teacher to analyze such things as the following: What he said and how much of the time he was talking, what the students said, how many students participated, the kinds of questions students raised, if any. Also such mechanical features as the quality of the teacher's voice and the speech of students can be helpfully studied under some circumstances. Some teachers have been amazed at the sounds of their own voices in the classroom. Where a teacher has not used this approach it can be very stimulating.

[3] R. H. Simpson, "Reading Disabilities Among Teachers and Administrators," *The Clearing House*, 17 (1942), p. 12.

Another related type of tape recording can be made of an evaluative class session in which strengths and limitations of the class are analyzed by the students. This type of recording is usually made during the middle of a semester or year so that the teacher can use the leads that are picked up in improving his instruction. Such a discussion may be led by the instructor himself, or by a student, or by a panel of students, or in some cases by a colleague who has been invited into the class for this particular purpose and who is known to be able to quickly establish desirable rapport with students. Such an atmosphere is necessary for an evaluative class session to be a frank revealing of how students feel about various class activities.

Use of the Whole Class for Getting Self-Evaluation Leads

A variety of techniques are available for use with the whole class in alerting the teacher as to what his students consider to be relatively strong and weak aspects of his performance. Such evaluation can be useful to the instructor who desires to know where to begin to work on improving his effectiveness.

Postclass reaction sheets, filled out in the last two or three minutes of a particular class period or at the end of the morning or afternoon, with appropriately selected questions can give the teacher some indication of students' reactions to what is happening to them in the classroom. Such questions as the following can elicit useful leads: What did you like about today's class period? What part of today's class period do you think should be changed, if any? In today's class period did the teacher give sufficient opportunity for discussion? Did the teacher clarify issues? Was too much time used by a few students? Did the teacher encourage all to participate in discussions? Did the teacher maintain a good balance between pupil and teacher participation? If such questions are asked at appropriately spaced intervals during the semester or year, the teacher at least can see how students are reacting to some class activities.

Another whole class activity is to encourage students to elect a committee that will develop a learning-evaluation questionnaire to be answered by the whole class. The construction of such a questionnaire in and of itself can be useful in developing a consciousness on the part of class members of the purposes involved in the learning and also tends to help develop student responsibility. The school may itself want to encourage the student council or some representative student group to construct a learning-evaluation instrument. In all cases, teacher guidance should be given in the consideration of goals to be checked and in the development of the instrument. Also, a battery of suggestive evaluative items such as those in *Student Evaluation of Teaching and Learning*[4] can suggest to students and teacher what to include in a questionnaire.

[4] R. H. Simpson and J. M. Seidman, *Student Evaluation of Teaching and Learning* (Washington, D.C.: The American Association of Colleges for Teacher Education, 1962).

Another stimulating way to get ideas for self-improvement is to have one class period, or a part of such, periodically devoted to course planning. This may involve planning for the present class or may take place near the end of the year to give 'the teacher suggestions for the following year. Such planning sessions can give the teacher some idea of student-perceived strengths and weaknesses of the current class. Such topic areas as the following can provide a basis for discussion: To what extent have the goals and purposes of this class been clear? What are reactions to the text materials we have been using? How have you reacted as students to the assignments that have been made? Have they given you sufficient opportunity to make choices and decisions so that you would not be doing busy work? Have you seen the importance of the types of activities you have been asked to do in this class? Has the amount of time you feel you have been expected to spend on the class been reasonably appropriate?

Some teachers have found that asking students to write answers to such questions as the following is useful: What do you regard as this class's major strengths? What possible weaknesses do you see in the work of the class to date? How could these weaknesses be diminished? What do you consider to be the one or more best features of this course? What are the one or more least satisfactory features of the course? What suggestions do you have for improving this course?

The growing body of research literature on the use of students' rating of their teachers indicates that pupils can and do make reasonably accurate ratings of teachers. As Howsam[5] reports:

> Their ratings tend to agree with each other, and the teachers who are rated best by the pupils tend to obtain the highest pupil gains. Pupil ratings often do not agree with ratings by principals, supervisors, or other teachers. (This has not been considered an indication of weakness [of student ratings], however, since ratings by superiors and peers have not been shown to agree with pupil-gained measures or to be satisfactory in other ways.) Teachers have indicated their belief that pupil ratings, as obtained in research studies, are both fair and accurate.

These research findings would seem to indicate that teachers should consider making more use of evaluative questionnaires, checklists, or inventories which either are self-constructed or have been borrowed from such sources as *Student Evaluation of Teaching and Learning.*[6]

Use of Selected Individual Pupils

There are several techniques involving individual learners that some teachers have found helpful. One of these is to have a nonclass member who is an

[5] R. B. Howsam, *Who's a Good Teacher?* (1705 Merchanson Drive, Burlingame, California: Joint Committee on Personnel Procedures, 1960).
[6] Simpson and Seidman, *op. cit.*

accelerated pupil periodically observe and evaluate selected class sessions. When this is done, it is usually necessary for the teacher to alert the observer to the dimensions on which he is to consider the class. Sometimes an observation sheet developed by the teacher will greatly facilitate the recording of the observer's reactions.

Another procedure is to have regular or periodic informal discussions with individual pupils. Consideration should be given to getting reactions from various levels of intellectual ability. For example, the reactions and opinions of some average pupils should be sampled. Also the teacher may wish to elicit the judgments of bright or "reliable" learners who seem to be quite perceptive and who are able and willing to talk about various aspects of the class. A third group of individuals that the teacher may want to make use of in this regard are poor or relatively weak pupils who may have quite a different perception of such things as assignments, class discussions, text materials, and work expected by the teacher.

Another technique is to have a different pupil each day assume the role of class evaluator. This learner would, at the beginning of the period, be provided with an evaluation sheet by the teacher. This sheet would indicate types of things at which the class evaluator is supposed to look. One advantage of this approach, aside from the aid it may give to the teacher in self-evaluation, is that it may help learners become more involved in the planning, leadership, and responsibility for the class, and consequently it may favorably affect motivation.

In addition to "keeping his ear to the ground" for various evidences of student reaction to classroom activities, the teacher may wish to have elected by the students an evaluation committee which will meet with him periodically and provide feedback to him on student reactions to various activities, assignments, marking procedures, testing procedures, and other important aspects of the class.

In conclusion, it may be pointed out that evaluation of teaching-learning situations is continuously being made by teachers, students, administrators, parents, and others. Whether this evaluation will be soundly grounded depends to a high degree on the type of evidence upon which it is based. If the teacher wishes to improve his base for evaluation, one of the best ways is to develop a familiarity with, and a use of, a variety of measurement tools. A few of these have been suggested in the preceding paragraphs.

Chapter 12

Improving the Profession

Not only is the truly professional teacher concerned with his own self-development; he also recognizes and accepts his responsibility for upgrading the profession to which he belongs.

What does it mean to be a member of the teaching profession? And what are the professional responsibilities involved? Dorros considers these questions in the introductory article of this chapter; and Hubbard, in "I Speak of a Spark," stresses the importance of dedication, sense of purpose, "the spark of professional devotion," and the fundamental urge to be a professional teacher.

Implementation of group professional responsibilities requires that teachers combine their individual efforts to work toward common goals. Professional organizations offer the opportunity for teachers to work together to achieve what would be impossible for the individual to do alone. In the third article Foster reviews the types of organizations available to teachers. Corey, in "Educational Power and the Teaching Profession," states that the teaching profession must, through its organizational structure, increasingly exercise leadership in the improvement of educational objectives, curriculum, and instruction.

The chapter concludes with a brief discussion of professional negotiations and collective bargaining.

Criteria of a Profession

Sidney Dorros

Criteria of a Profession

The typical dictionary definition of "profession" describes it simply as a calling or vocation, especially one that requires learning and mental, rather than manual, labor. But most writers on the subject identify several more specific characteristics of a profession. These include the following:

1. Concern for the welfare of society above the personal interests of members of the profession
2. Command and application of a body of specialized and systematized knowledge and skills
3. Control by practitioners of admission to the profession, standards of preparation, and performance of its members
4. A high degree of autonomy in making decisions about how to perform one's work
5. A strong professional organization which enables the group to meet the above criteria, to achieve satisfactory conditions of work, and to advance and protect the welfare of its members.

These criteria are not ends in themselves. Their major purpose is to assure that those who satisfy professional requirements are more competent to perform a particular service than anyone else. The members of any profession have the responsibility of helping to identify, develop, and maintain high standards of competence.

These criteria apply to any profession, but means of meeting them vary according to differences in the nature of the various professions. For example, many professional workers such as medical doctors or lawyers practice their professions primarily as individuals; whereas teaching is primarily a public or *institutional* enterprise. Therefore, teachers are even more dependent than doctors or lawyers upon group action to achieve and maintain professional objectives.

One of the most widely accepted definitions of the respective roles of the public and the teaching profession in making decisions about education is reproduced in Figure 1.

Professional Responsibilities

Fulfillment of the preceding roles of the teaching profession depends upon how well teachers, as individuals and as members of organized groups, perform the following ten professional responsibilities:

Figure 1

The Profession's Responsibility		The Public's Responsibility
. . . joining with the public in	{ establishing public policy regarding education determining purposes of education providing working conditions conducive to productivity }	. . . joining with the profession in
. . . assuming autonomy for	{ determining and utilizing best means for achieving agreed-upon purposes ensuring competent professional personnel }	. . . granting the profession the right to make and carry out decisions in
. . . joining with the public in	{ evaluating achievement of purposes appraising public policy regarding education }	. . . joining with the profession in

1. Cooperative determination of goals of education
2. Adoption, observance, and enforcement of a code of ethics
3. Research and accumulation of professional procedures
4. Education in professional procedures
5. Accreditation of professional schools
6. Recruitment, selection, and orientation of candidates for the profession
7. Certification of members of the profession
8. Maintenance of economic welfare
9. Maintenance of a desirable work climate
10. Maintenance of effective professional organizations.

Source: National Education Association, National Commission on Teacher Education and Professional Standards, *New Horizons for the Teaching Profession,* Margaret Lindsey (ed.) (Washington, D.C.: the Commission, 1961), p. 23.

Reprinted by permission of Sidney Dorros and the National Education Association from *Teaching as a Profession,* pp. 1-3. Columbus, Ohio, Charles E. Merrill Publishing Co., 1968.

I Speak of a Spark

Frank W. Hubbard

No teacher worthy of the name has ever lacked an intangible spark of professional idealism. It is that something which makes one say, and really mean it, "I am proud to be a teacher—a professional teacher." Being a *professional* teacher involves a great deal more than being employed in teaching.

In early America the status of teachers did not kindle the spark of professionalism. Years ago, the well-meaning, kindly, and often elderly women who taught in the dame schools rarely thought of themselves as members of a profession. In colonial communities, many indentured persons went through the motions of teaching so as to move toward the end of their servitude. Only here and there did a strong, dedicated personality emerge. Not until well into the nineteenth century were there many counterparts of Ezekiel Cheever.

Soon after 1800, educational statesmen saw that the nation could not depend upon chance for its teachers. As the normal-school movement formed and moved ahead, teaching began the long, hard pull toward professional standards. The graduates of these schools were recognized as a selected group. They had pride in their skills and competence; they had a driving purpose in their lives; they brushed aside the notion that just anyone could teach school.

Systematic teacher preparation took a long stride forward when, despite opposition in the academic circles of universities, teacher education won a place in those institutions. The growth of public schools created a demand for teachers with specific preparation for their duties. Young people "found themselves" as they acquired new knowledge of the history, theory, and applications of instruction.

The characteristic idealism of youth leads to a sense of dedication. Perhaps the most important contribution of teacher education is to flame this spark—this sense of mission. Many graduates of teacher education today have the desire to be truly professional. Whether or not they keep this desire depends in large measure on what happens during their first years of employment. Placed among dedicated, experienced teachers and supported by a truly professional administration, the young teacher has an excellent chance of retaining his idealism and of growing to the point where he can share it with others who follow.

Unfortunately, however, everyday practice too frequently tends to smother the professional spark that the beginning teacher brings. He may be given teaching assignments regardless of his preparation and wishes. He may discover

Reprinted by permission of the National Education Association, Washington, D.C., from *NEA Journal,* 51:37, December, 1962.

that administrators offer little or no supervisory support. He may find that the custom of the school is for the new teacher to carry more than a fair share of the necessary, but less attractive, tasks of school management.

We hold no brief for pampering the young teacher, for only by becoming a student of his obligations and difficulties can he become truly professional.

The beginner should be expected to bring some degree of fortitude to his work and to build up his own inner resources. He must learn to study the problems in his classroom and to draw upon his technical preparation. He is expected to seek advice from those with more experience. He must seek in clinics, workshops, and conferences the clues to better teaching. But he must also have inner resources that will carry him on even when his preparation and experience offer no guide lines.

In other words, behind preparation and experience must lie a sense of purpose, a feeling of loyalty to the primary task of instruction, a belief that teaching is important.

There are many today who discount the spark of which we speak. For them, sparks merely cause smoke that obscures the real purposes of life—financial success, welfare benefits, publicity, and honors. Their goals are *primarily* materialistic and economic. The spark of professional devotion may remain, but its light is dimmed.

No one would contend that materialistic goals are of no importance. Teachers cannot eat idealism. The thought stressed here is that in the teacher, nothing can be *first* except his fundamental urge to be a professional teacher. The spark behind this urge must be constantly tended and replenished. The flame and light it provides is the way to public and professional esteem. Such esteem is the foundation of the teacher's influence on the present and the future.

Professional Organizations for Teachers

Walter S. Foster

One of the most important responsibilities of every teacher is that of selecting and supporting one or more professional organizations. Since there is a great diversity in types and numbers of organizations it is essential that the teacher become familiar with the nature, philosophy, goals, and procedures of the various associations from which he can choose.

Written for this volume.

Three broad categories of professional organizations are general purpose associations, special interest and teaching-field groups, and teachers' unions. The National Education Association (NEA) and the state and local education associations affiliated with the NEA are general purpose organizations. Special interest and teaching-field organizations include such groups as the Association for Childhood Education International, the Council for Exceptional Children, the Department of Classroom Teachers, the Department of Elementary-Kindergarten-Nursery Education, the National Council of Teachers of English, the National Science Teachers Association, and the Student National Education Association. The American Federation of Teachers is the major union organization available to teachers.

The oldest and largest teacher association in the United States is the National Education Association, which is, in a way, a confederation of affiliated state and local education associations. In 1970 it was 113 years old, and it now has more than one million members. Basic goals of the NEA include improvement of teaching, teaching conditions, and facilities and instructional materials; upgrading of professional standards; improvement of teacher welfare and protection of teachers' rights; and public support of education. To accomplish its goals the NEA conducts research; publishes research reports, journals, and other professional materials; assists state and local associations and its various units; works to achieve federal legislation favorable to education; defends teachers, as individuals or groups, and school programs; operates a public relations program; holds conferences and conventions; establishes procedures for professional negotiations; and invokes sanctions.

Every state has a state education association affiliated with the NEA. State associations tend to have the same general objectives as the parent organization and to engage in similar activities. Although services that are provided to members vary, it is generally agreed that the state education association should work for the development and maintenance of high professional standards, professional improvement of the members, the advancement of teacher and public welfare, and service to the schools and communities in the state. Since public education is a function of the individual states, many of the important decisions affecting education are made at the state level; therefore, state education associations have the responsibility and the opportunity to influence educational policy and practices to a very great extent. They are among the most effective of all organized teachers' groups.

The local education association is the organization to which the largest number of teachers belong and in which they participate most actively. Just as the strength of the national organization depends upon strong, active state units, so does the effectiveness of the state organizations depend upon the support of the local groups in such areas as membership drives, financial support, legislative campaigns, sources of information, and improvement of local school systems.

The local organizations provide teachers the opportunity to understand the problems and needs of their communities and to acquaint their communities with the problems and needs of the school and its teachers. The local association is the primary agency through which teachers negotiate with boards of education for improved conditions. Objectives and activities of local organizations generally include advancement of the profession and professional improvement of its members, school and community service, improvement of salaries and conditions of work, and social fellowship.

Many of the special interest and teaching-field associations are affiliated with the NEA. The Department of Classroom Teachers is one organization of this type to which many teachers belong and in which they participate at the local, state, and national levels.

Of the independent special interest organizations, one that appeals to many elementary school teachers is the Association for Childhood Education International. The ACEI is composed of approximately 100,000 members belonging to local branches which elect their own officers and meet periodically to study the growth and development of preschool and elementary school age children. The ACEI publishes *Childhood Education,* its official magazine, plus a number of bulletins and other publications.

The American Federation of Teachers (AFT) was formed as an affiliate of the American Federation of Labor in 1916. During the past twenty years it has grown steadily, particularly in the large metropolitan areas, to a membership estimated to be in excess of 140,000 in approximately 700 local units. These units are affiliated with their state federations and with the national organization, and members of locals automatically belong to the national and state federation. Members receive the official monthly publication, *The American Teacher,* and the quarterly professional journal, *Changing Education,* and are entitled to the services of the national office of the AFT.

According to the AFT Constitution, major objectives of the AFT appear to be similar to those of the NEA, focusing on protection of teachers' rights and interests, improvement of conditions of work, raising of professional standards, promotion of the welfare of children through increased educational opportunities, and promotion of democratization of the schools.

Although major differences exist in patterns of organization, philosophies, and procedures of the AFT and the NEA, the two organizations have become somewhat closer in their practices since the NEA passed its professional negotiations and sanctions resolutions in 1962. Certainly, one big difference between the organizations is that the AFT, although relatively autonomous with respect to its policy and program, is aligned with the AFL-CIO, while the NEA is an independent organization. Another difference claimed and stressed by the AFT is that it is controlled entirely by classroom teachers, since administrative personnel are excluded from membership; whereas the NEA is an all-inclusive association which accepts membership of all educators, including administrators.

Teachers' organizations furnish valuable services, among which are opportunities for personal contacts and service with other members of the profession, assistance with improvement of instruction and working conditions, and benefits pertaining to personal welfare. Each teacher is free to make his choice of associational groups, but only after evaluating the organizations available in terms of history, philosophy, objectives, program, and services should that choice be made. Then, when he has chosen, his support can be wholehearted.

REFERENCES

American Federation of Teachers, The Commission on Educational Reconstruction. *Organizing the Teaching Profession.* Glencoe, Illinois: The Free Press, 1955.

Dorros, Sidney. *Teaching as a Profession.* Columbus, Ohio: Charles E. Merrill Publishing Co., 1968.

Hubbard, Frank W. "Teachers' Organizations," *Encyclopedia of Educational Research* (3rd ed.), Chester Harris, editor. New York: The Macmillan Co., 1960. pp. 1491-96.

Stinnett, T. M. *Professional Problems of Teachers.* Third edition. New York: The Macmillan Co., 1968.

Weaver, J. F. "Professional Organizations and Education," *Review of Educational Research* 37:50-56, February, 1967.

Educational Power and the Teaching Profession

Arthur F. Corey

The constant use of the term "black power" has given a new connotation to a word which has in the past usually derived its meaning from the context in which it was used. Yesterday one might have asked, "What kind of power?" Today the word "power" is defined as the organization and implementation of the activities and influence of a somewhat homogeneous group in an attempt to gain conscious and desirable ends.

We often find illustration or parallel for human relations in mechanical principles. In the physical world, raw force is usually disorganized and uncoordinated energy. A tornado, an earthquake, or a huge waterfall exert unbelievable amounts of energy. They possess great force, but in a mechanical sense they

Reprinted by permission of the *Phi Delta Kappan,* Bloomington, Indiana, from *Phi Delta Kappan* 49:331-334, February, 1968. Copyright 1968 by Phi Delta Kappa, Inc.

develop no power. Natural sources of energy—that is, natural forces—must be concentrated and organized and channeled to accomplish desired ends before they can accurately be called "power."

In human relations, individuals have influence. Personal influence is social energy; it is tremendous force. When personal influence is so organized and concentrated and directed that it affects other people, it can rightfully be called "power." Good teachers have unique opportunity to exert such power over their students. If children are significantly different because of the influence of a teacher, then that teacher is truly "powerful." This is what Thomas Jefferson meant in ascribing to William Small, one of his teachers at the College of William and Mary, a "powerful" effect on all his later life.

Teachers have opportunity for "power" in all their personal relations. They can affect the opinions and attitudes of their family, neighbors, friends, tradesmen, and parents of their pupils. They may even have acquaintances within the power structure of the community. They can, if they will, have influence with a congressman, a state legislator, a city councilman, or a school board member. In all these relationships there is the possibility of "power." One of the negative aspects of today's larger school districts is the fact that personal relationships are less intimate—more tenuous and fragile—and therefore personal "power" is more difficult to establish and maintain.

It is not to deprecate the challenging possibilities of the influence of the individual teacher to accept the fact that the profession cannot be effective in directing changes in the schools unless these "units" of individual influence are organized, concentrated, and directed to desired ends.

The term "pressure group" is an epithet which has no definite meaning, usually applied to a group with which one disagrees and which one wishes to castigate. Most organized groups have common interests to advance and protect, and so long as their activities are honest there is nothing inimical or unethical in group activity. It must be expected that evil men will get together to further their nefarious ends. Edmund Burke once said, "When bad men combine, the good must associate." In fact, the political chicanery of certain economic groups was rampant until thwarted by the emergence of other groups strong and courageous enough to thwart them. Pure democracy in which every man as a unit speaks his own mind and controls his own destiny is a political ideal never yet approximated, and more and more difficult of realization as society becomes more complex. The play of group against group is the process of modern democracy. There is little profit in decrying this condition. We must be interested in making it more effective for the common good.

The only possible cure for the evils of organized pressure is more and better organization among honest and intelligent men and women of good will. We can be sure that economic interests will continue to organize for pressure and we accept their right to do so. Professional groups have also learned to organize to accomplish their cherished objectives. The real danger in American life is that large segments of our people will continue to be unorganized, and will have no effective voice in government and public affairs. The man who has no share in organized "power" is certainly not independent of it. He is consistently the victim of the organized pressures which shape his way of life. The teacher who wishes to have real influence must get himself into an effective group and work in it.

Tyranny, in modern times, begins by exploiting the unorganized mass and then uses this instrument to destroy all other organizations. The strongest guarantee against authoritarianism is the presence in society of many strong, voluntary organizations. The most corrupt political machines usually have developed where the unorganized mass is largest. Huey Long's reign in Louisiana is an excellent example. The decline in the power of Tammany Hall resulted from the development of many voluntary pressure groups which could not easily be exploited. Organization which is voluntarily supported by its members, and whose program is cooperatively developed by those members, is the only thing in modern life which we can justly call self-government. Self-government is the essence of individual liberty.

The professional not only knows his field; he applies his knowledge to the control and direction of some aspects of the lives of others. In short, the conception of a profession, when expressed in terms of its function as it bears on others in a society, implies that, in relating thought to action, power is exercised in a certain way in that society.

If in more and more areas of life today people are discovering that they can get more dependably what they most basically want by forging more effective power structures, the profession of teaching should develop, with some clarity, ideas about where its weight is to be felt.

Despite some recognition in our literature that the work of a profession involves the use of power, the analysis of power as it is related to the knowledge and service of the professions, especially the teaching profession, has been neglected. This neglect has meant that efforts to professionalize teaching have had no theory of power to support and guide them. They have had no theoretical analysis sufficient to discriminate between the functions of power in different contexts and no analysis to identify its uses and abuses.

Power obviously presents awkward problems for a community which abhors its existence and disavows its possession but values its exercise. Despite this convention of reticence and understatement, which seems to outlaw ostensible pursuit of power and which leads to a constant search for euphemisms to disguise its possession, there is no indication that, as a profession, we are averse to power. On the contrary, few things are more valued and more jealously guarded by their possessors in our society.

Teachers, like other Americans, are in fact very eager for power. They enjoy its possession, but would prefer to wield it quietly behind the scenes. This reticence has a basis in the fact that many teachers have a somewhat uneasy conscience based upon the assumption that organized power and democracy are not compatible. The truth is that democracy cannot function without organized power. Our political parties, the foundation stones of our representative government, are in themselves examples of organized power.

Many teachers seem to assume a scarcity theory about power. This theory is not dissimilar to the now outmoded scarcity theory of wealth. It was long thought that the only way in which one man or one social segment could improve his or its economic status was to lower the economic status of someone else in society. Just so, the scarcity theory of power unconsciously held by many assumes that the amount of power in society is a fixed quantity and therefore, when it is assumed by one group, it is *ipso facto* removed from some other group.

With obeisance toward these complexities, we shall take "power" to refer to organized and sustained social influence or control exerted by persons or groups on the decisions and actions of others. It relates to effectiveness in influencing action, decision, and policy in the entire range of human association. However, it is with the political aspect of power that this statement addresses itself.

America probably faces a generation of unprecedented political turmoil. The great issues will have to do with educational and social objectives and increasingly the people will begin to see that the kind of society they are to have is inescapably linked with the kind of education offered. America is heavily committed to more and more education for more of its people, but there is little consensus about what kind and quality of education this is to be.

Alvin Toffler[1] in a recent article calls the years between now and the turn of the century "The Age of Transience." Says he, "Rapid change will characterize every aspect of life. Time and space will collapse." People and things will come and go—in and out of one's life—at a faster rate than ever before. Man must learn to live with impermanence. There is ample evidence that even our ideas about goodness and badness—our sense of values—will change along with our environment. Impermanence will be further accelerated as science and technology advance and transience will permeate every aspect of life. The significant thing for us today is that in 1968 this acceleration is just barely beginning. The next third of a century will almost certainly be marked by scientific and social changes so severe that we must virtually abandon our habitual ways of thinking and doing and feeling. When society changes, education must inevitably change, and it will require great quantities of "educational power" to win this race with

---

[1]Alvin Toffler, "Can We Cope with Tomorrow?" *Redbook Magazine,* Jan., 1966.

catastrophe. If teachers are to lead educational change, or even influence it, they will do it through political power.

Teachers have been distressingly naive in their insistence that "schools must be kept out of politics." It may be that such people tend to confuse "politics" with patronage. Politics is the science of determining *who* gets *what* and *when*. No segment of American government is so thoroughly political as the public schools.

There is nothing inherently unethical in political power if it is broadly based, consistent, and responsible. The insistence that group power must be broadly based leads many into erroneous conclusions. Not every member of a large group can vote on every issue but all must still be involved in decision making. Power, to be effective, must be applied speedily and effectively and by responsible leaders, but must be based upon generalizations which have been picked in advance with the broadest possible group participation. The platform of an organization, broad-based and democratically determined, should be comprehensive enough to guide the on-the-spot decisions which must be made by its leaders.

Politics is the process through which organized power is, in the final analysis, applied in a free society. The effective methods for group political action have drastically changed in California in recent years. There was probably never a teachers' organization in America which enjoyed the political power possessed by the California Teachers Association (CTA) a generation ago. However, exactly the same methods would today be completely ineffective. The abolition of cross-filing, the sharp increase in the number of voters in legislative constituencies, and the unbelievable rise in campaign costs have combined to force groups which aspire to operate within the power structure to share the high campaign costs which otherwise keep all but the rich from running for legislative office. Time was when a pleasant letter praising a legislator for his support of public education was appreciated and was accepted as support. Those times are gone. Political support of public education is often measured in dollars, and if teachers are to stay in the game they must play the game under the new rules. This is the practical condition which gives rise to professional political action arms. Political forces are in flux. Labor and agriculture are gradually losing dominant places they once held in American politics. The present moment is indeed auspicious for the expansion and refinement of "educational power."

The expansion of educational power must be viewed and defended in terms of its objectives. Such power seeks to improve the quality of the educational experiences offered to American children. The ultimate end must always be improvement in the school program. Politicians instinctively respect that which they fear. They respect "power."

In the past the state teachers associations have generally been considered to be among the most effective groups in the legislative field. California has been no exception. The Golden State may also be typical of new conditions and new factors which must be faced if educational power is to be effective enough to give the profession some voice in educational decisions which may determine the nation's future.[2]

The unity which characterized professional legislative programs during the last decade is no longer so evident to legislators and to the public. The teachers union has been more disruptive to these programs than have the activities of organizations which have traditionally opposed public education. Although notoriously unsuccessful in attaining its own legislative objectives, the union has given legislatures the image of a house divided against itself and the excuse to defeat programs favored by a large majority of teachers. The schism between teachers and administrators, with the latter often maintaining independent representation at the capitol, has also tarnished the image of the united profession. In spite of these negative factors, the legislative record of state teachers associations has remained dramatically successful in the fields of school finance and teacher welfare.

The sad truth is that money for schools and economic security for teachers will not be enough in themselves to create the kind of schools which America now needs. These factors are basic and necessary, but well-financed schools with well-paid, secure teachers can still be woefully inadequate.

Educational power demands not only unity but commitment. Legislators have learned by experience that teachers really care about their own welfare, but lawmakers are not yet convinced that teachers are deeply motivated toward educational innovation and instructional improvement. This was painfully evident in the 1961 session of the California legislature.

Senator Fisher, and the Democratic Party which he represented, had no reason to believe that the members of the California Teachers Association would be vitally interested in a bill which sought to revolutionize the preparation of teachers. Assemblyman Casey had no reason to believe that the profession would be angered by his legislation, which mandated curricular detail. In opposing these bills, the CTA was operating outside its traditional sphere and legislators simply didn't take the opposition seriously. If these bills had attempted to weaken tenure, reduce retirement allowances, or cut state aid, they would have been killed in committee or never given a hearing. The politicians couldn't believe that the teachers back home really cared about certification or curricular detail. The fact that Senator Fisher, by his own admission, was defeated for reelection by angry teachers and that Assemblyman Casey is no longer in the

---

[2] "Legislative Policies and Procedures Used by State Teachers Associations," Corey and Strickland, an unpublished dissertation, University of Southern California, 1956.

legislature may be some slight assistance in correcting such legislative miscalculation in the future. However, educational power cannot be built by the occasional defeat of a recalcitrant legislator. The commitment of teachers to educational improvement must become traditional and hence accepted.

In an age of transience, society cannot permit a lag of a generation between important social and economic change and the resultant adjustment in education. The teaching profession must, through its organizational structure, be far more active in leading, or if necessary pushing, the reorganization of educational objectives, curriculum content, and teaching method.

With the collapse of space and time, we must give relatively more importance to the future than the past. The traditional argument that one learns to understand the future by knowing about the past has lost much of its validity. There is little precedent in the past for what our children face in the future. This fact is profoundly disturbing to many people and gives rise to the irrational demand from the far right that we continue to educate for life in a kind of world which has ceased to exist. It will require educational power to counter these misguided pressures.

The most important change in professional association programs in the immediate future must be increased involvement in the improvement of instruction. This responsibility has long been recognized, but it must be given high priority in teacher association budgets and hence in program emphasis. No group can develop or maintain professional status when its right or competence to have a voice in basic decisions regarding its own work is challenged or denied.

The teaching profession must assert that education in America is too important to leave in the hands of the prejudiced or the uninformed. It is a specialized field, the details of which are far too complex to leave to the average citizen. When professional organizations show as much interest in improving instruction as they now do in improving salaries, the public will be more willing to accord the profession a voice in determining educational policy. This is to say that if professional organizations really assert themselves in stimulating innovation and improving instruction, this very activity will be self-serving in that it will go far in developing the professional power to secure acceptance of their proposals.

Negotiating or Bargaining

Professional negotiating is a topic of high interest among teachers, school administrators, and boards of education. Actually this is a euphemism for collective bargaining; why disguise the term?

In championing the inherent right of bargaining, we are not saying that human values and individual integrity have always been guiding forces at negotiating tables. Faculty associations are facing the challenge of carrying on this operation in tune with the moral and spiritual values that have long characterized the teacher.

The profession must bargain without imperiling its unique talents in working with children. It must be ready to police its own profession, and in some areas to cure ills of overprotection caused by tenure. In negotiating, the teaching community is laying its professional image on the bargaining line.

Increments based almost entirely on years of service are a problem. A 75 percent salary differential may exist between the teacher with three years' experience and the one next door with twenty-five, though both may have the same responsibilities. In industry, years of service yield small if any increments, with a worker advancing to a better job to improve his salary. Yet a school salary schedule should be aimed at keeping able teachers in the classroom.

What is negotiable must also be decided. Most administrators and many teachers would limit it to salaries and "working conditions." But class size is a working condition. With a contract calling for twenty-five children per class, could a school have groups of twenty-eight normal or bright children to make possible a section of fifteen to twenty disturbed or disadvantaged children?

After-school duties are a working condition, but does the dedicated teacher want to define his services in terms of the hours he is paid to teach? And, once this becomes negotiable, can the teacher who wants to give additional time withstand the pressures from colleagues who feel he is weakening their bargaining position?

Another problem is the restricted power of boards of education. In industry, management can open new markets, retire inefficient machinery, and introduce new methods of operation so that improved productivity can provide salary increases. A school board is in a different position. Tax limits are often fixed by law and the taxable assets of the community must be considered. Many boards

Reprinted by permission of The Instructor Publications, Inc., Dansville, N.Y., from *The Instructor* 76:12, May, 1967. ©The Instructor Publications, Inc.

would increase salaries substantially if they could, for higher salaries improve competitive position when hiring teachers.

These problems, however big, still do not negate the principle of collective bargaining. Both sides should exert leadership to establish this right and to avoid climates of fear and suspicion. A few strikes have already occurred with accusations hurled on both sides. In Detroit, the Board has retained an attorney as chief negotiator, and in past years, contract negotiations in New York City have hardly gone smoothly. Even so, faculties in many districts are now bargaining quietly and effectively.

As a faculty, you may face the problem of two groups competing for the right to represent you. If so, be on guard against unfortunate acceleration of the bargaining process. An attempt by one group to wrest control from the other can result, regardless of the winner, in a committee's hastening to the bargaining table with poorly defined purposes and extravagant demands—partly to impress the members with its intentions.

Enough time must be provided to establish the validity of requests. Procedures must be set up based on the inherent goals of education as well as the dignity and integrity of the bargainers.

Any posture less than this is out of keeping with the democratic tenets of our society. And it is those tenets that the public school and its teachers are charged with improving and perpetuating.

Chapter 13

Becoming a Citizen of the Community

One of the major responsibilities of the beginning teacher is to learn about his community and establish himself as a responsible, participating member. He needs to recognize his obligations as a citizen of the community, become interested in its activities and problems, and take part in its enterprises, organizations, and political activities. He must, also, be aware of the role that the community expects him to fulfill and of the conflicts that can occur when he deviates from expectations.

In "The Teacher in the Community" Havighurst and Neugarten cite several studies revealing the pattern of participation of teachers in community activities. The rather limited nature and extent of involvement in the past is explained as being due, in part, to the reluctance of the public, and of teachers themselves, to have teachers engage in political activities. That some educators believe that change is needed and is occurring in this area is evidenced by the content of the following articles.

McGuigan, in "The Teacher and Politics," uses the word "politics" to mean the teacher's role in the community as a citizen and a member of society. He recommends that teachers assume leadership roles in service, fraternal, and religious organizations and that, in addition, they become involved in government and partisan politics in order to fulfill the responsibilities they are qualified, and obligated, to assume. Finally, Stinnett looks beyond the goal of achieving political involvement to the larger goals of directing political activity toward solving in an orderly manner the major, current problems of our nation.

The Teacher in the Community

Robert J. Havighurst and Bernice L. Neugarten

The Participant in Community Affairs

Since the teacher is an educated person and possesses certain skills that are useful in conducting the affairs of the community, teachers have been in demand for church work (teaching Sunday school classes, singing in the choir), for volunteer jobs with the Red Cross and other welfare organizations, and for other useful community services. Vidich and Bensman have characterized teachers as being, in this respect, "a replacement pool for spare talent as it is needed for various organizational jobs." (Vidich and Bensman, 1958, p. 270.) This role has, however, been circumscribed; it is usually limited to the "safe," noncontroversial community affairs and to activities to which little prestige is attached. There is likely to be resistance and criticism, especially in small towns, if the teacher takes an active part in politics or starts a business "on the side." Women teachers in many communities find it difficult to be accepted in the more prestigious women's clubs. The few men teachers who are accepted in the service clubs of the community are usually principals or superintendents or athletic coaches.

In a study of over 1,100 teachers in 66 communities in Pennsylvania, Buck (1960) found that one-third participated in community organizations at or above the rate of top business and professional people (the latter group has consistently ranked highest, as compared with other occupational groups, with regard to participation in community affairs), and 80 percent had participation scores higher than the average for white-collar workers. Rates of participation were approximately the same in large as in small communities.

Because a majority of the teachers had grown up in homes where community participation was low, the implications are that many teachers change their life styles to meet the expectation that the teacher will take part in community life beyond the school.

More recently, in a nationwide sample, four out of every five teachers were found to be active in one or more organizations, and over two-thirds of the active members belonged to one or more groups besides church. The amount of time spent in organizational work was considerable, given the average work week of over 47 hours reported by these same teachers. Teachers spent close to two hours a week, in organization work not counting attendance at religious services. Table 17.1 shows the proportion that were active and non-active members of various types of organizations. The table indicates that at the present time there is little administrative pressure upon teachers to join outside organizations, other than teachers' associations. Religious affiliation is the most usual type of membership, a fact that was pointed out also by Ryans (1960) in summarizing his findings from an elaborate study of teachers' characteristics.

Community Leadership

Such findings say nothing regarding the quality of the participation or the extent to which the teacher is a powerful person in the community. Studies made in 1940 by Cook and Greenhoe (Cook and Cook, 1950) showed that teachers participated in community affairs, but not as leaders.

While the picture with regard to community participation may be changing as teachers, like other professional groups, become more actively concerned over civil rights, efforts to eliminate poverty, and other national and international problems, it is unlikely that the overall picture concerning organizational leadership will be reversed. As the number of teachers from lower-middle and working-class levels increases, teacher participation in community life may well be more varied; and the number occupying leadership positions in the community, positions typically held by upper-middle-class people, is likely to be proportionately smaller.

There are, of course, various factors that interact to produce this pattern of participation, only one being the prevailing attitude in the community as regards the teacher's qualifications for leadership. Another factor that operates to curtail

*Table 17.1 Teacher Membership in Religious, Civic, or Other Organizations

Type of organization	Active member and workers	Inac- tive member	Not a member	Feel administra- tive pressure to take part[a]
Teachers association	54.1%	40.7%	5.2%	13.0%
Church or synagogue	53.2	34.0	12.8	0.5
Youth-serving group	15.8	5.4	78.8	0.3
Fraternal or auxiliary group	14.7	17.9	67.4	0.1
Political party organization	6.6	24.2	69.2	0.4
Women's group	20.1	11.5	68.4	0.1
Men's service club	13.4	6.2	80.4	0.2
Other organizations	24.1	12.7	63.2	0.4
Number reporting	a	a	a	1,852

[a] For all types of organizations, except women's group and men's service club, columns 2, 3, and 4 are based on the number 1,881, and add horizontally to 100%. For women's group the number is 1,291; for men's service club, 590.

Source: National Education Association, April, 1963, p. 27 (adapted).

* Reprinted in this volume by permission of the National Education Association.

the teacher's participations, especially in political and economic affairs, is the expectation that the teacher as a public servant should remain neutral on controversial issues. Possibly this is the reason why only two percent of the teachers in the NEA sample of 1960-61 (the sample reported in Table 17.1) had ever run for public office and less than seven percent were active workers in a political party. (NEA, April, 1963.) In many communities, teachers are barred by state law or by local requirement from participation in political activities. These restrictions often stem from the desire to protect the teacher from political influence. In other instances, they stem from the assumption, still unproved, that the teacher who participates in partisan politics loses his objectivity in teaching.

Other factors are derived from the teaching situation itself. One of these is the teacher's relative inability to control large blocks of time, as compared, for example, with other professional men or business executives. It is one thing, in terms of time required, to teach a Sunday School class; another thing, to organize and direct a Community Chest drive. In some instances, limited finances may operate against certain types of community participation.

While there are many individual exceptions, there is little evidence that teachers as a group are straining for fuller civic participation. Not only are teachers influenced by community tradition in this respect, but there has been, in general, little in their professional training that prepares them for community leadership.

The Teacher and Politics

J. Lorne McGuigan

Before embarking upon a discussion of this topic, it is necessary to define what is meant by the terms "teacher" and "politics." The teacher is the person who is endeavouring to the best of his ability to provide his students with an education. His teaching and training goes far beyond the academic field. Politics, as used here, relates to the teacher's role in the community as a citizen and as a member of society. It is not limited to partisan politics, although this is a part of the broader field.

Reprinted by permission of *Educational Review,* New Brunswick Teachers' Association, Fredericton, New Brunswick, from *Educational Review* 81:107-108, March, 1967.

In our North American history the teacher originally held an exalted position. He was looked upon, because of his superior education, as a leader in the community. This role he accepted, and his contribution to society and his influence went far beyond that of the classroom. Later, when his educational pre-eminence declined with respect to the society around him, the teacher seemed to retreat from the outside world behind a cloak of pseudo-dedication. While low pay, poor working conditions, and a low general level of professional qualifications undoubtedly contributed to this withdrawal, the withdrawal itself helped to perpetuate the very ills which retarded his professional advancement.

Today increasing salaries and qualifications happily are reversing this trend. However, it will take more than better working conditions, and more than an excellent job in the classroom before teachers gain the prestige they desire and deserve, and before they fulfill their complete role as citizens.

Participation in activities outside the framework of the school is essential to the good mental health of the teacher. It is not good that a mature adult be relegated to a society of children or adolescents only. Since teachers spend a great portion of their time in the company of the young, it is essential that they provide themselves with an opportunity to work with adults as much as possible. If this is not done, then over an extended period there may be some truth to the statement that, "teachers tend to become men among boys, and boys among men."

The first area where participation and leadership from teachers should be forthcoming is in organizations—service, fraternal and religious. In such organizations, with their ever diversifying programs and objectives, there is a great need for the type of contribution which teachers are equipped to make. It is true that teacher membership is great in such organizations, but all too often the teachers involved stand aside to let others provide the leadership on the executive level. The same applies to civic boards and committees and to community organizations.

The first stage of public politics is the civic level. Here the record of teachers has been somewhat better. In Saint John teachers have and currently are playing a significant role in civic government. Unfortunately such individuals are a rare exception.

Teachers, before endeavouring to teach citizenship, must be good citizens. They comprise a significant segment of the population and possess qualifications far above the average. But teachers shirk their responsibility as citizens when they are not concerned and active in the making of local decisions that affect all of us. It is true that not everyone can or should run for public office, but there is a need for more to offer than have in the past. And certainly strong positive action to seek out, support and elect worthy representatives to civic government is as much the prerogative of teachers as of any of the other "prestige" professions.

It is in the field of partisan politics that strong opinions regarding teacher involvement are heard. Many would suggest that it is "improper" for teachers to engage in such activity. Although "improper" is rarely if ever defined, two reasons for this belief are most often advanced. First the teacher is supposed to be some sort of a symbol who must not act as other persons, even when away from school. There is a real double standard at work here. While this double standard is breaking, especially in urban areas, there is need for public re-education in this matter. It must be shown that entering teaching is not entering a monastery. And it must be shown that when the teacher is not neglecting his primary job, and providing his actions are ethical and moral, there is no justification for endeavouring to restrict his life after hours.

The second reason advanced for keeping teachers out of political activity is that they would influence the school population to their way of thinking. This is simply not valid. There is no reason to assume that a teacher active in politics would seek to influence his charges more than one interested but inactive. In fact experience has shown that an active teacher will tend to the other extreme. It is strange too that many people who are afraid their children would be indoctrinated politically by such a teacher will not object to these children being taught by a teacher of a different religious persuasion.

Teachers must be interested and involved in government and politics. To be indifferent is to abdicate our duty as a citizen, both to ourselves and to our fellows. Regardless of what we may think of individual politicians or parties, qualified people have a moral duty to make whatever contribution they can in this field. Spreading bureaucracy has already eliminated a major segment of our population from the opportunity to serve. It would be most unfortunate if the teachers were to ignore their duty or were to be prevented from contributing their share.

Of course anyone elected to the Provincial or Federal Government House can hardly continue to teach on a regular basis. The question of the teacher in politics, for him, becomes academic, even though it could be argued that such people could contribute as much to society as they could have in the classroom. But the elected representative is only one small factor in the field of partisan politics. There is need today in all parties for an uplifting of the tone of political endeavour. There is a need for people with new ideas to shape the policy which will determine the course our country and province take as we enter our second century. Here, and in the functioning of the parties themselves, is a major role teachers can play if they so desire.

But what is to be the attitude of School Boards to such activities on the part of teachers? Progressive people in the field of education have long recognized that good sound leadership in any field helps the profession in general. Since Board members hopefully are all progressive, such activity should be welcomed. Generally it is welcomed—at least until the problem of lost time because of such activity arises.

The problem of lost time has been handled, I feel, with integrity and intelligence over the past years by one School Board in particular. Although they moved slowly because they were breaking new ground, they looked with favor on any activity which would enhance the prestige of the profession as a whole. If the endeavour in any way was connected with education, there was no loss of salary for lost time. If it were not connected with education, a day lost meant the loss of a day's pay. However approval of such activity was shown by allowing the teacher to have the time off provided, of course, the privilege was not abused. If the endeavour required the loss of only part of a session and no substitute was required, there was no loss in salary. Certainly one could not expect a more just and progressive policy.

In our society the teacher must bear a double responsibility. A dedicated teacher must continually strive by every means at his disposal to improve his qualifications, his work in the classroom, and the stature of his profession. And he must live up to the responsibility which is naturally his as a highly qualified member of a democratic society. A reasonably large degree of endeavour outside the classroom is essential if the teacher is to adequately fill both these roles.

This outside endeavour will contribute significantly to the development of the individual teacher. It will answer a great need for informed and thoughtful leadership at all levels in our society. The willingness to contribute, and the contributions made, will enhance the prestige of a profession continually in search of increased recognition. The increased prestige of the continually developing teacher will make his job within the classroom easier, especially with older students. But most of all the teacher will be fulfilling his full role as a citizen—an active role which good citizenship demands of all people—a role in line with his capabilities—a role which will take the hollow ring out of his admonitions to his students regarding good citizenship.

Thus the teacher does have a role, and a most important one, to play in his community. The fulfillment of this role is politics in the broad sense. This fulfillment will come in various fields, and will manifest itself in various endeavours and on different levels. Ours is but to find our area and to make our just contribution.

In conclusion, I would like to pay tribute to the many fine teachers of the present and past who, through their efforts outside the classroom, have contributed and are contributing so much to society and to the teaching profession. Unfortunately it appears that the total contribution of teachers—fine as it has been—has been small indeed in relation to the abundance they have to offer if they are but willing.

Teachers in Politics: The Larger Roles

T. M. Stinnett

Teachers are aiming at many goals in their drive to become politically active citizens. They seek to be voters, party volunteers, even office holders—to influence legislation. But politics is not a final goal. It is a means to achieve larger goals. For teachers especially, these larger goals have to do with the alarming problems facing this nation. The imperative task facing Americans and America's teachers is to recapture and exemplify that moral grandeur which we claim has been at the core of our being.

In the past, we have sung with great vigor and great emotion, "Thine alabaster cities gleam, undimmed by human tears. . . . And crown they good with brotherhood from sea to shining sea."

The realists among us know that if these beautiful figures of speech were ever true, they, and the ideals they encompass, are now in disturbing disarray. This nation is in trouble, and it is not going to be set right by milksops or by people who are unwilling to give up their biases for the welfare of the country. Clearly, we face but one choice—the resurrection of the dream and the full implementation of its sweep.

This is no easy task. It will require extraordinary courage, forbearance, tolerance, and patience.

Teachers ought to be, and can be, the essential leavening force in this resurrection. I think we miss the boat if we assume that the role of teachers is only that of educating the public. Doing this is important, of course. But teachers must do much more: To help move the nation toward its destiny, they must present a united, vigorous, activist front.

Reprinted by permission of the National Education Association, Washington, D.C., and T. M. Stinnett from *Today's Education* 57:37-38, October, 1968.

Adapted from a speech prepared by Dr. Stinnett for the second annual T. M. Stinnett Chair of Criticism Lecture during the NEA Citizenship Committee's Teachers-in-Politics Weekend. The full speech is available in booklet form from the Citizenship Committee, NEA Center. Single copies free.

What, specifically, are the larger goals that teachers must strive to sell to the people?

Teachers must fight to induce our people to shift from their traditional interests to the great social issues of our time.

They must fight for a shift from obsession with equality of opportunity (which has become something of a sterile cliche) to an all-out effort to eliminate the deadly conditions of life that make opportunity wither on the vine for so many.

They must fight to balance concern for property rights with equal concern for the rights of people.

They must set their wills against the ugly face of racism. Racism, be it black, white, yellow, brown, or whatever, has no place in an openended society.

No nation on earth and no group within a nation can long exist as an affluent island in the midst of racially based cultural, social, and economic deprivation. Nor can any of our national groups operate as if they and their kindred are members of an exclusive club. And this is just as applicable to any of our minority groups as it is to the majority.

There is an innate dignity about a decent human life, with its aspirations and its God-given potential of living in the upper reaches of the human spirit, that ought never to be violated by another living being. This dignity in others ought to be as sacred to us as our own. Again, this is as applicable to minorities as it is to the majority.

To foster this dignity in our modern social setting means providing occupational opportunities that are as equal as a just society can make them, in consonance with divergent talents. It means equal protection under the law and equal treatment before the law.

It means that undergirding all this is full education in the best sense, including compensatory education for those neglected children we imperfectly categorize as deprived. Educational deprivation is not an ethnic problem; it applies almost all across the board, to all races and cultures. Compensatory education should be available to all those children who have been denied the birthright of high quality education. Many of these are children of our rural areas, where the cruel and still-lingering inequalities of local controls have bequeathed inadequacy to the local children. The problem of our ghetto children of all races is that they migrated to the city slum schools as fugitives from country slum schools.

Providing a full education means providing compensatory reeducation for teachers who come into the schools from deprived backgrounds.

It means a teacher in every classroom with an almost fanatical zeal and the understanding and skills to make certain that each child has his chance at a good education.

Teachers must lead the fight to persuade our people to embrace an open-ended society in the full meaning of the term. This means convincing our people that we can have an authoritarian society *or* a free society, but not both.

We must convince our people that fixed goals and diminishing alternatives are marks of the authoritarian society. We must convince them that an open-ended society is characterized by a proliferation of alternatives.

We must convince them that an open-ended society will always be marked by controversy, dissent, and some intramural quarreling—because these are the means by which the majority makes wise decisions and determines new and ever-shifting objectives.

To do these things, however, teachers must themselves have a sense of enduring values and must exercise an abnormal amount of self-restraint.

I have said that this country is in trouble. One of the chief symptoms and symbols of this trouble is the almost total absence of self-restraint among many of our dissatisfied people. The voice of reason is being shouted down by something glibly called the right of dissent. The moderate is being derided and hooted at and trampled underfoot by far-left activists. Reason and moderation are being intimidated into silence and inactivity by intellectual lynching parties.

In the language of Sidney Hook, the right of civil disobedience has been escalated by extremists into the right of uncivil disobedience. The right to peacefully assemble and petition for redress of grievances has been distorted into the right to form mobs for the purpose, wittingly or unwittingly, of forcing redress by violence. It is frightening how many Americans are uncritically accepting the excuse that this nation began in rebellion. So it did. But we forget that there was then no recourse to the changing of laws or the government by the orderly process of the ballot.

Teachers have a deep responsibility in the process of dissent. If they run with the mob, if they indulge in the hysteria of unreason, if they embrace the current madness of lawlessness, then the country is in trouble so deep and bitter it may not survive.

The popular thing for me to do would be to present the alluring picture that teachers are on the glory road by virtue of a newly found activist vigor, by virtue of a newly found political muscle. But the future of teachers cannot be more hopeful than the future of the nation itself.

The greatest of all possible triumphs of the involvement of teachers in politics, in my view, is for us—all of us—to set our faces, our wills, and our actions against the mob spirit and for the achievement of human justice through orderly change in laws that do not serve this end.

If ever there was a time in the history of this nation when its people could identify without a doubt a crossroads and choose the direction they must pursue, it is now. I covet for teachers a vital part in blazing the new trail that must be traveled.

Suggested Additional Readings

Bohning, Roger D. "New Twist to Parent Visits." *The Instructor* 77:60, December, 1967.

Denemark, George W. "The Teacher and His Staff." *NEA Journal* 55:17-19, 70, December, 1966.

Dineen, Russell. "The Teacher as Active Citizen." *Educational Leadership* 22:83-84, 131, 133, November, 1964.

Doherty, Robert E. "Letter to a School Board." *Phi Delta Kappan* 48:272-277, February, 1967.

Donaldson, Marion G. "Teachers as Active Political Citizens." *Childhood Education* 44:482-486, April, 1968.

Dorros, Sidney. "Economic Welfare of Teachers," pp. 57-77 in *Teaching as a Profession.* Columbus, Ohio: Charles E. Merrill Publishing Co., 1968.

_____. "Professional Organizations,"pp. 94-116 in *Teaching as a Profession.* Columbus, Ohio: Charles E. Merrill Publishing Co., 1968.

Fast, Betty. "Teachers and Librarians: Stage Managers for the Learning Program." *Childhood Education* 43:73-75, October, 1964.

Fine, Marvin J. "What Can You Expect from a Guidance Counselor?" *Grade Teacher* 84:152, 154-155, September, 1966.

Fox, Raymond B. "The Committed Teacher." *Educational Leadership* 22:18-20, 72, October, 1964.

Garrett, Henry E. "Evaluating Yourself as a Teacher," pp. 73-85 in *The Art of Good Teaching.* New York: David McKay Co., 1964.

Griffin, Mary D. "Teacher Organizations as Change Agents." *School and Society* 96:242-243, April 13, 1968.

Hain, John. "Research in the Classroom." *The National Elementary Principal* 44:49-51, November, 1964.

Harrison, Raymond H., and Lawrence E. Gowin. "Relationships with Parents," pp. 84-88 in *The Elementary Teacher in Action.* San Francisco: Wadsworth Publishing Co., Inc., 1958.

Johansen, Vera Emmert. " 'A' Is for Aide." *Illinois Education* 57:149, December, 1968.

Langdon, Grace, and Irving W. Stout. "What Parents Think of Homework." *NEA Journal* 52:9-11, December, 1963.

LeFevre, Carol. "Face to Face in the Parent-Teacher Conference." *The Elementary School Journal* 68:1-8, October, 1967.

Ozmon, Howard. "What 'Professional' Means." *Illinois State University Journal* 28:17-20, February, 1966.

Peters, Herman J., Collins W. Burnett, and Gail F. Farwell. "Learning to Live in the Community," pp. 101-121 in *Introduction to Teaching*. New York: The Macmillan Co., 1963.

_____. "Professional Pointers," pp. 172-205 in *Introduction to Teaching*. New York: The Macmillan Co., 1963.

_____. "Teachers Work with Parents," pp. 148-171 in *Introduction to Teaching*. New York: The Macmillan Co., 1963.

Riedesel, C. Alan. "Every Teacher Is a Researcher." *The Arithmetic Teacher* 15:355-356, April, 1968.

Shermis, S. Samuel, and Donald C. Orlich. "Teaching as a Profession," pp. 288-314 in *The Pursuit of Excellence: Introductory Readings in Education,* Donald C. Orlich and S. Samuel Shermis, editors. New York: American Book Co., 1965.

Stinnett, T. M. "Professional Organizations of Teachers," pp. 367-403 in *Professional Problems of Teachers,* Third Edition. New York: The Macmillan Co., 1968.

_____. "The Changing Scene in Teaching," pp. 471-526 in *Professional Problems of Teachers,* Third Edition. New York: The Macmillan Co., 1968.

_____. "The Profession of Teaching," pp. 49-71 in *Professional Problems of Teachers,* Third Edition. New York: The Macmillan Co., 1968.

Tolbert, E. L. *Research for Teachers and Counselors.* Minneapolis: Burgess Publishing Co., 1967.

Unruh, Glenys G. "Parents Can Help Their Children Succeed in School." *NEA Journal* 55:14-16, December, 1966.

Walker, Tom T. "Teacher-Image." *Peabody Journal of Education* 43:40-41, July, 1965.

Willatts, Elizabeth. "Involved Parents Aid to Achievement." *The Times Educational Supplement,* No. 2705, p. 989, March 24, 1967.

Yauch, Wilbur A., Martin H. Bartels, and Emmet Morris. "Ways to Improve on the Job," pp. 238-262 in *The Beginning Teacher.* New York: Henry Holt and Company, Inc., 1955.

Part IV

TEACHING IN A CLIMATE OF EDUCATIONAL CHANGE

Introduction

The day is long past, we hope, when the teacher can enter the classroom, shut the door, and teach as he was taught. Too much has happened since then, too much has happened since yesterday, too much will happen tomorrow, and every tomorrow, for the teacher to go on teaching in the same old way. It hardly needs to be said that "times are changing," and education is changing right along with the times. The teacher who closes his eyes to change and ignores its implications for teaching is failing not only to face reality but also to avail himself of opportunities to improve his teaching.

The formation of an attitude is the teacher's first step in teaching in a climate of educational change. He must begin by questioning: What are the changes that have occurred, are occurring, and seem likely to occur? In what ways does and should change affect the teacher's decisions in determining what and how he will teach? These are pressing questions that the teacher must confront and seek to answer.

Almost any educational periodical that one picks up has articles on innovations and instructional technology. And one has only to observe the exhibit areas at educational conferences to be almost overwhelmed by the sheer number of technological devices available for instructional purposes. How does the teacher proceed, then, in planning and deciding how to work with various types of organizational patterns and with curricular and instructional innovations? Certainly he must keep up with the times by reading and study, and he must obtain all the in-service training he can get to help him utilize innovations effectively.

Quite possibly, one of the most important steps the teacher will need to take will be that of building a philosophy of education that can guide him in deciding what and how he is going to teach in today's technological age.

In the chapters that follow, a number of authors express their views on determining curriculum content and instructional methods, working with educational innovations, and developing a philosophy of education.

Chapter 14

Deciding What and How to Teach

Change has been with us always, but only recently have we had so much of it so rapidly; and as we look to the future we are inclined to believe that what we have experienced so far is only a small indication of what is to come. In a world of inevitable, universal change, the teacher must seek to determine how societal changes influence educational change in general and the individual teacher in particular. The many changes that have occurred in educational opportunities, teaching practices, instructional resources, and facilities make it mandatory that teachers learn to direct change to raise the quality of education and improve instruction for all, according to Myers in the opening article of this chapter.

"What shall be taught?" is a continuing question that does not lack for answers, although the answers differ according to the times and to the respondent. There seems to be agreement that the schools should teach knowledge, skills, and values, but controversy exists as to the specific knowledge, skills, and values that should be included in the curriculum. How, then, can the elementary school teacher decide what and how he should teach? What can he use as criteria for making his decisions? The National Committee of the NEA Project on Instruction believes that the most effective direction comes from analysis of values and goals, contemporary society, learners and the learning process, and organized knowledge. In the second selection of the chapter it identifies significant values, goals, social changes, and concerns about learners, learning, and knowledge.

Recognizing that we cannot give children all the knowledge they will need to answer the questions of the future, Lee recommends that they be taught processes which they can use to find their own answers, and some fundamental concepts about their world. She elaborates on what she considers to be some of the more important processes and content areas.

Deen believes that the past offers guidelines for deciding what and how to teach—that traditional American education provides time-tested ideas that can be used as a basis for modern-day curriculum and instruction. She describes what she calls a "modern-traditional program."

To help him make decisions about what and how he will teach, the teacher will want to consider the attitudes and wishes of parents. This chapter includes a report of a Gallup Poll surveying parents' reactions to educational innovations. It appears that they are ready to accept changes in content and methods to make education more realistic with the times.

The final article in the chapter is concerned with the teacher's role in curriculum planning. According to May, teachers can operate at the manipulative level, the source level, or the process level in curriculum making. The professional teacher is not satisfied to be manipulated by the planning of others; he wants to work at the source and process levels—to have a vital part in planning what he is going to teach and how he is going to teach it.

Mandate for Change

Allen Myers

Not many years ago, the word "education" was popularly defined in terms of the three "Rs" and the little red school house. Some say that there are now six "Rs," reading, writing, and arithmetic and remedial reading, remedial writing, and remedial arithmetic.

In the days of the little red school house, educational opportunities for all children were fairly limited. The primary purpose was to educate children to master the language of words and the language of numbers. This training was fundamental to the exercise of civic responsibility in a democratic society and formed the foundation for higher education for those who could take advantage of it. Children who did not adjust to this kind of an educational program did not profit readily in a school with these goals. If they were poorly motivated or learned with difficulty, the school had little to offer them. They soon dropped out and learned or were taught such skills as the need dictated. As they grew into adulthood they took their place ultimately in the community, performing a wide range of tasks for which little ability in the three "Rs" was needed. Such practices were acceptable because the structure and the fabric of society was so patterned.

Today, education means learning written language and number concepts and much more. It means taking together all of the experiences that children have

Reprinted by permission of the Illinois Association for Higher Education, Springfield, Illinois, and Allen Myers from *College and University Report* 2:1, 5, Winter, 1968.

that contribute to their growth whether at school, or at large in the community, and calling these total experiences education. But the changing educational scene, "the quiet revolution," reminds us that the past is prologue. We are expected to teach more and more to a greater number of students and at the same time individualize instruction. Moreover, a shortage of qualified personnel, lack of funds, and the information explosion demands that different and improved methods of instruction must be found and utilized.

Accompanying the educational transformation is the principle of *acceleration* at all levels of human organization. As Marshall McCluhan reminds us, "when information moves at the speed of signals in the central nervous system, man is confronted with obsolescence of all earlier forms of acceleration, such as road and rail. What emerges is a total field of inclusion awareness. The old patterns of psychic and social adjustment become irrelevant." If we recognize the short period of time that man has been on earth and the brief span of time that written and recorded information has existed, our senses are charged by the electrifying speed at which the word becomes manifest. Between 1896 and 1947 (51 years) the amount of information in printed, written and other storage forms doubled. It doubled again between 1947 and 1957 (10 years) and doubled again between 1957 and 1964 (7 years); and it is predicted that it will be doubled again by 1969 (5 years). We may be confronted by the fact that the book is now the most outmoded form of information retrieval. Thus, new and different methods of instruction must be found and implemented on all learning levels so that the quality of education and instruction can be improved.

We are comfortable with the tools and techniques so dear and familiar and we tend to rely on textbooks, workbooks, paperbacks, tests, films, transparencies, magnetic tapes, projection equipment, recorders, learning laboratories, teaching machines and television. More recently the advances are even more dramatic with enormous import for education. The new *armamentarium* will include the electronic computer with numerous modalities for computer assisted instruction. The corollary technical advance of computer technology is the development of technical equipment for the input and receipt of information at locations remote from the computer. Its potential is so great that it threatens our traditional ideas about time and place for the delivery of instruction.

As we comfortably watch the instant replay of the fights or football games we are little aware of the dramatic advance in the development of video tape and video tape recording now available at a cost so low that it is within easy reach of many school budgets. Numerous other techniques such as satellite television, 8mm optical sound track, programmed instruction, and the systems approach permit the welding of the components of technology, the purposes of education and the objectives of instruction into a meaningful relationship so that a maximum instructional effort can be obtained.

If we couple these technological advances with the educational time sequence change such as flexible scheduling, team teaching, modular scheduling, independent study centers, tutorials, small group seminars, independent four-phase instruction (large groups, laboratory, seminars, independent study) middle school development, ungraded and nongraded schools—the potential expands. Juxtaposed are methodological techniques and curricular innovations such as the "new match," I.T.A., PSSC, programmed instruction, dial axis systems, packaged progress and structural management, sensorium environment, the daily demand schedule, schools as community centers, and pre-school developments, all of which produce a heady acceleration and opportunity.

Further revelation of this celestial elevation reveals a preview of new concepts of school plant design. In our time schools no longer need be compartmentalized into conventional type classrooms. The new trends provide for arenas of learning with flexible zones of space. These space zones, acoustically treated, eliminate the need for walls, for acoustical developments have made walls obsolete as sound barriers. Our excuse for walls now is to provide for visual privacy and thus walls need not be extended from floor to ceiling. The "new purpose" for walls is to serve as a sight barrier for a group of students who are seated and engaged in a learning activity.

The new schools, the educational parks, the consortium, the comprehensive approaches, educational technology and information retrieval, federal legislation, and the private foundations, mandate for us change. Change—so that the quality of education for children can be improved. Change—to provide more flexibility in the educational organization and process. Change—to fulfill the promise and hope for each learner in achieving for himself the full realization of his talent and capacity for growth. Change—to relieve teachers of responsibilities which can be performed by others or by technicians, so that teachers can devote more of their time, energy, and talent to teaching functions that require professional and personal attention. Change—so that education may see its challenge, not only in the technical aspects of educating people to execute a task competently, but continuing the educational imperative in teaching people how to function as human beings while at the same time instilling confidence and courage in the midst of organizational complexity, in order that free-thinking individuals may emerge motivated by worthy purposes.

And so *change,* an inescapable fact of life, is our handmaiden and the question is not whether we choose to change, but how we can master the intricacies of "productive change," taking comfort in the wisdom of Jefferson who wrote, "if a nation expects to be ignorant and free in the state of civilization, it expects what never was and what never will be."

Data for Decisions

Decisions cannot be made in a vacuum. The questions posed in this report can be resolved only on the basis of a deliberate analysis of the forces which shape education.

In formulating its recommendations, the Committee has sought direction from three major sources: social trends and forces, knowledge of the human being as a learner, and the accumulated body of organized knowledge about the world and man. In these areas are the forces which determine the setting and the possible method and substance of education. These forces must then be screened against the values and objectives which society sets for education, the guides which influence the translation of what could be into what shall be.

These bases for decision—values, objectives, the society, the learner, and organized knowledge—are constant in the sense that each must be considered whenever and wherever fundamental educational decisions are made. But they are also changeable, for times and people change, evolving different data for educational decision making.

The following sections—"A Statement of Values," "Essential Objectives of Education," "Society as a Base," "The Learner as a Base," "Organized Knowledge as a Base"—summarize the Committee's appraisal of these major considerations and briefly review the reasoning underlying its recommendations.

A Statement of Values

Every society is directed and sustained by a core of values which represents its ideals, its standards, and its norms of what is desirable. There are also, in every society, values which are a reflection of human preferences, of what people actually want and seek to obtain. These operational values develop from personal needs and sometimes conflict with the society's normative values; what people *do* want is not always consistent with what they believe they *ought* to want.

Today the racial situation in our country points up such an inconsistency. Freedom, justice, equality have always been ideals of America; as citizens, we pledge allegiance in the words "with liberty and justice for all." Yet, lack of freedom, injustice, and great inequalities exist in this country because personal

Reprinted by permission of the National Education Association from *Schools for the Sixties.* A Report of the Project on Instruction. New York: McGraw-Hill Book Co., 1963, pp. 6-12.

values about race and religion, bolstered by custom and habit, override the patriotic ideals of many of our people.

Actual wants are modified by changes in society and culture. Today people value many things which earlier generations did not, simply because these objects of desire did not exist as genuine possibilities. Values in terms of material comforts are quite different than they were before the fruits of mass production and technology were available. Values in terms of attitudes and behavior will change as more and more people, Negro and white, recognize that traditional roles cannot forever be maintained comfortably.

Educational values should, and do, reflect the generally accepted ideals of society. Our standards of what ought to be should be a guide to both teaching and learning. Equally necessary, educational values should reflect the needs and interests of the learner. Education must comprehend what *is* before it can broaden and relate the immediate to the ideal. The educator's task is to build continuity between the interests of the learner and the standards of excellence which transcend the immediate desires of the immature.

The values against which the multiple possibilities for educational practice are screened must be made explicit. To do otherwise would be to make decisions without reference to what we seek to obtain and without sufficient heed to the actual needs of those for whom we seek to obtain it. The National Committee believes that the following values are vital as criteria for assessing present practices and as guides to future improvement of our common schools:

- respect for the worth and dignity of every individual
- equality of opportunity for all children
- encouragement of variability
- faith in man's ability to make rational decisions
- shared responsibility for the common good
- respect for moral and spiritual values and ethical standards of conduct

Essential Objectives of Education

The schools should not, and cannot, provide all of the learning opportunities that students need in order to live fully and effectively. Other agencies have particular responsibilities in the education of youth and learning also takes place outside of the school—and continuously throughout life. Furthermore, school time and facilities are finite, making it impossible, as well as undesirable, that the schools be the source of all necessary learning.

Education is a process of changing behavior—behavior in the broad sense of thinking, feeling, and acting. As a result of education, students should acquire ideas they did not have, skills they did not possess, interests broader and more mature than they had known, ways of thinking more effective than they had employed. From this viewpoint, educational objectives may be stated in terms of behavioral change, and the responsibilities of the schools may be differentiated from those of other educative agencies.

It is necessary for the schools to choose relatively few important objectives, to work toward them consistently, and to review them periodically in the light of changing times. The additive approach—putting more subject-matter areas into the curriculum and adopting a multitude of educational goals—is ineffective.

The basic criterion in establishing priorities should be an assessment of the contributions which education can make to the individual, to our society, and to the improvement of mankind. In this swift-moving world, such choices are not easy. What knowledge will today's ten-year-old need three decades hence? What skills will he require to live successfully? What problems will he have to solve? In what social context will he need to reinterpret basic human values? Education must help the individual to identify and maintain values that are relatively constant. It also must equip him to cope with change.

The essential objectives of education, therefore, must be premised on a recognition that education is a process of changing behavior and that a changing society requires the capacity for self-teaching and self-adaptation. Priorities in educational objectives should be placed upon such ends as:

- learning how to learn, how to attack new problems, how to acquire new knowledge
- using rational processes
- building competence in basic skills
- developing intellectual and vocational competence
- exploring values in new experience
- understanding concepts and generalizations

Above all, the school must develop in the pupil the ability to learn under his own initiative and an abiding interest in doing so.

Society as a Base

The Committee reviewed dominant forces in contemporary society in an effort to anticipate some of the social changes which will create a new setting for education—changes which need to be comprehended in making educational decisions. The forces are: science and technology, economic growth, large bureaucratic organizations, leisure time, television and other mass media, urbanization, population growth, and international interdependence and conflict. Discussion of these forces is interwoven throughout this report in the brief analyses of the Committee's recommendations. They are also dealt with in the Project's three supporting volumes; specific attention is paid to each force in one of the volumes, *Education in a Changing Society*.

The forces mentioned above are apparent not only in our own country but throughout the world, particularly those concerning economic growth, population growth, and the cold war. One of the most fundamental changes that is occurring in the world—the effort of the colored races to throw off the dominance of the white race—is accelerated by and transcends many of the forces listed. This change is manifested in Africa and Asia by the number of new nations rapidly carved from former colonies and by their rejection of white leadership; here, at home, it is apparent in the increasing vigor of the Negroes' struggle for equal civil rights and in their impatience with gradualism.

These changes affect the lives of students profoundly; an intelligent awareness of them is only the beginning toward shaping them to positive rather then negative effects. The schools cannot correct housing patterns, employment practices, voting registration laws any more than they can alter the bitter residue of a "white-man's-burden" colonial policy or call back the scientific discoveries that presage man's control—or destruction—of nature. But the schools can help students to gain a knowledge of the world in which they find themselves, with a more complete history of all its cultures and as many possible solutions to its problems as mortal men can now foresee. This much, *at the very least,* the schools can and should do.

The Learner as a Base

An important fact, which is not always easily recognized by educators, is that every child has an inner push to become a more complete self, to learn what can become meaningful to him. The art of teaching lies in stimulating this force and in keeping it alive, free, and developing. To do so, it is essential to understand the learner, to know what he is working on, what he is up against, what his basic assets are.

Investigations by psychologists during the last fifteen years have provided much significant information about thinking, learning, and personality. Their findings are helping to lay a better foundation for changes in curriculum and methods of teaching. Today there is a closer connection between psychology and the practice of education than there has been for many years, and more academicians are becoming interested in ways children learn.

It seems clear now that development is achieved through learning, probably constrained by biochemical processes that probably in some sense are genetically regulated. The idea of development as emergence according to a precise timetable is withering on the vine. Most forward-looking psychologists now see the child not as the innocent victim of society but as the creative product of society. It is appropriate in our society to consider education as a demand upon the individual rather than as a privilege or as therapy. Progress and happiness can both be served, it is conceded, when adults get behind the child and push. There can be both excellence and mental health provided we do not go overboard, letting the push become abuse, and believing that mind is everything.

Some of the concerns that seem most significant in educational planning and practice, in terms of the learner, are:

- recognizing and nurturing creativity
- promoting the development of responsibility
- promoting the development of positive self-attitudes
- relating learning to development in children
- evaluating the learner's motivations
- acknowledging inter-individual differences
- acknowledging intra-individual differences
- acknowledging social-group differences

Organized Knowledge as a Base

Probably the most important single factor forcing change upon education is the explosion of knowledge—the "information revolution." Furthermore, because scientific and scholarly work is now quite extensive and many people are engaged in it, the rate of revision is swift. Teaching the disciplines in this situation clearly requires teaching something more permanent and more pervasive than a catalogue of factual knowledge, although some facts are essential, and it is clear that there is a continuing need for drill and repetition for learning of basic information.

Educators are not only concerned with the *amount of knowledge* students possess but also with students' *lack of understanding* about what they presumably know. Since about 1955, a vivid awareness of this latter problem has led some scholars and researchers to explore ways of selecting, organizing, and teaching available information to make it more intelligible and more usable. In general, the recent studies shift the balance in learning from *inventory* to *transaction.* The structure of a discipline, its methods of inquiry, and the styles of thinking of its scholars and specialists offer important keys to this educational task.

Developing structure in generalizations, rules, and styles of thought in the elementary and secondary school curriculum requires the talents of the teacher or curriculum worker as much as those of specialists in the academic disciplines. It imposes a great responsibility on the teacher to keep current with the frontiers of knowledge, even though the general principles best learned by pupils may be broader and simpler than those of specialists.

What Shall We Teach?

Dorris May Lee

A changing world requires a changing role and a changing educational pattern for our schools. What we shall teach cannot be decided merely on the basis of what we were taught to deem valuable. The elementary school child of today will be operating in the society of 1966 to 1972 on for the rest of his life span. Increasingly, we are aware that we cannot predict the state of the world in the future or the specific needs of its citizens. In light of this, it seems imperative that we reconsider what we teach children.

It seems fairly obvious that we cannot give children many of the answers they will need. Therefore, we must give them command of the processes by which they can determine their own answers in light of the situation at the time. They will also need some fundamental concepts about the world in which they live. Thus, we might well plan our teaching under the dual headings of processes and content.

What Processes Are Important?

What are the processes which the school should teach? Some of the more important may be:

- the process of communicating
- the process of conceptualizing
- the process of seeing relationships
- the process of generalizing
- the process of making applications
- the process of problem solving
- the process of self-direction
- the process of creating
- the process of appreciating
- the process of memorizing.

It is apparent that these processes all represent certain skills in thinking. Too often when we have thought of developing skills, it was the mechanical skills to which we referred. Skills, however, are at all levels of behavior—from skill in letter formation to skill in human relationships. They may be more than mechanics.

Reprinted by permission of Department of Elementary School Principals, National Education Association, Washington, D.C., from *The National Elementary Principal* 40:12-16, December, 1960. Copyright 1960 Department of Elementary School Principals, National Education Association. All rights reserved.

The process of communicating: Each facet of communication—reading, writing, speaking, and listening—is primarily a thought process. This fact should continually be uppermost in the teacher's plans and procedures. Equally important, it must be uppermost in the awareness and activities of the learners. *Reading is the process of bringing meaning and feelings to the printed page.* Many of the thought processes other than communicating are obviously involved, such as seeing relationships between what is being read and knowledge gained from previous experiences and enriching and developing concepts.

In order to develop this process of reading, a variety of skills need to be learned. Some of these are the mechanical skills of analyzing word and sentence structure. Others are of a different order having to do with understanding—for example, the use of context clues. When a child reads orally and miscalls words in such a way that the material is quite meaningless, it is a dead giveaway that reading is not a thinking process for him.

Writing is a process of expressing thoughts and feelings so they are meaningful to others. Obviously here, too, there are mechanical skills involved, mainly penmanship and spelling, with a certain amount of skill in word derivatives. Most so-called poor sentence structure stems from unclear thinking and can only be strengthened by improving the clarity and sureness of the child's thought processes. Other skills needed are the ability to consider and empathize with the intended audience and modify the writing so it will be most meaningful to them; the capacity to have clearly in mind the idea to be communicated and plan ways of expressing it most effectively; and the ability to select words and compose sentences and paragraphs in a way that will help one work through an unclear problem.

Speaking is the process of exchanging thoughts and feelings orally with others in order to improve understanding. Included here are the mechanical skills of sound production so that words are intelligible. However, many articulation problems are the result of lack of clarity and sureness in the thinking being expressed. Other skills needed are the ability to organize ideas into meaningful sequence and, as with writing, gauge the listening abilities and interests of the audience and adjust to them. Development of these skills in school needs to begin in kindergarten and continue thereafter.

Listening is the process of interpreting others' statements, ideas, and feelings. Schools have done a minimum of teaching this very important process. We continue to hope for greater cooperation all the way from between classmates to between world powers. Yet the ability to listen and understand how the other person is thinking and feeling, an imperative basis for cooperation, has received very little attention. We tell children to listen quietly and courteously but seldom do we say, "Listen to find out how another is thinking or feeling about something." Neither do we often say, "Listen to see what you think and feel about what someone is saying."

The process of conceptualizing: This process involves increasing differentiation. Throughout life, every concept deepens and sharpens from the first inkling one has of its existence. The school needs to be keenly aware of the important concepts in all areas of living. Teachers need to know what stage each child has reached in developing these concepts so as to correct misconceptions and advance the depth and sharpness of thinking.

The process of seeing relationships: The school should so teach and organize learning that children are constantly being helped to recognize interrelationships. Teaching the fact that in some way and to some degree all things are related stimulates children to look for relationships. And seeing them increases effective learning many fold.

The process of generalizing: This might be called the process of integration for it involves finding common elements among concepts. Research has long documented the fact that generalizations are far more effective learnings than specifics. When children are led to make their own generalizations, the effectiveness of the learning is increased. They also learn how to make generalizations for themselves and test their accuracy.

The process of making applications: Since generalizations are better remembered, then surely children must learn how to apply them to new situations and do it accurately. Since the only value of anything we learn in or out of school lies in the success with which we can apply it in various situations, the school must deliberately and consciously teach such a process of application.

The process of problem solving: Life is a series of different kinds of problems to be solved in varying contexts. The greatest difficulties we have stem from an inadequate solution of such problems. By using significant problems, both valuable content and needed processes can be learned. Also a procedure will be established which will help children recognize and deal with the innumerable problems of living at which we now can not even guess but for which they must have answers in the future.

The process of self-direction: Almost everyone agrees that learning the process of self-direction is important. Yet we have far to go in teaching it adequately. On the development of this process depends the continuing growth of each child in accordance with his potential, the habit of lifelong learning which is essential, and the amount of freedom which teachers will have to give guidance to individuals and small groups.

Self-direction includes the more negative aspect of self-control but puts emphasis on the positive, constructive, forward-moving activity of the child under his own steam. He has this self-direction to some degree on his first day of school. It can be strengthened and developed in his subsequent learning experiences, or it can be so inhibited that he becomes more dependent on teacher direction.

The process of creating: Much confusion has resulted from the failure to separate consideration of the creative process from that of the created product. The former is a way of thinking, an approach to life and its problems. It involves always being ready to take a new look, to search for more adequate alternatives.

The creative process depends on a healthy self-concept, a confidence on the part of each child that *his* thinking and ideas are valuable. This may be one of the most important learnings in the elementary school. It is an approach to living which is essential for the adequate development of each individual and our national life. Skill in the process of creating can be developed in some aspect of every content area, in every process to be taught. It means seeking new ways of looking at situations, new relationships and their implications for action. Only as the child develops confidence and trust in his own thinking and ability to solve problems in ways that are new to him, will he develop these processes to the point where they make larger contributions in later years.

The process of appreciating: Richness of life comes from the enjoyment of the good, the true, and the beautiful wherever we may find them. This is far broader than an appreciation of the Old Masters, Shakespeare, or Beethoven. It is a way of life and can be a part of every hour of every school day.

How does one learn appreciation? Perhaps through respect for others and the products they achieve. We can learn to appreciate certain aspects of nearly anything while at the same time recognizing their inadequacies. We also learn to appreciate in terms of the effectiveness with which a purpose is served. Most of all, we can learn to appreciate differences.

The process of memorizing: In the early schools, memorization was the main process that was taught. With greater understanding of how children learn and, even more important, how they learn to use what they know in life situations, memorization has taken quite a different role. We know that rote memory produces mechanical performance. And with certain skills this is important. We also know, however, that for intelligent application even these skills must be based on understanding. We know further that many of the learnings that require memorization are much more usable if experiences requiring understanding and application are provided.

What Content Is Important?

Processes are fundamental. But none of them can be developed without content for they have no content of their own. This content is derived from the society in which we live—both present and future as far as we can predict. It is indefensible to teach content which is inaccurate or superfluous. Even though a "good case" can be made for any particular learnings, it is always necessary to ask if they will be more important to children tomorrow than other things that might be put in their place. It is equally indefensible to omit learnings which it is almost certain children will need as they take their place in adult society.

What is this content? Or perhaps, how do we determine it? All content deals with the world in which we live—a world which can be divided into the physical-biological world and the world of people. Basic information about both and ways of dealing with them are essential.

For instance, certain content in science may be used to develop the processes of thinking, such as forming concepts, seeing relationships, making generalizations and applications, and communicating all these. All the facts about the physical world can never be taught to any one person. However, basic information can be learned when content is selected to develop overriding concepts and essential thought processes with material meaningful to the child. Understanding why something is so and what the consequences and implications may be for himself and others are fundamental learnings for the child.

All this is equally true in relation to the world of people. Since this science is newer and less fully developed than the science of things, it has been even less well organized for the curriculum. The older disciplines of history and geography have been included, but the newer ones of sociology, anthropology, psychology, and economics have only begun to be tapped for the elementary school. Yet these developing sciences perhaps involve more concepts and understandings necessary for effective living than do the older ones. We should look carefully at these disciplines—determine basic principles appropriate for elementary school children and weigh their potential contributions against the goals of the elementary school.

Implications for Curriculum

What does the foregoing mean as far as what the schools shall teach? It means that teachers would be far more conscious than they are today of the processes they are developing. They would realize that any of these processes can be developed through a wide range of content. Thus, content can be selected on its own merits.

It would mean that nothing needs to be retained in the curriculum just because it has "always been there." In no other area of life do we believe that what was good enough for us is good enough for our children. And certainly, this is not true in education. Our infinitely increased knowledge, including our understanding of how children learn to live effectively, must rule this out.

Certainly, it means we will teach the skills of communication—reading, writing, speaking, and listening—and of arithmetic, and teach them better than ever before. But we will realize that only an extremely small portion of these skills are mechanical. The art must be taught along with the mechanics since there is no value in and of the mechanics themselves. And we will remember that a child has not learned a skill until he has learned how to use it artfully and effectively for his own purposes in a "real" situation.

The social studies program needs most careful consideration as to content for it breaks the most sharply of all with tradition and goals are often not clear. As it fits into the total program, its purpose seems to be to help children live more successfully in the world of people. The child needs to understand himself and his associates, why they do what they do and how to deal with both himself and them more effectively. He needs to understand groups of peoples in both near and far places—how they live, how they have solved their problems, and why they do as they do—for they are all becoming his neighbors in this shrinking world.

He cannot possibly begin to know all of these things about any one group, nor much of consequence about all groups. A decision needs to be made as to whether studying a few representative groups in some depth or surveying many groups leads to greater understanding. A meaningful study of a group needs to include all the major activities of living: communication, transportation, food, clothing, shelter, education, creative efforts, values, and other cultural factors. It should consider the political, economic, geographic, and cultural forces which have influenced their historical development; their place in the family of nations today; the likenesses and differences between their situation and ours; and the implications of their life and development for understanding our own.

Such study could only be undertaken for a limited number of groups. Hence, in making our selection, we should choose representative groups and those which have the greatest significance for understanding our own and world history. As time brings changes to the world scene, so may the choice of what should be studied change. A program of this nature may contribute extensively to the development of all the processes mentioned earlier as well as provide extremely important content.

Science will be a part of children's learning in school from kindergarten on. It will be a matter of continually developing concepts and understanding through observation, experimentation, and research which at the same time will be developing the processes of thinking. Children need to know mathematics as the language of science.

Scientists and educators working together need to help teachers by outlining basic concepts and providing illustrations of ways and materials through which they may be developed. The use of a structured science program depends on whether or not teachers use situations in other content areas and in daily living to provide continuity in developing the important concepts.

The foreign language program in the elementary school has made considerable headway in the last decade. It has met with much lay approval, partly because of the status factor. This needs to be recognized and taken into account in our evaluation.

The greatest weakness in our elementary school foreign language programs is probably the lack of a clear purpose. Is it for communication purposes? Then selection of the language is important and should meet either local need or national need in the international field. Is it for appreciation of another culture? Then quite different content, procedures, and goals need to be established. While the study of any language may give the basis for understanding a culture different from our own, efficiency seems to demand that a culture which most needs understanding at this time should be selected.

Implications of answers to the above questions are significant. If communication is the aim, then continuity of language instruction is essential. What about mobility of students? of teachers? Would all children participate? If not, on what basis would they be selected? What does this mean for teacher education programs? For new skills for teachers in service? The new mechanical aids could help, but all studies show these to be simply aids, in no way ruling out teacher skill.

If appreciation is the aim, then a different procedure would be more adequate. Diversity rather than continuity might be the goal. Could some familiarity with the language become a part of the study of any people? How would mechanical aids fit into such a program? Would teachers need more information on the interrelationships of language and culture, the interrelationships and basic differences in the languages themselves, and the implications for the enrichment of our own language?

The most crucial question of all is this: Are the benefits which come to children from the study of a foreign language greater than those which might be attained in other ways? Are there better ways of spending the child's time and effort during these elementary school years?

The arts contribute to the processes of appreciation, and enjoyment, and creativity. How clearly does the school distinguish this in its content? There is considerable content and skill in the field of music, as well as in the other arts. To what extent are these areas taught also as bases for creativity?

Graphic art is probably the area in which greatest creativity is encouraged. Are children being helped to use it as a basis for appreciation and communication? The number of small storms kicked up today by those who are unable to appreciate art different from the traditional or to gain communication from it certainly indicates a lack in the development of these processes.

Now, what shall we teach in the elementary school? Will the *content* need to be continually re-evaluated in terms of the needs of a rapidly changing society and in light of continually expanding and altered knowledge? Will the *processes* become ever more important as skills to be used in discovering solutions to current problems of living together in this contracting world? We have had much experience in teaching content, but how well do we know how to teach processes? Or will the deliberate teaching of processes alter our methods of teaching content?

Shades of McGuffey

Lou Emma Wright Deen

Modern techniques based on a century of time-tested ideas can provide a program design for individualized elementary education.

I am a member of a species that is rapidly nearing extinction. Before the advent of consolidated unit schools, I was a rural school teacher—one of those antiquated creatures that you read about who taught 50 pupils in eight grades in a one-room country school.

Times have changed and I have changed with them. Any old teacher can learn new tricks, and there are always new tricks. We have learned that it is too late to use a walking plow to cultivate the field of education if we expect to produce a bumper crop of solid American citizens. We need innovations to improve education. The population explosion and technology seem to have headed us for mass-production methods in the classroom. These involve new educational media, which have met with some resistance because of fear of uniformity.

Traditional American education has required a certain amount of conformity. Our ladder system of education and promotion, standard tests, our goal of equal educational opportunity, the size of our country, and extensive transiency have made basic standardization necessary. Standard textbooks and comparative courses of study have helped to maintain our national level of education.

Basic conformity has not led to uniformity because schools have operated under local control. Programs have varied according to faculties, facilities, and community demands. As long as schools remain under local control there is little danger of uniformity.

There is also fear that new media may swallow local schools. Local schools should set up their programs to consume new media before the media consume them. Efforts to fit educational television into existing programs have been discouraging. Piped aids are flat if there is no correlation with existing programs. Special offerings can't be squeezed into programs that are already full. When it comes to a choice between make-over and take-over we had better alter our programs.

New educational media needn't be the end of traditional American education. An innovation in program design can facilitate new media without changing the traditional pattern of education. The new trick is a base pattern for the

Reprinted by permission of *Illinois Education,* The Illinois Education Association, Springfield, Illinois, from *Illinois Education* 55:386-388, May, 1967.

organization of all subject matter. The new design was gleaned from courses of study from the McGuffey era to the present time. Evolution is safer than revolution. A scientific course for the unknown future can be charted safely by utilizing information that has already been proved. The proposed course could have been used universally for the past hundred years or more, and can be used indefinitely.

Controversial Issues

Before we go into program planning, we need to air some petty controversial issues that stink. Too much time has been wasted in arguing over them. The continuous hub-bub has interfered with the normal progress of education. We keep getting sidetracked from the main line. Critics use minor issues as a sort of tug-o'-war game that keeps education see-sawing back and forth and prevents it from moving ahead.

We keep wasting time over such antiquated issues as the phonic versus the word method, ability grouping, graded and ungraded schools, and combining subjects. Some people seem to think these are current issues but they are really hang-over issues from the era of William Holmes McGuffey. Time has proved that such issues have little, if any, bearing on the general quality of education.

The phonic versus the word method of teaching reading has been debated for more than a century. Phonics is just one method of teaching one subject. Superior teachers have success with any method. *McGuffey's First Reader* suggests, "This reader may be used in teaching reading by any of the methods in common use, but is especially adapted to the phonic method, the word method, or a combination of the two."

Organizers of courses of study of a century ago ignored minor issues and dealt only with basic subject matter. An 1854 course of study states, "No attention is given to the details of the work, all that being left to the judgment and discretion of the teacher."

A century ago, school children in the Midwest attended ungraded elementary schools; ability grouping was the common practice. One textbook writer, C. J. Barnes, spoke for succeeding generations when he recommended his readers "for graded or ungraded schools, there evidently being nothing in the one not readily adaptable to the other."

Some critics object to the combining of subjects, calling it a trend of the Progressives. To these critics, the combining of reading, writing, spelling, and language into "language arts" is taboo, as is the combining of geography, history, and civics into "social studies." Some of these same critics are McGuffey fans and laud his readers—which crossed subject lines and combined reading, writing, spelling, language, science, health, history, civics, morals, manners, humanity, and what not.

If combining subjects is a Progressive trend, and being a Progressive is a sin, then shame on McGuffey and other textbook writers of his day. Combining subjects is a very old traditional practice. Someone has purposely or unwittingly confused the public and interfered with traditional American education. Don't look now, but it could be the person directly behind the fellow in front of you, and the name is not John Dewey. John Dewey can't be blamed for all of the so-called "Progressive trends"; combining subjects was popular before he was born.

Somebody has said wisely that we rise to greater heights by standing on the shoulders of giants. John Dewey must have been a giant or so many critics wouldn't be able to hide behind him. Educators are human and humans err. Grains of wisdom are gleaned from many sources and we don't have to buy the whole crop.

Organization of Material

Traditional American education is based on the natural sequence of learning. Textbooks, our leading source of educational subject matter, have been organized according to the learning sequence. The same basic material is presented at increasing levels of difficulty at each successive grade.

The unit method of instruction is very old and very efficient. There has been a trend to base courses of study on a series of units of work. Some units cross subject lines and involve several areas of learning. Such integrated teaching pulls the areas together and allows both vertical and horizontal organization and parallel planning of subject matter.

Snowballing subject matter makes it imperative that educational materials be organized in order to simplify education. John Dewey was in search of "the roots out of which would grow more elaborate technical and organized knowledge in later years."

There seem to be four roots which incorporate all of the core subject matter to be taught at the elementary level. These four basic units of work can be used simultaneously, schoolwide, which allows us to reach all children at individual levels of learning regardless of grouping plan.

The root units and their best sequence for teaching purposes are: Unit 1: Our World; Unit 2: People of Our World; Unit 3: Living In Our Country; and Unit 4: The Work of Our World. Each unit should be taught at all levels, grades one through six.

A Modern-Traditional Program

Simplicity is the magic word for efficiency in education. When organizing a new course of study, we can use the following simple modern-traditional design. Used throughout a wide area, it would facilitate new educational media.

1. Follow the traditional pattern of American education. Since all textbooks follow this general pattern, a variety of textbooks in any area can be used without losing the common thread of basic content. Some teachers seem to be married too tightly to textbooks; but a quickie divorce is not the answer. At present, textbooks are indispensable.

2. *Pre-plan the base.* In the past, a pre-planned base has been available for elementary programs, from which modified local school programs were developed to meet local needs. A base is necessary as a standard and guide. A pre-planned base allows all teachers concerned to get the over-all picture of elementary education, to see the continuity, and to discern their part in the total program.

3. *Deal only with subject matter.* Details should be left to the judgment and discretion of the teacher.

4. *Use the root series of basic common units of work in their fixed sequence as a base.* Elementary programs are usually based on standard textbook subject matter. The new design suggests that programs be based on this same subject matter organized into common units of work that are life problems. Education has been based on facts which time and change often cancelled. By shifting from facts to problems we broaden the base which will allow us to carry the increasing load. The series of root units of work allows the efficient organization of all pertinent subject matter from textbooks, current materials, programed materials, ETV, films, etc.

5. *Use the integrated unit method of instruction.* This method is necessary because it allows the parallel organization of all pertinent subject matter; allows enough vertical and horizontal spread to meet individual differences; and allows longer blocks of time, which allow pertinent subject matter from many sources to be introduced at any time during a unit period. This solves the bugaboo of timing and correlation that has hindered mass media efforts.

6. *Explore the units simultaneously, schoolwide (grades one to six), at successive levels of learning, allowing two months for each unit.* No unit is ever completed. The units are lifetime problems which are explored but never solved. Each year they are continued on a higher level. Simultaneous exploration of each unit makes the application of mass media more efficient, allows for individual differences by letting children participate at individual levels, and simplifies mass instruction by making it possible to combine groups or grades. It simplifies instruction and supervision. Allowing two months for each unit leaves the remainder of the year for drill, review, and individual work. Exploring the same units at successive levels may sound like repetition but it need not be. Each year the child participates at a higher level of learning and is introduced to more advanced material, in our traditional spiral pattern of education.

S. C. Weber has said, "Education is not information: it is the ability to use information." Whenever feasible, basic tool subjects such as reading, writing, spelling, or language should be applied to core content and mastered through daily use. The integration of art and music when possible adds depth and feeling to the total program. The functional application of subject matter provides a related program that gives purpose to learning and motivates pupils. No subject except arithmetic need be isolated and taught abstractly.

The result of integrated teaching is everything but uniform. The teacher is striving for individual accomplishment as well as group progress. Group progress is limited by the slower pupils. Individual progress is boundless. The suggested program design allows the superior child to soar in any direction while the slower child will find the shortness of his tether and remain close to the fundamental base. Equal educational opportunity does not guarantee equal results because of diversities of abilities over which we have little control.

A Multiple Solution

Teachers and school board members seem inclined to follow traditional lines. Tax objectors want technological innovations to cut rising educational costs. Traditionalists demand the fundamentals. Progressives insist upon improved methods of instruction. Mass media need a logical design to contain them. Teachers need a simple program that will entice them to adopt modern techniques which will require more efficient use of textbooks, encourage the incorporation of new materials, and allow sufficient time for the fundamentals. Children need a more stimulating functional program. The nation needs a universal design to supplement local school programs without domination.

This new design is offered as a logical one-shot answer. It contains choice techniques from more than a century of American education. It stems from the correlation, integration, coordination, combination, and other manipulations used by teachers in old country schoolhouses where you had to know all of the tricks of the trade. The new design is a composite of old time-tested ideas put together with a new twist. There is really nothing new in education except new tricks.

Parents Are Ready

"While there is general satisfaction with the educational system itself, many changes are favored by an overwhelming proportion of parents. In fact, the conclusion seems warranted that educators have not appreciated the extent to which the public is ready to accept change."

So reports a recent Gallup Poll surveying attitudes of parents toward education. Sponsored by the Institute for the Development of Educational Activities (IDEA) of the Charles F. Kettering Foundation, the poll in particular investigates parents' reactions to educational innovations. The findings and conclusions are eye-opening in some respects.

The poll states: "Parents of school children reveal an amazing capacity to accept new educational ideas, even though some of them are far-reaching in character. This is all the more surprising, since there is rather little active opposition to present practices, and an overall feeling that the present school system is quite satisfactory. Parents are by no means experts on education, either in respect to curriculum or methods of teaching, but as consumers of education, they have a right to help delineate the kind of education which they believe best meets the needs of their children in this present era. In some instances, their views may be regarded as somewhat naive. On the other hand, their thinking is likely to be less chained to the past than the thinking of those who have made education their profession."

Parental Approval

There is much discussion, both pro and con, of the "good old days" vs. "the changing times." But exactly how do parents feel about schools today as compared to their own days? A majority believe they are improved. Here is how they replied:

Better 75%
Not so good 12%
About the same 11%
No answer 2%

And what in particular do parents like about the schools their children are attending? Where do they think the schools are doing a successful job? The

Reprinted by permission of The Instructor Publications, Inc., Dansville, N.Y., from *The Instructor* 76:149, 154, October, 1966. ©The Instructor Publications, Inc.

following are a few of the responses given when parents were asked in what ways they think the schools are good:

Good teachers (help develop individual child, good teacher-child relationship, know their subject matter, inspire students, and so on)	29%
Generally good in all respects	21%
Good basic education (reading, writing, spelling, math, and so on)	12%
Varied curriculum (language, science, and so on)	10%
Keep up with new changes	5%
Good physical facilities (laboratories, libraries, and so on)	8%
Good discipline	5%

On the other hand, when parents were asked to specify some ways in which they felt the schools are weak, the following opinions were offered:

Poor teachers (don't retire old teachers, preponderance of very young teachers, salaries so low cannot attract good teachers) ·············	10%
Large classes	10%
Small or inadequate curriculum	9%
Poor physical facilities	8%
Poor discipline	8%
Poor basic education	4%
Expect too much of children	4%
Schools not weak in any respect	21%

From these findings, it appears that less than one-quarter of the parents find the schools generally good and without weaknesses.

Are Parents Well Informed?

According to the Gallup report, well over half the parents of school children are familiar with one or more new educational practices, but many are unaware of, or unfamiliar with, many innovations being carried out in schools. The one which has the highest publicity and awareness is "New Math." The next most widely recognized is the concept of nongraded schools.

Parents said they had read or heard about these innovations:

New math	28%
Nongraded schools	11%
New reading systems	9%
Teaching machines, films, visual aids, and so on	6%

Team teaching 4%
FLES 4%
Changes in courses 4%
Television teaching 4%
New alphabet 1%
Longer school year 1%
Sex education 1%
Miscellaneous 5%
No answer 42%

The large percentage of "no answer" might indicate a need of many school systems for a parent-information campaign.

What Parents Want

Parents stated a variety of ideas when asked, "If you were the one to decide, what changes would you make in the elementary school curriculum, or in the way the elementary schools are run?" Below are a few of the replies:

More time on basic education 11%
Better teachers 7%
Smaller classes 6%
Varied curriculum 6%
More discipline 4%
Nongraded schools 3%
More help for below-average students 3%
Changes in homework: more, less, none 2%
Not try new systems until proven
better than old 2%
Better physical equipment 2%
Less pressure on students 1%
Less emphasis on sports 1%
Television teaching 1%
No answer 22%

How Parents React

Educational innovations can generally be measured in two dimensions. First, the overall acceptance or rejection of the idea; and second, the significance or the important additions of the particular innovation. The parents interviewed in the Gallup Poll were asked to indicate if they thought certain innovations were either good or poor. Results show two ideas receiving the highest approval.

Parents approve of teaching pupils how to organize their work and their thinking, how to concentrate, and how to analyze problems. A remarkably high percentage would like to have a regular part of the school day set aside for this problem. The idea of using schools as community centers for adult learning centers received an equally high percentage of acceptance. Rating was tabulated as follows:

Classes on how to think and study
Good idea 93%
Poor idea 6%
No answer 1%

Schools used as community centers
Good idea 93%
Poor idea 6%
No answer 1%

Team teaching
Good idea 84%
Poor idea 14%
No answer 2%

Guidebooks for parents
Good idea 84%
Poor idea 15%
No answer 1%

Vocational training
Good idea 76%
Poor idea 22%
No answer 2%

Nongraded schools (classes assigned
by level of achievement)
Good idea 70%
Poor idea 27%
No answer 3%

More independent study time
Good idea 70%
Poor idea 27%
No answer 3%

Movable partitions for classrooms
Good idea 63%
Poor idea 34%
No answer 3%

Programed instruction
Good idea 59%
Poor idea 34%
No answer 7%

Reduce summer vacation to 4 weeks

Good idea............................ 30%

Poor idea 68%

No answer 2%

Marks "Pass" or "Fail"

Good idea 15%

Poor idea........................... 83%

No answer 2%

Increase school day by one hour

Good idea 45%

Poor idea........................... 53%

No answer 2%

From these responses, it appears that more parents approve of incorporating new educational innovations than might be anticipated by many educators. In fact, a greater number of parents favor such innovations than the percentage of their schools carrying them out. As far as the parents are concerned, they are ready for more new practices than the schools are giving them.

After testing reactions to several different innovations, the Gallup Poll then asked parents of school children: "Now, of all these suggested changes in education, which one appeals to you most? Which would you most like the schools in this community to adopt in the near future?" The following answers were made:

Classes in how to think and study 31%

Guidebooks for parents 13%

Vocational training 12%

Classes assigned by levels

of achievement 10%

Team teaching 7%

Increase school day by 1 hour 4%

Reduce summer vacation to 4 weeks 4%

Schools used as community centers 4%

More independent study time 3%

Programed instruction 2%

Movable partitions for classrooms 1%

Marks "Pass" or "Fail" 1%

Undesignated 11%

Look at this list again. How are the schools in your community, or those you know, fulfilling these ideas? Do you know if about 10 percent of your schools are nongraded? Are a third of the schools you know conducting classes in how to think and study? Are educators in your area ready for some of these ideas as much as the parents of school children are?

Who Resists Change?

A healthy attitude toward change and innovation must exist in a community for improvement to take place. Parents were asked their opinion of the innovation they favored.

"Just how difficult would it be to get the schools in this community to adopt this idea? Would it be extremely difficult, fairly difficult, or rather easy?"

Extremely difficult 18%
Fairly difficult 39%
Rather easy 36%
No answer 7%

"In making changes in the educational system, four groups must be considered: the school board, the school administrators (superintendents, principals, teachers), the parents of schoolchildren, and all the others who make up the general public. Just your own best guess, which of these four groups would be hardest to "sell" on some new idea—that is, to get some new idea accepted and used in the local schools of this community?"

General public 36%
School board 25%
School administrators 18%
Parents of school children 16%
No answer 5%

From this response, it appears parents feel almost half (43%) of the resistance to change would be found in the school personnel. This figure gives food for thought.

Parents Are Ready for Change

The Gallup report reflects "the general satisfaction of parents with the elementary and secondary schools of the nation. At the same time, it reveals that the public is ready to accept innovations which would change substantially the present type of education which their children receive. In fact, it is accurate to describe their views as revolutionary.

"Every profession has strong bonds with the past and has difficulty keeping pace with the present. This is particularly true with education. The pressures for change have never been great in this field; in fact, the pressures to maintain the status quo have often been stronger."

If parents were to have their way, "both the content of education and teaching methods would be changed, if the ideas which they favor were to be widely adopted. For example, part of the school day would be devoted to teaching students how to study, how to organize their work and their thinking, how to analyze problems. The schools would adopt team teaching. They would let the children in the upper grades spend nearly half of their time in independent study; they would adopt the idea of the nongraded school and assign each student to the class or kind of study in keeping with his level of achievement. They would make use of teaching machines for courses requiring much drill work, and they would redesign school buildings to make this new kind of individualized custom-tailored education possible. Acceptance of these innovations is not confined to any small segment of the public. Parents of school-children in all areas of the nation express favorable attitudes towards them. Those with college backgrounds hold the same views as the less well-educated.

"If the wishes of parents of children now enrolled in educational institutions were to be fully implemented, the role of education in our society would be vastly changed. In fact, the conclusion seems warranted that the public, in respect to education, may be as far ahead of present-day educators. . . .

"It would be a mistake to draw a conclusion that parents want only a strictly utilitarian type of education. Their attitudes towards the development of cultural interests and personal qualities refute this. What they want might best be expressed as education which is reality-related. They want the type of education which fits the needs of present-day life in America."

The Teacher as a Curriculum Maker

Charles R. May

New national studies are raising critical questions about the role of the teacher in curriculum making. I believe that all teachers are basically interested in improving themselves and in doing a good job. However, this does not mean that all teachers perform at the same level. In fact, teachers generally perform at three different levels and, consequently, assume three different roles in curriculum making.

These three roles can be seen as points on a continuum. At one end of the continuum is the teacher who is a "manipulator." Teachers at this level are manipulated by curriculum planners and by the textbooks they use. In turn, these teachers manipulate their students in much the same way. While operating at this level, teachers do those tasks which have been determined for them.

Reprinted by permission of *Ohio Schools,* Ohio Education Association, Columbus, Ohio, from *Ohio Schools* 43:12-13, 45, December, 1965.

Consequently, the decisions that they make are those delegated to them. For the most part, those decisions are restricted to their immediate area of operation— their classrooms.

This pattern would indicate that others have the responsibility for planning the curriculum, and the function of teachers is to see that this planning is carried out in their classrooms. Therefore, "covering the content" in the ways determined by the curriculum planners and textbook writers is the main responsibility of these teachers.

Teachers operating at the manipulative level behave more like technicians than members of a profession. In accepting a minor role in curriculum decision making, these teachers relinquish the status of a professional person. I have not always held this view. For example, in my first year of teaching, I found myself overly dependent upon my textbooks and the ideas of others. The teacher, I felt, was the "doer," putting into operation the plans of the experts. I reasoned that the expert had the time, knowledge, and experience to determine and organize the content and methods which teachers should use in their teaching. Thus, if a teacher could read the teacher's guide that accompanied a textbook, he should do at least an average job of teaching.

This view, I now believe, restricts the teacher to a minor role in curriculum decision making. Primarily, the tasks given a teacher at this level are those of serving on textbook committees and deciding which of several activities suggested by the experts should be used in teaching a lesson. Teachers who are interested in becoming professional people, however, are not satisfied to operate at this minor level of decision making, nor are they willing to be manipulated by others.

Toward the middle of the continuum are teachers operating at a level above the manipulative stage. These teachers have no need to use their textbooks and teacher's guides as though they were recipes or blueprints. They have an understanding of the textbook author's purposes and philosophy. Furthermore, they have an understanding of children's needs and interests. With these insights, they know when and where to supplement or deviate from the text. In other words, the teacher at this level is a "source" just as the textbook or curriculum guide is a source of content and method.

This level is therefore characterized by teachers who take an interest in curriculum planning. Frequently such planning is carried out through committees and through in-service workshops. At this level, the administration often assumes the leadership role. The following conditions foster this level of activity: time during school hours for planning, encouragement, guidance, recognition, and putting the results of planning into operation.

From my own experience, I found operating at the source level much more satisfying than operating at the manipulative level. Although there is security in following the textbook and in doing the suggested activities, this level of operation proves to be .rather routine and unimaginative. Therefore, as I gained knowledge and experience, I changed my emphasis from covering the text to that of using learning activities designed to meet the needs and interest of my students. As a result, I found my role in curriculum decision making changing also. For example, in teaching reading I switched from a basal textbook approach to an individualized approach, which required me to make many of the decisions that had formerly been made by the textbook authors. But because I knew my students, our reading objectives, and the variety of methods we could use, I was secure in using this approach. The reactions of the students toward reading revealed that the change was desirable, especially for that particular class.

Working at the source level requires much of the teacher; many more demands are placed on him. But the rewards are greater, too. Primarily, it is the difference in knowing that one is working as a professional person rather than as a technician.

At the opposite end of the continuum is the process level. Teachers operating at this level are fully professional. These teachers are characterized by a sound understanding of the following: teaching objectives, content, and methods. Moreover, they are aware of children's needs and interests. They are further characterized by their "open" attitude toward experience, their view of living and learning as a process, and their belief in the worth of each individual. They have a positive attitude toward themselves, their profession, and mankind in general.

A teacher at this level is considered as a "process" person. He views his function as that of bringing "raw materials" of learning—including himself—into the classroom. Together the teacher and the students then build concepts and understandings from this "raw material." Each student is involved in the process.

Teachers operating at this level have a vital part in curriculum planning. They assume leadership roles along with the administrators in making revisions in the curriculum. They are, indeed, the most important people involved in curriculum planning. By utilizing research and experimental studies, these teachers determine the best educational procedures and then work to incorporate these procedures into the curriculum.

As we mature and grow as a profession there will be fewer teachers operating at the manipulative level and more will come to function at the source and process levels. I am convinced that the type of teacher training that our future teachers now receive will shape more professional attitudes both toward teaching and toward the teacher's responsibilities in curriculum making.

Chapter 15

Working With Organizational Innovations

In the preceding chapter the results of a Gallup Poll surveying the public's reactions to educational innovations were reported as indicating that parents are ready to accept changes in what and how their children are taught. Society is saying that changes must be made—that we must innovate. But lest we rush too fast to accept as good anything and everything that is new and different, we need to find ways of evaluating and selecting. Criteria for measuring educational innovations are offered in the selection "The Teacher Evaluates Innovations." The reader will do well to keep these criteria in mind as he considers the organizational, curricular, and instructional innovations discussed in the selections that follow in this chapter and the next.

It may be that there is no one best type of organizational design for grouping pupils for the purpose of instruction. The three patterns most often employed are the self-contained classroom, the departmentalized school, and the ungraded plan. Of the three, only the ungraded plan is new enough to be considered innovative in itself, but when combined with team teaching, departmentalization can become innovative also.

Thomas and Crescimbeni discuss the ungraded elementary school, two teacher classes, multilevel assignments, departmentalization, team teaching, and team learning. McLoughlin claims that many schools purporting to be nongraded are really graded schools in which "homogeneous grouping and semidepartmentalization of instruction in reading and arithmetic are frequently passed off as nongraded programs." A truly nongraded program is based on instructional procedures that recognize and provide for individual differences among children. Olson examines the nature and demands of team teaching, tells why he thinks many teaching teams do not succeed, and offers suggestions for avoiding failure.

Expounding on his statement, "Two of the greatest needs in American education today are those of individualizing instruction and utilizing the staff more efficiently and effectively," Fox, in the concluding article, describes several organizational innovations that he feels offer considerable promise in meeting these needs.

The Teacher Evaluates Innovations

Gary A. Griffin and Rev. Joseph Devlin, S.J.

There was a time when attempting educational innovations was somewhat like drinking during Prohibition. The innovator stealthily entered a classroom, furtively looked around, pulled down the shades, locked the door, and INNOVATED. But, like liquor, innovation has become socially if not universally accepted. And overindulging in innovation can sometimes produce the same effects as those of the evil corn—dizziness, bleary eyes, slowed-down intellectual reflexes, and the resolution never to touch the stuff again.

Along with the population and knowledge explosions has come an explosion in the number and kinds of practices and materials from which educators can choose. We are no longer limited to one method of intoxication. Many, all neatly labeled, stare down at us from the shelf, urging us to sample them: team teaching, the nongraded school, computer-assisted instruction, national curriculum projects, programed instruction—the list grows as theoreticians and practitioners join forces on the common meeting ground of the school. The purpose of this article is to suggest some criteria against which the teacher can measure educational innovations.

Today's teacher is being given ever greater opportunity to participate in decision making on educational reform. As a professional, he should therefore feel a distinct mandate to use his expertise and intimate knowledge of day-to-day teaching to make these decisions. This does not mean, of course, that he should sit in on seemingly endless committee meetings in which each member expresses his biases and from which no product is forthcoming. It does mean that he should use his valuable store of information to provide a framework for making wise and well-founded choices for his students.

The implication here is an important one: namely, that the teacher is responsible for possessing relevant and reliable information—not opinion, hearsay, or conventional wisdom. He should share valid information with his fellows and use that information when necessary.

All teachers have innumerable opportunities to assess innovative practices informally: We can carp about them over the lunch table; we can raise our eyes heavenward at faculty meetings; we can put that new curriculum guide to the back of the bookshelf; we can, as in the Prohibition days, lock the door, pull down the blinds, and go on our merry way. But morning may bring with it woes

Reprinted by permission of the National Education Association, Washington, D.C., and Gary A. Griffin and Rev. Joseph Devlin, S.J., from *NEA Journal* 56:26-28, December, 1967.

that no simple remedy can cure. There must be a better way to make our influence felt and there must be sounder reasons for evaluating directions and innovations.

The following questions and answers are not prescriptive. They are designed to provide a framework for developing additional criteria and a firmer meeting ground for innovators and practitioners.

1. Is the innovation appropriate for the learner? National curriculum projects and other large-scale programs will have far-reaching effects on millions of young people. We must resolve the fundamental question of appropriateness for *which* learner. Are the prepackaged programs, with their slick and attractive trappings, for example, the best educational tools for the disadvantaged child of the inner city? If we are to answer the question of appropriateness, we must answer it in terms of our comprehensive knowledge of the learner and his social and economic environment.

2. Is the innovation economical of time, space, and human resources? In some instances, studies of new approaches to an educational task show no statistical difference in the students' level of learning after using the innovation. Unfortunately, this "no difference" has meant to some that the innovative practice is a failure and should be discontinued. But the assessment should not stop there. Improved efficiency in achieving the same level of accomplishment should also be a consideration when one chooses to adopt or reject an educational innovation. Surely the savings bank of time, space, and materials provided by some new techniques will yield a high rate of interest for the learner and the school.

3. Is the innovation in line with the goals of the school system? In all too many school systems, this question may receive little attention. But emphasis on categorical goals, although not new, is gaining increased recognition from educators. The reason for this is simple: Until a task has been defined, one cannot effectively develop procedures and practices to accomplish it. Few school systems have not stated as a goal: "To train responsible citizens for a democracy." But what does this mean? Each of us could interpret this goal, but each definition would probably be different.

School systems must carefully list their problems and their goals and then devise a plan that shows promise of solving the problems and achieving the goals. In doing so, they should develop a framework for innovative decision making. Within this framework, teachers can measure each innovation in terms of its prospective effectiveness as it relates to the objectives and procedures defined by the school system. The teacher in this process assumes an all-important role. He must *know* the goals as well as the procedures, and he must have a voice in their implementation.

4. Is the innovation aligned with the philosophical position of the society and the schools? This question, although it might be read into the above comprehensive scheme, is important enough to merit special consideration. Learning theory, for example, tells us that material rewards can increase the learner's involvement in a task: Paying money for grades has produced better learning for some children. Does this mean, then, that the teacher should distribute silver to his students on the successful completion of an arithmetic lesson? A philosophical position on the relation of the individual to his environment will help us answer this rather facetious question. Obviously, most philosophies of education would answer *No!*

Some school systems have produced statements of educational philosophy to guide their schools. In most instances, however, it is up to the individual school, the professional association, and even the teacher standing alone to develop a philosophical filter through which innovations can be screened. The position of the teacher must be clearly stated and readily defensible. To fight for a principle in the philosophical arena takes a kind of courage that some teachers and teacher groups have yet to develop. When we stand up and are counted, we must be able to offer valid reasons for our positions.

5. Is the innovation firmly rooted in sound educational theory? Far too prevalent on the educational scene has been the ascendancy of superficial, expedient, so-called practicality over promising, if challenging, theory. Few faculty meetings go their full measure of rhetoric without at least one person's saying, "It sounds great, but it won't work in *my* classroom."

It is up to the teacher to discover in any proposed innovation the theory on which the proposed practice is based. This simply means: What indicates that this practice will be more effective than any other? With the present-day proliferation of methods, materials, and techniques, the teacher must become more and more familiar with the major learning theories in order to assess innovations successfully.

Why innovate? Some fear that school systems may be too ready to innovate, as they jockey for federal funds, seek prestigious national curriculum projects, or try to gain a reputation as a progressive system. Before instituting changes, the needs of the school should be clearly identified, and no one can do this, in its most literal sense, as well as the teacher who confronts learners each day. Merely because the neighboring school system, for example, is using faddish materials is no reason for your system to do so. It would be far better for teachers and administrators to work as partners in identifying problem areas and seeking solutions to the problems.

The list of criteria does not end here. Each of you will think of ways in which teachers, as individuals and as members of groups, can participate in the selection and assessment of educational innovations. The topics mentioned above can apply to many school systems. It is up to you, after intelligent evaluation, to make the process of application and the definition of criteria pertinent to your own school.

We mentioned the explosion of educational innovations. Let us be sure, finally, that the glare from that explosion does not obscure our ultimate goal—the best education for the most children.

The Changing Nature of the Elementary School

George I. Thomas and Joseph Crescimbeni

Education in the elementary schools has been characterized by a change in the philosophy of education underlying our schools and the way teachers teach. The elementary school of today is not the same school it was two decades ago. Teachers have many more teaching aids. They can make learning more interesting and more effective when they base their methods upon a knowledge of the "nature of the children." Children are more likely to be recognized as human beings with strong feelings and drives. They have many more opportunities to acquire good work-study habits, because more teachers are interested in a type of teaching which calls for multiple textbooks and references. Also, children today are encouraged to work both independently and cooperatively.

Teachers in many schools are interested in individualizing the teaching process, but they are not going back to the type of individualized teaching found before the start of the graded school. There are times when teachers find it highly desirable to work with boys and girls individually; however, children have many common needs, abilities, and interests which should enable them to share group experiences. So today we are seeing a modified return to the ungraded school.

Ungraded Elementary Schools

A large number of school systems have been exploring the ungraded elementary school concept, but have restricted themselves to the ungraded primary stage. In such school systems children in Grades 1, 2, and 3 of the traditional school are grouped together without grade levels. These ungraded primary groups allow children to make continuous progress through the ungraded unit until it is time for them to move into the intermediate grades. When the children leave the ungraded primary school, they may go into a regular fourth grade or they may advance to a new ungraded unit which extends through the equivalent of Grades 4, 5, and 6. A school which takes children through the primary and intermediate levels without actual grade designations may be called the ungraded elementary school, but the true test of ungradedness will depend upon the philosophy of the teachers as they work with children in the classroom.

Advantages of the Ungraded School. Since many factors influence the achievement or growth of boys and girls, it is not always easy to prove claims for the ungraded school pattern. However, educators who have been experimenting and working to improve the ungraded pattern of organization believe that achievement has improved and that the amount of failure and pupil dropout has decreased in their schools. Some of the specific advantages claimed for the ungraded school are:

1. It recognizes the individuality of children. Due to emotional, mental, physical, and social differences, boys and girls progress at their own rates of speed, even at junior high school levels. The ungraded program provides better than the graded school for the lags and spurts which accompany children's growth.

2. It attempts to provide a program of continuous and sequential learning experiences. Children gain confidence and satisfaction from success at each learning level.

3. Pupil academic progress has been reportedly faster. (Further studies may be desired here since many teachers in the ungraded school are using teaching techniques which are not new, but which have just been neglected in all but the better graded schools. This advantage may not be real where comparable teaching methods are used.)

4. Slow pupils are not pressured to work beyond their normal rate of growth. They do not have to contend with the problem of repeating grades since they always move on to new levels from the point where they left off the previous year. Bright pupils or fast learners are not held back to await slower-progressing pupils, nor are they accelerated. They work in higher levels or special enrichment levels where they can continue to find challenge as they work and grow.

5. Pupil achievement is more likely to be considered in terms of expectancy levels for the pupil's *mental age* than in terms of normal grade standards, since pupils and teachers may work with materials extending over several years.

6. A higher quality of reading results from more complete mastery, leading to better achievement in other subjects. For example, problem solving has improved where children really mastered reading comprehension.

7. There is greater flexibility of movement within and between classes.

Pupils can be transferred to higher or lower learning levels during the school year without having a major adjustment problem.

8. Teachers are not restrained from using textbooks and work materials normally reserved for higher grade levels. They use materials appropriate for given learning levels regardless of grade designations by publishers and others. Teachers are expected to work with pupils with advanced materials if they are ready for such experiences.

9. The ungraded school is easy to administer and is no more expensive than the traditional graded school, yet it gives children opportunities to grow with fewer frustrations.

10. Experience with the ungraded school organization shows that parents favor it once they understand its goals.

The Ungraded Primary Easy to Adapt. The curriculum of the first, second, and third grades can be adapted, without too much difficulty, to meet the format of the ungraded primary unit as long as the teachers are prepared to think in terms of *continuous progress* instead of grade standards. Since reading is frequently used to group boys and girls in the ungraded primary school, progress through the school is related to the speed with which pupils move through the developmental reading material. The average pupil goes through the ungraded primary unit in the space of three years, fast learners in less time, while slow learners may require four years.

After they complete kindergarten, children are usually assigned to the primary unit, but without grade designation. In some schools, parents are asked to refer to the child as being in his first or second year of school rather than in a specific grade. In other schools the parents merely refer to the fact that a pupil is in the primary division, e.g., "Johnny is in Miss Howell's primary section."

When children attend kindergarten prior to starting to work in an ungraded primary, the ungraded school teachers have a pupil record to guide them. Where a school system does not have a kindergarten, the teachers have to work very slowly with their new children. They have to (1) expose the pupils to readiness activities and (2) accumulate a fairly complete record about each pupil.

Continuous Progress in the Ungraded School. The theme of this book will stress the concept that children should be grouped so that progress can be continuous for *all children,* even within the confines of a graded school, although the nongraded approach may be ideal for individualizing the learning process. The ungraded school organization owes its success to the fact that children progress through these various achievement levels at their own rate of speed. Bright pupils or fast learners do not have to wait for slower pupils, nor do they have to read and reread books or special materials which no longer challenge them. Average pupils do not have to keep up with faster learners, nor do they have to wait for the slower.

The issue of promotion or nonpromotion can be eliminated in the ungraded elementary school since there is never a question about where the pupils are going to be in the fall. Each individual is expected to continue with the learning stages at the point where he left off when school closed for the summer. In many graded schools teachers feel pressure to get their boys and girls through a prescribed series of learning activities by the close of the year. With true grouping, neither the pupil nor the teacher feels this pressure. The children tend to continue their work with other pupils who are similar in ability and achievement. If a pupil is overachieving in terms of the other pupils in his group, he is phased out and put into the next higher level. There is no question about "skipping" grades as such.

If these pupils are socially and physically mature, they may leave the primary unit a year earlier than their chronological peers, but many schools have introduced extra achievement levels or an enrichment level to challenge such pupils before they are allowed to move ahead to another group. Thus, one may find the brighter pupils reading fewer preprimers, first readers, second readers, or third readers. To occupy their time, they may read from a wide variety of advanced books with the teacher or independently. In other cases, their vertical growth will be slowed only for a short time before they are allowed to move into higher levels of instruction. In such schools one may find pupils leaving the primary unit who have mastered the fourth-, fifth-, and even sixth-grade curriculum. There may be some pupils leaving the intermediate unit who have mastered the books normally assigned to the seventh- and eighth-grade classes.

Pupils who complete the books of a designated level, but who show that they have not mastered them, are not asked to repeat the book they have read. The pupil works with a reinforcement reader to develop skills essential to his continued growth. Surprisingly enough, studies of schools which have adopted the ungraded primary program show that many pupils who may be labeled "slow starters" catch up with pupils who progressed at a faster rate in their first year in the primary grade unit. Through a program of continuous progress there seems to be a decrease in the amount of actual retardation in the three-year span. In some schools this may be due to the elimination of mass reteaching when specific children in a learning group have trouble. If a child seems to be making slow progress in a learning level, the teacher tries to identify what is responsible for the slow progress. Thus, a teacher may work with a child on the improvement of auditory recognition of sounds that are causing trouble, or place the pupil in learning situations that stretch out the program.

To guarantee that all pupils are making continuous progress, the teachers must study carefully the achievement of their children and in some instances shift them to higher or lower levels. Each child should be placed in a learning situation which will enable him to achieve a continued measure of success. The teacher who is working with 25 to 30 pupils will have two or three reading or arithmetic groups, so children may be shifted from one group to another at almost any time during the year. Occasionally, however, some children may be shifted from one teacher to another during the school year to place them in a desired learning level without forcing the teacher to form another instructional group. Teachers often try to group children so no child is more than one year younger or older chronologically within a classroom, and some pupil shifting may therefore result from other than academic achievement.

Children in ungraded primary classes reportedly are happier and make better progress due to the absence of the pressures encountered in schools where grade standards have to be met by the close of the school year. By breaking the curriculum into small segments or steps, boys and girls experience success at more frequent intervals and then proceed to the next learning stage when they are ready for it.

Reading Is Often the Basis for Grouping in the Ungraded Primary School. A pupil's placement in an ungraded primary unit is usually determined by his reading accomplishment. Where the pupil stands at the end of a given year of schooling depends upon the speed with which he masters the *sequence of learning skills* of the various reading levels established by the teachers. There is considerable variation in the number of levels established by different school systems, but a typical reading program may resemble the following:

Levels of Learning	Representative Reading Levels of a Basic Reading Program	Probable Rate of Progress of Children		
		Fast Learner	Average Learner	Slow Learner
Level 11	Fourth reader or reading for independence	3rd year	4th year	5th year
Level 10	Third reader—hard (3-2)		3rd year	4th year
Level 9	Third reader—easy (3-1)			
Level 8	Reading for enrichment	2nd year		
Level 7	Second reader—hard (2-2)		2nd year	3rd year
Level 6	Second reader—easy (2-1)			
Level 5	First reader (1-2)	1st year	1st year	2nd year
Level 4	Primer (1-1)			
Level 3	Preprimer			1st year
Level 2	Chart reading			
Level 1	Readiness or prereading			
Kindergarten	Orientation and readiness			

Each child works with other children on a given level until he masters the skills of that level. The work is sequential, so he does not skip nor repeat a level if his readiness to go to higher levels has been properly evaluated. Each pupil's success is carefully measured through regular reading tests. In one school where some pupils failed to pass the tests, provisions were made for work in a parallel reader. Pupils rating high on the tests could bypass the reinforcement materials, but pupils who rated low would have to work with them until they mastered the skills outlined for their reading levels. In other schools, slow learners skip the enrichment levels which rapid learners complete before going into higher reading levels. The enrichment levels allow bright pupils to broaden their background and strengthen their skills before going too far ahead of their peers. Enrichment reading should not be reserved for only bright pupils, because all children would be exposed to a progran of enrichment at each reading level. For example, some schools develop reading lists composed of basic readers, supplementary books, and library books to guide teachers at each level.

Some teachers have advocated the ungraded primary plan in hopes of eliminating subgrouping. In terms of achievement, the number of groups that have to be taught is decreased with the ungraded primary, but teachers are still expected to work with their children in small groups for reading and other subjects. The difference lies in the narrower range between the top and bottom reading subgroups within a section. This range may be kept small by transferring pupils to other sections if they are isolated in a given classroom. If a school is large, teachers will often teach overlapping reading levels to give greater flexibility in grouping. Thus, one teacher may be working with levels 4-5-6 while another is working with levels 3-4-5 and still another is working with levels 5-6-7. This overlapping makes it easy to place transfer students from another classroom or another school.

Transfers Not Made Without Considering the Impact. Studies seem to indicate a tendency to transfer *groups* of children from one teacher to another much more readily than to transfer *individual* pupils. This does not mean that individual children are not transferred—because they are. With subgrouping in each classroom, the teacher has some flexibility when it comes to placing pupils in an appropriate learning situation. In some schools, children are changed at the end of a semester or at the conclusion of the work in a given level. Special changes are made, but the transfers are based upon consultation with the principal, other teachers, and, frequently, the parents.

Other Criteria Besides Reading Used to Assign Children to Ungraded Sections. Some educators reject the idea of using reading as a basis for assigning children to ungraded sections since it connotes or resembles a form of homogeneous grouping. To achieve a more heterogeneous pattern, children are assigned to teachers on the basis of random selection or chance. Other educators study kindergarten records and then make selective pupil assignments to ensure balanced heterogeneity. A few schools use chronological age as the basis of assignment. For example, the younger-aged kindergarten children are placed together in a beginning primary section, and the older pupils go to another section. Through chronological age grouping, educators attempt to keep together those children who should have common needs. Some educators consider such grouping as too unrealistic. They prefer a balanced heterogeneity which takes into account the interests, personalities, and backgrounds of the children assigned to given sections. Unfortunately, the amount of information about six-year-olds is often sparse and not too reliable for truly balanced groupings of this sort. Apparent differences disappear due to the leveling influence of the school. Yet other differences become noticeable when pupils are in learning situations which call for decisions and actions based upon physical and mental exercise plus different experiential backgrounds.

A number of schools attempt to place children into class sections on the basis of mental age or expectancy levels for their mental age. Group intelligence tests are administered in an attempt to determine the readiness of individual children for learning levels. As children work together, the teacher observes their growth in terms of their actual progress in various subject fields and their expected progress for their intellectual capacity. From time to time pupils are transferred to other class sections to bring together children who have common educational needs. IQs are not used for grouping since they do not tell a pupil's potential at a given period of time. However, if the mental age is used to compute expectancy levels, and if achievement test scores are interpreted in terms of these expectancy levels, parents and teachers can more effectively follow the progress of children through a sequence of learning activities. Pupils who are working close to expectation levels should not be pushed, whereas pupils who are working one or more years below expectation levels may need extra help in one or more academic areas.

Standardized achievement test results may be used to determine the level to which boys and girls should be assigned as they go through an ungraded primary unit. Thus:

Level 1. Pupils whose test scores range from 1.0 to 1.4 (grade equivalents)
Level 2. Scores from 1.0 to 1.4
Level 3. Scores from 1.5 to 1.9
Level 4. Scores from 2.0 to 2.4
Level 5. Scores from 3.0 to 3.4
Level 6. Scores from 3.5 to 3.9
Level 7. Scores from 4.0 to 4.4
Level 8. Scores from 4.5 to 4.9

The authors are reluctant to recommend achievement test results for placement unless flexibility is guaranteed through consideration of factors other than a single test score. This is especially true of children at beginning levels.

Two-Teacher Classes

When space is at a premium, large numbers of children are frequently assigned to a classroom. In an attempt to provide them with a more individualized program, experimentation with two teachers to a classroom has proved highly effective. Excellent results have been obtained when two teachers worked together as partners, planned together, and divided their responsibilities equally. This is a form of team teaching, because the success of the program depends upon constant cooperation of two teachers whose educational goals are compatible. The authors have seen success with such a program with kindergarten children and third- and fourth-grade pupils. While not advocating this type of organization, the authors do feel it is possible to provide children with a broad enriched program if two average-sized classes are combined to work in a large-sized classroom, with the teachers making every effort to teach subgroups elsewhere in the building at some other time of day.

For this type of organization to be effective, the two teachers must understand their responsibilities and must be willing to share them under conditions that can be most trying. Work must be divided so that no teacher feels that she is doing more than her share. There will be times when all children will work together with one teacher. At such times the other teacher can correct papers, confer with parents, put assignments on the board, study test results and cumulative records, plan activities for special subject teachers, or prepare materials for demonstrations and experiments. During skill development periods the class is divided into groups on the basis of homogeneity or readiness for an activity, with each teacher taking two to three groups. In arithmetic there will be times when all pupils work together in introductory activities; then they may be divided in terms of need for additional practice, need for review of lower-level skills, or ability to work with higher-level concepts or skills. In any case, pupils requiring remedial help should be taken out of the class.

Fifty children can work together in some areas of the curriculum where numbers are insignificant, but for activities that call for free expression, teachers find it advantageous to divide their work so that one teacher can work in the classroom with a limited number of pupils. During the course of the week there are many free areas in a building if one looks for them. This is especially true if recess and lunch periods are staggered for a two-teacher class. For example, half the class may go to the gym or cafeteria while the other children work in their homeroom. Study groups may go to the library to work with research materials. Thus small groups are left behind to work on creative activities or to engage in discussion. In one school, large second-grade groups found it advantageous to go to the cafeteria because they could spread out art materials.

Multilevel Assignments

Pupils from all ability levels gain in general achievement when teachers individualize their teaching by making multilevel assignments. Teachers have been most successful in meeting the needs of pupils in homogeneous or heterogeneous classes when they have planned the work in terms of ability, interest, achievement, attitude, and drive. Varied assignments can meet these differences within a class without having to subdivide it into intermediate and upper grade pupils. Some teachers have been most successful with assignments which called for work in one of three different level social studies books. The pupils in one such class never had assignments given in terms of *pages* to be studied. History books of different degrees of difficulty were used, and the pupils learned to locate the appropriate pages using the index.

Departmentalization and Team Teaching

For more than half a century, educators have been arguing about the pro and con of departmentalized teaching versus the self-contained classroom. While upper grade and high school teachers are firmly committed to departmentalized teaching, elementary school teachers have been divided as to its merits. It has an appeal to subject-matter-minded teachers and parents; so one finds pressure exerted from time to time to departmentalize the teaching in the intermediate and even the primary grades. Between 1910 and 1930 there was considerable experimentation with departmentalized teaching in the elementary schools. During the 1930s feelings ran high between teachers favoring or opposing the plan, but during the 1940s many schools gave up departmentalization only to see a new surge of interest appear during the 1950s and 1960s. Recent attempts to narrow the range of reading or arithmetic instruction at the intermediate grade levels have helped to stimulate interest in some form of departmentalized teaching.

Opposition to departmentalized teaching is often based on the following arguments:

Departmentalization tends to develop subject matter specialists who fail to see the relationship between what they teach and what the next teacher teaches. There is no continuity in the curriculum when several teachers teach separate subjects. Their work cannot be integrated so that children can see and understand relationships between subjects of studies.

Teachers work with so many children that they fail to get to know their students as individuals. By not seeing the children working under different conditions, it is impossible for teachers to understand thoroughly their children's basic needs.

Departmentalized teachers think in terms of adult needs more than they do in terms of children's needs.

Some of these arguments, however, can be met through a form of team teaching that has been used successfully in some elementary schools. While there are a number of departmentalized school systems which claim to have adopted a team teaching approach, the concept may vary within these schools. In its simplest form it may consist of nothing more than two or three teachers meeting together regularly to plan their work and to talk about the progress of the children with whom they work in a departmentalized program. If the teachers are conscientious about their work and can get together fairly regularly, they can counter some of the arguments listed above. Through repeated evaluations and through joint planning teachers can get acquainted with boys and girls and can interpolate their own subject matter with what the other teachers are teaching. They can see the desirability for continuity as pupils go from class to class or even to the next grade. This is possible at the elementary school or junior high school level where the teachers assigned to a team work with the same children as they teach different subjects. It is not necessarily true where the teams consist of teachers teaching the same subjects to different groups of children.

Team teaching should be used as a means to improve the quality of education. It should be ignored if the objective is to save money. In a proper setting, team teaching at the elementary school level can help eliminate some of the handicaps under which the teachers work in a departmentalized program. There are some persons who are opposed to bringing large groups of children together for lectures or motion pictures, but this can be one way to free teachers from routine so they may give special instruction to pupils who need it. Better teacher planning and cooperative planning can result from team teaching, particularly where large-group activities are alternated with small-group seminars and individual work or study periods.

Team Teaching in a Given Subject

Team teaching can be considered a much higher phase of joint teacher activity than team planning. Here teachers who work in a common subject field plan a program which may be based on both large group and small group instruction. Thus, a social studies teacher with a special interest or background may elect to teach all of the students from four, five, or more classes. The large group of children may be supervised with the assistance of one of the other members of the team. This releases the other social studies teachers to prepare their own lessons or to work with small groups of students or with individuals. When the large group instruction is over, the pupils may then discuss the lecture, picture, or demonstration in their regular classrooms with their regular teacher.

Team Planning

In its simplest form teachers may be assigned to teach four classes of students. The pupils go to a different teacher for reading, arithmetic, social studies, and language arts where instruction may be directed to the elimination of problems identified in the weekly or biweekly planning session of the teaching team. In this school the teachers do not combine classes; however, they will try to direct their efforts to the basic problems they identify when they meet to discuss their work with the children assigned to their teams, as the following illustration shows:

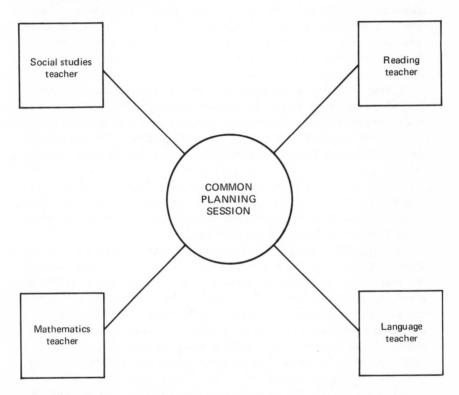

Team Learning

Parents and teachers have a tendency to frown upon having children work together when they do their work, yet many boys and girls find that it helps to work with others. Teachers will find that they often assume added burdens by not taking advantage of what may be described as team learning. There are times when teachers have to teach, but there also are times when boys and girls can teach each other if they are left to themselves or are encouraged to help each other. Teachers who are overly concerned about the wide range within an intermediate class can delegate some of the responsibility for learning to pupil learning teams without reverting to the faults of the old pupil monitorial system. This was illustrated in a group experiment conducted at Dedham, Massachusetts, under the direction of Dr. Donald D. Durrell of Boston University:*

In the Dedham experiment, forty-five teachers worked with 1200 intermediate grade pupils in a special team learning approach. Each class was divided into two or three work teams for instruction in subjects like arithmetic, spelling and social studies. The pupils in each classroom were divided into sub-groups or work teams on the basis of ability, with the understanding that they could move ahead as fast as they were able to do so. As a result, about one-third of the fourth, fifth, and sixth graders finished the equivalent of two years of arithmetic in one year.

A report on pupil performance based on the result of comparative tests showed growth in all subjects beyond the normal rate for pupils in a given grade. Fourth graders exceeded the normal growth for the year by 4.3 months, fifth graders by 5.3 months, and sixth graders by 3.4 months. As a result of the team learning approach, there was a definite increase in the proportion of pupils making a full year's growth in school. It was estimated that team learning had resulted in a jump of from about 50 to 74 percent in achievement. This growth was not limited to selected classrooms. Every class which was involved in the experiment showed an increase in the percentage of pupils making at least a full year's growth.

The experiment called for flexible grouping with all pupils working on a team in terms of ability and congeniality. Some of the pupils were on different teams for arithmetic, spelling, history, or geography. Instead of competing with each other, team members provided mutual help and support to each other. Discussion frequently took the place of drill. Because pupils continued to help each other in team learning activities, classroom teachers often had fewer papers to correct. While group activities were stressed, each pupil was always on his own when it came time to take the tests which were given every ten days to judge their mastery of basic skills.

From time to time the teachers instructed the whole class as a unit, but most of the class work was performed by small teams of pupils working at their own rates of speed. Individual pupils or groups of pupils did not spend their time waiting for the teacher. As a result, they did not waste time with busy-work. Teachers found that they had less disciplinary problems to cope

---

* Donald D. Durrell and Viola Palos, "Pupil Study Teams in Reading," *Education*, 76 (May 1956), 552-56. Reprinted by permission of The Bobbs-Merrill Company, Inc., publisher.

with than formerly. Usually, discipline was meted out by the working unit. Pupils who acted up were isolated by the learning team. This was most effective since team learning capitalized upon the natural desire of the students to work together. Most pupils accepted the leadership of the other students and learned to carry their own share of work and responsibility rather than lose the respect of their classmates.

Here one finds another illustration of what happens when boys and girls in a learning situation are encouraged to progress at their own pace. They can, under the right stimulus, make a mockery of traditional grade standards. The problem is what to give these fast learners who demonstrate their ability to master traditional bodies of knowledge or skill at twice the rate of speed of average-learning pupils. Educators have often used the term "enriched curriculum" for the faster learners, but the term is inadequate to express what is desired. Modern children are living in a world which is changing daily. To live in it they must be prepared to solve problems undreamed of by their fathers and mothers when they went to school. To solve them they must have a background of information and skill far beyond traditional grade standards, yet it is virtually impossible to think of this new knowledge and skill in terms of grade levels or age levels. One has to cope with elements of interest and background or readiness for new learning at all levels of our schools; therefore, it may be necessary to think in terms of optional units or even new courses of study for our faster learners.

Team learning is another example of what happens when continuous progress becomes the accepted pattern. Grade lines, as such, tend to be eliminated. Unless the teachers teach a multiple-track curriculum, some of them will find themselves hard pressed to challenge their faster learners. Furthermore, team learning points up a possibility that many classes have been too teacher-dominated in the past. Teachers have to see that boys and girls often learn from each other as well as from the teachers. This does not mean that a teacher can ignore his leadership role in the classroom, but if the right type of environment is created, many of the pupils can help him extend the range of pupil interests and achievement and, in doing so, may help him resolve the issue of grouping or balancing out classes in an artificial attempt to narrow the teaching range.

For decades the good disciplinarians were teachers who could keep children quiet and orderly in class. This problem has plagued most teachers from time to time in their teaching careers. One of the complaints about group instruction has been that teachers have to interrupt good group activity to quiet the talkers or to stop some pupils who are working together from copying or wasting time. In spite of the desirability of modern movable school furniture, one still finds desks and chairs lined up in rows, largely to keep pupils from getting too close to one another. Teachers reason that it is easier to preserve discipline by separating children as much as possible in order to discourage talking and copying.

This philosophy fails to recognize a natural tendency of both children and youths to work together on many types of projects or problems. Team learning calls for an end to the silent classroom. Pupils in the new setting are not only going to be permitted to talk and work together, but they are actually going to be encouraged to talk out their problems without teacher intervention. Studies have shown that boys and girls not only prefer to work in teams or in small groups, but they can work successfully without constant admonitions to be quiet while they are working. Students have shown that they prefer to work in small teams instead of an all-class or a large subgroup basis. If they can be given an opportunity to work in meaningful activities, the teacher does not have to worry so much about problems of discipline such as those that haunt teachers in the traditional teacher-dominated classroom. Much of the need or desire to copy or waste time with idle talk will disappear once pupils have experience working closely with selected students with similar problems and learning needs.

How children react to the new rules and procedures becomes a matter of training and experience. Pupils can learn to work cooperatively with each other and with the teacher from the day they start school in the kindergarten or first grade. They can learn that there is a time for individual work as well as a time for all-class or large group activity. If, after three or four years of close work, boys and girls have not learned to accept responsibility for the way they work, one may question whether they have learned the true meaning of words such as "responsibility," "self-discipline," "leadership," and "cooperation."

The Phantom Nongraded School

William P. McLoughlin

Few propositions for educational change have generated and sustained as much interest as the nongraded school. It is discussed at nearly every major educational conference, and symposiums on the nongraded school are increasing in popularity. Furthermore, the body of available literature is increasing rapidly; most leading professional journals have published several articles on this topic. Through these and other means, educators have learned more of the promises of the nongraded school than they have of its accomplishments.

Reprinted by permission of the *Phi Delta Kappan,* Bloomington, Indiana, from *Phi Delta Kappan* 49:248-250, January, 1968. Copyright 1968 by Phi Delta Kappa, Inc.

This is understandable, for nongrading appears to be preached more than practiced and practiced more than appraised. In fact, few dependable estimates on the present status and anticipated growth of the nongraded school are currently available and sound studies on its accomplishments are even more difficult to come by. From what is available one would be hard put to determine just how many schools have nongraded their instructional programs and how many are seriously contemplating the change. If findings in these areas are obscure, the outcomes of the evaluations of existing nongraded programs are even less definitive.

The available estimates of the number of schools with nongraded programs fluctuates from 5.5 percent[1] to 30 percent.[2] These, it must be pointed out, are unqualified estimates; they do not consider the quality of the programs purporting to be nongraded. When this element is added, estimates of the number of schools with *truly* nongraded programs shrink considerably. Goodlad, in 1955, estimated that less than one percent of the schools in the country were nongraded[3] and in 1961 he felt there were probably fewer than 125 schools to be found with *truly* nongraded programs.[4]

If uncertainty marks present estimates of the number of schools operating nongraded programs, certainly forecasts for future growth are dubious. In 1958 the NEA reported 26.3 percent of the respondents to its survey saying they intended to nongrade their schools.[5] Five years later, however, this estimate had dwindled to 3.2 percent.[6] On the other hand, the USOE's pollings reverse this trend. Of schools queried in 1958, only 13.4 percent expected to become nongraded,[7] but two years later this estimate doubled and 26.3 percent of the respondents reported considering nongrading their schools.[8] With these conflicting findings it is difficult to know if the nongraded school is coming into its own or passing out of existence.

---

[1]Lillian L. Gore and Rose E. Koury, *A Survey of Early Elementary Education in Public Schools, 1960-61.* Washington, D.C.: U.S. Department of Health, Education and Welfare, 1965.

[2]National Education Association, *Nongraded Schools.* Research Memo 1965-12. Washington, D.C.: Research Division, NEA, May, 1965.

[3]John I. Goodlad, "More About the Ungraded Plan," *NEA Journal,* May, 1955, pp. 295-96.

[4]National Education Association, *Nongrading: A Modern Practice in Elementary School Organization.* Research Memorandum 1961-37. Washington, D.C.: Research Division, NEA, October, 1961.

[5]National Education Association, *Administrative Practices in Urban School Districts, 1958-59.* Research Report 1961-R10. Washington, D.C.: Research Division, NEA, May, 1961.

[6]NEA, *Nongraded Schools, op. cit.*

[7]Stuart E. Dean, *Elementary School Administration and Organization: A National Survey of Practices and Policies.* Washington, D.C.: U.S. Department of Health, Education and Welfare, 1963.

[8]Gore and Koury, *op. cit.*

One thing seems clear from these surveys, however: nongrading is related to district size. Nearly all available surveys confirm this; the larger the district, the more likely it is to have one or more nongraded units. Here we should stress that this does not mean that nongrading is the principal organizational pattern in large school districts. It simply means a nongraded unit is operating in one or more of the district's several elementary schools.[9]

Studies of the influence of nongrading on students are rare, too, and their composite findings somewhat bewildering. Thirty-three empirical studies of the influence of nongrading on student academic achievement have been identified. Not all of these, however, consider the same variables. About half of them assess the influence of nongrading on reading achievement, while 25 percent look at its influence on arithmetic performance. Only 11 percent of the studies question the impact nongrading has on the student's development in language arts. Nine percent report on the total achievement scores of children. The remaining studies are spread so thinly through the other curricular divisions that a detailed consideration of their findings is hardly profitable.[10]

Judged by these studies, the academic development of children probably does not suffer from attending a nongraded school; there is some evidence, admittedly sketchy and tentative, to indicate it may be somewhat enhanced. One thing is certain; children from graded classes seldom do better on these measures than children from nongraded classes. More commonly, children from nongraded classes excel their contemporaries from graded classes.

For example, 15 studies considered the influence of nongrading on the general reading achievement of children. Seven of these report no significant difference between children from graded and nongraded classes. In other words, nothing is lost by having children attend nongraded classes. But only two studies found children from graded classes outscoring children from nongraded classes, while six studies found the general reading attainments of children from nongraded classes superior to that of children in graded classes.

Similar though less distinct outcomes are attained when the reading subskills of comprehension and vocabulary development are examined. Again, the principal finding of 14 studies is that there are no marked differences in the accomplishments of children in these areas regardless of the type of organization in which they learn to read. Furthermore, for every study showing greater gains for children from graded classes, there is an equal number of studies counter-balancing these findings.

[9]William P. McLoughlin, *The Nongraded School: A Critical Assessment.* Albany, N.Y.: The University of the State of New York, The New York State Educational Department, 1967.
    [10]*Ibid.*

The mirror image of this picture emerges when the arithmetic attainments of children from graded and nongraded classes are contrasted. Eleven studies considered the influence of nongrading on children's general arithmetic achievement, and their findings are inconclusive. Three report differences favoring children from nongraded classes, five found differences favoring children from graded classes,[11] and three found no difference.

But when the arithmetic subskills of reasoning and knowledge of fundamentals are examined, different outcomes appear. Of the 12 published studies in these areas, one reports differences favoring children from graded classes but six report differences favoring children from nongraded classes. The remaining five show no real difference in the achievement of children in these areas, regardless of the type of class organization.

In language arts, too, there is scant evidence to demonstrate that organization influences achievement. Seven of the 10 studies in this area report no true differences in the language skills developed by children from graded and nongraded classes. One reports achievement test scores of children from graded classes as superior to those of children from nongraded classes, while two studies found the observed differences in the achievement of children from nongraded classes indeed significantly superior to that of controls in the graded classes. Apparently, nongraded classes are no more effective in developing language arts skills than are graded classes.

Total achievement test scores, too, seem remarkably immune to change because of changes in organizational pattern. Half of the eight studies using them to measure the efficacy of the nongraded school found no significant differences in the achievements of children from graded and nongraded classes. The remaining studies divide equally: Two reported differences favoring children from graded classes while two found differences favoring children from nongraded classes. So here, once again, the influence of nongrading on the academic development of children is indeterminate.

Better student achievement is not the only claim put forth for the nongraded school. Its advocates maintain, implicitly or explicitly, that superior student adjustment is attained in the nongraded school. Certainly student adjustment and personality development are crucial concerns of educators and, quite reasonably, they are interested in developing learning settings which foster this goal.

Unfortunately, studies assessing the influence of nongrading on student adjustment are even more rare than studies assessing its influence on their academic achievement. Moreover, the diversity of procedures utilized in these

[11]*Ibid.*

studies to measure adjustment lessens their cumulative value. Sociograms, adjustment inventories, anxiety scales, and even school attendance records have all been used as indices of pupil adjustment. But no matter how measured, there is scant evidence to support the contention that superior student adjustment is realized in nongraded schools. On the 32 separate indices of adjustment used in these studies, the overwhelming majority, 26, indicate that there is no significant difference in the adjustment of children from graded and nongraded classes. Only four of the measures (general adjustment, social adjustment, social maturity, and freedom from age stereotypes) showed differences favorable to children from nongraded classes, while the remaining two (social participation and freedom from defensiveness) were favorable to children from graded classes.[12]

Research, then, finds little to impel or impede practitioners interested in nongrading. Under either organization children's adjustment and achievement appear to remain remarkably constant. For those to whom the nongraded school is a magnificent obsession, these findings must come as a numbing disappointment. Taken at face value, current research on the nongraded school seems to say that its contribution to the academic, social, and emotional development of children is marginal.

But should these findings be taken at face value? It might be naive to rest the fate of the nongraded school on past research. The validity of these studies should be rigorously tested, for they depend on one tacit but critical assumption: that the experimental schools, those purporting to be nongraded, are *truly* nongraded. If this assumption is not met and the experimental schools are not nongraded, then research has told us nothing about the efficacy of the nongraded school.

Too often, on close inspection, one finds that schools credited with operating nongraded programs are not nongraded at all. Homogeneous grouping and semi-departmentalization of instruction in reading and arithmetic are frequently passed off as nongraded programs. These techniques must be recognized for what they are. They are administrative expediencies developed to make the *graded* school work. They are not nongraded instructional programs.

If these are the "nongraded" programs represented in these studies, then researching their effectiveness is an exercise in futility, for the *experimental* schools are as graded as the control schools and no experimental treatment is being tested. Research has done nothing more than contrast the performances of children from graded schools called graded schools with the performance of children from graded schools called nongraded schools. Essentially, we have simply researched the age-old question: "What's in a name?"

---

[12]*Ibid.*

The nongraded school is defensible only because the graded school is indefensible. Its justification flows from its efforts to correct the instructional errors of the graded school. It is reasonably unlikely that any amount of manipulation of the physical arrangements of schools will produce discernible differences in the academic or psycho-social development of children. Every grade label can be cleansed from every classroom door in the school without influencing the school's attainments with children as long as graded instructional practices prevail behind these doors.

Nongrading begins with significant alterations in instructional, not organizational, procedures. As long as schools seek practices designed to group away differences they are *not* nongraded. The nongraded school never held this as a goal, for it is impossible. Rather, nongrading says: "Accept children as they are, with all their differences, and teach to these differences. Don't try to eradicate them!" Until educators develop instructional programs that will meet this challenge they are not nongrading. They are simply masking their old egg-crate schools with a new facade.

Why Teaching Teams Fail

Carl O. Olson, Jr.

Although team teaching is certainly not a new form of school organization, there has been a tremendous emphasis on team teaching in recent years. Virtually every school district has something labeled "team teaching"—a few schools are completely organized on a team teaching basis. Generally teaching teams are organized to: (1) utilize better the talents and interests of teachers, (2) increase grouping and scheduling flexibility and (3) improve the quality of instruction. In theory, team teaching has merit and there are many excellent teaching teams in operation.

As an administrator I have helped organize elementary and secondary teaching teams and have taught on teaching teams. I have observed teaching teams in operation and have discussed team teaching with many educators actively involved in team teaching. *My experience with team teaching has led me to conclude that: quite a few teams are dismal failures, many teaching teams do*

Reprinted by permission of *Peabody Journal of Education,* Nashville, Tennessee, and Carl O. Olson, Jr., from *Peabody Journal of Education* 45:15-20, July, 1967.

not make a significant enough contribution to the education of students to warrant the time and effort devoted to them and a few actually retard the educational development of students. Surely, a sterile, ineffective teaching team is a failure even though it may retain the "teaching team" label.

Teaching teams fail for a variety of reasons. Many teams devote entirely too much time to large group lecturing and others spend too much time in meaningless small group discussion. Very few actually provide significant independent study experiences for students. On many teams the students have much less intimate contact with their teachers than they might normally enjoy in a self-contained classroom. Some teams are dominated by one or more members of the team. For a variety of reasons many teams are rigidly bound to an inflexible schedule. For example, they may be forced to have large group instruction on Monday, Wednesday, and Friday and seminars on Tuesday and Thursday week after week regardless of the needs of the students or the desires of the team members. Although teaching teams may lose vitality and purpose and cease to make a significant contribution to the education of students, all too often they remain in existence.

I recognize that my observations and my main conclusion are purely subjective. (It would be extremely valuable but very difficult to conduct a "scientific" study of the reasons why teaching teams fail. Unfortunately, we educators are usually quite reluctant to admit our failures. Our "experiments" are almost invariably successful; newly established programs rarely fail.) I am not necessarily opposed to team teaching. In fact, I enthusiastically support good team teaching. My primary purpose in exploring the reasons why teaching teams fail is to enable educators considering the formation of teaching teams to examine the "other side of the coin" realistically in the hope that they may be spared some unnecessary disappointment, frustration and work. Secondly, I would hope that the article would be of some value to anyone examining the operation of existing teaching teams.

The Nature of Team Teaching

Many teaching teams fail because those responsible for creating and operating them simply do not understand the nature and demands of team teaching. The theoretical advantages of team teaching will obviously not materialize unless a genuine teaching team is created. Therefore, it is imperative that those planning to organize a teaching team really understand team teaching. In addition, they must agree on their own operational definition of team teaching.

Team teaching is one form of "cooperative" teaching. Although all definitions of team teaching necessarily vary somewhat, essentially team teaching may be thought of as *an instructional situation where two or more teachers possessing complementary teaching skills cooperatively plan and implement the instruction for a single group of students using flexible scheduling and grouping techniques to meet the particular instructional needs of the students.* Cooperative planning of curriculum content and methods of instruction; mutual evaluation of instruction by the entire team; flexible scheduling and grouping and an effort to capitalize on teachers' skills and interests are usually considered the essentials of team teaching.

Many forms of organization labeled "team teaching" are simply not teaching teams in the sense of the commonly accepted definition presented here. Although they may be excellent examples of "cooperative teaching" they cannot produce the theoretical advantages of team teaching. For example, if two history teachers each having 25-30 students in a given period are able to bring their groups together they may be able to provide some excellent large group instruction but their student-teacher ratio will not enable them to achieve the flexible scheduling and grouping expected in team teaching.

All too often teachers and administrators expect a teaching team to produce miracles. Team teaching is no panacea. It will not make slow learners bright. It will not reduce the range of individual differences in student achievement and ability. It will not automatically create a spark of interest in the disaffected student. And, finally, it will not automatically convert mediocre teachers into outstanding teachers.

Many teaching teams have not produced the expected results of team teaching simply because a genuine teaching team was not created. This has led to a great deal of unnecessary and unfair frustration for teachers and students. Everyone involved in team teaching must have a realistic understanding of what may be expected from team teaching.

The Demands of Team Teaching

Additional problems result when those involved in team teaching do not understand the considerable demands of team teaching. Although a viable, effective team will make more intelligent use of the teacher's time and talent and permit more flexible scheduling to better meet the needs of students, such a team requires a great deal of work and sacrifice on the part of its members. *Team teaching is not a labor-saving device.* In many, many ways team teaching requires much more effort and sacrifice on the part of teachers than teaching in the self-contained classroom. This point cannot be overemphasized. The difficulties of team teaching may vary from subject to subject. For example, a "Problems of Democracy" social studies team may have to devote more time to planning than a geometry team simply because there probably would be less general agreement on the basic nature of the social studies curriculum and the methods of teaching.

As indicated above a team must be well-planned in order to operate successfully. The teachers must begin by clearly defining their goals. They must understand exactly what they expect from team teaching. Basic instructional materials must be selected. Schedules, techniques, and criteria for grouping and methods of evaluation have to be discussed thoroughly and agreed upon *before* the team begins to work with students. This kind of planning requires time. It is unreasonable and unfair to expect teachers to plan a teaching team while teaching a full load and totally unrealistic to expect it to occur after a team has actually begun to work with students. If a team is to be properly organized the planning should be done on pressure-free "release time." Although release time during the course of a school year may be sufficient, a significant period of summer planning time can contribute a great deal to the success of a team.

After a team has begun to function much day-to-day planning must take place. The planning of truly flexible grouping (with students grouped and regrouped according to their needs, interests, or abilities), the creation of instructional materials and the planning of instruction are very time consuming if done properly. Team activities must be evaluated and future activities planned. When insufficient planning time is provided, the teachers are forced to settle for less than what they would normally believe to be the proper approach to instruction. More often than not this means too much reliance on large-group lecturing. Frequently the scheduling becomes much too rigid. When team teachers do not have enough planning time they simply cannot capitalize on the inherent advantages of team teaching. Team teachers must have a common planning time so they can work together on virtually a daily basis. If planning time cannot be made available during the day, after school time, at the very least, must be kept free for planning.

Periodically, (possibly every summer) teaching teams should be provided with release time to evaluate and, if necessary, change the operation and curriculum of the team and to evaluate and create instructional materials.

Sufficient planning time is vital to the success of a team. If a team does not have adequate planning time or if the members of the team do not devote the necessary time to planning, the team will fail.

A critical factor in the failure of some teams is often the nature of the people selected to be on the team. All teachers are not qualified by virtue of their experience, temperament, or attitude to be members of a teaching team. Team teaching is decidedly different from teaching in the self-contained classroom and, therefore, team teaching requires a special kind of teacher. As mutual evaluation of instruction is an important aspect of team teaching, the members of a team must observe one another teach and, more important, they must be willing to give and accept constructive criticism without ill-feeling. They must respect one another and be able to work together in harmony. This requires much more than the ability merely to "get along" with one another. As constant change is an important aspect of team teaching, the teachers must be flexible. The members of a teaching team must be willing to spend the extra time and effort required of real team teaching. Team teachers find themselves in a variety of instructional situations. As all teachers are not equally capable of performing all the teaching tasks required of a teaching team, the members of a team must possess complementary backgrounds, interests, and teaching skills. To take an obvious example, if all members of a team would prefer to be large group lecturers and none enjoys small group activities, friction and failure may result.

Many teachers prefer the self-contained classroom to team teaching because they feel they can create a more intimate relationship with their students in the self-contained classroom. This kind of relationship can develop in team teaching, although unfortunately it often does not. Teachers who are convinced that an optimum student-teacher relationship can be obtained *only* in the self-contained classroom should not participate in team teaching.

Only teachers sincerely interested in at least giving team teaching a fair trial should be selected for teaching teams. Certainly no teacher should be assigned to a team against his will or, as more commonly occurs, no teacher should be cajoled into team teaching. Team teaching demands too much of teachers. Reluctant or antagonistic team members can and usually do cause teaching teams to fail.

A teaching team must have a continuity to insure a smooth operation. If a team has a high rate of turnover, continuity will be lost. Therefore, teachers with a high probability of remaining with a team for a significant period of time should be selected. However, as absolutely no turnover may inhibit the infusion of new ideas and insights, some provision must be made to bring new teachers into existing teams from time-to-time.

The members of a teaching team must be chosen with care if a team is to be successful. The teachers must collectively possess a balance of experience, interest, insight, patience, and ability. They must understand and accept what will be required of them in team teaching or they should not become involved in team teaching.

Poor leadership often contributes to the failure of a teaching team. *A teaching team cannot function successfully without good leadership* any more than a school or an athletic team can be successful without good leadership. Many educators believe leadership will ultimately "evolve" or "emerge" from any social group and, extending this to team teaching, they believe that out of a group of teachers selected to be members of a team, a team leader will ultimately evolve. To a certain extent this is true. However, in team teaching leadership may evolve out of the wreckage of the team. Because the first year of operation is usually difficult and always critical, a team requires good leadership from the very beginning and cannot afford the luxury of waiting for a leader to "emerge." A team leader should be formally designated (either through election by the team or by administrative appointment) and given sufficient authority and time to expedite and coordinate the activities of the team. *All successful teaching teams are built on a foundation of good leadership.*

Some Additional Factors

Inadequate physical facilities, instructional materials, or other resources can cause the failure of a team as readily as any of the factors mentioned above. Some of the current literature on team teaching indicates that special facilities are not required for team teaching. In my judgment this is not very realistic. Team teaching *does* require special facilities as well as a different attitude toward the use of available space. Team teachers require flexibility for small group activities and large group instruction. A teaching team must have an adequate place for large group instruction, and, just as important, at least as many small group teaching stations as there are team members. To be truly flexible the team must have control of its instructional facilities. For example, large group instruction should take place when and as often as it is needed and not just when the facilities are available. Instructional facilities must be adequately equipped. A teaching team should have its own planning area. The best physical facilities will not automatically guarantee the success of a teaching team, but inadequate facilities will definitely contribute to its failure.

The building principal has an important role to play in the success of a teaching team simply because a successful team usually cannot be established or maintained without his continual, enthusiastic support—mere acquiescence is insufficient. It is the principal's responsibility to see that the team has the time and the resources to be successful. In particular, if he does not provide his teachers with sufficient planning time, the team will contribute far less than it should and may even fail. The principal must make sure that his entire faculty understands the nature and purpose of the team. If team teachers are valued more highly than others simply because they are team teachers or if the team becomes a public relations device, faculty harmony will be reduced and the entire school program may suffer.

All too frequently adverse parent reaction arising out of ignorance of the nature and the purpose of team teaching has contributed to the failure of the team. Parents should understand the nature of team teaching and particularly that the main purpose of team teaching is to improve instruction for their children. A carefully planned parent orientation program conducted *before* a team goes into operation will prevent problems from arising and will elicit support for the team.

The organization of a teaching team is not a step to be taken lightly. *Teachers and administrators who expect the benefits of team teaching must be willing to pay the price good team teaching demands.* Good team teaching is a solution to many, but certainly not all, of the problems we face in our schools today. Team teaching can be rewarding and enjoyable for all involved if the members of the team understand what they are trying to accomplish and are given the time and means to accomplish their objectives. Poor team teaching can harm children, frustrate teachers, alienate parents, and destroy staff morale. There is no justification for establishing a team if it is predestined to fail.

Innovations in Education

Raymond B. Fox

"Two of the greatest needs in American education today are those of individualizing instruction and utilizing the staff more efficiently and effectively."

A key word in educational circles today is *innovation.* Almost every educational journal seems to have at least one article extolling the merits of the latest instructional innovation. The reader of such articles is often left with the impression that his school has little choice: Either it must adopt the latest innovation or the children who attend the school will obviously be educationally deprived.

As a consequence, schools often appear to be competing with one another to see which one can adopt the largest number of innovations in the shortest period of time. In fact, almost every imaginable innovation, not to mention a few unimaginable ones which the federal government has been willing to support, has been adopted by some school.

Since American schools have changed slowly in the past, it is natural to wonder why they have changed so rapidly in recent years. Several of the changes have been made in response to criticism of the schools which began with the launching of Sputnik in 1957. Many Americans believed that the Russian victory in the space race proved that American schools were inferior. Navy admirals and products of private schools who had never spent a day in an American public school suddenly became experts on American public education. Their criticisms, such as "The three T's (typing, tap dancing, and tomfoolery) have replaced the three R's," often made the headlines in newspapers across the country.

Reprinted by permission of *Illinois Education,* the Illinois Education Association, Springfield, Illinois, from *Illinois Education* 57:293-296, March, 1969.

Those of us in the teaching profession have been partially responsible for the increase in criticism. By and large, we have failed to offer any rebuttal to the critics. Of course, it is difficult for an objective answer to get the same newspaper coverage that spectacular criticism gets. Nevertheless, we should not hesitate to defend American education.

In general, today's schools are doing a tremendous job. Even though we are educating a larger percentage of the population than ever before in our history, studies comparing the achievement of today's children with that of children in the past consistently find that today's children are learning more than those in the past when the two groups are equated on the basis of intelligence. They read better, speak better, write better, spell better, and know much more about such specialized fields as mathematics and science. In fact, they even look better. They are both taller and healthier than their predecessors.

The fact that the schools are better than in the past does not mean that they should resist change. They must change. However, it is important to realize that a change may or may not be for the better. Too often changes and innovations are automatically considered to be improvements; consequently, no method of evaluating an innovation is established at the time of its adoption. As a result, much of what we know about the effectiveness of specific innovations is based upon testimonials of administrators, teachers, and students rather than upon the findings of objective studies. The best justification for adopting innovations may well be that many facets of our present educational program can not be justified.

Another difficulty in attempting to determine whether an innovation has value is that a specific innovation, such as team teaching, may be very successful in one school but fail completely in another. How teachers feel about the proposed innovation, whether or not they accept it, and whether or not they believe it is superior to the present practice seem to be the principal factors in determining whether or not an innovation will be successful. If the teachers do not accept a curricular change or are not prepared to practice it, the innovation is doomed to failure. Most innovations require a re-definition of the roles of the teacher and the student. If the new roles are understood and accepted by the teachers and the students, the innovation will probably be successful. However, if the teachers and students continue to do essentially the same things as they did in the traditional program, the innovation has little chance.

It is absolutely essential for a community to understand that a school's curriculum is never any better than its teachers. The most important criterion is what a teacher does in his classroom. If he is still using the methods and materials which were used 20 years ago, he is as out of date as a farmer who uses agricultural methods and materials which were used 20 years ago. If a community wishes to improve its schools and the achievement level of its students, the surest way for it to do so is to hire and retain the best teachers available.

Because innovations are being developed at such a rapid rate, it would be impossible even to list all of them in an article of this length. Readers who are interested in a comprehensive listing of innovative practices should see two recently published books of abstracts, *Instructional Innovation in Illinois— Elementary Schools* and *Instructional Innovation in Illinois—Secondary Schools*. These excellent publications contain brief descriptions of innovative practices in Illinois schools, the names of the schools, the numbers of teachers and students involved, the method of funding, and the name and address of the person who can supply additional information concerning any specific practice described. The publications were developed by the research committee of the Illinois Association for Supervision and Curriculum Development under the direction of Prof. Henry Knapp of Eastern Illinois University, in cooperation with other professional organizations and the Office of the Superintendent of Public Instruction. A review of the practices described will give the reader an idea of what the schools of tomorrow may be like.

Some Promising Practices

Two of the greatest needs in American education today are those of individualizing instruction and utilizing the staff more efficiently and effectively. A few of the most promising innovations designed to meet those needs are described here.

Differentiated Staff. Many cries of protest are heard each year concerning the large amount of time that teachers must spend on non-instructional duties. The National Education Association Research Division, for example, recently asked a nationwide sample of public school teachers the following free-response question: "If you could make one change that you think would improve your own morale or professional satisfaction as a teacher, what would the change be?" The most frequently mentioned response was, "More time to teach." Since other studies indicate that teachers spend almost 50 percent of their time on non-instructional duties, it should not be too surprising that teachers are demanding more time to teach.

To meet that demand and to provide for the wide differences which exist among teachers in knowledge of their subject, teaching ability, interests, and experience, some schools are identifying different tasks which the schools must perform; are determining what qualifications a person must have to perform specific tasks; and are employing persons for differentiated assignments—clerical aides, teacher aides, teaching assistants, para-professionals, interns, beginning teachers, experienced teachers, and master teachers. Such specialized or auxiliary personnel as social workers, school psychologists, subject-matter supervisors, counselors, and curriculum coordinators are also essential members of the staff.

Differentiated staff plans enable a school system to individualize instruction and to reward outstanding teachers by promoting them to master teachers, thereby giving them greater responsibilities and prestige as well as higher salaries. Master teachers in Temple City, California, for example, can earn up to $25,000 a year. The salary schedule there categorizes teachers as beginning, staff, senior, and master teachers. Each category has its own salary range.

If classroom teachers have the opportunity to earn salaries which are commensurate with their education and abilities, the teaching profession may be able to attract and retain a larger number of outstanding persons as classroom teachers.

One of the difficulties of instituting a differentiated staff plan in Illinois has been that most teacher-education institutions have not assumed the role of preparing teacher aides and teacher assistants. Many community colleges, however, are now developing specialized courses for interested persons—one-year certificate programs for teacher aides and associate of arts degree programs for teacher assistants.

Readers who are interested in more information concerning differentiated staff plans should read the articles which Dwight Allen, dean of the School of Education, University of Massachusetts, has written on this topic, and also his paper entitled "Needed: A New Professionalism in Education," which was published by the American Association of Colleges for Teacher Education, Washington, D.C., in May, 1968.

Continuous Pupil Progress Plan. Don Davies, associate commissioner of education, Bureau of Educational Personnel Development, recently told a group of educators meeting in Chicago that the most important direction for change in education at all levels, from pre-school through the university, is to move from a mass approach to teaching and learning to a highly individualized approach. The continuous pupil progress plan is an attempt to move in that direction.

The plan is based upon the developmental concept of learning. A diagnosis of each child's abilities, strengths, weaknesses, and interests is made. Then an individualized program of sequential blocks of learning is designed for each child. Such a program enables the child to move through levels of achievement at his own rate.

Many variations of the continuous pupil progress plan exist in Illinois schools. Some schools follow the plan in only one or two content areas, usually reading, language arts, or mathematics. Others use the plan in nongrading, multi-aged grouping, or dual-progress structuring.

An important feature of the plan is that it eliminates the need for failing students. Unfortunately, even though the findings of numerous research studies indicate that a child usually does no better when he repeats a grade and that his self-concept is often irreparably damaged, many schools continue to fail a large number of students each year.

In addition to being educationally indefensible, the cost of failing students is prohibitive. For example, in a very small school district having 30 teachers with a 30-to-1 student-teacher ratio, if each teacher failed just one student in a year, in the following year that district would have to employ an additional teacher to maintain its student-teacher ratio. It would also need an additional classroom, textbooks, and other materials for 30 additional students. Obviously, such funds could be more profitably and wisely used to support educationally sound practices.

Learning Centers. The primary purpose served by a learning center is to provide a place where all children can develop their responsibility for individual learning. It provides every student with the opportunity to direct his own learning activities and to determine the rate at which he learns.

Learning centers usually contain instructional media which support the school's curriculum, enrichment materials, programed materials, reference books and materials, conference rooms, work or project areas, and independent study areas. Some have individual study carrels equipped with audio-visual aids, auto-instructional materials, and computer-assisted instructional programs.

Learning centers provide resource materials and services for both teachers and students. Resources are available for reinforcement, enrichment, and remediation so that every child can profit.

Elk Grove School District No. 59 is an excellent place to see learning centers in operation. The district has 20 learning centers in 18 schools, including the Juliette Low School which has a learning center as the heart of the school. The building was specifically designed for individualized instruction and won a national design award from the American Association of School Administrators. It consists of two hexagons. The only permanent walls are in the corner sections of each hexagon, thereby providing a large open area at the core of the building which serves as the library-learning center. Visits can be arranged through the Elk Grove Training and Development Center, 1706 West Algonquin Road, Arlington Heights.

The Community School. Based upon the belief that the typical school, operating six or seven hours a day, five days a week for nine months a year, is a luxury which most communities cannot afford, many communities have adopted the community school concept.

According to Peter Clancy, director of the Mott Program, Flint Community Schools, the Mott Foundation developed the community school concept to achieve the foundation's primary objective of developing "the human resources of Flint, Mich., to such a degree that Flint becomes a model community, worthy of emulation by other communities around the world."

Community schools mobilize the human and institutional resources of a community to attack the educational, social, and economic problems of the community. The community schools operate throughout the day and evening to serve persons of all ages. With little additional cost, and in some cases at a reduced cost, communities find that they can greatly increase school plant use and the number of people they serve. Costly and unnecessary duplication of community services is often eliminated.

Because the problems and needs of communities or neighborhoods served by community schools vary, the programs also vary. However, in all cases, the community involves its members in the process of solving its problems. The problems of the functionally illiterate, the unemployable, senior citizens, youth, and the family are confronted. Educational and recreational activities are provided for all members of the community, young and old. Teen counseling, family education, marriage counseling, civic discussions, and job counseling and placement services may also be provided.

More than 160 communities throughout the United States have emulated the community school plan developed in Flint. For example, 20 community school programs are now in operation in Dade County, Florida, to serve the full continuum of educational, social, and economic needs. More than 92,000 people per week, of all ages, use the Flint schools after school hours, because the community school operates 3800 hours annually as opposed to the 1400 hours a typical school operates.

Readers interested in extending the school day and year or in the community school concept are encouraged to visit the Community School Program in Flint, Michigan.

Sex-Segregated Primary Schools. The average girl is physiologically and psychologically ready for school sooner than the average boy. She not only matures at a faster rate but also has the advantage of remaining in a feminine environment when she enters the primary grades. Almost all primary teachers are females, and much of the primary curriculum tends to be feminine-oriented.

Some educators have advocated that girls should be admitted to the first grade earlier than boys. This is not considered to be a satisfactory solution, however, since boys eventually catch up with the girls. In fact, there is no significant difference in standardized achievement test scores for boys and girls by the end of the intermediate grades.

The principal advantage of segregating the sexes in the primary grades is that the curriculum can be oriented toward a specific sex, thereby enabling the child to maximize his appropriate sex role in the learning experiences.

Obviously, if male teachers were employed to teach the boys, the advantages of segregating the sexes would be even greater. There is no father in many lower socio-economic homes, and many middle-class fathers are away from the home during most of a young child's day. Therefore, daily contact with a male teacher could be very beneficial.

Unfortunately, few males prepare to be primary grade teachers at the present time. However, if they knew that they would be teaching a masculine-oriented curriculum to boys, more men might prefer to enter the field.

During the past year, Professors Joseph Ellis and Joan Peterson of Northern Illinois University conducted a study sponsored by the US Office of Education in which seventh- and eighth-grade boys and girls in the university's laboratory school and in the Belvidere public schools were segregated. A pilot project is also being conducted this year in the laboratory school in which the first-graders are segregated according to sex.

Work-Study Programs. Although work-study programs are not new, the earlier ones were designed for non-college-bound students who were maintaining at least a "C" average. Their primary purpose was to prepare the participants for jobs immediately after graduation from high school.

Realizing that work experiences are important for all students, some schools have expanded their work-study programs to permit various degrees of involvement. Some students work only a few hours a week or month; others—who participate in such programs as Diversified Occupations, Distributive Education, and Office Occupations—usually work a half day and attend classes the other half.

Some students work in school offices and in the school cafeteria; others work in local businesses and industries. The supervisor of the work-study program and the employers cooperatively supervise the students in the program.

In addition to providing valuable work experience, participation in work-study programs enables the student to earn money and also often makes the academic classes more meaningful. Potential dropouts are given an incentive to remain in school, and college-bound students who participate are better prepared to obtain part-time jobs when they enter college. Many Illinois community colleges are also offering work-study programs.

Continuous In-Service Education. Too often in-service education is limited to institute days and consists of listening to speeches. Faculty meetings during the year are too often devoted to reading announcements and discussing specific problems.

Members of all professions must continue to keep themselves informed of changes and new developments in their professions. Teaching is no exception. Therefore, continuous in-service education is necessary.

Because many of the changes occurring in the schools require the teacher to play a different role, in-service programs designed to change teacher behavior are essential. Before the teacher can assume a new role, it is necessary for him to have an accurate perception of himself. Several innovative techniques have been developed for that purpose.

One which has proved to be a very effective way of giving teachers greater insight into their classroom behavior is that of video-taping them while they are teaching. The video-tape enables the teacher to observe his own teaching methods and procedures and also provides him with the opportunity to study the reactions of students whom he may not have had time to observe during the regular class.

Another technique which is being used effectively in some schools to gain greater insight into teacher-learner interaction is Flanders' Interaction Analysis. A trained observer using this technique is able to establish the patterns of student and teacher behavior in a classroom. Teachers who believe that their classes consist largely of student discussion are often surprised to learn how much of the class period is spent in "teacher talk." More important, an analysis of the interaction matrix for a class often enables the teacher to see what types of verbal behavior on his part are most effective in eliciting desirable student responses.

A number of other innovative techniques, such as sensitivity training, are being used to give teachers a better understanding of themselves. The success of such techniques, however, is largely dependent upon the skill of the group leader.

Another important aspect of a teacher's self-perception is the manner in which he perceives students from various socio-economic groups, ability levels, nationalities, and races. Continuous in-service education is needed to discuss the implications of recent findings in this area.

One of the most interesting studies was conducted recently by Prof. Robert Rosenthal of Harvard University and Lenore Jacobson, principal of a San Francisco elementary school. Several children in each class of an elementary school in south San Francisco were selected at random. There were no significant differences between these children and their classmates; however, their teachers were told that these children could be expected to show considerable intellectual and academic gains during the year.

The children were tested throughout the year, and the results indicated that the children whom the teachers expected to make the greatest gains made such gains. In addition, the teachers indicated that these children were better adjusted, more appealing, more affectionate, less in need of social approval, had a better chance of being successful in life, and were happier and more interesting than their classmates.

The findings of this study strongly support the concept of the self-fulfilling prophecy in education—that a teacher's prediction of a child's behavior somehow comes to be realized.

All of the innovations described in this article require administrative or organizational changes; however, many innovative practices do not. Unfortunately, teachers often wait for administrative or organizational changes before attempting to improve instruction in their own classroom.

Teachers sometimes complain, "They never try anything new in our school." If we accept the contention that teaching is a profession, then certainly the teacher, as a professional person, must assume the responsibility for improving instruction in his own classroom. If the reader accepts that premise, it should be fair to ask, "What are you doing in your classroom this year that you have not done in the past?"

Chapter 16

Working With Curricular and Instructional Innovations

Numerous innovations in curriculum and instruction have been heralded during the past decade. A few appear to be really new, creative, major innovations that promise to be of help to the teacher in accomplishing his goal of improving instruction for boys and girls. Many more are ideas and techniques that have been introduced in the past, have been ignored, abandoned, or misinterpreted, and are now being reconsidered. These need to be analyzed and evaluated to ascertain their value for improving curriculum and instruction. Many of the ideas upon which basic innovative change must build are probably accepted, valuable concepts that simply need to be clarified and implemented.

Changes in curriculum and instruction must be measured by what they do for children. Miel, in "Let Us Develop Children Who Care About Themselves and Others," proposes seven items that should be emphasized in curricular change. As she points out, her proposals are not panaceas; rather, they are slow but steady ways of improving the curriculum.

Increasingly, educational technology is moving into the classroom. There is cause to be optimistic about the role of technology in improving the quality of education, especially if educators move positively to make the most effective use of it in curricular and instructional improvement. Teachers need to consider carefully the place of instructional technology in the classroom, they need to be aware of technological devices and of how they can be used to improve teaching, and they need to examine and clarify their own role in the technological age. Miller considers these concerns in "Educational Technology and the Classroom Teacher." Chastain and Seguel attempt to actually place the reader in a type of learning environment as they explore the multimedia approach to learning and teaching in "Learning Environments for Teaching."

One of the newest terms in instructional technology is "computer-assisted instruction." Computerized instructional devices offer significant potential for the individualization of instruction in the regular classroom. In the last selection of this chapter, Suppes discusses some of the ways that computers can be used in teaching, and he poses and answers questions about computer-assisted instruction.

"Let Us Develop Children Who Care About Themselves and Others"

Alice Miel

Many changes are being made or are strongly urged today which really are not curriculum changes at all and which, in fact, make it more difficult to achieve some of the curriculum changes we advocate. Some changes that I wish could gain ground were made years ago by a few people in education. Other changes that I will advocate would require work far out on an unmapped frontier. I prefer, then, to make some proposals on enhancing the quality of the curriculum at the elementary-school level.

Concept of Self

The item I have put first in planning a better curriculum at the elementary level is fostering in each child a healthy concept of self. By this I mean that the child feels that he has the worth and dignity, the basic rights, of any human being. By this I mean, also, that he realizes the extent to which he depends on others and they on him for that very humanness—how inextricably interwoven are the self and the other.

A child who is maintaining a healthy view of himself as he changes with each year of living is a child who approaches most new situations with a feeling that "I can (or I can learn to) cope with this." The "I can'ts" for this child are based on realistic assessment of self and requirements and not on false teaching by others.

The elementary school can just as easily offer opportunities for girls to learn that they can run a projector, or use a hammer and saw, or do arithmetic or handle a snake, or perform an experiment in science as it can reinforce the belief possibly held by their mothers that certain learnings are too difficult for girls. The elementary school can just as easily offer opportunities for boys to feel

Reprinted by permission of *Audiovisual Instruction,* Washington, D.C., from *Audiovisual Instruction* 7:355-357, June, 1962.

successful in handling needle and thread, or running a sewing machine, or preparing a simple meal, as it can reinforce the helplessness about household matters they may be picking up from the males whom they admire.

Both boys and girls have a right to opportunities in the elementary school to find that they can read, that they can understand poetry and art and music and dance, and that they can take responsibility for managing their own conduct and learning. All children have a right to build a view that any kind of honest work they find themselves interested in and capable of performing in later life will be a worthy extension of themselves.

The concept of self which the school helps a child to develop is so basic to all of education that the most recent yearbook of the Association for Supervision and Curriculum Development was devoted solely to this aspect of the curriculum. Those of you who have not yet read *Perceiving, Behaving, Becoming: A New Focus for Education* will find there many of the things which must be left unsaid today because of lack of time.

Creativity

The second item we have selected for emphasis in our improved curriculum is *creativity*. It should not be necessary to make a case for creativity to an audience such as this. With the increasing mechanization of our society, the tendency toward depersonalization that comes from crowded living, and the increasing complexity of situations faced by human beings in this age, creative approaches to problem solving and to life in general are much needed by all members of the society.

Some do not agree that creativity can be developed in all persons, for they reserve the quality for a few truly original individuals. However, what harm can it do to treat every child as if he had the potentiality for creativity and to give him opportunity and encouragement for engaging in a creative *process?* The creativity of the product may range all the way from something new under the sun to something new to the individual making it, yet the process seems to be the same. The imagination produces a new way of seeing something, a new combination of familiar elements. The individual judges that the new idea is potentially useful and proceeds to work at it until he has expressed it in what is to him a satisfying finished form in some medium—materials of some kind, sounds, movements, or words. The product may be a new tune, a mobile, or a plan for improving flow of traffic.

Those interested in fostering creativity in children will want to consider carefully where some of the new applications of technology to education may be leading. Some of you may have heard or read Calvin Taylor's paper presented at the seminar on a theory of instructional materials sponsored by the ASCD in St. Louis in April 1960. The paper was entitled, "Possible Positive and Negative

Effects of Instructional Media on Creativity." One possible negative effect Taylor pointed out was that "the largely ignored areas in education will continue to be ignored." Here he referred in particular to the development of creative talent. Another danger is that "of producing single views, single structures, single approaches in the minds and experiences of students." Creativity requires, of all things, that the individual play around with various approaches, gather data from many sources, and do his own ordering and structuring. Taylor suggests ways in which instructional materials can be made to stimulate diversity of response and also cautions that certain instructional media, such as teachers, should perhaps specialize in creativity, allowing other devices, such as machines "to specialize in those things for which they are so efficient in the total learning situation."

Commitment

The third emphasis we wish to suggest in changing the curriculum is working for *commitment*. We realize that psychologists use this word to cover the case where an individual is so bound by one approach to a problem or one way of viewing a situation that he is blinded to other possibilities. This is just what must be avoided if the individual is to be creative. However, when we say that a person is *committed* to a democratic way of life, we have a useful meaning in mind. We think of a person pledged to uphold the basic values of our society, of someone who cares deeply about people, and who is willing to work hard and intelligently to help democracy to fulfill itself. In the 1962 yearbook of the ASCD referred to earlier, Maslow writes, ". . . character disorders and disturbances are now seen as far more important for the fate of the world than the classical neuroses or even the psychoses. From this point of view, new kinds of illness are most dangerous, e.g., the diminished or stunted person, i.e., the loss of any defining characteristics of humanness, or personhood, the failure to grow to one's potential; valuelessness." "The human being needs a framework of values . . . to live by and understand by," Maslow goes on to say, "in about the same sense that he needs sunlight, calcium, or love."

Maslow uses the expressive term "value-illnesses" for conditions like apathy, hopelessness, and cynicism.

We know that values cannot be taught to children in the way that facts are taught, we know also that adults in this period need help in clarifying their own values. Thus the task is doubly difficult. The responsibility of education for helping children develop a useful commitment to guiding values will not be fulfilled unless we work deliberately toward that end. Again, participants in this conference will want to think of the role of instructional materials. It will be equally important to do two things: (1) develop commitment that opens the way for more humane living; and (2) take precaution against developing commitment that narrows vision and closes doors.

Content

The fourth curriculum emphasis we wish to propose is development of *content* that is comprehensive enough to help a modern child deal with his many-faceted environment and significant enough to mean all that is *contained* in opportunities for experience provided by the school. We must include within the term not subject matter alone, but also skills for searching out, organizing and using information and skills for handling various types of symbols, media, and tools.   We must include also thought processes such as reasoning and criticizing and both analytical and intuitive approaches to data taken in by the senses.

The strengths and limitations of various media and instruction must be judged on the basis of their promise to develop some of this broad range of content. A special caution relates to what Taylor describes as using so many channels simultaneously for input of information that children have "too few channels free for scanning." A research study now in progress at Teachers College, Columbia University, has revealed the confusion of many of today's young children as a result of unexamined and unorganized information collected here and there in the process of growing. (Dorothy Mugge, *Social Studies Information of Seven-Year-Old Children.*) When the seven-year-old children in the study were asked what countries they had heard about, some of their replies were:

. . . I just see countries but never heard of any. I saw when we went to New Jersey.

. . . There's a country school in this book, I know.

. . . You mean a country that's in a state?

. . . We live in a country right now.

. . . What's a country? Is Allentown a city or a country?

Asked about oceans they had heard about, the children said things like this:

. . . Pocono Ocean. I think that's the ocean around here.

. . . Mississippi Ocean, "Elantic" City Ocean, New Jersey Ocean, Delaware.

. . . I only heard of a bay ocean at the seashore—bay and ocean together.

Confused time concepts were revealed in answering the question, "How often do you attend the movies?"

. . . About twice some days.

. . . Sometimes a week or five times a week.

. . . Sometimes eleven days and then we go.

. . . A whole bunch of times.

. . . About a few months.

. . . Two times a week or month.

Hearing such replies raised questions in the mind of the investigator about the great amount of information children supposedly have today and the desires of some scholars to introduce their disciplines to the very young. It caused her to wonder how these children could be helped most at school—by having a great deal more information fed in, or by assistance in getting order out of information already introduced?

Communication

The fifth item in our list is *communication.* Under the heading of content, I have already included a broad range of skills, many of which are essential for communication. At this point, let us attend to the essence of the act of communication—having a real conversation with another human being. We say in elementary schools that we should give children "listening" experiences. Some of the activities we think of for this purpose are useful as far as they go, but how often do we help children really to listen to one another in ways that result in sharing and thus shifting their perceptions? The one-way communication of most media of instruction, including teachers at times, must be amply supplemented by provisions for genuine two-way communication. Much of this communication will be through language used as a means of clarifying one's own thoughts, quite as much as a means of conveying ideas to another. However, children will be cheated in school if they do not experience the many ways there are, in addition to words, for people to communicate.

Counseling

The sixth item for consideration is *counseling.* The elementary school, organized to provide one teacher as coordinator of all the experiences and as instructor for many of the experiences of one group of children, has a built-in opportunity for counseling by a familiar person as need arises. Not all teachers make good use of this counseling opportunity and not all problems of children can be handled by the classroom teacher. However, the direction of change that seems most promising is to make better use of the counseling advantage afforded by the so-called self-contained classroom and to build additional counseling services on that base.

Continuity

The seventh and last point of emphasis, *continuity,* is like the rest, overlapping and pervasive. We hear a great deal nowadays about the proper sequence of learning tasks. Programing of subject matter so that one idea is established before the next was the concern of textbook and workbook writers for many years before the latest revival of interest in the teaching machine. In the word "continuity" there is quite a different idea from the straight line of progression conveyed by the word "sequence."

Continuity is a better term to use when thinking of the learning of an individual. We may say there is continuity in learning only when an individual is maintaining wholeness of his unique personality as he moves forward in life. Continuity is not just continuing in the same way. The individual must be achieving an integration of the different facets of his experience and distilling useful ideas and generalizations for testing in new situations. He must be transforming his ideas and his skills of relating to others as he grows up and moves into wider and different circles of people, each year of his life. Exposure to external sequences of subject matter may or may not hinder continuity within the individual. But in any case, the setting up of such sequences cannot be expected automatically to foster continuity. Some of the best opportunities for helping a child to maintain continuity in his learning occur in the in-between times in a school, the times unfortunately devoted in some schools largely to passing to another room or activity.

Conclusion

These seven suggested emphases in changing the curriculum have been reviewed all too briefly. Yet you must have noted that each of them suggested a slow, difficult way to improve rather than a panacea. In concluding, may I leave this statement in your mental notebook? Let us develop children who care about themselves and others around the world and who care also for the higher values of our society; children who are competent and therefore moving into the future with continuing confidence; children who (and here I run out of appropriate words beginning with the letter "c") are masters, not slaves of channels of communication, in school and out.

Educational Technology and the Classroom Teacher

Richard I. Miller

The important contribution of science and technology to our way of life is well known and does not require elaboration here. Almost every living moment of our lives is touched by the more or less constant thrust forward of the inventive genius that has given the United States its unique posture among nations of the world.

Reprinted by permission of Richard I. Miller and the Association for Childhood Education International, 3615 Wisconsin Avenue, N.W., Washington, D.C., from *Childhood Education* 43:276-278, January, 1967. Copyright ©1967 by the Association.

The relationship of technology to education, however, is somewhat clouded with mystery and apprehensions—in most cases based upon lack of rational knowledge rather than upon facts. Certainly the role of the classroom teacher is changing as the conditions of our national life change. The teacher as a catalyst, as a prompter of learning, will become increasingly apparent as the knowledge industry continues to refine and develop presentations of facts. The relating aspect of teaching will become more important in the future.

Even as recently as twenty or thirty years ago, teachers relied upon limited sources of knowledge to pass on to the student. And at an earlier date, when textbooks were not the individual possession of each student, the teacher was the sole middleman between the source of knowledge and the student. This middleman role will become increasingly unnecessary in the future as more emphasis is placed upon bringing the student into firsthand contact with the knowledge itself. This places the teacher in the role of consultant to the student, helping him to relate and to understand. In short, the teacher will become involved in higher intellectual processes than just describing facts and figures.

As the rise of instructional technology becomes more apparent—and this rise has been very rapid indeed—some fears have arisen as to whether or not the teacher will become a bureaucratic functionary. This might well be the case *if* teachers permit it. It is in the hands of teachers and educators to maintain the dynamic and qualitative dimension of education at such a level as to solicit the cooperation of those involved in technological developments. Most educators will agree that mechanical teachers should be replaced by mechanical devices but that nothing has ever been developed to replace a creative and dynamic teacher. At the American Management Association's Conference this summer, U.S. Commissioner of Education Harold Howe II made this point:

> *Sophisticated computers may eventually help us answer some of education's hard questions, and they will undoubtedly be programmed to present conventional subject matter very effectively. The essence of education, however, is beyond the capacity of a machine, and always will be. A computer cannot develop a student's ability to associate effectively with other people. It cannot train a pupil to originate ideas, to present them and defend them against criticism, or to talk confidently before a group. It cannot foster creativity, stimulate thought, encourage experimentation, teach students to analyze.*

A great deal of fuzzy thinking has taken place as to the role of instructional technology in the classroom. The fear that the teacher may be replaced by the machine is farfetched and unrealistic with respect to what most reasonable educational technologists desire. As educators, however, we do need to approach the question rationally and with a strategy for action. Ralph W. Tyler, director of the Center for Advanced Study in the Behavioral Sciences, speaking at the

American Management Association's Conference, highlighted several important factors in considering the role of instructional technology in the classroom:

- the educational objectives toward which the learning in a course or subject is directed
- the abilities, interests and relevant backgrounds of the students
- the extent to which the environment of school, home and neighborhood encourage or discourage school learning
- the extent to which the student's friends and respected associates encourage or discourage school learning
- the extent to which the technological device appropriately fits in with the total pattern of conditions required for effective learning.

These criteria suggest a framework for approaching the problem that heretofore has been lacking. Teachers need to develop a systematic approach to the problem by raising a number of questions relevant to *their* situation. Since every situation varies, the questions need to be general and yet specific. For example, a technological device that has been tested in suburban schools cannot be assumed to be appropriate for central city schools. Environmental conditions as well as the students' backgrounds may vary significantly and therefore may render ineffective research done in a different environment.

We need to look more toward a systems approach to the use of instructional technology. In addition to the points raised by Ralph Tyler, preservice education needs to look sympathetically and realistically at the role of instructional technology in the classroom. Any technological device introduced should be accompanied by extensive inservice training of the teachers involved. Airline pilots are given extensive check-out training on new models of airplanes, but in education we have somehow gotten into the position of not checking out or retraining teachers and others for new developments.

The relationship of the technological innovation to curriculum development needs to be carefully meshed. For example, it will do little good to introduce educational television and not consider the total curricular development in terms of where the television can be most effective for students and the total program.

A final aspect of a systems approach to the introduction of instructional technology relates to periodic inservice review and redirection. Somehow we have missed this important aspect of evaluation. When program instruction is introduced, teachers should be given an opportunity periodically at certain agreed-upon dates to share experiences among themselves and to gain expert advice. Proving effective is the American Association for the Advancement of Science's Science Inquiry Project for elementary youngsters which has built into the program periodic study sessions for teachers.

Three points are made, in conclusion:

1. Educational technology will become more effective and more pressure will be made upon school systems at least to try it. Teachers and educators should not be dragged into this arena but walk in ahead of those manufacturing the hardware. It is important that a positive attitude toward the value of instructional technology be taken by the education profession as a whole.

2. Technological companies should be encouraged to involve selected teachers in their work. Too often programs have been developed by those with little experience in the schools and with no real knowledge of what goes on in the classroom. Our profession needs to speak up for involvement of our brightest and most effective teachers.

3. The fundamental role of instructional technology is to free the teacher and to extend the resources of the classroom. Increasingly the teacher's role needs to be examined in terms of developments in various aspects of our society, including increasing specialization in all walks of life, education not excluded. There is no reason for the teacher to do things that can be done better by a machine; but, as the Commissioner mentioned earlier, there are some important aspects of learning uniquely within the province of the teacher-learner transaction. We need to know where each belongs and to move positively toward making use of what can be a valuable resource for the improvement of education.

Learning Environments for Teaching

Shelt Chastain and Mary Louise Seguel

Hello!
You are now at the door. Please come in and examine the room. When you take your seat, you become a part of an isolated learning environment.

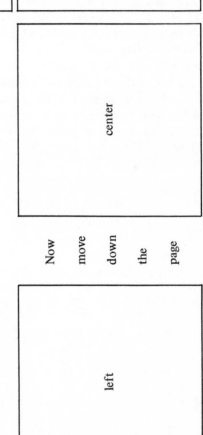

left	center	right

Now

move

down

the

page

You are seated before the three screens as drawn above.

Written for this volume.

You are seated here.

The lights go out.

Look first to the center screen, then left as that screen lights up, then to the right screen as it lights up.

environment: that which surrounds—all the external conditions & influences affecting life & development of an organism
learning: knowledge or skill received by instruction

learning environment

natural—not artificial or contrived
apart from the usual

The three screens are darkened.

isolated or contrived: to separate, to design separately

ISOLATED

ISOLATED

Look first to the **left** and follow the action there. . .

Then look to the _right_ screen and become involved in the action there. . .

Then look to the center screen—it will fuse and complement the **left** and _right_ screens. . .

Hello, Darkness,

my old friend

A film begins above which depicts three college students watching three screens. The silence of their darkened room is broken by soft music. Quietly a low voice begins, "Hello, Darkness, my old friend." On their left screen a film on the history of communications begins to run. On their right screen a series of stills are flashed, showing a man with a lantern, a child on tiptoe, and others. On the center screen captions are flashed such as "We deal with trivial matters because they are safe." jump to the *right* screen

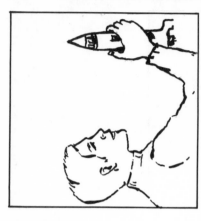

The film on this screen shows teen-agers firing small rockets they have made on a simulated rocket range. A boy acting as fire control officer checks a panel of lights & switches. All seems "go" at his station. The telephone rings. "All clear for firing! T minus 5...., 4...., 3...., 2...., 1.... We have ignition!" Smoke forms around the base of a rocket which immediately speeds toward the upper atmosphere. Ground crews of teen-agers begin the work of tabulating speed, elevation and azimuth angles to relay to the computing center.

now go to the center

The center screen silhouettes a person who by his actions makes himself part of both media. Sometimes he talks, sometimes the center screen talks through captions or pictures, sometimes both he and the screen are silent. What he and the screen are communicating may be about the film on the **left** and the contrived environment it is creating or it may be about the film on the *right* and its natural environment. Through speech and silence, color and darkness, word and music he points up the similarities between these two learning environments, but also the unique effectiveness of each one.

When the technology of a people's natural environment is so much greater than the technology employed in their schools, youngsters sense and react to this disparity. Perhaps the greatest problem facing today's teachers working in their isolated learning environments in schools is that of rebuilding learning environments that can match for effectiveness or even exceed the learning environments found in children's day-to-day living. In far too many schools today, for example, learning experiences are built almost solely through words. Words are valuable, but they are less, far less useful than the experiences they refer to. Words alone tend to support a simplistic, one-dimensional approach to content. Language often fails to say what a speaker wishes to communicate because the objects of the words are not shared by both speaker and listener, or, more critically, because the experiences with the objects of the words are not shared. Quite often a youngster knows what he knows only because he was told, not because he really knows. As Gertrude Stein once asked, "Do you know because I tell you so, or do you know, do you know?"

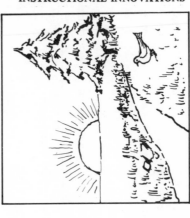

In an effort to bridge this technological gap between the school and society, teachers have often turned hopefully to the natural learning environments found in the culture and have tried as much as possible to exploit them. Thus there are educational programs which use the city as a classroom, the city employees and businessmen as teachers, and which develop the curriculum around the human activities which engage men from day to day. Schools often try to use parks, governmental offices and their materials, museums and their resources, and other culture milieu to provide direct experiences in natural environments. Such experiences in natural environments, however, although valuable, contain certain hidden pitfalls in some cases.

The day-to-day reality of any given group of people is their natural environment. And this same environment is a constant testing ground for their experience. Their most effective learnings are those which are generated naturally, but which also tend to enhance the life of the group. The culture usually teaches most effectively ideas about differences within the culture: morals, cleanliness, language, worship, fear, honesty, bravery, organization, sex, time, occupations. This can be illustrated by considering the blacks in our culture who maintain that they have been invisible. Few people have ever said the black person did not exist. Few people overtly denied the black person a place in our culture. However, many, many people and cultural institutions were a part of the effective teaching which excluded blacks from the culture. The culture has taught racism most effectively, possibly without consciously intending to do so. Thus natural environments, although valuable for their multidimensional nature, may easily be both too overwhelming and too parochial for learners.

Teachers will continue to use both school-isolated, one-dimensional learning environments and multidimensional learning environments as described above in ways that enhance children's learning. A third kind of learning environment, however, the multimedia contrived learning environment, is an important addition to the teacher's repertoire. This kind of environment enables the teacher to extricate significant pieces of the culture from their natural setting and through the use of a variety of media present these pieces in a manner that permits the participants to gain new and better insights with which to return to the complex cultural setting in which these insights are to operate.

one, two, three, four

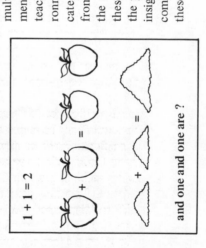

1 + 1 = 2

and one and one are ?

These multimedia, contrived learning environments, should be so constructed that, like natural learning environments, they contain multisensory stimulation fashioned to appeal to the several levels of reality which function simultaneously in individuals. An individual's levels of reality are appealed to in varied ways: at the social level he may reject the conditioned fear symbol of a black cat, but at the subconscious level he is still sympathetic to the cultural teaching that the black cat is an omen of bad luck; at the childish level he feels the joy of fur, the delight when the cat chases a spool; at the dream and memory level he calls up associations with previous experiences with cats; and for that part of the individual which prefers to remain uninvolved, there is the stimulation to understand the appeal cats may have.

Often a teacher in the primary grades presents a picture of a cat and names it. Youngsters are then expected to be stimulated by the word cat in a story. Another teacher may bring a cat to the classroom. Most of us are inclined to feel that the teacher who brought the cat to class may be doing more for the youngsters. Perhaps. However, if a teacher's goal is to assist youngsters as they build an "educated" approach to understanding and appreciating cats, the several levels of reality outlined above must be stimulated to grow through interaction. These levels are best stimulated through sensory experiences in a multimedia approach. One

to bell the cat
to let the cat out of the bag
the cat's pajamas

one of the smartest of tame animals; want to have their own way

ancient Egyptians thought cats were gods; made mummies of cats anyone killing a cat received death

eyes shine at night because of layer of cells in the inner eye

Hey, diddle, diddle!
The cat and the fiddle,

c a t

whiskers are delicate sense organs which help cats feel through bushes

sounds:

purr for happiness; hiss and growl for

or more colorful motion pictures may be shown which follow cats at play, fighting, hunting, eating, and cleaning themselves. Still pictures may be employed to deal with ideas of why some people dislike cats. Words and pictures may be used to present the ancient folklore responsible for the black cat as an omen. Darkness and a cat's scream may help learners to understand why fear is sometimes associated with cats. Certainly several youngsters might be encouraged to bring cats.

In order to gain a greater appreciation for a story of people at a large airport, a teacher might plan a field trip if there is a busy airport nearby. In addition, the teacher might use multimedia techniques to build a contrived learning environment that will stimulate the sensory channels which expand awareness. The contrived environment must be planned to reach participants' multiple levels of reality. There must be the stereo-sound excitement of the take-off, the buzz of planes taxiing to position for take-off. There must be the sound of the crowds with talk noise must be there. The learners must sense the dramatic possibilities of arrivals and departures, must empathize with the workers who serve so many people on the move. Motion pictures are needed to simulate flight, still pictures presented with taped sound are used to implant ideas of the services offered and the emotions of the travelers. Some media may provide background during the youngsters' silent reading and for any dramatizations they might perform as a result of the experience.

Simultaneity is an important consideration in multimedia presentations. Not only is it possible to present stimuli in such a manner that free associations may be made, but a small part can be realized in its entirety, aside from its entirety, and for contrast with related material. For example, an art teacher using a three-screen technique can show simultaneously a complete picture, a detail, and a contrasting or similar style. The presentation can have movement, be accompanied by music, and be in and out of focus at times. An English teacher can involve an entire class in recreating the sensory stimulation that existed in the Elizabethan theatre on the afternoon a new play by Shakespeare was first presented. A history teacher can project a color film on our Declaration of Independence while feeding in opposing ideas, challenges, period paintings, current ideas and some of the magic of the Broadway musical *1776!* Many areas of the school curriculum can best be experienced through multimedia learning environments rather than through verbal blandness.

Reality for any of us is personal, personal because a reality is a summary of sensory experiences, and words are only a small part of that experience. It is important to consider when building learning environments exactly what is to be isolated, how it is to be isolated, and why, in order to heighten any given area of awareness. All of these considerations indicate that the teacher must be conversant with all the ideas outlined—the youngsters and their levels of awareness, the culture, the content as an organized system of clues to be subjected to a multisensory study, the methods for moving objects of words into experience, and the media which may most effectively do the stimulating.

Marshall McLuhan has pointed out that the visual sense for youngsters who live in what he calls today's tribal age (the world of all-at-once-ness as in televised events) is not so dominant as it has been in the now rapidly fading world of print. The visual has taken its place as only one among other sensual modes, such as audible, tactile, spatial, and olfactory. McLuhan has also called our attention to what must be most apparent: that youngsters want roles, not goals. These roles are to be built around contemporary literature, contemporary music, and contemporary events, all of which proclaim youth's appreciation of sensory experience.

Youngsters of the tribal age learn in a multimedia environment because they assume the responsibility for integrating and extending themselves within the media. When the school ventures into the types of isolated multimedia learning environments that have been described, such environments must be constructed so that youngsters enjoy the same freedom for interaction that they have in the natural multimedia environments. This freedom implies that teachers must confront a youngster's personalized learning and responses with the full realization that any synthesis of experience the youngster communicates solely through words probably is somewhat different from and inferior to the sensations which were the experiential building blocks for his synthesis. In short, the teacher's words are not the learners words—and even the learner's words are but a pale representation of the initial experience itself.

The presentations end for the multimedia lesson on communication. The college students volunteer such remarks as, "The film seemed trite." "Real communication took place in the still pictures!" Or simply, "It's all so

C O N F U S I N G !"

When the youngsters in the film gather to discuss their experiences, they volunteer such remarks as "Golly, what a surge of power!" "My wind tunnel test really did not check with the firing today." "Wasn't that chute a beauty as she brought her down!"

natural environment
for learning
and
for testing
isolated learning

words are abstract
symbols for
manipulating
E X P E R I E N C E

multimedia
isolated learning
environments for moving the
objects of words directly into
experience

the screens are darkened
you go out the door
PLEASE JOIN US IN TESTING AND REFINING THE IDEAS

The Teacher and Computer-Assisted Instruction

Patrick Suppes

Educators have shown increasing interest in the use of computers for classroom teaching, especially during the last year or two, and they have raised a number of fundamental questions that need analysis and discussion. The purpose of this article is to acquaint the reader with some of the ways that computers can be used for instruction, and to answer, at least briefly, some of the questions that are frequently asked about computer-assisted teaching.

Some of the most important questions are: How can the computer help in individualizing instruction? How might it change the teacher's role? How will computer-assisted instruction change teacher-administrator relationships? Will it lead to impersonality and regimentation in the classroom? How can teachers play a part in planning and using computers for instructional purposes?

Let us begin by looking at a student seated at a console or station that is connected by a telephone line to a central computer. The console will usually contain a typewriter keyboard that the student can use to "talk to" the computer and a television screen that can display written messages as well as drawings, equations, and other graphic material. In many cases, the student will also have a "light pen," which he can use to select answers to the problems shown on the screen; he can even erase or change the images that appear. The computer talks to the student through a pair of earphones or a loudspeaker, thus providing him with the verbal communication necessary for effective learning, particularly when new concepts are being presented.

The central computer, which controls the presentation of information and evaluates the students' responses, need not be in the school but can be located at a central point in the school district. Because of its great operating speed, one large computer can serve many students, and a number of students can "time-share" the computer simultaneously.

Computer-assisted instruction is possible with only one console per classroom, which would be shared by many students during the school day. In a more expensive and elaborate arrangement, a classroom would have a large number of consoles, and each student could spend considerable time—as much as an hour and a half a day—at the console. It is important to emphasize, however, that in either arrangement the student would still be spending most of this time in the regular class setting, directly under teacher supervision.

Recent research indicates that students at all age levels come to feel at home

Reprinted by permission of the National Education Association, Washington, D.C., and Patrick Suppes from *NEA Journal* 56:15-17, February, 1967.

with this sort of equipment and are quite willing to make its use a part of their daily school experience.

The student and the computer program may interact at three distinct levels, each of which comprises a particular system of instruction. (This use of the word *system* also corresponds to its use in the computer industry.)

Individualized drill-and-practice systems. This kind of interaction between the student and the computer program is meant to supplement the regular teaching process. After the teacher has introduced new concepts and ideas in the standard fashion, the computer provides regular review and practice of basic concepts and skills. In elementary school mathematics, for example, each student would receive 15 or 20 exercises a day. These would be automatically presented, evaluated, and scored by the computer program without any effort by the classroom teacher.

In addition, these exercises can be presented to the student on an individualized basis, with the brighter children receiving harder-than-average exercises, and the slower children receiving easier problems. One important aspect of this individualization should be emphasized: In the drill-and-practice computer system, a student need not be placed on a track at the start of school in the fall and held there the entire year. At the beginning of each new concept block—whether in mathematics or in language arts—a student can be "recalibrated" if the results indicate that he is now capable of handling more advanced material.

Drill-and-practice work is particularly suitable for the skill subjects that make up a good part of our curriculum. Elementary mathematics, reading, and aspects of the language arts, such as spelling, elementary science, and beginning work in a foreign language, benefit from standardized and regularly presented drill-and-practice exercises.

Tutorial systems. In contrast to the individualized drill-and-practice systems, tutorial systems take over the main responsibility for helping the student to understand a concept and develop skill in using it. Basic concepts, such as addition or subtraction of numbers, can be introduced by the computer program in such systems. The aim is to approximate the interaction a patient tutor would have with an individual student.

In the tutorial programs in reading and elementary mathematics that we have been working with at Stanford University for the past three years, we have tried hard to avoid having slower children experience any initial failures. On the other hand, the program has enough flexibility to avoid boring the brighter children with too many repetitive exercises. As soon as the child shows that he has a clear understanding of a concept by successfully working a number of exercises, he is immediately introduced to a new concept and new exercises.

Dialogue systems. Dialogue systems are computer programs and consoles that enable the student to conduct a genuine dialogue with the computer. It will be some years before we are able to implement dialogue systems in classrooms, because a number of technical problems remain unsolved. One problem is the difficulty of devising a computer that can "understand" oral communication, especially that of young children. We would like to have a computer that would respond to questions. To attain this interaction, the computer would have to recognize the speech of the student and to comprehend the meaning of the question. It will be some time before a computer is developed that will be able to do either of these with any efficiency and economy.

Dialogue systems have been mentioned here in order to give readers an idea of the depth of interaction we ultimately hope for. Drill-and-practice systems and tutorial systems, on the other hand, are already in operation on an experimental basis and will no doubt find an increasing application throughout the country in the next few years.

Effective programs of computer-assisted instruction now exist for elementary school mathematics, parts of language arts programs (particularly reading and spelling), and various topics in mathematics and science at the secondary and university levels. The programs have been developed primarily at universities, the following of which are currently the main centers of activity: Stanford, Illinois, Michigan, Texas, Pennsylvania State, Pittsburgh, Florida State, and the Los Angeles campus and the Irvine campus of the University of California.

Let us now look at some of the most frequently asked questions about computer-assisted instruction:

What role can computers play in individualizing instruction? The theme of individualized instruction has been prominent in American education for over 50 years. Psychologists have shown that individuals differ in their abilities, their rates of learning, and often even in their general approaches to learning. Unfortunately, the cost of providing individualized instruction that adapts to these differences is prohibitive if it depends on the use of professional teachers. For example, consider what it would cost to reduce present classroom size to four or five students per teacher.

The computer offers perhaps the most practical hope for a program of individualized instruction under the supervision of a single teacher in a classroom of 25 to 35 students. The basis for this practical hope is the rapid operation of the computer, which enables it to deal on an individual basis with a number of students simultaneously and thus lowers the cost per student of the computer.

How will the computer change the teacher's role? Drill-and-practice systems will modify the teacher's role only slightly. What they will do is relieve teachers of some of the burden of preparing and correcting large numbers of individualized drill-and-practice exercises in basic concepts and skills and of recording grades.

The teacher will be more significantly affected by tutorial systems. Let us consider a concrete example: teaching addition and subtraction of fractions at the fourth grade level. The computer will provide the basic ideas and the procedure of how to add and subtract the fractions. The program will probably be written so that if a student does not understand the basic concepts on first presentation he will receive a second and possibly even a third exposure to them.

The new role of the teacher will be to work individually with all students on whatever problems and questions they may have in assessing and handling the new concepts. Tutorial systems allow teachers greater opportunity for personal interaction with students.

How will computer-assisted instruction affect teacher-administrator relationships? Teachers and administrators should be able to develop even closer relations in a setting where computers are used to aid instruction. The information-gathering capacity of the computer enables administrators to have a much more detailed profile and up-to-date picture of the strengths and weaknesses of each area of curriculum. As they develop skill in interpreting and using the vast amount of information about students provided by the computer, administrators and teachers should be able to work together more effectively for improvements in curriculum.

Is there a danger that the computer will impose a rigid and impersonal regime on the classroom and even replace teachers? Contrary to popular opinion, the computer's most important potential is to make learning and teaching *more* an individual affair rather than *less* so. Students will be less subject to regimentation and moving in lockstep because computer programs will offer highly individualized instruction. In our own work at Stanford, for example, we estimate that the brightest student and the slowest student going through our tutorial program in fourth-grade mathematics have an overlap of not more than 25 percent in actual curriculum.

The computer program is neither personal nor impersonal. The effect and feeling of the program will depend on the skill and perceptivity of those responsible for constructing it.

There seems to be little reason to think that computers will ever replace teachers or reduce the number of teachers needed. The thrust of computer-assisted instruction is to raise the quality of education in this country, not to reduce its cost. In any sort of computer-assisted instructional system used in classrooms in the near future, teachers will continue dealing with children on an individual basis and doing most of the things they are now doing during most of the school day with only slight changes.

Finally, we emphasize once again that no one expects that students will spend most of their school hours at consoles hooked up to computers. They will work at consoles no more than 20 to 30 percent of the time. All teachers everywhere recognize the help that books give them in teaching students. The day is coming when computers will receive the same recognition. Teachers will look on computers as a new and powerful tool for helping them to teach their students more effectively.

Chapter 17

Building a Philosophy of Education
in Today's World

It seems likely that it always has been important for a teacher to have a clearcut, well-thought-out philosophy of education to guide him in his educational practices, but probably there never has been a time when the need was greater than it is now. The rapid changes in today's society, the ever-expanding body of knowledge, the increasing demands on the public schools, the growing number of crucial issues and problems of contemporary education, and the widely divergent points of view regarding educational goals and procedures, all demand of the teacher a coherent philosophical system to provide a framework for answering his questions, resolving his conflicts, and providing consistency in his theory and practice.

The building of an educational philosophy is an experiental process necessitating continued learning, interpretation, and evaluation. It is an individual, personal pursuit that begins as preparation for teaching begins and that must continue for as long as experience lasts. In the articles that follow, the authors recognize and stress the importance and value of a personal philosophy and encourage and direct the teacher in his development of a working philosophy of education.

Importance of a Philosophy for Teachers

Fred G. Walcott

There is a common misconception abroad, it seems to me, concerning the nature of philosophy and how it is learned. When I see a school staff set itself the task of drawing up a school philosophy, my interest wavers. I envision the countless hours of committee work and staff meetings devoted to discussions of trivia, all ending in a statement so sanctimonious and so general that it threatens no one.

When I see this kind of project proposed, my impulse is to suggest quickly: "Don't begin with this kind of thing; instead, start experimenting right now to improve a practice that offends you."

The fact is that a philosophy emerges from experience. It would be more accurate to say that a philosophy results from reflection on experience. Once acquired, it constitutes a *sense of rightness*—an organic attitude that looks both toward the past that nurtured it, and to the future where tentative actions are to be considered.

There is an inevitability, too, in everyone's present philosophical position— that is, it could not possibly be different. One cannot deliberately take a position contrary to his present sense of rightness. His attitudes will continue to change, of course, as the impacts of new experience affect them. Realizing this fact of inevitability should enjoin us all to tolerance for the present points of view of others.

Reflection on Experience

Because a philosophy comes from reflection on experience, it seems quite doubtful whether we can teach a new one indirectly—that is, theoretically—in detachment from the learner's reflection on his own questionable acts. We may be able to teach *about* philosophy; we might, for example, be able to teach the philosophy of Socrates, so that the learner would be able to tell something of what Socrates believed.

This would be quite different, however, from what Dewey spoke of as integration into one's own being—that is, having a built-in, emotion-freighted memory of one's own actions and their personal and social consequences. Dewey's comment on moral training[1] is quite apropos here; it is, he said,

Reprinted with permission of the Association for Supervision and Curriculum Development and Fred G. Walcott from *Educational Leadership* 23:556-559, April, 1966. Copyright ©1966 by the Association for Supervision and Curriculum Development.

[1] John Dewey. *My Pedagogic Creed.* Washington, D.C.: National Education Association, 1896. p. 14.

"precisely that which one gets through having to enter into proper relations with others in a unity of work and thought." It is only during a poignant weighing of one's own or another's genuine emotional perplexity that such an integration can take place.

I draw these thoughts, now, for example, from a reflection on my own past involvements. When I began to teach, I lacked both practical experience and a dependable philosophy of education. I had already tried to read John Dewey and William James for a college course, but I only understood them dimly because my experience was not abreast of their ideas.

For my own practical guidance, I had only some illusory notions drawn from a primitive folklore based on force. The teacher must be a strong dominant figure, I thought, and he must have the strength, physical and otherwise, to maintain his control. And so I acted like a martinet, commanding obedience and anticipating trouble even where it did not exist. The pupils reacted to this treatment in a predictable human manner. While they obeyed outwardly, they began to practice an underground resistance exactly like that of my own callow youth. This eventually led to physical clashes with suspected leaders, which I won through superior strength and position.

The community, which of course had fostered my illusions, thought that I was a good disciplinarian. Yet looking back from my present experience and its ancillary philosophy, I would give a good deal if I could live those years over. I know, now, that had I been a kindly, encouraging, helpful person, those fine pupils would have loved me. In every case of physical violence, I now see that I was tragically wrong.

Work with Remedial Pupils

Perhaps the most telling experience in my professional life was my work with so-called remedial pupils. I began this work without any special preparation, and I doubt whether special training given before the real encounter would have helped me very much—unless, of course, it had been genuine laboratory work under the direction of a person of better experience that mine. As it was, I followed the stereotyped practices of the day: testing; assigning remedial exercises, many of which I devised myself; re-testing; and using motivational tricks of one kind or another.

My own enlightenment came whan I began to observe the habits of the pupils themselves. Trapped in a system that was deliberately competitive, these young people were the chronic failures. Their pitiful defenses against their predicament were quite obvious. All of them sought to hide their inability under various false pretenses. Tests of any kind were, in their eyes, only methods of a cruel exposure. If, for example, I would ask them to report the number of pages they had read during a class hour, they would turn in fantastic figures.

One boy of large, awkward stature had developed a skill in making wisecracks. His classmates always rewarded him with appreciative laughter. I stepped up beside him one day to help him with his reading before the class. Despite his silly antics, I discovered that he was trembling violently, and sweat stood out in drops on his forehead.

I remember another boy of small stature—often a very significant factor—whose mother was a patient in a mental hospital. This boy would invariably come to my room late, with a huge pile of textbooks in his arms. Every day he would poise this load with maddening deliberation and let it come crashing down upon the desk. One day it occurred to me that probably what he needed was to be in the limelight. "Billy," I said, "would you like to help me take the roll every day?" He came up beside me and stood there facing the class. I helped him spell the names of the absent pupils. When he had finished, he put the slip in the slot of the door. The scheme worked like magic. He was always on time after that, and his annoying manner ceased.

I began to ask myself what we had been doing to these young people throughout the apparently dismal years of their schooling. I was thrown back inevitably upon a sobering self-scrutiny. And obviously I saw the single remedy that might restore their well-being: humane acceptance and kindly encouragement. The school, I saw at once, must withdraw its standard expectations; it must seek to discover and to honor their simple ambitions to learn and to grow up.[2]

A Congenial Drift

The resulting parallels of philosophy were simply automatic. I found not only clear directions for my own professional improvement, but I could discover everywhere the supporting thoughts of others. As my own experience has changed, I have felt a congenial drift toward the pragmatic philosophers. It was they, I found, who had a warm current of compassion in their veins. The earlier ones, it seemed to me, came to stand as posthumous critics of my own shortcomings. Listen, for example, to William James:

> Now the blindness in human beings, of which this discourse will treat, is the blindness with which we all are afflicted in regard to the feelings of creatures and people different from ourselves.
>
> We are practical beings, each of us with limited functions and duties to perform. Each is bound to feel intensely the importance of his own duties and the significance of the situations that call these forth. But this feeling is in each of us a vital secret, for sympathy with which we

2 See Earl C. Kelley. *In Defense of Youth.* Englewood Cliffs, New Jersey: Prentice-Hall, Inc., 1962. Chapter 10: see also Jesse Stuart. *The Thread That Runs So True.* New York: Charles Scribner's Sons, 1954. p. 270-80.

vainly look to others. The others are too much absorbed in their own vital secrets to take an interest in ours; hence the stupidity and injustice of our opinions, so far as they deal with the significance of alien lives. Hence the falsity of our judgments, so far as they presume to decide in an absolute way on the value of other persons' conditions or ideals.

That is James speaking out sixty-seven years ago in his *Talks to Teachers.* How clear today, how pertinent, how humane! Could one who had learned this lesson through experience ever serve again the authoritarian role? James understood the iniquity of rigid, mass-administered curricula. To me he seems to say that we need more humanity, more freedom for the personal ambitions of others, more respect for the child who hears a different drummer. Accordingly, I have drawn up a new definition of the teacher's role: I see him now as a helper, as one who makes possible children's dreams.

And Dewey, too, now came to stir my mind as with a trumpet. Listen to his repudiation of the formal regimen:

> *Save as the efforts of the educator connect with some activity which the child is carrying on of his own initiative independent of the educator, education becomes reduced to a pressure from without. It may, indeed, give certain external results but cannot truly be called educative. Without insight into the psychological structure and activities of the individual, the educative process will, therefore, be haphazard and arbitrary. If it chances to coincide with the child's activity it will get a leverage; if it does not, it will result in friction, or disintegration, or arrest of the child-nature.*[3]

Here, I think, is illustrated the true value of philosophy. Speaking out of his own experiences with the children in the University of Chicago Elementary School seventy years ago, Dewey sounds the universal note of compassion. Hearing his dicta—drawn from his experience—I find an echo of my own. I liked Gardner Murphy's peroration in 1961:

> *John Dewey, it is to you to whom we are chiefly obligated for this vision of active and democratic education in the public schools, the instilling of socially significant habits derived from the common needs of ordinary people.*[4]

And thus the world moves on—slowly but surely, toward a more abundant freedom. We swim in the same social stream as the prophets of old, but a little farther down. The office of philosophy is to bind their times and ours together in a commonality of reflection on experience.

---

[3] *My Pedagogic Creed, op. cit.*

[4] Gardner Murphy. *Freeing Intelligence Through Teaching.* New York: Harper and Brothers, 1961. p. 31.

Building a Philosophy of Education
for the Pace-Setting Seventies

William R. Speer

Little imagination is needed to realize that the new decade into which we are now entering will, like the sixties, be characterized by continued conflicts, perplexities, tensions, readjustments in thinking, and realignments of arrangements in society, politics, and education. But the seventies will bring also new challenges, new hopes, and new opportunities. Man will doubtless continue to probe the cosmos beyond our planet, perhaps with greater success than he will explore his inner self.

Traditional values, customs, and beliefs will continue to be reevaluated and revised, and some will doubtless be forced to yield in favor of new ones, some better, some worse. Man's institutions, among them education, will come under closer scrutiny and critical examination than in the decade just ended. Continued change is the one absolute upon which the beginning teacher can depend with certainty.

A growing number of young adults is coming more and more to reject the idea that there must always be wars and rumors of wars, that each night half the population of this earth must go to bed hungry, that illiteracy cannot be eradicated, and that man must be morally degenerate. Such is the context within which the beginning teacher is invited to view his new role in professional education and the appropriate place of philosophy of education in his personal and professional life.

Socrates once asserted that the unexamined life is not worth living. Philosophy begins with this assumption. Those who reject it feel no real conscious need to pursue the subject further. For Socrates did not say that man cannot live without examining his own life. Of course he can. In the sense that he can continue some sort of existence—he can survive—he can live. But Socrates simply expressed a value judgment concerning the quality of human life when it is not examined. By the same token, he seems to have implied that man can improve the quality of his life by first examining it. And this is what philosophy is all about.

Does life have meaning? Is life inherently purposeful? Is man innately good? Evil? Neither? Did God make man or did man make God? Is man rational? Irrational? Rational some of the time; irrational some of the time? Does man really have a free will? Is choice really free choice? Such are the substantive

Written for this volume.

concerns of general philosophy which call for examination by the beginning teacher as a person if he chooses to live the examined life.

What is education? What are the purposes of education? Who shall become educated? Who should teach? By what means? To what ends? With what resources? What role shall freedom play in the education process? These are some of the substantive concerns of philosophy of education to which the beginning teacher as a member of the teaching profession is asked to address himself.

Although the lower forms of animal life are not endowed with the capacity to discover the answers to questions like those posed here, fortunately man is. The quest to know, and the joy of adventure which goes with it, have been reserved for man alone. This is precisely what separates man from the lower animals.

Man is endowed with two capacities which fit him uniquely and well to search for knowledge of the good, a quality life. First, he is endowed with the capacity to think—to think rationally, logically, purposefully, intelligently, and creatively. Second, he is endowed with the capacity to believe—to possess a faith of some kind. These two capacities can be used by man as a means of attaining a quality life, both as a person and as a teacher, but he must first will to do so.

A word needs to be said here about man's capacity to think. John Dewey referred to philosophy as "a habit of mind in the exercise of which one tends not to take the conventional and customary for granted, but always to see possible alternatives." Dewey's abiding faith in the perfectibility of man is not justified merely because man possesses the capacity to think, but rather because he has the capacity to think creatively and this creative kind of thinking can become a habit. If teachers themselves can acquire the habit of not taking the customary and conventional for granted, if they can develop the habit of constantly seeking other and better alternatives, and if teachers can instill this same habit in their students, then the purposes of education might well be summed up in this sentence. For with Dewey, the purpose of education is to "shed some light on the path that lies ahead." This can be done only if teachers think imaginatively and creatively.

Man's second capacity, his capacity to believe, is no less important than the first, and yet it frequently seems to escape man, particularly the agnostic or atheist. For believing through faith picks up where knowing leaves off. Everyone believes in something; everyone places his faith and trust in some object, some person, or persons. His faith may be in material goods, or it may be in power, in himself, in a Higher Power, in love, in sensual desires, in a here, or perhaps in a hereafter. It is not a question of whether or not man has faith of some kind. It is rather a question of the object or objects of his faith. A faith of some kind is an undeniable fact of life—it is with us now and doubtless will remain so. Since this is so, might it not be argued that we may as well place our faith in whatever objects will enhance the quality of human life—all human life everywhere?

CONCLUSION

As we enter the pace-setting seventies with the radical changes which will inevitably occur on this planet, as we explore further into outer space and within ourselves, building a philosophy of education attuned harmoniously to the exciting age in which we live can bring quality to the professional and personal life of the beginning teacher. In the final analysis, the hope of man lies in his two capacities—his capacity to know and his capacity to believe. Better we should concern ourselves less with the kind of a world we live in and more with the kind of world we want. Man already possesses the means of attaining it. These means need only to be put to work in experience.

Suggested Additional Readings

Adams, Sam, and John L. Garrett, Jr. "Some Basic Philosophies of Education," pp. 134-140 in *To Be a Teacher: An Introduction to Education*. Englewood Cliffs: Prentice-Hall, Inc., 1969.

Anderson, Robert H. "The Nongraded School: An Overview." *The National Elementary Principal* 47:4-10, November, 1967.

Brameld, Theodore. "Illusions and Disillusions in American Education." *Phi Delta Kappan* 50:202-207, December, 1968.

Calvin, Allen D. "How to Teach with Programmed Textbooks." *Grade Teacher* 84:94-95, 128-137, February, 1967.

Dawson, Kenneth E., and Morris Norfleet. "The Computer and the Student." *NEA Journal* 57:47-48, February, 1968.

DeYoung, Chris A., and Richard Wynn. "Educational Materiel and Technology," pp. 388-417 in *American Education,* Sixth Edition. New York: McGraw-Hill Book Co., 1968.

Featherstone, Joseph. "Schools for Children: What's Happening in British Classrooms." *The New Republic* 157:17-21, August 19, 1967.

Frankel, Charles. "Philosophy." *NEA Journal* 51:50-53, December, 1962.

Fraser, Dorothy McClure. "What Content and When?" *The National Elementary Principal* 42:13-19, September, 1962.

Fullerton, Bill J., and LeRoy H. Griffith. "Organizing Teaching Teams," pp. 4-9 in *The Student Teacher and Team Teaching,* AST Bulletin 25. Washington, D.C.: The Association for Student Teaching, 1966.

Gaskell, William. "The Inservice Education Potential of Team Planning-Teaching." *Peabody Journal of Education* 45:152-155, November, 1967.

Gleason, Gerald T. "Computer Assisted Instruction—Prospects and Problems." *Educational Technology* 7:1-8, November 15, 1967.

Goodlad, John I. "Implications of Current Curricular Change." *The North Central Association Quarterly* 41:179-183, Fall, 1966.

————. "The Schools vs. Education." *Saturday Review* 52:59-61, 80-82, April 19, 1969.

Gorman, Burton W. "Changing Ideas and the Teacher." *Peabody Journal of Education* 44:199-203, January, 1967.

Hamilton, Norman K. "TAG and the Teacher." *The Instructor* 77:102-103, October, 1967.

Hearn, Norman E. "Change for the Sake of Change: Why Not?" *The National Elementary Principal* 46:50-52, September, 1966.

Heathers, Glen. "Influencing Change at the Elementary Level," pp. 21-53 in *Perspectives on Educational Change,* Richard I. Miller, editor. New York: Appleton-Century-Crofts, 1967.

Hurd, Helen Bartelt, *Teaching in the Kindergarten,* Third Edition. Minneapolis: Burgess Publishing Co., 1965.

Johnson, Robert H., Jr., and John J. Hunt. R_x *for Team Teaching.* Minneapolis: Burgess Publishing Co., 1968.

Lambert, Philip. "Team Teaching in Today's World." *Teachers College Record* 64:480-486, March, 1963.

Lee, J. Murray. "Technology Improves Learning," pp. 114-128 in *Elementary Education Today and Tomorrow.* Boston: Allyn and Bacon, Inc., 1967.

Lippitt, Ronald, and Colleagues. "The Teacher as Innovator, Seeker, and Sharer of New Practices," pp. 307-324 in *Perspectives on Educational Change,* Richard I. Miller, editor. New York: Appleton-Century-Crofts, 1967.

Martin, John Henry. "Kaleidoscope for Learning." *Saturday Review* 52:76-77, 86, June 21, 1969.

Morris, Van Cleve. "Building a Personal Philosophy of Education," pp. 463-473 in *Philosophy and the American School.* Boston: Houghton Mifflin Co., 1961.

National Education Association. "Deciding What to Teach," pp. 27-61 in *Schools for the Sixties.* A Report of the Project on Instruction. New York: McGraw-Hill Book Co., 1963.

Ozmon, Howard. *Challenging Ideas in Education.* Minneapolis: Burgess Publishing Co., 1967.

————. *Utopias and Education.* Minneapolis: Burgess Publishing Co., 1969.

Richey, Robert W. "Controversial Issues and Problems in Education," pp. 550-578 in *Planning for Teaching: An Introduction to Education,* Fourth Edition. New York: McGraw-Hill Book Co., 1968.

Rounds, Sue. "Fifth and Sixth Graders Program a Computer." *The Instructor* 77:53, April, 1968.

Schell, Edith. "Existentialism and the Classroom Teacher." *Elementary School Journal* 69:7-16, October, 1968.

Short, Edmund C. "The Importance of a Guiding Philosophy," pp. 150-151 in *Contemporary Thoughts on Public School Curriculum,* Edmund C. Short and George D. Marconnit, editors. Dubuque, Iowa: Wm. C. Brown Company Publishers, 1968.

Stinnett, T. M. "The Emerging Revolution in American Education," pp. 25-46 in *Professional Problems of Teachers,* Third Edition. New York: The Macmillan Co., 1968.

Suydam, Marilyn N. "Teachers, Pupils, and Computer-assisted Instruction." *The Arithmetic Teacher* 16:173-176, March, 1969.

Thomas, George I., and Joseph Crescimbeni. "Innovations Affecting the Teacher-Learner Situation," pp. 50-63 in *Individualizing Instruction in the Elementary School.* New York: Random House, Inc., 1967.

Tillman, Rodney. "Self-Contained Classroom: Where Do We Stand?" *Educational Leadership* 18:82-84, November, 1960.

Torkelson, Gerald M., and Emily A. Torkelson. "How Mechanized Should the Classroom Be?" *NEA Journal* 56:28-30, March, 1967.

Tumin, Melvin. "Teaching in America." *Saturday Review* 50:77-79, 84, October 21, 1967.

Van Til, William. "The Temper of the Times." *Childhood Education* 45:243-246, January, 1969.

Wilson, Charles H. "Educational Innovation." *Nation's Schools* 80:66-68, November, 1967.

Yeazell, Mary. "Phads and Phantoms in American Education." *Peabody Journal of Education* 44:333-340, May, 1967.

Author Index

Ashcroft, Samuel C., 165
Barr, David L., 175
Beatty, Walcott H., 78
Beauchamp, George A., 38
Bromberg, Susan L., 212
Camp, William L., 246
Chamberlin, Leslie J., 57
Chasnoff, Robert E., 55
Chastain, Shelt, 376
Cholden, Harriet B., 209
Collier, Calhoun C., 19
Corey, Arthur F., 275
Crescimbeni, Joseph, 113, 333
Cruickshank, Donald R., 229
Davis, Sara, 28
Deen, Lou Emma Wright, 315
Deep, Donald, 132
Devlin, Rev. Joseph, S.J., 330
Dinkmeyer, Don, 72
Dorros, Sidney, 269
Douglass, Harl R., 30, 104
Douglass, M. Genevieve, 46
Duffey, Robert W., 89
Dunfee, Maxine, 205
Ferguson, Arthur Louis, 63
Fleming, Robert S., 182
Foster, Walter S., 256, 272
Fox, Raymond B., 357
Furst, Norma, 106
Garcia, Elvira T., 253
Geston, John M., 250
Gowin, Lawrence E., 218
Griffin, Gary A., 330
Grindle, John L., 46
Grubman, Annette, 177
Hanna, Nancy W., 250
Harrison, Raymond H., 218
Haupt, Charlotte, 83
Havighurst, Robert J., 285
Hedges, William D., 139
Herman, Wayne L., 89, 236
Houston, W. Robert, 19

Hubbard, Frank W., 271
Hubbell, Ned S., 200
Jacobs, Norman C., 96
Jarzen, Cynthia, 116
Lee, Dorris M., 128, 308
MacGorman, Ruth Stephens, 173
McGuigan, J. Lorne, 287
McLoughlin, William P., 346
McQueen, Mildred, 146
Massialas, Byron G., 110
Mattleman, Marciene S., 106
May, Charles R., 326
Mehl, Marie A., 30, 104
Miel, Alice, 367
Miller, Richard I., 372
Mills, Hubert H., 30, 104
Myers, Allen, 300
Neugarten, Bernice L., 285
Olson, Carl O., Jr., 351
Reiss, Ira L., 153
Rillo, Thomas J., 162
Schmatz, Robert R., 19
Schrag, Peter, 234
Schuhmacher, Elisabeth, 89
Scobey, Mary-Margaret, 30, 104
Seguel, Mary Louise, 376
Simpson, Ray H., 4, 259
Speer, William R., 395
Stinnett, T. M., 11, 291
Suppes, Patrick, 385
Teigland, Elizabeth, 60
Thomas, George I., 113, 333
Trubowitz, Sidney, 168
Veatch, Jeannette, 135
Walcott, Fred G., 391
Walsh, William J., 19
Williams, David L., 89
Williams, Robert L., 189
Wolfson, Bernice J., 125
Wrightstone, J. Wayne, 121
Zachary, Lillian B., 89

Subject Index

Administrators (See Relationships, teacher)

Afro-American history, 146,177-181

Aides, teacher, 134,234-239,258

Applying for a position, 4,11-17

Attitudes
child
formation of, 173-174,177-181,201
multi-ethnic, 177-181
teacher
toward children, 28, 53-54, 62-63, 76, 80-82, 89-94, 107, 170, 255
toward teaching, 60-63, 255, 271-272, 298

Bargaining, collective (See Negotiating)

Behavior
child, 89-94 (See also Growth and development, child)
teaching, 90-94, 106-110 (See also Competence, teacher)

Change, 23,113, 278, 298-308, 320, 325, 333-346, 357-359, 367, 395

Child development (See Growth and development, child)

Choosing a position, 3-17

Christmas (See Holidays)

Class control (See Discipline)

Classroom climate, 28-30, 60-63, 72-73, 77, 106-110, 254

Classroom routine (See Routine, classroom)

Community
citizen of, 284-293
leadership in, 286-290
participant in, 285-286, 288-290

Community school, 323, 361-362

Competence, teacher
developing, 7-9, 198, 240-267
levels of, 96-103, 106-110
qualities identified, 253-255
teacher's perception of, 256-259

Computer-assisted instruction, 385-389

Conferences, parent-teacher, 199, 201-202, 209-217

Continuous pupil progress, 335-337, 345, 360-361

Contracts, 17

Controversial issues, 173-177, 287, 316-317

Counseling, 77, 371

Creativity, 23-24, 100-101, 113-119, 311, 368-369

Curriculum (See also Innovations, curricular)
content, 178-181, 299, 308-319, 370-371
planning, 133, 326-328
processes, 308-314
time allotment, 33

Decision-making, bases for, 19, 299, 303-307

Departmentalization, 329, 341-342

Development (See Growth and development, child)

Differentiated staff, 359-360

Disadvantaged child, 87-88, 145, 150-152, 168-172, 212, 292

Discipline, 46-52, 57-59, 89-94, 254-255, 344-346

Discovery approach, 118

Discussion teams, 241-244

Early childhood education, 75, 145-153, 178-179, 212

Emotional health, child, 78-88 (See also Self-concept)

Environment
classroom, 28-30, 37, 83-84, 118, 254
learning, 28-30, 376-384
outdoor, 162-165

Ethics, 12, 54, 219-221, 227

Evaluation
and grading, 49, 189-193
and parents, 207, 324
competitive, 189-193
forms of, 182-193
of learning, 182-194
of pupils, 49, 182-193, 207, 254, 261
of self, 4-10, 230-232, 244-246, 255-267
of teacher performance, 240-246, 256-267
techniques of, 182-189, 259-267

Excellence, qualities of, 253-255

Failure, child, 83-85, 169, 360-361

First day of school, 37, 48-49

First weeks of school, 49-50

Flag salute, 173-174
Ghetto school, 168-172
Grouping
    ability, 121-124, 189
    homogeneous, 75-76
    in individualized program, 128-132
    in non-graded school, 337-339
Growth and development, child, 20-23, 28,
    70-77, 147, 306-307
Guides and manuals, 32-34
Handicapped child, 88, 145, 165-168
Holidays
    activities for, 176-177
    religious, 175-177
Home visits, 202, 215-216
Homework, 138-144, 322
Human relations, 53-54, 218-234, 241-246
    (See also Relationships, teacher)
Independent study
    activities, 135, 137-138
    centers of interest, 137
    criteria for, 136-137
Individual differences, 21, 71, 75-77,
    120-144, 166, 206, 257
Individualized instruction, 125-138, 258,
    359-360, 385-387
Innovations
    curricular, 302, 366-389
    evaluation of, 127, 329-333, 346-358
    instructional, 302, 366-389
    organizational, 329, 333-365
    parents' reactions to, 320-326
    technological, 301-302, 372-389
    working with, 127, 329-389
Inquiry teaching, 110-113
In-service education, 5, 240-249, 363-365
Intelligence, 74
Interest centers, 29-30, 37, 137-138
Interviews, 4-13
Law, school, 53, 63-65, 175-177
Learning center, 29-30
Learning environment (See Environment,
    learning)
Lesson plan (See Planning, lesson)
Liability, teacher, 63-65
Manuals, teacher (See Guides and manuals)
Multilevel assignments, 341
Multimedia, 376-384
Negotiating, 282-283
Non-graded school, 329, 333-339, 346-351

Non-teaching responsibilities (See Responsi-
    bilities, non-teaching)
Objectives
    behavioral, 24-27, 133
    for handicapped child, 167
    importance of, 19
    of early childhood education, 148-150
    of elementary education, 19-27, 126,
        304-305
    preparing, 19, 24-27, 304-305
    taxonomy of, 24-26
Orientation (See Preschool, orientation)
Outdoor education, 145, 162-165
Parents
    as helpers, 209, 234-235
    conferring with, 201-202, 209-217
    informing, 49, 200-217, 321-322
    opinions of, 202, 320-326
    relationships with (See Relationships,
        teacher)
    telephoning, 203, 213
    visiting, 202, 215-216
    working with, 199-217
Performance, levels of teaching, 96-103
Periodicals, professional, 250-253, 263-264
Philosophy of education
    building of, 298, 390, 395-397
    generally accepted, 154-155
    importance of, 390-394
Placement services, 4, 11, 13, 15-16
Planning
    cooperative, 134, 262, 342-343, 353-354
    curriculum, 133, 326-328
    lesson, 38-44, 49, 52, 110, 257
    preschool, 30-37
    teacher-pupil, 104-106, 257, 266
    team, 342-343, 353-354
    unit, 41-42
Pledge of allegiance, 146, 173-174
Politics
    definition of, 279, 284, 287, 291
    professional involvement in, 278-279,
        287-293
Preschool
    orientation, 31-32
    planning and preparation, 30-37, 47-48
Problem solving, 101
Profession, teaching
    criteria of, 269-270
    improvement of, 268-283

organizations of (See Professional organizations)
power of, 275-281
responsibilities of, 269-272, 275-283, 291-293
Professional magazines (See Periodicals, professional)
Professional organizations
objectives and activities, 272-275, 281
power of, 275-281
responsibilities of, 203-204, 275-281
types, 272-275
Public relations, 200-209 (See also Relationships, teacher)
Question techniques, 85, 107-108, 111
Relationships, teacher
with administrators, 5, 221-224, 388
with board of education, 226-227
with noncertificated personnel, 225-226
with other teachers, 54, 218-221, 229-234, 262
with parents, 49, 54, 199-209
with supervisors, 47, 59, 221-224
Religion, study of, 175-177
Research
child development, 71-77, 81-82, 89-94
conducting, 240, 246-249
using, 71-94, 208, 240
Responsibilities, non-teaching, 6, 47, 224, 236-238, 359

Role, teacher, 19, 28, 107-112, 126, 132-134, 287, 290, 293, 326, 373, 387-388, 394
Routine, classroom, 37, 46, 48, 55-56, 58, 105, 169
Schedule, daily, 33, 35-37, 43
Self-concept, 21-22, 60, 73-75, 78-82, 190, 367-368
Sex education, 145, 153-162
Sex segregated primary school, 362-363
Society, dominant forces in, 305-306
Starting the school year, 45-65
Success, child, importance of, 82-83, 86-87
Tape recording, of teacher, 244-245, 264-265, 363
Teaching inventory, 245-246
Team learning, 343-346
Team teaching, 262, 341-346, 351-357
Technology (See Innovations, technological)
Textbooks, 34, 317, 318
Tradition, 70, 315-319
Two-teacher classes, 340
Ungraded school (See non-graded school)
Unit teaching, 41, 115, 317-318
Values, 19, 22, 60, 112, 293, 303-304
Video-taping, of teacher, 264, 363-364
Volunteer helpers, 234-235
Work centers (See Interest centers)